Naked Screenwriting

Twenty-two Oscar-Winning Screenwriters Bare Their Secrets to Writing

Lew Hunter
with Meg Gifford

ROWMAN & LITTLEFIELD
Lanham • Boulder • New York • London

Published by Rowman & Littlefield
An imprint of The Rowman & Littlefield Publishing Group, Inc.
4501 Forbes Boulevard, Suite 200, Lanham, Maryland 20706
www.rowman.com

6 Tinworth Street, London SE11 5AL, United Kingdom

FRANCIS FORD COPPOLA (*Patton, Godfather I, II, III, Apocalypse Now*)
BRUCE JOEL RUBIN (*Ghost*)
WILLIAM GOLDMAN (*Butch Cassidy and the Sundance Kid, The Princess Bride*)
JULIUS EPSTEIN (*Casablanca*)
ALEXANDER PAYNE and JIM TAYLOR (*Sideways, Election, About Schmidt*)
ALFRED UHRY (*Driving Miss Daisy*)
OLIVER STONE (*Midnight Express*)
IRVING RAVETCH and HARRIET FRANK JR.* (*Hud, Norma Rae*)
TOM SCHULMAN (*Dead Poets Society, What About Bob?*)
TED TALLY (*The Silence of the Lambs*)
RUTH PRAWER JABVOLA (*A Room With a View, Howard's End*)
ERNEST LEHMAN* (*Sabrina, North By Northwest, West Side Story*)
ERIC ROTH (*Forest Gump, Benjamin Button, Munich*)
JEAN-CLAUDE CARRIÈRE (*The Unbearable Lightness of Being, Belle de Jour*)
FRANK PIERSON (*Dog Day Afternoon*)
DAVID WARD (*The Sting*)
HORTON FOOTE (*To Kill a Mockingbird, Tender Mercies*)
CHRISTOPHER MCQUARIE (*The Usual Suspects*)
RON BASS (*Rain Man*)
ALAN BALL (*American Beauty*)
CALLIE KHOURI (*Thelma and Louise*)
ROBERT BENTON (*Kramer Versus Kramer, Places in the Heart*)
BILLY WILDER (*Sunset Boulevard, Ace in the Hole, Some Like it Hot*)

British Library Cataloguing in Publication Information Available

Library of Congress Cataloging-in-Publication Data

Names: Hunter, Lew, author. | Gifford, Meg editor.
Title: Naked screenwriting : twenty-two Oscar-winning screenwriters bare
   their secrets to writing / by Lew Hunter with Meg Gifford.
Description: Lanham : Rowman & Littlefield, 2021. | Summary: "Through
   interviews with world-renowned UCLA screenwriting professor Lew Hunter,
   Oscar-winning screenwriters and multiple award-winners reveal their
   Hollywood secrets in crafting brilliant stories and methodology.
   Interviewees include Francis Ford Coppola, William Golden, Alexander
   Payne, Ernest Lehman, Horton Foote and Billy Wilde"— Provided by
   publisher.
Identifiers: LCCN 2020037389 (print) | LCCN 2020037390 (ebook) | ISBN
   9781538137956 (paperback) | ISBN 9781538137963 (epub)
Subjects: LCSH: Motion picture authorship. | Screenwriters—United
   States—Interviews.
Classification: LCC PN1996 .H755 2021 (print) | LCC PN1996 (ebook) | DDC
   808.2/3—dc23
LC record available at https://lccn.loc.gov/2020037389
LC ebook record available at https://lccn.loc.gov/2020037390

Naked Screenwriting

Once again, garlands and potted plants to
my beloved, Pamela Hunter;
my many students, including Meg, Shelley, and Rita;
the screenwriters who comprise this tome;
and the screenwriting *art* and *craft*—
all beloved by yours truly in exactly that order.

Contents

Acknowledgments

The world's most beautiful (inside and out) wife, Pamela Hunter
The world's greatest agent, Richard Curtis
Richard Ray Walter, super research associate
MBD Shelley Ray Anderson, super research associate
Rita Ray Augustine, super research associate
Kathy Ray Fischer
Editor and make-believe daughter Meg Gifford
MBD Maren Mason Chumley
Michael Hoeft
Vincent Tsu
Mike Sakamoto

Thank you to Dean Rosen, Gil Cates, Howard Suber, John Young, and Lonnie Senstock.

Thank you, LouAnne Wright, for the title because your dumb-shit (sweet) husband turned it down for his book. A tremendous merci beaucoup to the above and the giants in the index for their inspirational roles in my screenwriting, book writing, and professing career, and much gratitude to Doe Miller and Arthur Ripley, both resting in peace. Thank you to all of my favorites: Eileen, Marty, Scott, Denny, Amy, Michelle, Heather, Adam, Hilary, Hollie, Nicole, Hadley, Hannah the banana, and Christiana Pamela Marie.

Introduction

FADE IN:
INT. UCLA 434 GRADUATE SCREENWRITING CLASS DAY

LEW: What is a screenwriter? Somewhere between the pulsating pentameters of a poet and the humdrum hindsight of a historian, there lives a curious and wondrous creature known as a screenwriter. Working screenwriters can be found at Vegas, the racetrack, the tennis courts, their favorite bars; nonworking screenwriters, same or at the keyboard.

A writer would rather smoke, eat, drink, play golf, crochet, fix the toaster, or even make love to their mate than face what comes after fade in. A writer thinks he or she can act better than an actor, direct better than a director, produce better than a producer, but the butcher, the mailman, and the rotten kid next door each knows he or she can write better than the writer. A writer can write comedy when he or she is heartbroken and tragedy when he or she is happy. Some writers, like Stirling Silliphant and Calder Willingham, have elaborate names. Other writers are called Mel, Jane, Lew, or insert yours here.

Writers win Writers Guild Awards and Oscars and Emmys for their writing achievements, and yet, all a writer really does is rearrange the words in the dictionary. The most handsome star, the most beautiful lady, must wait in the wings while a scrawny or pudgy man or woman, with or without glasses, stares at a blank screen or piece of paper and slowly, laboriously dreams them into bed with each other.

The art of the screenwriter is compounded of frustration and misery, of neurosis and pride, of hunger and fear, and for what? To see on a screen that one credit that enables him or her to say to his or her parents and verily all the world, "I am a screenwriter!" True, the sight lasts but for an instant and is soon overwhelmed by sound and image and fury, but at least there is that one fleeting moment of immortality in this everlasting commercial known as life.

Since 1979, every UCLA master screenwriting class taught by yours truly has heard "What is a screenwriter?" in their first session. Our authors are Rocky and Irma Kalish, wonderful comedy screenwriters who were challenged to write this paean to screenwriting for Arthur Hill to deliver at a 1976 Emmy Awards broadcast. "To deliver" are the preceding key words. I suspect and verily hope you realize by now that actors do not make it up.

Directors? I give you the following about a novice who asked Harry Cohen, the legendary tyrant/maven of Columbia Pictures in the forties, "Harry, a rich Texan comes up to you and says 'I've got $5 million I want to invest in a movie. You choose the movie and do whatever you want to it. There's only one thing. I have a young son who is mentally slow, and I want him to have a significant credit on the film.' What do you do, Harry? Maybe refuse the money?"

"Hell no," replied the gruff Cohen. "I'd be happy to take the money, and I'd make his boy the director."

"The director?"

"Absolutely. Any place else he could screw up everything. I'd take him to the set and set him in those high, canvas-backed chairs. I'd say, 'You sit right here, and when that guy behind the camera gives you the go nod, you say, "Action!" loud. Then sit there very quietly until the actors stop talking, and the operator again nods, then yell, "Cut!" And don't forget, you little bastard, in between, you don't open your mouth.'"

That's most directors. The loneliest man in the world is a director wandering the halls outside the writer's office, waiting to find out how the script works.

If the past Columbia tyro Harry Cohen doesn't convince, how about Irving Thalberg, the "genius" of MGM during their halcyon days: "The writer is the most important person in Hollywood, but we must never tell the sons of bitches."

Today, in our new century, the script *is* God. I am continually astonished and thrilled so many of our ex-UCLA students command

$1 million plus per script. Shane Black (*Lethal Weapon*) is far beyond that mark. Oh, and let me add Eric Roth (*Forrest Gump*), David Koepp (*Jurassic Park*), and Francis Ford Coppola (*The Godfather*).

In television, please know, the writer rules. Period. End of statement. The showrunner is always a writer. Dear Barney Rosensweig was the last producer (*Cagney and Lacy*) who did not start screen life as a writer: Steven Bochco, James Brooks, Steve Cannell, Linda Bloodworth-Thomason, Dick Wolf, Chris Carter, Kathy Ann Stumpe, Les and Glen Charles, Diane English, Aaron Spelling, David E. Kelley, Aaron Sorkin, David Chase, Tom Fontana, Larry David, Mike Jacobs, David Milch, Matt Groening, Marta Kauffman, David Crane, and on and on and on.

Theater? Well, you probably well know the writer has ruled since the thirties, with Eugene O'Neil, to Tennessee Williams and Arthur Miller in the forties, up to Neil Simon, Wendy Wasserstein, David Mamet, Andrew Lloyd Webber, and David Rabe today. Ibsen, Shakespeare, Moliere, Pirandello, and the Greek theater cats generally also had their way. All performance writing artists—*all!*

Sixty-plus years ago, I landed on the storied shores of Hollywood. Oh yes, I saw or knew Marilyn Monroe, Jimmy Dean (not the sausage king), Mae West, Humphrey Bogart, Bette Davis, Clark Gable, and Fred Astaire from close and far. But my real idols were Charlie Chaplin, Mankewicz, Dudley Nichols, Frances Marion, James Poe, Paddy Chayefsky, Ernest Kinoy, Billy Wilder, Julie and Phillip Epstein, Ernie Lehman, John Paxon, James Agee, Irving Ravetch and Harriet Frank Jr., and enough to fill the next three pages.

I was a young, trying-not-to-be-foolish NBC executive in the seventies with the instructions to give Paddy Chayefsky "notes" on a pilot he had written for our perennial second network. In front of this personal "god," I weakly cleared my voice. It still broke, as I said, "Mr. Chayefsky, I'm here to give the network notes on your script, and I, oh, I so admire you. I feel totally foolish doing what I'm supposed to do." This screenwriting and playwriting giant smiled, also cleared his throat (to probably hold back a small laugh), then assured me, "Lew? It is Lew?" I nodded in maintained awe as he called me by my first name when he could have just called me "kid." "Lew, tell me what you have to tell me. I'll take it from there."

Did Mr. Chayefsky ever take it from there. His ensuing rage and passion became the Oscar-winning *Network* screenplay and subsequent seminal movie. His wrath was obviously aimed at those far above my network status yet, possibly in terms of history, below my status, as even though I'm still going, "they" are either dead or selling real estate.

I revere screenwriters. As the late and wonderful Oscar-winner UCLA professor Stirling Silliphant once said, screenwriters are the bottom of the barrel in this business. Perhaps each extreme bursts the envelope, but we should and must put our professional lives on the line and daily claim our rightful due. We. Are. Artists. We are the ones who write *The Godfather, Citizen Kane, Dr. Strangelove, Casablanca, 2001: A Space Odyssey, American Beauty, Annie Hall,* and on and on. We are the ones who write such iconic lines as

"And so we beat on, boats against the current, borne back ceaselessly into the past."
"Frankly, my dear, I don't give a damn."
"This could be the start of a beautiful friendship."
"We'll always have Paris."
"I'll make you an offer you can't refuse."
"Badges—we don't need no stinking badges."
"Make my day."

We are the ones who write the stories that will significantly define the public and popular future of the twenty-first century. I've professionally worked with Chayefsky, Simon, Rose, Bochco, Cannell, Oliansky, Bloodworth-Thomason, Spelling, Bradbury, Sowards, Harris, Baldwin, Link, Levinson, and hundreds more who were perhaps less famous but many as talented. In my concurrent professor career at UCLA, Coppola, Epstein, Uhry, Stone, Ravetch, Frank, Tally, Lehman, Roth, Nava, Werb, Rosenberg, Pierson, Ward, Bass, Khouri, Campion, and Wilder have spoken to my screenwriting classes.

Have I "outed" myself? I love screenwriters and am so humbled to be included in that species as a result of more than one hundred hours of television and movie work of my own, shown around the world. Would it be more, but the goddess of screenwriting seems to have designated me to celebrate the screenwriter via my *Screenwriting 434* book, my classes, my workshops, my seminars, my writer's colonies, and this not-so-humble *Naked Screenwriting* treatise. I say "not-so-humble" because the words of my past, present, and future gods and goddesses are in the subsequent pages.

For the rest of this book, motion-picture yourself at UCLA in Mac-Gowan Hall, room 23, at 3:00 p.m. on a Thursday at my 434 Master Screenwriting class. You're with eight master's graduate students between ages twenty-five and thirty-five. All have written four to fourteen feature-length scripts. All are seated around a long, Formica-topped, dull gray table. Around the outer perimeter of the square room, another great eight, anticipating auditors sit with distinguished but nonstuffy UCLA professors led by my fellow Screenwriting Department chair, Richard Walter. The world-class Matisse-Rodin-Moore-filled sculpture garden reposes outside the windows, unwatched by all inside this efficient, hallowed room. Hallowed because many world-class screenwriting warriors received their basic training here. Hallowed because most of the people between these pages shuffled, strode, crept into the room to be greeted upon recognition by yours truly.

They accept my words and gesture to sit beside me, backed up to a never-used blackboard. After a small hello to all and obligatory pleasantries, we hunker down to our mission possible: to have each Academy Award–winning writer tell us how he or she writes. Not how they became rich and famous with accompanying war stories. Not anecdotes about Humphrey or Audrey or Marlon or Marilyn or Cary or Barbra or Hanks or Redford or Pacino or Peck. But "How do you write screenplays?" And Bill Goldman says, "The horror of it is we all do it so differently!!" I'll save replying to Bill for my third act, the "Fadeout," of this giant compilation. Giant, not because of size. Giant because of who these writers are, what they represent, and how fucking hard they've worked for it.

"The most important sons and daughters of bitches in Hollywood!" They know it. I know it. You and the public must now know it. Legendary Oscar-winner Ben Hecht said that, in a story conference, he so angered Sam Goldwyn, who never used scatological language, transposed into a red-faced madman who stuttered and blustered and finally got out his most vehement curse: "You, you, writer!"

My ordering of these screenwriting giants is not alphabetical but completely subjective. My pedagogical objective is to have one dialogue flow into the other for rhythm; pace; and a variety of thought, age, experience, and rage. What you are about to read or devour is just marvelous—no thanks to me but to these Academy Award–winning screenwriting human beings.

1

Francis Ford Coppola

I have known Francis since he was an eager kid studying directing at UCLA while I was studying in the UCLA screenwriting program. He already carried an aura of hard-working, obsessed with creativity and every UCLA film student wanted to get their scripts into his capable hands even then, as he was rumored to be the strongest writer in our program. He remains one of the strongest of writers and directors in Hollywood and it's an honor to have him back in these hallowed halls to discover what he's learned along the way, and to hear his secrets to writing, directing and just living a creative life.

LEW: Happy to have you here, Francis. We have photographers who are going to take a couple of pictures and leave if that's okay with you. My next book is going to be called *Naked Screenwriting: Academy Award–Winning Authors Bare Their Art, Soul, Craft, and Secrets.* Oliver was here; Billy Wilder was here; Ron Bass, Julius Epstein, Frank Pierson, Ernie Lehman, Tom Schulman, Bruce Joel Rubin, Irving Ravetch were all here.

FRANCIS: You all got to listen to these?

LEW: It's over a period of multiple 434s. This is my current graduate class. The rest are distinguished visitors and Shelley Anderson, who has been coordinating this affair. Professor Caruso and Hal Ackerman from our screenwriting department. Terry Bond Michael, in charge of UCLA public information; Marina Goldovskaya, our distinguished documentary professor, who comes to us from beautiful uptown Moscow; and Maren and Vincent, our research associates. But the people around the table, Francis, will be professional screenwriters. Our average age is thirty. As you can see, they're fairly grown up. Old is another way to put it.

FRANCIS: They look young to me.

LEW: Well, me, too, but I'm pretending. These particular people audition to get into this school and were selected from about five hundred applications, although the pool is growing each year. They also audition to get into our classes. We put these great eight together, and this class is the best I've ever had here, so that's why I say every one of them will be a professional screenwriter.

Ah! Come on in, Robert. Are you going to stay with us or are you going to be diplomatic and say hello and then leave? You're going to stay? Good, good, good. We're trying to inculcate him with the concept of writing being important to film school, and he's learning. Most of you know our dean, Robert Rosen. Okay? Let's see. Let's go back to 1960. I was going out of graduate school as you were coming in.

FRANCIS: Yes, it was 1960.

LEW: I remember you as a little, skinny Italian kid who had all the keys. He would be shooting at three o'clock or four o'clock in the morning, and then when he wasn't shooting at three o'clock or four o'clock in the morning, he'd be cutting. We both shared the wonderful director and professor Dorothy Arzner as one of the true pinnacles of our young experience and actually our entire lifetime.

FRANCIS: She was totally wonderful.

LEW: We want to talk here about process. I want to first ask you the same question I asked Billy Wilder: Do you consider yourself a director or a screenwriter?

FRANCIS: I consider myself a writer. That's the point of view I started from, and that's always at the root of my aspiration.

LEW: How do you feel about screenwriting being mostly in the oral tradition of storytelling? Does that track, or do you have another view?

FRANCIS: Well, as a kid, I started writing plays. Dumb little plays for the high school and college musicals. My family were a musical comedy. My dad actually conducted. I saw shows sitting in his orchestra pits. I was interested first in plays, specifically musicals, because of this. I had a brother who was a philosophy major, reading Andre Gide, James Joyce, and all. He was an older brother I looked up to. From him, I got a sense of the literary. He gave me books like *Brave New World*. To top it off, I was a kind of kid scientist. That was my own natural thing when I wasn't imitating my brother or my father. That ultimately got me into theater because in theater they needed someone to do the lights, which is why I had all the keys. I was always the one who controlled the technology.

I only became a director because I never was very high on my writing. Writers can be very tough on themselves. I was as a kid, certainly. I was just heartbroken because I felt I had no writing talent. I remember that drove me more into directing. I would be hanging lights, and I'd see the professor who was directing the play give directions. I thought, "Well, gee, I could do that." So I became more of a director because of my great tragedy, of my failure as a writer when I was nineteen or twenty. I can remember weeping over it, really, literally, because talent was a very important thing in our family. That was more important than anything, whether or not you had it, an issue none of us will ever satisfy in our lifetimes.

I became knocked out by film one afternoon when I was on the Hofstra campus and in their little theater. At four o'clock, they were showing Eisenstein's *Ten Days That Shook the World*. I didn't know much about it, so I went and sat and saw. I think it's, what, three or four hours long? It's long. I came out after that and wanted to make film, which is eerily logical because Eisenstein had been a theater designer, and in his biography he says, "In that moment the cart broke. The driver fell into the cinema." Well, I felt I didn't have to write novels like my brother or musicals like my father. Now I had something of my own. That's when I changed my desire in attending the Yale Drama School to UCLA's film program.

I found, however, when I got here, it was a real advantage to have tried to a write a lot. I wrote so many little stories and plays when I was sixteen and was always despondent that they weren't as good as I'd hoped or even good period. Yet here at UCLA, I found my writing experience was an advantage. I was known as the student more interested in screenwriting. I was able to get to make a short film because, I don't know if it's like that now, but you submit a script, and you compete to be one of the three productions that actually got funds. Writing was my edge throughout the early part of my career.

I became a screenwriter as a relatively young person. When I got out of school, I was twenty-five years old. I wrote important projects, like *This Property Is Condemned*. My dream became to write original work for film and then get to direct it, something that only Woody Allen has really been able to do, and among all the other directors, only a few people, like Oliver Stone, who really write their own work, could do that. But what a wonderful thing to do, if you could—to imagine what films are like. You know, in the past, it would be novels or plays but real original works of literature for the cinema. Not from a book, not from anything—originals. That was always my dream and my aspiration. When I started my career, that was my intention. The early movies I made, *The Rain People* and *The Conversation*, in a sense, come from that idea.

However, I had the great fortune, or misfortune, to be very success-ful very quickly with *The Godfather*. Suddenly, all the other dreams I'd had in college were put aside. I was now like the head of the drama department, the czar of that theater school, because of this. Extraor-dinary thing that happened with *The Godfather*: I had some money for the first time in my life. I could build a company that was sort of like that drama department I had going early on. Do original things and stuff. That's what Zoetrope was, in a sense. But there's a terrible price you pay. If you have a little company or you have these kinds of dreams, you can't take eight months off and write an original screen-play because you've got to have a production. We've got to make film. So you get into directing films from scripts that you didn't write or you worked on them or maybe in some cases you didn't work on them at all. I'm giving you this as a preamble because I do want to talk about the process.

My preamble is that all those years I worked, I always thought, "One day I'm going to make enough money where I don't have to work for two years. Then I'm going to write." I would really try after we made *One from the Heart*, a movie written by Armyan Bernstein. I adapted that, but fundamentally, it wasn't something I had written. I kept saying, "I'm going to write this thing that's fifty times too ambitious for me to really pull off," but nonetheless, if you're going to have a dream project, why not? You know, make it hard. And I would try to work on writing two or three weeks after I finished films. I did that off and on for fifteen years, and I even had a fragment of a draft as a result.

It was only recently that I have fulfilled the requirements where I could say, "Okay, this year, I'm not going to travel. I'm not going to do anything. I'm going to take this thing on. I'm going to do it one way or the other." I wake up every morning and write without fail. This morning, I'm at the typewriter by 7:00 a.m. I do it every day, six days a week. I've done it now for a month. So from that perspective, it might be fun to talk to me about screenwriting.

Lew: And so we will. Ron Bass says he gets up at three o'clock to write. Sigh. Yet he writes nine scripts a year. Back to UCLA, Francis, when we were crisscrossing as students, I remember we wrote for the cinematography class what we're going to shoot and our scene to edit for that class, and we wrote for our acting classes. We wrote, wrote, wrote. Our chair, Arthur Ripley, kept saying, "It's writing. It's writing. Every piece of writing you do is an investment in yourself." Now, you did *You're a Big Boy* here, at UCLA, or just immediately after.

Francis: That was my thesis.

Lew: It was released by—

Francis: What is now Warner Brothers.

Lew: How did *Patton* get to you? Wasn't that one of your first screenwriting assignments?

Francis: I won the Samuel Goldwyn Writing Award as a student. That award had never before been won with a screenplay. It had been novels and plays. That got a lot of play in Hollywood, and I was immediately called up by all these agents and stuff.

Lew: It's still going on, you know, the Goldwyn Award.

Francis: Sure. And you know how it goes. Before I know it, I had a job at Seven Arts as a staff writer. Seven Arts was a kind of, well, then the equivalent of an independent company. And hot, you know. Ray Stark was our leader. My job was to write scripts, which was the most wonderful thing that could happen because that's what I wanted to learn how to do anyway. Usually they gave me a book to adapt. They'd say, you know, write a script for *Reflections in a Golden Eye* or whatever. So, for two years, I basically wrote three scripts a year as a staff writer. From those days came the *Patton* assignment.

LEW: How did you get to writing *The Godfather*?

FRANCIS: Well, Paramount had a script that Mario Puzo had written, but oddly enough, it wasn't much like the book. For instance, it wasn't set in the 1940s. He must've listened to what someone told him to do. So I went to Paramount and said, "Well, let's put it back in the 1940s." I basically wrote the first draft, which was quite a bit like the book. I got along quite well with Mario. We sort of worked together.

LEW: When you were developing yourself as a screenwriter, did you have any books you read? Was Aristotle's *Poetics* or Egri particularly useful to you?

FRANCIS: You know, I had read a wonderful book on playwriting by the old dean of the Yale Drama School, George Baker, but I always had a tough time digesting things about writing from reading. Maybe it's like riding a bicycle. You're constantly trying to learn. In recent years in Hollywood, there's an obsession with these quick weekends in dramaturgy.

LEW: That's the thing I admire about these graduate students They commit to two to three years, and by the time they finish, they've done five to eight scripts. They ride the bicycle.

FRANCIS: The problem with this concern over dramaturgy, even with Aristotle, is that the rules are very manipulatable. It's great to understand the rules as to how you get from here to there, but it's all the things you do in and around that which sometimes defy gravity that makes a script come to life.

LEW: Let's now talk process. Do you have a particular litmus test for yourself in terms of how you say, "Hey, I want to spend a couple years of my life on this particular notion or this particular book or this particular whatever"?

FRANCIS: Which is where I'm at, sort of. I think you really have to cultivate your intuition because that tells you what you love and what you like to be immersed in the vicinity of, and the project I've chosen for this original screenplay is something I knew I would like to live with for a long time because it was so interesting to me. That interest would see me through all those times of self-doubt. That first choice is really important.

I've been working on this current project off and on for almost twenty years. Unfortunately, I never got to spend three weeks or four weeks in a row on it, but I keep coming back to it. The world has changed, yet the story is always very contemporary to me. So choosing the right thing that's going to continue to feed you is very important, which means you have to choose from your heart and not because they're making a certain kind of movie.

LEW: Me, along with my fellow professors Richard, Dee, and Hal here, were cursed with the student Tarantino imitations. Prior to that, with *Die Hard* in a grain silo or *Die Hard* in an elevator. Was doing something commercial ever meaningful to you as a writer?

FRANCIS: In the earlier parts of my career, I didn't really see things that way. I knew that if you made a movie and it was a hit, that was good. You could get a nice car. I understood it that level. But the level of commerciality in the last ten years, where the box office reaches twenty million, I never think of it that way, ever.

LEW: Of course, we were blessed with running like Pamplona bulls down to the Laemmle Theater on Hillhurst, checking out Antonioni's doing this year or Bergman or Truffaut.

FRANCIS: That was a wonderful era. Today, Steven's such a bright example to young people. You know, they say, "Wow, I can do that." This idea now is there is also an art to making movies that are incredibly popular. This idea that you should write something that you could ultimately sell makes sense. You can just as easily fall in love with a rich man or woman. When we were young, our idea was to be Fellini or Kurosawa. We wanted to make films our work, our novels, to give the world our take on it. We wanted to ultimately address the question "What is art?" I feel the purpose of art is to imitate life, to illuminate life, so people can understand and see that there is illumination even in our times. We're living in such interesting times. So many things are changing so suddenly, more so than perhaps any other time in history. The old things, a remake of this or that television series, what does that have to do with the era we're moving into?

LEW: I'm crazed with the concept of what you just said about screen-writing as art because that's my crusade with the Writers Guild. We will never become serious artists if we keep whining about how the studios have fucked us over.

FRANCIS: We're in school. What kind of language is that?

LEW: As you just said, Francis, eras change.

FRANCIS: I remember a screenwriting class at UCLA. It was in the evening in one of those bungalows. We were reading the text, and there were, if you'll excuse me, lots of *fucks*. We were all debating whether or not the writer should use other words like *friggin*. Then all of a sudden, our teacher, Hugh Gray, turns red and shouts, "I don't care what any of you say! You're never going to say the word *fuck* in a movie in your lifetimes!" This was in 1963.

LEW: Ah, Hugh Gray, bless his departed soul.

FRANCIS: I was considered really smart because they needed that obscenity in some movie I worked on. I said, "Some bakery goods sounded sexy," so I had stuff in it like, "Bring your . . ." I can't even say it now, but if you use any bakery good name with that attitude, it works!

LEW: We had Julius Epstein here, and somebody came late, after I promised him we wouldn't talk about *Casablanca* or anything related to this wonderful movie because he gets it all too often. A latecomer says, "Mr. Epstein, tell us about *Casablanca*." I hurriedly say, "Oh, no no! We promised—but as long as she brought it up, do you have anything to say?" He said, "Lew, you used a scatological word before. May I use one now?" Then he looks directly at the camera and he says, "Slick shit." Going from scatological language to structure, is structure different today in the way you write versus when you were starting out?

FRANCIS: There are profound differences. In my experience, I've worked on lots of scripts between writing a screenplay that you're adapting from another source or rewriting a screenplay that someone else has written. So different. The latter is very interesting discussion because it's ulti-mately about writing, be it a screenplay, short story, novella, or novel. In terms of adapting a screenplay, what I was doing at Seven Arts was trying to get an original work to fill you with sensations and emotions and then to put them out in a very different form. You have to use what you know about storytelling in the cinematic form. The visuals tell you much, much more than just descriptions. The ultimate memorable stuff comes from dramaturgy and how the behavior of the characters let you learn about them. Oh, I have a funny story to illustrate this.

There's a little girl where I live in San Francisco. I think she's seven. She's a genius, really a genius. Her parents say she gets into fights with other kids because she knows all this stuff and she doesn't abide like a normal kid. I said, "Well, drop her off with me, and I'll play with her for a few hours." So she comes over, and she's a nice little girl. Eventually, she tells me she wants to write a screenplay. I say fine. She says to me, "It's called *The Adventure of Mozambique*." Then she dictates to me, "The little girls go, the Arabs are in the car, they're all following him, and so and so." I realized that most of what I would say to her was, "But how are we going to show that?" She would say, "You know, they have the bags of stolen gold." I'd say, "Well, how do we know what's in the bags?" She says, "We'll write 'Money' on the bags." I realized in trying to translate this little child genius into a screenwriter, the issue was always, "Well, how are you going to get that across without just saying it?"

ROBERT ROSEN: But how do you write about what it's going to look like? You'd have to be real sparse on the dialogue.

FRANCIS: A screenplay is the most horrible reading experience that has yet been devised. By contrast, reading a short story is a pleasure. You have to keep in mind and really help the reader. So many times, I'm reading a script, and I'm thirty pages in, and I say, "What? Who is this?" Then, I'm spending my time going back and looking for a name. As a writer, you have to try and give the reader the experience of reading a story, even though it's going to end up as a movie. You want it to be like the actual experience of seeing it, as much as you can, if you can. Strive for that.

The punch line on this little girl is when we get to the part where she says, "And they run into a copse of trees." I said, "A what?" She's seven years old. She says it again, "They run into a copse of trees." I said, "There's no such word as *copse*." She says, "Of course there is. Like a gander of geese or a pride of lions. A copse of trees." I said, "I'm getting a dictionary." Sure enough, there it is: a copse of trees. That was my little screenwriter. Write to show in a script. Cinema is a language.

The screenwriter knows and understands that language and knows that the best way is to show things to the audience and to get them to feel. The best way to get them to feel is with the interaction of great characters or the value of a great action sequence with brilliant cutting. You start to be savvy as to what the film language actually is. Today, there is pretty much a unified script language. Most movies, as Godard said, "If you cut the titles off of them, you wouldn't know who made them." Some of the best people, you can see their style. Generally, movies are turning into this more generic product. What I'm interested in these days is the idea of writing that reaches into your feelings, your intuitions. Write something that in some way makes us all understand things, like the relationship of men and women, the effects of family being scattered all over, whatever. Something that really can help you understand life or participate or get emotional. That to me has to come from original writing. Writing from your heart, your soul.

LEW: Like Faulkner said in his Nobel Prize speech, "There are no longer problems of the spirit. There is only one question: When will I be blown up? Because of this, the young man, young woman writing today has forgotten the problems of the human heart in conflict with itself, which alone can make good writing because only that is worth writing about, worth the agony and the sweat."

FRANCIS: So right. I have lots of nieces and nephews. They're all directors and writers and actors. I'm always saying, "Don't write something because they're going to do that kind of movie. Write something you know, something that's a part of you." So that's the kind of writing that I'm interested in. Did you guys know we have a short-story magazine? Have you seen it? You should get it. It's only stories. The form of the short story or the novella that we want to do, that I want to do. The screenplay, the part of it where you get to illustrate various things by giving the director suggestion as to how he might film it—that's the least of it. The most important are the characters.

LEW: Is that what you start with: with the characters, once you have the idea?

FRANCIS: As you know, so many people have written books. There are nineteen dramatic situations or twenty-six; one guy says forty-two. However it is, there are not a lot of dramatic situations. You can buy the book, like the famous Georges Polti, who says thirty-six. What makes it infinite is that the characters in different situations are all so different. How they connect to the plots will make it different. It's ultimately through character that an audience will become focused and remember. Working with a wonderful plot through these characters is when it becomes a supreme thing. I would very definitely emphasize character and try and find ways to help the actor so that the actor can use behaviors as exposition or interaction with other characters. Something happens to so and so, and you realize, "Oh, I get it. That person did that because they're that." Then you get a shiver because you realize you've become so intimate with these characters.

Character and practice doing character. I suggest everybody have a notebook. Just write character sketches all of the time, whether you're on an airplane, whatever. See how skillful you are in just a paragraph or two in bringing out this character you're observing and feeling something about. That notebook becomes ideal when you're trying to write a script. You say, "Oh, I had this great guy!" and you can copy him right out of there. The other thing is to keep a similar book of characters that you've encountered in literature. Write about characters in books. It's a slightly different perspective, but you also learn a lot from that.

LEW: Do you outline?

FRANCIS: Well, I work in a kind of never-ending platforming technique, which is to say that I don't develop a story in any logical way. I do it in an emotional way. When I feel like writing, I'll venture out, like when you build a bridge without anything on it. Then I'll stop and go back up and often do it again. It's a constant process of forging ahead into uncharted territory, and then, usually in the afternoons, I look at it and build myself an outline. I have an outline now, from beginning to end, but I don't have the ending worked out well enough just yet.

LEW: Do you sometimes get to the third act and just think, "Fuck it, I'll get there eventually"?

FRANCIS: Definitely. I think the name of the game is to reach into yourself and find something in you that's alive, that isn't all worked out, that's just emotional, and use those parts for your writing. Those are the things that give rise to art. How do you know to do this or that? For me, and for other people I've known, you look for life because if it has life, it doesn't matter if it's imperfect. Life is what you're trying to do. So on the other side, use your real stuff. Then you use your head to figure out so and so. The beauty of writing is that you can always rewrite. I tell you, when you don't have it and you get there in the morning and you start out, and it's uncharted territory, you think, "I had this thing and there were going to be great events, but now, where are they? What does my character say?" Okay, they're in a room.

Wait a second, here's a good example: I saw a wonderful old clip of Jane Fonda when she was like eighteen or nineteen. She was talking about acting. She was really beautiful, too, I might add. She explained how she thought about stuff that you love to do or things that you always wanted to do and you dream about it and one day you get to do it. It can be hard, painful work, but it's worth every second. That's how I feel. I have never started to write an original screenplay and then finished it, set it aside, and said, "Okay, I'm ready to make that."

I started *The Rain People* at UCLA. Then I abandoned it three-quarters through and then picked it up again when I was trying to write another original. I worked on that a little bit, and then I saw *The Rain People* more clearly. That's when I finished it and then made it. After *The Godfather*, I went back and found a fragment I had abandoned when I went to make *The Rain People*, and that turned into *The Conversation*. So for me, there's a two-tiered thing I write on. There is this gene in the writer's body that is activated when you're writing that makes you think it's terrible, and you just have to say, "I know." What I do when I finish a page: I turn it over and don't look at it again because it's not important what I wrote. What's important is more the journey I'm on. I can always go back and revise it.

In fact, let's say I'm thirty pages in, and I want to make a major revision. I won't use that as an excuse to go all of the way back to the beginning. That's bad. What I do is I say, "Okay, from now on, he's really a woman." Then later on, if it works out, I'll go back and do it from the beginning. It's very important not to sabotage yourself when you're in this original writing mood. Now I'm happy because now I'm going to rewrite this mess, but I have something I can look at. I'm telling myself that I can do better. As soon as I'm lost, I can go back and say, "Ah, that was that scene. That's important to me."

LEW: George Lucas once told me that he considered the first draft the most important draft. I've always used that idea in the classroom because once you get the first draft, it's a downhill run from there. You've got an emotional blueprint.

FRANCIS: In a way. I work differently from many other people. I do a lot of rewriting. I do lots of drafts. I mean, I do like thirty to thirty-five drafts. I'm constantly doing another draft.

LEW: Are there substantial changes in each draft?

FRANCIS: Sometimes they're far-out changes. What it is, I guess, I'm like a car engine. A car engine has no strength until it reaches a high RPM. I don't have any good ideas until it starts to really come to life for me. I'm not confident before that.

LEW: This is what you mean when you said, "layering in tiers." Have you always done this? Even in the beginning?

FRANCIS: I think it's the way I think. I'm not patient enough to sit there and analytically make a step outline. I like to make it after I put my hand in, a little bit, and get a feel for it. Then I can imagine the steps. Usually, what I do is, I'm just about to finish, then I take the drafts and make a step outline from it. I'll use that to pin on a bulletin board, and then I rewrite.

LEW: Jack Sowards is one of our people. He wrote the second *Star Trek*, *The Wrath of Khan*. Jack says he does the first draft, then tosses it, then does his first real draft.

FRANCIS: I can understand that.

LEW: And one of his students asked, "What if there's something in that first draft?" Jack said, "Then I'll remember it."

FRANCIS: It's funny. You do remember the good stuff. That's my theory in cutting a movie or cutting a script. A lot of things you face in a script are, well, you have to decide to eliminate the characters and scenes. I always say when I cut something that should be in, that it's going to nag me and nag me, and it will find a way back in.

LEW: Now when you get into a script, your outline is just sort of evolving, though I'm sure you have a beginning, middle, and end?

FRANCIS: Not in that order.

LEW: Let's talk script. Have you always started at seven o'clock in the morning?

FRANCIS: I get up at ten till six each morning. I mean, the alarm rings then. I'm sort of out of bed by six o'clock.

LEW: Those are your most creative hours? First thing in the morning?

FRANCIS: Well, all hours are good, but for writing, for me, early in the morning I have no emotional biases. Someone hasn't hurt my feelings, someone hasn't said something stupid, someone hasn't made you sad. So you're basically still water. Your emotions are fluid and very influence-able. Plus you've slept, so you're not sleepy or drowsy. You're rested, and you're at your full thing. Nobody else is up, so no one is going to call you or distract you or annoy you. You have at least three hours. You could do your whole day in three hours, but I'll keep going, and in the afternoon, I like to review because my work is based on such a lot of research. I mean so much research. I like to think through what I'm really doing and what the influencing sources are. I always have many, many books that deal with my subject, and all have interesting things to reference.

LEW: Do you set goals for yourself?

FRANCIS: I've been thinking about that. I was feeling a little nervous, and I thought I would. However, I've made good, natural progress. So I don't feel as pressed as I did. I have no goal. I just think I'm going to work on the script. Maybe I'll spend the rest of the year.

LEW: Floyd Mutrux said he works by page rather than by hour. He had a daily five-page goal. Do you have a page count?

FRANCIS: Well, if you do five pages of screenplay a day, you can feel okay if you want to chuck it. My experience is, I usually have five terrible pages. That's not the same. I mean, you want to work with those pages and to look at them. If you do five pages in the morning, either you're the type who thinks it out well and then the five pages are really there, or you just kind of write. Gore Vidal says, "You just turn up the tap," which I think is very good for myself. That's when you get all of the exotic stuff. You think, "Well, maybe this isn't really a scene. What if I moved it here? What if she doesn't come in there? What if she's already there?" There are so many what-ifs. A good thing to do for writing character is to know a little about acting. The craft of acting very much covers the same material as in creating characters. Certainly motivation and behavior, and also you can write roles actors like to do because they don't want to just stand there and talk. They want to behave.

LEW: Gore Vidal said, "Turn on the tap." Contextualize that a little.

FRANCIS: Well, you just go at it, and it comes out. You don't think about it.

LEW: You don't intellectualize it.

FRANCIS: You just write.

LEW: Does creativity come from your subconscious? Is that what you're saying?

FRANCIS: What creativity? My greatest talent is I'm a great idea person. I come up with a thousand ideas an hour. That's why I have wineries and hotels and stuff. I can't shut it off. I have faith. I'm at the point now, when I write, I just write it the way I want, and I don't care about whether it's good, bad, or indifferent. I know that later on I'll have a great idea that will fix it. In other words, I have faith in my ideas.

LEW: To drop a Hemingway line, what's your bullshit detector? Do you have a clear thing you do to say, "Wait a minute, that's bad"?

FRANCIS: Eventually, it just comes to me as I read it through. I make many passes, and without even thinking about it, I make it better. I also act out scenes in my head, or sometimes I even say them like an actor improvising.

LEW: Do you often read your scenes out loud? I covertly saw Neil Simon reading aloud.

FRANCIS: A little bit. I do when we're about to make a movie or even early in the writing process. We sometimes invite actors to read the script. I've read this script in its earlier form eight years ago.

LEW: You told me three or four years ago you had a company, and you had actors read scripts in front of an audience, like the old days of radio.

FRANCIS: I have experimented with more techniques in writing and rehearsing actors and casting actors and preparing movies than any other human being I can think of. I've tried everything to learn. Where I'm at now, oddly enough, is the most simple. It's sort of like at the very beginning. Maybe it's not quite the same, but when you go through all those, you learn more of what the essentials are.

LEW: Is writing in isolation important to you?

FRANCIS: I can rewrite around people. People could be having fun, and I could be rewriting.

LEW: My wife is always playing up my writing by saying, "I'm by my mother's dying bed, with my daughter giving birth," and I'm sitting there working on scenes. Do you do that sort of thing?

FRANCIS: No, I don't think I can concentrate quite like that. I mean, when something is going on, I'm usually going on with what's going on.

LEW: Were you at a particular point in time more precious? I'm trying to get out of an old Noël Coward line: "I adore professionalism. I loathe writers who can only write when it is raining."

FRANCIS: I have the panic in the morning, but it doesn't mean it will last more than ten or fifteen minutes. Then I start writing. The pitfall I find both in writing and with acting is to stop and start writing about what it is you're trying to write about. When you're working with actors, they're always trying to say, "Okay, well, you're Mary, you know, and I'll be Mary. Hi Mary. Now, let's do this." And then they'll say, "Yeah, but I think that she," and then I say, "No, no, no, stay in character and tell me the same thing." Force yourself to do that. Just like the writer.

I notice, at the end of a day's work on a screenplay, it suddenly turns into, well, what I'm really trying to do is understand time. Time is not reliable. This whole essay at the end thing. That's just me being uncomfortable being in it, like actors are. Stay in it as long as you can because for every actor, every moment, every emotion that you experience within the character, you're getting like a bank deposit. The same with writing. You're getting stuff that's probably got something. That's a little foible of mine.

LEW: In the years that I've been here, I've always had my students do character sketches before they start developing step outlines. We've just started doing them in—where is she?

SHELLEY: Tyler?

LEW: Yes, it was Tyler's fault. She did her characters in first person, and that ties into what you're saying. So now it's required that all are in first person.

FRANCIS: Well, whenever you go through that, it's a magical thing. To be able to put yourself in another frame of mind, it's almost ritualistic for me. You get a kind of energy and magic from your resources that are not normally available to you. It's good to go through that.

LEW: Of course, Francis has something going for him, having come through UCLA with a really strong background in theater. I can't impress enough upon any of you to get into theater as much as you can. It will give you more writing skills than you realize.

FRANCIS: It's also fun. Every so often, at my place in Napa, we'll do three or four one-act plays. We have a place that can be a nice theater. All of the kids will play a part. It's sort of like a Mickey Rooney movie because at the end of the summer, a hundred or so neighbors come over, and we put on the plays. I think working in one-act-play form and writing short stories is what people who want to be writers should be doing. The screenplay is easy, if you can tell a short story. What did Orson Welles say? Didn't he say you can learn a whole lot in a day or something?

LEW: Oh, that was on directing.

FRANCIS: Some people want to be directors, and I always tell them to direct a few one-act plays. It's cheap. You get two or three people. You could either write it, or there's a whole wonderful bunch of one-act plays already written.

LEW: We encourage students to come in with some knowledge of the playwrights, and what he's saying is true. Now, let's have questions for fifteen minutes or so, okay? Anybody got to say anything? They're grumbling because they all wanted to go to Napa.

FRANCIS: We'll go tonight. Where's the jet?

LEW: They were so excited about the possibility of going to be with you in Napa.

FRANCIS: Where's the UCLA jet?

LEW: And one said, "Why do we want to go to Napa?" And I said, "When you and I were film students, we would have killed to go to the vineyards to be with Orson Welles."

FRANCIS: No wine before their time.

LEW: Yes, Cindy?

CINDY: I rewatched *Apocalypse Now* and *Hearts of Darkness*, and I was just watching you. I mean, you were obsessed, and that was like twenty-some years ago. Does that ever fade? Not to sound horrible, but does age change anything in your enthusiasm?

FRANCIS: I think age, what it does bring, it lets you shed some of the stuff you went through that isn't necessary. Basically, what you have to realize is that in those situations, the person, myself in that case, was terribly insecure. That's what it really all comes from. So the more secure you can be, the more you can be effective with less strum and drum, I think.

LEW: My feelings about Francis—because I do remember him when he was a young, shave-tailed Italian boy—he was always enthusiastic.

FRANCIS: Always.

LEW: We had him to UCLA about four years ago, and I hadn't seen Francis in fifteen or so years. I was so worried that he was going to be the great, "I am the director." He wasn't at all. He was just a graduate student again. Mazel tov, dear Francis.

FRANCIS: I think I still have the feeling I had then. I'm now very, very interested in the idea of having the rest of my career being that I just write and then I direct what I've written. I would love that to be possible. I would like to do a musical, too.

LEW: John Shaw.

JOHN: When approaching, say *Patton*, an autobiographical subject, so you have to almost immediately just treat him as a character. How was your approach to taking someone whose life was as large as *Patton*?

FRANCIS: My approach was to take about thirty books on Patton and just sit down and read all of them. From that, he became a character. I think in the research, I got this feeling that he was a Don Quixote out of his time, in another era. Usually with screenplays, it's like one thing opens up for you. I saw this image of him by a windmill, and that became my concept for how to do it. That's true of actors, too.

Gene Hackman once told me that when he was working on *The French Connection*, he didn't have a character for the first three weeks. He just didn't know what the hell he was doing. He was very bad, but then they're in the alleyway, and he goes over to craft service, and he takes a cup of coffee, and he takes a donut. He dunks the donut, takes a bite, and throws it away. Billy Friedkin said, "That's him!" Sometimes that's all. Actors find their characters at different rates. Some are in already. Some are looking for it.

Freddy Forrest was the last one to get on it in *Apocalypse Now*. I knew he was so unhappy, so I said, "Well, come up with me, and have dinner and talk." "Francis," he says, "I'm not really here. I'm in Beverly Hills with my things, going with my dog to the so and so." I said, "Well, that's who the guy is. Whenever you're lost in the movie, just say, 'I'm not here,'" which is what he did. So, it's just something that opens up as you're in a project, and that can happen with writing, too.

LEW: Basically, the sense of what the character or even the movie is about. I mean, we're always ragging on students to define what their movie is really about.

FRANCIS: I have a hunch I didn't answer your question.

JOHN: No, no, no, you did.

LEW: Kris Young.

KRIS: You've had a really long and successful career. Do you have any tips about how to keep a career going for a long time? Also, some people say you have to reinvent yourself every few years. Wondering if you've had times where you did reinvent yourself, and if so, what was that?

FRANCIS: I don't think I consciously said, "I've got to reinvent myself." I think I just have so many interests, and I'm so enthusiastic about a lot of things.

LEW: Shelley Anderson.

SHELLEY: This is back to more of the acting thing. I heard an interview with Wayne Wang, and someone was asking him, "What did Harvey Keitel teach you in *Smoke*?" He remembered Harvey saying that it's all about secrets. I thought that was pretty interesting. Do you ever think about the secrets before you write your characters?

FRANCIS: Well, actors are very much like—well, Mickey Rourke had this thing, when he's playing in a scene, there's usually something he's brought in that morning. Maybe a piece of jewelry or something he's got in his pocket. At first I thought that was very weird, but then I said,

"Well, that's great, if he's thinking about that, then whatever's happening is going to kind of happen as it's happening." So then I started to bring him little things. The whole art of working with actors is much more interesting and full of things and options that many directors don't consider because they've never been actors. Actors tend to be pretty good directors. This is a big reason for it.

LEW: Secrets. Is there a secret behind the string on your wrist?

FRANCIS: I was in Brazil, and they put this on my wrist and tied it with three knots and said, "I should make a wish." I wished for, you know, profound things, of course, good health, but other meaningful things. I tried to make altruistic wishes. So, now I have to wait until it falls off. I kind of pull at it though.

LEW: Kimberly Simi.

KIMBERLY: You said artists should illuminate life. I'm just curious, what type of life do you want to illuminate? Are you finding you are going back to your childhood experiences or your family?

FRANCIS: Well, one thought: I feel ultimately doing that is the only way I can really write something from the heart. I have such strong feelings about members of my family that sooner or later, I would love to do my *Long Day's Journey into Night*. What I'm doing now, of course, I make use of anything I've got, but it's not the story directly related to my life.

LEW: Paul John Castro.

PAUL: When you write dialogue, do you have a particular actor in mind once you've established the character? Like Al Pacino's voice with Michael?

FRANCIS: No. Of course, at that time, he didn't have that voice. I tend to think of actors more visually. I also play the parts myself. I'll pretend I'm the character.

LEW: Somebody else, please. Robert Rosen, say something if you want. You have a million questions bubbling inside you. Oh, yes, Alexander Cassini.

ALEXANDER: You talked about doubt when you're writing, the self-doubt. Has that changed over the years? And if it hasn't changed, is that maybe the source? Not of creativity but of keeping it fresh?

FRANCIS: I think you're onto something. I mean, my experience now tells me that in those terrible moments when I'm writing it, even though I think it's stupid and dumb, usually a day later, I look back, and there was something there. So maybe the doubt is some sort of, I don't know, displeasure or fear. You have to learn to keep on going. Then it can take off. Then things can start happening, and you can start enjoying it. But I, of course, I'm going back to original writing after twenty years, so I'm nervous I can't do it.

LEW: Larry Gelbart talked about the constant worry of having someone discover him to be a fraud.

FRANCIS: But when you cook, you know there's a phase when you're doing certain kinds of things that it doesn't look like anything. You're still putting in this and that, but you have to have faith that if you keep cooking and you keep stirring, it's going to be good sauce. That's what I feel about writing.

ROBERT ROSEN: When you were here a while back, you talked about a real interest in live television. It was interesting when John Franken-heimer was here. Somebody asked him, "How many pages a day did you shoot when you were doing television?" He said, "All of them." What's your interest in television, particularly in relationship to the issues of writing?

FRANCIS: I've always had this feeling there was almost a whole other form which I think of as live cinema. That's what *One from the Heart* was supposed to be. We weren't able to really do it, but we tried. I made some fundamental mistakes. I love the idea of doing an entire complex, articulate, beautiful work of cinema live. Literally, the actors go in and do the whole thing, and that's it. People are amazed when someone does a six-minute scene. But actors used to do the whole hundred minutes at once.

ROBERT ROSEN: The way Frankenheimer used to.

FRANCIS: I saw things in Frankenheimer that no one's ever seen because they didn't have video tape then. Like *Farewell to Arms*.

LEW: I remember *Old Man and the Sea* for *Playhouse 90*.

FRANCIS: They were unbelievable. Did you ever see *The Comedian*, with Mickey Rooney? All live, all in one shot. Amazing.

Lew: Dee Caruso.

Dee: What's it like working with Marlon Brando?

Francis: Oh, Brando is an extremely brilliant man. If I've gotten, in my lifetime, to meet two or three geniuses, I would make him one. Not necessarily because of his great acting but just because of the kind of things he thinks about and talks about. He can really suck you into that world, and that's a great pleasure. He's a very affectionate man. He loves kids. He's sort of childish himself, kind of, you know, selfish. But I think he's brilliant.

Dee: How much of *The Godfather* was Brando, and how much was in the script and directing?

Francis: Well, it was substantially in the script.

Lew: Paul John.

Paul: I'm sure you look back on your career and wish you could have done some things differently. As a writer, what would you have done differently? And what would you advise us not to do?

Francis: Well, in my case, I would have wished that I only directed movies where I had written the story and the script. That's the only regret I have in life. I'm going to try now. I'm fifty-nine years old, so I have this date with myself that before I'm sixty, I am going to get back on that track.

Kris: As a screenwriter, sometimes I wonder if I have what it takes to direct. Is there something inside yourself as a writer that makes a good director? How do you know you're going to be able to direct?

Francis: Writers, oddly enough, have less of a need to become directors than, say, actors. It depends if you're the kind of person that really is interested in acting and knows about it. It really comes from your personality. I would direct a one-act play or something just to see how you like it.

Lew: We've actually gotten more, with David Koepp being the last one, directors out of our screenwriting department than actually all of the directing schools in the United States combined. These writers after a while said, "Fuck it, I want to do it myself." Is that kind of what you did too? Oh, that's right. Sorry, I keep forgetting, you didn't really have to go through the trouble in the '60s. Call me any scatological thing you can think of. I taught in the '60s, okay?

FRANCIS: I pay a dollar to any woman in my presence when I say a word like that. My secretary, she's got about—she doesn't have that much.

LEW: Oh, one more please.

FRANCIS: She has ten dollars, maybe nine.

LEW: Katherine Hollis.

KATHERINE: The worlds that we create are all on paper. You've had the opportunity of taking those and translating them into film. What is the gulf between what you imagine when you're writing and what you direct or produce that's on film? Do they match up?

FRANCIS: Usually it's much more wonderful because you have the talents of a great production designer. And, well, it's a collaborative art. All of these other people are so gifted. You can be very gentle about suggesting shots unless it's an idea that is important because you know you're going to have this wonderful photographer who's going to talk over things with this wonderful director. They're all going to add to it.

LEW: David Plieler.

DAVID: I like to read the script and watch the movie and really tear it apart and see what they ended up with on the screen. Is it better for me to write long form more?

FRANCIS: I think you should write almost a novella, something of the length that will give the reader of the story the impact you want.

DAVID: Not what we think the final cut might look like?

FRANCIS: Well, you know, a script becoming a movie is like a chemical process in that it can't be looked at. Your script is not going to be like the page because it's going to come to life.

LEW: My publisher said that when people buy all these screenwriting books, they look for the secret in them. Like the bachelor who says, maybe I missed the secret on being a successful bachelor because I missed the February 1984 issue of *Playboy*. Are there any secrets you think that are particular to screenwriting?

FRANCIS: There are many techniques you learn and pitfalls you learn to avoid. For example, it's very difficult to have a lot of characters. Mine tend to have a lot of characters. I've overdone it in that department. Based on that, this is an epic movie, where I've focused on protagonists but less on plot lines. I've done that more than anything in *The Godfather II*. There were two stories with lots of people. That's a real juggling act. Audiences tend to want to get some emotional satisfaction, and that's hard to do when you're always switching characters. Maybe you're making a wonderful intellectual or a cinematic idea, but audiences really want to stay with characters and see them have experiences and go through their feelings with them. That's easier to do when you focus on fewer characters.

LEW: It says here in this magazine interview—

FRANCIS: Oh, nice smile.

LEW: Yeah, same tie? "I know the thing I'm writing, ultimately, is ambitious." It's original, but it's the same guy who wrote *The Conversation*. You all here must realize there are two people who have won three screenwriting Oscars. This gentleman here and Billy Wilder. We're rooting for number 4 here, particularly because he's one of us. What's that line in *The Freaks*? "You are one of us now." Remember that? At any rate, back to the article "The same guy who wrote *The Conversation* on the scale of *Apocalypse Now*. It's contemporary. It tries to illuminate where we are, where mankind is today, where this civilization is going."

FRANCIS: I'm making a movie about the meaning of life.

LEW: Somebody asked me yesterday what you were doing, and I said, "He's making a movie about the meaning of life!"

FRANCIS: I'm tackling that every day.

LEW: Any rate, we wish you the very best. We're so grateful you popped by. I'm empowered by my wonderful dean, here to offer you a screenwriting position for one minute, one hour, one year. Right, Robert?

ROBERT ROSEN: Anytime. We don't care about the directing department.

LEW: Come and see us anytime you're in the area. We want you in a multiplicity of ways. Right, Robert? When Billy Wilder left our 434, I said, "Mr. Wilder, having you come to our film school is akin to God visiting divinity school. May I say in your case, St. Paul or Jesus? Thank you so much for being at our 434."

FRANCIS: Well, I love Billy Wilder. He's such a wonderful man. He's so funny. Did you hear the Billy Wilder story about his wife asking him to get her a bidet when he was in Europe? Billy sends her a telegram: "Cannot find bidet. Suggest handstand in shower."

SHELLEY: At the Writers Guild, one of the reporters asked, "Mr. Wilder, do you think you could compete in today's market with all the special effects?" And he says, "Oh when we did movies, we had special effects. We called it dialogue."

FRANCIS: He's a funny man.

LEW: Three for Billy. Three for you. Number 4 on the horizon line. Thank you, thank you, thank you, dear Francis Ford Coppola. You are one of us, and we all aspire to be one of you.

2

Bruce Joel Rubin

Bruce J. R. is not a Hollywood archetype; he is the most spiritual man I have ever met. Bruce spent a year and one-half with the Dalai Lama, one of my idols, as you will read. It will seem clear that the Writers Guild of America should make it mandatory for all screenwriters to gain their WGA cards via walking mountains barefoot and chanting in robes.

Alas, that will not occur, so in reading the path that Rubin took, sit back and prepare to be a changed writer forever. He is that good! Kidding aside, this conversation is one of the best in this compilation of Oscar-winning screenwriters. I encourage you to get naked, with maybe a robe and bare feet, as Bruce Joel Rubin chants his way into your writing and your soul.

LEW: You know, Bruce Joel Rubin, when I went to school here in '59, the Sanders brothers were the big deal? They won an Oscar for *Time Out of War*. Then David Ward for *Sting*. A friend of mine I'm sure you all know as Lenny Bruce once said, "There's nothing sadder than an old hipster." Bruce, half of these 434 people, twelve out of the yearly enrolled twenty, will be professional screenwriters within the next three or four years.

ROBERT DAVENPORT: Perhaps.

LEW: No perhaps, Robert. We'll even include you in the pro half. Anyway, this is a very special group we have here because this is medical or law school for these screenwriters. I teach undergrads once a year, and I find I'm preparing them for life. Here, we prepare them for a career, and we're so pleased you're part of the process today, Bruce.

I want to start with the lead-in: "Bruce Joel Rubin's home is in a quiet section of the San Fernando Valley, characterized by its rustic care. It's almost farmland and not at all what one might expect from a man who has written one of the all-time profitable movies, *Ghost*. It's certainly far from the usual haunts of the successor. Our interview is punctuated by the sound of a train going by not far away, which is one of the reasons he stays here because likes the sound. Also, the neighbors have horses and other animals, and it's a good place for his children to grow up."

BRUCE: I don't know who this person was. They were not in my house. I've never been a slug in my room. He describes me as, I used to be a film curator at the Whitney Museum, and as I recall, he describes me as the janitor of the Whitney Museum. So I wouldn't trust what anybody writes, and this in particular. I have no idea who this person was. I mean, I know they must have come to my house and talked to me one afternoon, but I don't know what they're describing. I think they're just flipping back through their notes and trying to remember something.

LEW: Okay, how about this: "I think I was looking for a teacher but not just to learn writing; I really wanted someone to teach me the process by which one can go deeper into one's self, to really enter into the hidden centers of the soul. The whole purpose of living, in my mind, is to make that journey. To me, there is a deep significance in our presence, in this plane of existence, and so the journey I began is a kind of search without knowing exactly what I was searching for." Is that in the ballpark?

BRUCE: That's pretty good.

LEW: That was from a '93 purported interview with you. This is really what I'm coming to. I've been professing screenwriting now for twenty years, concurrently with my own screenwriting career, and I'm getting more and more people excited about the concept of getting into the soul of writing. I'm almost at a point in my teaching to totally go beyond craft. Screenwriting students are so knowledgeable. When I started teaching, a scrap of poetry, a bit of a short story, if it looked interesting it would get students into the program. We almost had to tackle people for admittance. Then we spent half of their master's career teaching them craft.

At present, people come in well skilled or four and five scripts already down the road. We're now mostly interested in them going out into the world and trying to do something other than just taking up space on the planet. We want our people to develop creative strength and confidence in their own ability. We believe the only real strength comes out of commercial detachment. If your happiness is based on material achievement, then you're going to be in grave trouble because you become addicted to the things "they" give you. I just came from a doctor's appointment. He kept on talking about "they." "They" are the people you can't identify. In this instance, "they" would be the HMO folks. They won't do this; they won't let him do this.

Okay, enough philosophy cum psychology. Let me give you the Bruce Joel Rubin credits: *Brainstorm*; *Deadly Friend*; *Ghost*; *Jacob's Ladder*; *My Life*; and, it says here, *Deep Impact*. Is that something on the shelf or about to be made?

BRUCE: It's in production.

LEW: Excellent. Who's directing?

BRUCE: It's produced by Spielberg. It was going to be directed by Spielberg, but it's being directed by a woman whose name I forget, but she's an Emmy Award winner for *ER*. I'm no longer associated with the project. It's a long story. I don't think it should be on camera, but if you turn off the camera—

LEW: That's all right. We really want to get into the process as opposed to—well, if war or horror stories come out, they'll come out. We're trying to maintain as much idealism as these 434-ers might have left. Most of these people, as you can tell, are over the age of twenty-five, so they've already had a bit of life experience and are familiar with war stories. We're interested in trying to figure out how to exist with these horrors or interpret them as something other than horror. What I'm also trying to say is that I've run for the board of directors for the Writers Guild, and my basic platform was that the screenwriter, I think, should be regarded as an artist. We're never going to be regarded as such if we continue bitching like little children saying how badly "they" screwed us over. In television they don't do that anymore because the writer controls the television medium, as in theater. Hopefully, feature writers will get there. What are you working on now?

BRUCE: Well, I'm on the eighteenth month of a screenplay with Jerry Zucker, who directed *Ghost*. This was going to be a four-month rewrite my assistant, David Salesman, had written. It's turned out to be an unbelievably demanding and frustrating process only because finding the story with two people is not necessarily an easy process. I mean, trying to find out what your movie is about, to make it into something worth telling, and starting out with what appears to be a single vision and discovering there are different visions. That's a very difficult part of the Hollywood experience. You have to be prepared for when you start writing for someone else, more for someone else. You really have to merge your voice with their voice. You're really developing a client relationship, and what you're going to do is try to serve the client. That's really been happening to me.

Jerry and I are such enormously good friends that I've been willing to allow our relationship, on this particular project, to extend itself far beyond what one normally would do. I would advise you to follow your contract as much as possible. You're usually dealing with ten weeks for a first draft, something like six weeks for a second draft, three weeks for a polish. There's an extraordinary problem in Hollywood called "draft inflation," in which it is not inconceivable you can write five or six or ten drafts for somebody and submit it to the studio as a first draft. Then write another four or five and submit it as a second draft. As writers, we tend to be weak in our ability to stand up for ourselves because we want the films to get made.

Then if you start to have a client relationship where you are working for somebody else, you want to make them happy. You should find the way to make yourself happy in writing. There are two kinds of writing in Hollywood: One is writing for someone. The other is writing for you, and you can't always when you write for someone else make that person happy. You also have to understand there's a lot of pure craft involved in those kinds of circumstances.

I entered into this project with Jerry, experiencing and anticipating a craft-like process. What I discovered in doing it, as I did with Spielberg and have in other cases, is that ultimately all projects are personal. They're all very important to me. If you are writing to satisfy a client, it's conceivable you will not write to satisfy yourself. And if you don't satisfy yourself, the money doesn't pay for the disappointment. There's a sense of betraying your own voice. I came to that position with Jerry about two weeks ago when I quit the project. I said that I couldn't write anymore on this project. I spent a year and a half of my life, and I have to tell you, you 434-ers are still young, but when you hit fifty-four years old, there comes a point when you realize you have a limited duration on this planet, and each year becomes precious. I had given a year of my life to Steven Spielberg and now a year and a half to Jerry Zucker. I have too many things I need to do. Jerry was deeply sympathetic because we had not been able to find the core of the script. We had written version upon version. Each has wonderful scenes, wonderful characters, wonderful ideas, and all sorts of delicious things you would have to see on screen, but somehow, this project does not work coherently.

Jerry described it last week as Frankenstein. It's got all the pieces but no soul. It's not breathing. I could if I wanted—in fact, I'm here from a meeting with Jerry—I could go back and try to fix it, as my relationship with this project is that I'm both a producer and a writer. I can now just sit and work as a producer and find ideas for what might work and bring in another writer who may feel fresher with the material than I do. On the other hand, there's always the temptation, once you see solutions, to go in and solve them.

My agent gets very disturbed at the possibility I may be pulled back under again for another several months or a year or whatever in trying to make this happen. I know it will happen because it's awfully good, and there is a lot of wonderful stuff. It's a love story, and I'm trying to make a love story about two people who fall in love, but it's not enough to watch them fall in love. You have to be in love with them and be hungry for their love to come together. And if you don't have a story in which you find your characters are compelling the audience to that love, then you just have a story about love, and it doesn't play. Although you position everything wonderfully and get all the right beats and the right elements in place, if you aren't hungering for this love to evolve, then something isn't there. What has happened to us in this movie is that love isn't earned in the end. They fall in love, but there's a beat missing; something's not working.

We're pretty seasoned pros in this business, and a lot of people come into the process of making movies thinking that the writer is a professional, so he or she should know the answer. You have to understand, in William Goldman's terms, "Nobody knows anything." Sometimes there's no answer in finding how to make it work, just like there's no answer in your own life as to, How do you fall in love with somebody else? What is the chemistry? You can have people talk about it all you want, but once you start to meet somebody and you find a way into it, it's magical; it's mysterious; it's about its own reality. It's not something you can impose on. You can't find rules or reasons. All you can do is follow the path.

So, what we're really doing in this movie is finding how to make a story about two people in love and make it real to an audience. The fact that it's taken a year and a half is painful on a certain level, but Jerry's belief is that a film has to work on paper first. I did a first draft in four months that I would have been happy to make and which I think any studio in Hollywood would produce. Jerry wants to carry it to a higher level. I'm not at all opposed to that. I think raising your work to the highest level possible is really worthy and valuable, but you also have to know when to say, "I can't figure it out. I don't know the solution."

If you're in year 3, then you've probably gone too long. The biggest problem I'm facing right now is that Cameron Crowe said to somebody that he spent three years on *Jerry Maguire*. Now every producer and director in Hollywood says, "Well, *Jerry Maguire* took three years. Why can't this take three years?" Because you can't necessarily afford three years in this business. On the other hand, if you really believe in the work and you're really committed to it, three years is of course worth your time. But this was a rewrite of another piece of material, an adaptation. I did it truly as a favor, so I had no idea what I was getting myself into. It's hard to walk away from something you have invested in that deeply. Sometimes you just have to do it. On the other hand, I'm telling you that I'll probably be sucked back into writing on it again, as early as next week.

LEW: This interview with you was done four years ago. It says, "Jerry Zucker said to me when we first met on *Ghost*, 'What's this movie about?' I said, 'It's about a guy who dies and comes back to save his wife.' He said, 'No, what's it really about?'"

I first came to Hollywood in 1955, and I used to hear the writer talk about breaking the back of the story or breaking the back of really what it's about. Larry Gelbart told me he found the "What it's about?" when he decided that you take a dress and put it on. The Dustin Hoffman character in *Tootsie*, he'll become a better man. Frank Pierson suddenly realized he broke the Al Pacino character in *Dog Day Afternoon* when he discovered that the guy lived for everybody but for himself. So, you, too, must push to find what the movie is about and what the story is about.

BRUCE: I never knew, when I first started to write, that movies were about anything. I always thought it was just a story. It had a beginning, middle, and an end. I later discovered characters and arcs. I didn't even know there was such a thing as an arc. I had a kind of organic sense of this, but I could not delineate it, and I couldn't explain it to myself or to anybody else. But as you start to work, what you have to realize is that there are all of these layers that make a film work. The most important end result is that it be a worthy experience for people. They come away knowing something they didn't know, not just that they've watched an adventure or they've seen something unfold. Movies that are going to have any cultural permanence have to be about something. They have to have a deep undercurrent, and this idea about breaking the back of a movie is really important because "what it's about" doesn't give itself up easily. It's not something you know automatically. Jerry and I have maybe 150 pages of notes on what this movie is about, but it doesn't mean anything because you can say what it's about, but what is it about?

A poet once said, "A poem must not mean, but be." It's not about meaning, but what is it? What does it communicate? What is it really saying to people? It's crucial you begin to understand as you work your movie that you know what it's saying. What is it trying to communicate to the world or to the audience? My feeling as a writer is that we have this enormous privilege, this unbelievable opportunity to talk to the world for two hours, to stand up in front of all humanity and talk to people deeply in the dark when they are at their most vulnerable, their most open and most unprotected because people just sit in the dark and give themselves over to the screenplay, the director, the performers. They're just completely available to you. You can put in their minds and their psyches and their souls whatever you want. I think the most important thing to understand, given how fast those two hours go by, what do you really want to tell people? If you could stand up at a podium outside today and speak to everyone at UCLA for two hours, what would you have to say to them? Do you have two hours' worth of anything to say? The thing about movies is that you're lucky to communicate a single thought or a single idea in a movie. You're really lucky to get one idea across. It's not like being at a podium and being able to say everything you've ever wanted to say.

My very first screenplay, the first one I ever wrote, the last eighty pages were a monologue. It was one man just talking to the camera and saying what life and love and joy and everything are. Someone looked at me and said, "This is very interesting, but this is not a movie." That's what I've been trying to figure out for the last thirty years.

What I finally came down to is that if you're lucky, each movie will communicate one sentence, and by the end of your life, you will have communicated maybe a paragraph's worth of knowledge for the world in terms of these underpinnings and important messages and feelings and statements you want to share with people. The problem is, what if you don't know that? A lot of people writing understand deeply that they want to say something. It used to be a terrible dilemma for me because I wanted to communicate. I wanted to write movies, but I didn't know what to write about. I didn't have a clue. I just wanted to have my name on the screen. I wanted to have pictures up there. I wanted to have this feeling of the power of being a screenwriter. I wanted all that, but I had nothing to write about.

So the journey into yourself is a journey into the realm of story, into what you are about, what your life is about. What is it you have learned from your own, very personal, very private, and probably painful and exhilarating experience? What have you learned that you can share with people that might be meaningful? And the truth is, and you've heard this from probably any book you've read on writing or from anyone who has ever talked to you, your experience is unique. Nobody has gone through life the way you have. Nobody else sees it the way you have. The only commonality you have with other people is that you're a human being, and somehow, in some very private recess, we all share extraordinary sameness. We all share the same experiences. We don't always express them effectively with each other. We often hide behind our egos, our masks, our protections. We particularly don't want to communicate our pain and our jealousies and our envies and all of our dark sides. But in truth, going into yourself, the inward journey, and seeing who you are and what you are, how you work and how you function, you may find you have something worthy to communicate to another person. This, as a writer, seems like what you have to do. But how do you go in? How do you start to find out who you are and what you are? Forgive me if it sounds like I'm pontificating.

I have, for many years, meditated. I'm a very strong believer in meditation. Meditation, to me, is essentially the process of being quiet, just sitting still. Sitting still is something that rarely happens in our culture. We have the capacity for endless noise. We can wake up in the morning with an alarm clock, which is aggressively noisy, or with music that startlingly blares into our life. You can let that music play as you go into the shower. You can even turn on the radio in the shower. You can get in the car, you can get the *Today Show*, you can get the *Howard Stern Show*, you can let noise carry you through to your workplace. You can have it in the hallway, in the elevator. It's possible never to be quiet in Western culture, never, for a moment, to hear yourself.

Consequently, I think it is really important to find a time in the day to weave in silence because when you start to get really quiet, what happens after a while is all of your stuff starts to surface. Believe me, within five minutes, you'll start to feel all of this "I want to get out of this. I can't stand this. I'm not comfortable. What am I doing?" Your crap will rise, and you will begin to see stuff in you that you never knew was there, and it may look like shit, but it's fertilizer. It is the stuff of your life. It's the stuff that makes you who you are, and what you need to do is examine you and look at that and then let it go because underneath this stuff is more extraordinary stuff. The deeper you go, the more you start to discover.

This sense I have is that when each of us goes back more and more to our center, we all discover we are going to the same place. We all talk about ourselves, "myself," this possessive, individual, unique thing. I believe when I dive deeply into myself, and you dive deeply into yourself, we come to this unexpected realization that we share the same self. We distinguish it as ours. We interpret it as having a direct and personal dialogue with us, but in fact, so much of our shared experience comes from the fact that we share a self. I'm talking in a sort of Buddhist and even perhaps Judeo-Christian terms, the idea of God as One or the sense of the one mind in the Buddhist tradition. We all, as we begin to go deep into ourselves, start to discover a commonality that is very profound. The deeper you go, the more you have to tell. If you really go into yourself and you get really quiet, what you will discover is that the journey inward is the journey, if you will, of the hero.

Everyone who makes the journey inward begins to discover, as Homer discovered in the *Odyssey*, as all great travelers and journeyers discover, that all of the pathways and all the obstacles and all of the challenges that one has in getting to the place of knowledge, that when you find that magical place, you will find you want to bring it back. That's what heroes do. They bring back wisdom to share with the world. And if you, as writers, because you have this incredible opportunity to share it, have anything to do that is meaningful, it will be to bring it back. If all you do is blow up buildings, I don't think that's a good use of two hours. You can do it, you might get paid well for it, you can have fun doing it, and there's nothing wrong with that at a certain level, but I'm not sure that it's the most valuable use of your time and your skill and your talent. So my suggestion to people is always go deep, and if you can't go deep into yourself and you cannot find what the journey is all about, then go into the world because our life in the world mirrors our life of the soul, if you will. Journeying in the world can be just as valuable as journeying into yourself. I always tell people to travel. Go to the most unfamiliar and uncomfortable and the most unknown place you can go. Reach out, and see what the world has for you.

My son, Joshua, who has become a wonderful writer, wanted to go to film school, and I said, "No, don't go to film school. I went to film school. I learned a craft that took me thirty years to put into practice. I found that very frustrating." I said, "Get an education, but get a really open liberal arts education. Learn history. Learn philosophy. Learn literature. Learn mathematics. Learn science. Learn whatever it is that sparks your interest and attention." After this, I said, "Travel. Just go. Go anywhere. Move around the world. Go to places that most attract you and the ones that most frighten you, and see what's there. What does this world have to offer?" He went for three years and has come back with journals and a deep capacity to describe his journey and to write about it, and he will, I think, be a wonderful writer. He is a wonderful writer, but I think, he will also be a successful writer because his journey has really been into the world around him. I think you can also journey into relationships, learning how to love another person, learning how to connect with another human being. It's a terrifying process for most people.

It seems easy and friendly at a certain level. For many people, the sexual level is very stimulating, and it brings you together in some other wonderful way. But then you're immediately into cigarettes and staring at the wall, not sure what to say to each other. Yes, sexuality brings us together, but the merging, the connection of souls, are what a relationship is. If you want to go on a terrifying journey, get to know another person. Be fearless in your capacity to explore love and what it means to have a life of relationships, not just sexually and not just with a spouse or a partner, but with anybody. Start to get to know other people; really get to live a life in which you can know them. Truthfully, what you'll discover is that the only way you'll get to know another person is by sharing yourself. That's where most people and writers really run into trouble because they're afraid to share. They only want to get inches deep into someone else because they're only willing to go that deep with themselves. You'll find the measure of perception of life has to do with your willingness to expose yourself. The more you can open yourself in depth, the more you can expose yourself to others, and the more they expose themselves to you or situations or aspects of life. You get what you put out. You mirror yourself. So going in, going out, going anywhere, *depth* is the key word. Pursue your life as deeply as you can. Reach in; take it in; drink it in; touch it; smell it; examine it; know what it is; feel it. Then you'll be able to write about it, the human experience.

What you find in many of the good screenplays that get made is they're about character. They're about real people and real experience. The great screenplays are about people who go on these journeys of their own and discover, as Dustin Hoffman did in *Tootsie* and Cage in *Moonstruck*. You have these people who come to know parts of themselves that are risky and unexpected, and they come out of surprise for us because these characters were invested by the writer. The writer wrote from character. They didn't write from plot. Writing from plot moves people around a board. Writing from character invents a world. When you start to write from character, you enter in their lives; your script will surprise you. It will stun you, and at the same time, if you're surprised and stunned, it will surprise and stun the viewer. You will find you created something really wondrous and unexpected rather than something structured and manipulated.

I think this is the hardest thing for writers in Hollywood. I see this more than anything when I look at screenplays. They're not character-driven; they're plot-driven. They're manipulated. That can be fun. It's okay. There's nothing wrong with that, and I don't mean to put down a shallower level of filmmaking, but if you're aspiring to anything more, and I think you should or could, then know you. By knowing you, you will start to know others. You will understand character. By understanding character, you will understand the conflicts of other people's lives. Then, you'll know how to tell stories.

LEW: Aristotle says, "Superior drama and comedy is drama and comedy that allows us to discover ourselves." That ties in exactly with what you're saying. Here's a sidebar that relates to character: I've traveled all around the world, and I find my relationships with people outside the contiguous United States are much more dimensional. We hug. There is passion and talking until four o'clock in the morning, night after night. No radio. No television. No distractions. Just communicating, and we're gone. Then, we see each other a day, a year, or six months later; we resume that passion and intensity, more so than in America. So you share that feeling?

BRUCE: To some degree. I know my travels were very enriching. I have experiences that felt very magical and unfamiliar, partly because I was in a place that was magical and unfamiliar. My first major traveling was traveling around the world. I started in Greece and stuck out my thumb and traveled ultimately to Japan. I went through Iran and Turkey and Afghanistan and Pakistan. I saw a lot of places you can't easily go today. The people you would see here were so "other." They were so other from the people I was comfortable and familiar with that I had to dig to explore.

The shorthand of our relationships in Western culture is such that we find ourselves second-guessing things, and we don't ask questions because we think we know the answers. You peg everybody. We can tell things about each other. We look at each other and go, "Oh, I know who that is." They fit in that category, that slot. I was in Kenya, engaging with tribal people in that place, and I've never seen anybody so other ever. I said, "This is really other. There is something going on here that doesn't work in any category I know." I didn't quite know how to get through. My son, Josh pulled out a cigarette, went over to one of these tribesmen, and offered him a cigarette. They sat down and started smoking and having a great time. Joshua understood a more primal way of connecting than I did. But I noticed that otherness opens you to possibilities, whereas familiarity keeps you locked in a room. If you stay locked in the norm, there is no exploration.

LEW: In my experience, most of my travel deals with seminars, workshops, and other writers. We have a commonality and some places to go to, which is so much more different than tribesman in New Guinea. Joseph Campbell—has he been influential in your storytelling life?

BRUCE: Not so much Joseph Campbell, although I really think he understood the nature of storytelling. I relate to Joseph Campbell mostly through a book that was written based on his work about screenwriting. I don't know if you know this book, but it's my favorite screenwriting book. It's called *The Writer's Journey* by Christopher Vogler, and it's completely based on Joseph Campbell's work. I buy endless copies of that book and give it to people who are trying to figure out the art of screenwriting. It talks about the journey and about all of us as the hero. It really makes you understand that the hero's journey is not just about the hero in your movie, but that it's really about you.

His book is really clear on the basic elements of storytelling. If you are having trouble with your screenplay, pick up a copy of his book, and look at your screenplay in relation to the paradigms he creates. You'll probably see where you have a problem, where you're falling down, because there is a classical structure to storytelling, and he has, through Joseph Campbell, come to understand an extraordinary amount of what that is. I find it very valuable. In that regard, Joseph Campbell was a great gift to a lot of us because he began to take all of storytelling, all of myth, and show us the archetypes and what they are, how they work, and how they worked, not only thousands of years ago, but are still totally present in our lives today.

LEW: I used to use Aristotle all the time, but now I've added Campbell because he does emphasize hero or heroine's call to adventure, the acceptance of the adventure, and then giving her- or himself up for the greater good and bringing something back and then having a Yoda-like mentor to talk to—the things that obviously, at Skywalker Ranch, Lucas and Campbell must have talked about for hours before George actually sat down and wrote *Star Wars*.

BRUCE: He really got it in *Star Wars*.

LEW: He really did. You're much more eloquent than I, but I always tell these screenwriting students to take their entrails and put a sword through them because that's the only thing that is unique. Everything else has been done before. It's your doing what's been done before that's special.

BRUCE: I don't think eloquence is required. I think what is required is that the message get across to all of us. It's not just something you do once and then you have it. That's the most frustrating thing about being a writer. Every writer you talk to who will admit it will tell you that every time you start a screenplay, it's the first time. You really have no idea about how to do it again; just because you've done it before doesn't mean you ever get it down. It really doesn't. Every time, there's a new adventure, and it's humiliating at a certain level and maybe humbling because how do you do it? You have to enter into, I guess, the Zen sense of the beginner's mind. You have to start over again every single time to learn how to write, and if you do that, if you're really willing to be humble in the face of this process and say, "Help me get through this. How do I tell a story?" then once you begin to let it come out, it really starts to happen. You slowly go, "Oh yeah, that's right. Oh, I remember." And as it all starts to come back together again; the process begins to enthrall you, and then you don't have to worry about how to do it because it takes over.

LEW: The Old Testament writers didn't need name credit.

BRUCE: That's right.

LEW: Matthew, Mark, Luke, and John needed publicity, I guess.

BRUCE: That's a really interesting point. I really don't ever believe the credit is ours. I really believe it's channeled. That's a bad word to use in our culture today because it's so New Age, but I think real writing comes through you. The most exciting process of writing for me has been that "through me" aspect. I especially had it with *Jacob's Ladder*, where I was simply the first person to see the movie. I got to watch it and describe it as it came through. I just sat there and started typing as fast as it came through. I thought this was an incredible story. I liked the story, but it didn't feel like it was mine. It felt like I had access to something that wanted to be told. When that happens, your ownership diminishes, and you feel much more humble in the face of your own creation, and when you do that, you will not be as troubled by the egoism of writers and owning your own material because it came through you, but you won't feel like you're the only one who knows the material. Especially when a director comes in and wants to change every word of it or every aspect of what you've done. You might fight for what you did, but you also know there are a lot of voices going into making a movie. You, as a writer of screenplays, are one of the voices.

That's one of the hardest things to understand: As opposed to a playwright or a novelist, the screenwriter is truly in a collaborative mode. That's why you kind of have to write one version for yourself and, somewhere along the line, put it aside and then know anything that comes after that is going to be adulterated, maybe for better or maybe for worse. But have one draft that you're proud of, one you feel represents you; then go out and do the dirty work of making it ready for an actor or director or a production company or whoever else. They can come to you, as they once did for me, and say, "We want to make a ninety-minute movie out of this, so cut out thirty pages." Well, that's what you do: You cut out thirty pages. You don't feel proud of it, but that's what you do. Hollywood is a business. Again, I fear I'm saying things you've heard from every other person.

LEW: Not in your way Bruce. You're saying exactly what I want these new screenwriting warriors to hear. Back to more practicality: In this one interview, you talk about calling up the next morning and saying, "I think I've found a new way to fix this particular picture." Ergo, your home is paid for. My daughter has a master's degree in social work because Irwin Allen and Columbia wanted me to write two things.

BRUCE: That's very important, and that's something I talk about a lot. I was offered a movie to write based on the worst horror story I'd read in my life—I mean, really horrible. I turned it down and felt very proud of myself. I don't need to write this crap. I didn't come to Hollywood to write this kind of movie. The next morning, I was meditating and feeling this pride in me, feeling really grateful that I was maintaining my integrity in the face of these temptations, when suddenly, I hear this voice in my head. The voice goes, "Schmuck. There is more integrity in providing for your family than turning down jobs." And the voice said literally, "Get up, go to the phone, call this producer, and tell him that you now know how to make this movie work." I literally got up from my cross-legged position, wobbled over to the telephone, called up this producer, and said, "I can do this film." I told him that I had all these great ideas. I hadn't a single idea. But he said, "Wonderful, we have another writer, but I think we can get you in instead." And so I said, "Terrific."

And I ended up doing this movie, which makes me wince when it's in my credits. It's called *Deadly Friend*. It wasn't originally called *Deadly Friend*; it was called *Friend*, and it was for Wes Craven, who had just finished *Nightmare on Elm Street* and was hoping to break out of his horror-film mode, so I took this film. It's so hard to imagine. It's a film about a little boy who is a scientific genius, who makes a robot, and who falls in love with the girl next door. She's abused by her father and ultimately is made brain-dead by her father. Our little scientist next door goes and steals her body out of the hospital, takes his robot brain out of his robot, plants it in her brain, and she comes back to life and kills everyone in the neighborhood. All I thought was, "How do I make this work?" I said, "In truth there is a love story, and it's a love story between this boy and this girl." So I wrote this movie with an emotional component that had a real heart and soul. In fact, when Lucy Fisher read it at Warner Brothers, she said she cried. I said, "What?" I couldn't believe it, but the film really did have something going for it. Wes was excited, and the studio wanted to make it. This is the one they said to cut thirty pages, which we did because we wanted a ninety-minute film to go into theaters. When the film was finished, the making of the film turned out to be one of the happiest experiences in my life. My kids were like mascots on the set and got to watch this film shooting almost every day.

Wes Craven was wonderful and very collaborative and a joy to be with. Then, when the film was over, it was screened for one of Wes's audiences. The people were brought into a theater and asked if they wanted to see a Wes Craven movie, and they hated it. They hated it because there was emotion on the screen; there was tenderness. There were all these things that they thought were not appropriate to Wes Craven movies. Mark Canton, the studio head, was sitting there with us and said, "Add blood. Here's money. Add six scenes. Each should be bloodier than the one before." We previewed it again, and the audience was so bloodthirsty, they were standing on their chairs cheering at the bloodletting in the movie.

Then, we took the movie to the rating board and they gave us an X. They said, "There is no way you can show this to the public." Wes started cutting frame by frame, and he said, "For every frame we cut out of the movie, we lose another million dollars at the box office." In fact, we ended up making no money at the box office. But the important thing for me, the screenwriter, is that it had given me enough money to purchase my house and pay for my son's bar mitzvah. Before the movie, I didn't have enough money for anything but peanut butter and jelly sandwiches for the bar mitzvah, which is not in our Jewish tradition. The film served me wonderfully, even though it didn't last more than three weeks at the box office.

Shortly after the film's release came the writer's strike. Five months into the strike, I was deep in financial trouble. My wife and I had both looked at our bank accounts one day and added up only four hundred dollars. We had no idea what we were going to do. I hadn't had any income all this time, and of course, I wasn't the only one. That afternoon a residual check arrives in the mail for *Deadly Friend*. The lesson for me from this movie is that there is nothing wrong in taking jobs for movies you may not think are worthy of your talents and your skills. The important thing is that whatever work you get, do it well. Your job isn't to determine what the universe brings you to do; your job is to write what you're brought as well as you can.

LEW: William Saroyan said that oftentimes, practically always, we work just as hard and with just as much passion for a bad play as a good play. Dan Pyne, one of our professors and a wonderful writer who wrote *Pacific Heights*, says, "Film school gives you a chance to be as good as you can be." When you get out there, other elements happen. Initially, write a script, put it out there, and once it's on the table, go back to it. Bring all of your critical faculties into play. When I was picketing on a Writers Guild strike, I walked with Jim Poe, who wrote the screenplay for *Around the World in Eighty Days* and *Lilies of the Field*. I said. "Jim, this wonderful small movie called *Lilies of the Field* you wrote—how did that ever get as good as it was?" He responded, "I had three weeks to write, a three-week window with Sidney Poitier to shoot it, and then three weeks for postproduction. We just didn't have time to fuck it up."

Talk to us about your screenwriting emotions when the intellect starts coming into play because that's what you're saying after getting that first draft down.

BRUCE: I refer to that first draft as getting the clay on the table. You can't shape something until it's there. It may not be good but full of potential. It will be full of this stuff that ultimately you need as writers to work with. Once it's sitting there, you can take this away, you can take that away, you can punch that, dig that, and then you can begin to shape with another view, another vision of what it now is because now it's there to be shaped. The problem with a lot of writers is that they spend so much time getting that first little piece onto the table and go, "It doesn't look good this way or that way."

There's a mound of stuff that's got to be on the table, and if you're fussing over every little piece you put out there, you may never get it all done. If you're sitting there being self-critical, analyzing, thinking, "This is no good. This is not going to win the Academy Award. Nobody's ever going to see this," and you're only on page 3, you'll never get to page 120.

LEW: This is one of the blessings and principles of this program. These folks here have to get a draft out in six weeks.

BRUCE: That's how it should be.

LEW: Then they go back and hopefully make it good. Of course, we were intimidated by Irving Ravetch, who sat here and said he likes to get it right the first time.

BRUCE: That's a wonderful thing, if you can do it. It's a rarity in the business. I don't think we should be afraid of rewriting anything. Rewriting is one of the great opportunities to enhance your material. I used to think, when I was young, if you don't do it right the first time, you didn't do it. Something is wrong. I also always believed in the purity of the first expression. However, I've now really come to understand that, in the first expression, what you really have is the instinct toward the thing, but you may not have the revelation or the realization of what it should be as a complete form. You have everything in place. It's still fermenting, it's still growing, but you need to come in and begin to work in order to really, really make it play. I'm no longer afraid of rewriting. I find rewriting the great pleasure of screenwriting. The hardest part is getting the first draft. The rewriting is where you get to really making it what you want it to be.

LEW: Talk to us about process. Go from your idea, through developing the idea, up to the point where you start working on the first draft. How do you do it?

BRUCE: The idea is usually a magical moment. Where the idea comes from no one can actually tell you. But suddenly, you're reading a magazine, or when I meditate, I get a lot coming through.

LEW: Do you have a notepad with you when you're meditating?

BRUCE: During certain periods of meditation, I put a notepad beside me. You see, meditation is rising or descending. As you get to a certain point, there is a layer of very active dream and mind state, out of which enormous ideas arise. When people write, I think that's the place they go. If you meditate, you have to let go of that and continue, and you go higher or deeper. As you pass through that state, you often get the most incredible insights in things you need. I used to let them go and kept meditating. Others said, "That's stupid. It's not going to be hard to stop for a minute and write stuff down." Now I have a pad whenever I'm in the writing mode, and I put it next to me. I write it down, very quickly. Then I can let go of that state and just continue with my pursuit. When an idea comes, I think it's important to write it down.

I have a file drawer full of ideas. They all have a title. Almost all of my ideas come with a title for some reason. I keep filling the file with new ideas whenever ideas come up. I'll be sitting in the car and I'll go, "Oh, that's a good idea for such and such a script." So what I do now, I keep this recorder with me all of the time because I need to be able to remember an idea if it comes, and I don't want it to evaporate, so I throw it in here. Then, I also buy flowers or stop at the supermarket, all those things, and then at home I write them down and put them in my file. When I go back to the script, I have all these scraps of paper with ideas I have thought of over the months or years I assemble.

When I decide to work on a script, I begin with what I call a bible, which is really a brainstorm series of pages where I just write anything I can think about concerning the movie: things I feel, scenes I'd like to see, a character I come into, anything, even a thought from another movie I saw, a quote from something I've read. I just keep filling these pages and it starts to have a living, vibrating quality. It's a place I can go to even late in the script, even after it's many times written, even when I go into production. I can always go back to this place and see what were the sparks, those moments that stimulated me in some real important way. When I go back, they often bring me insights into the material that have been long since forgotten.

It's a wonderful thing to create this bible. In the beginning of the process, I delineate a possible story, a way it can work. Sometimes I can't get to an ending; I can only get the premise. I'm usually very good with first acts. I think most of us must be good at first acts. Setting up a story is terrific. The second act is a complete killer. And the third act usually explains itself. The second act is where everybody runs into trouble. What I do is delineate the story as much as possible without trying to rob myself of spontaneity in the writing, so I write as much as I can. I'll often write a kind of treatment or a loose treatment and then put it aside. Then I'll sit down to write the movie. Often the treatment is out the window within the first scene. I didn't start that way. I started out in a completely different mode. I don't know why, and yet it seemed right.

Today, I use the treatment as a kind of guideline, a reminder of what I wanted it to be, but I let the story become what it wants to be. You just sit there and let it come through you, and you write as fluidly as you can, and when you're stuck, that's the worst part of writing to me: the stuck moments. And they come continually. You suddenly don't know what the next thing should be. Should I go to this character or that character? The hardest thing about writing a movie is how much possibility exists. You can go in 360-degree directions at any point in time, and how do you know the right direction? Well, you don't. So what you have to do is keep writing.

I often begin to write a movie almost knowing that nothing I'm writing in the first five or ten days will ever make it into the final script. I'm just writing to get a sense of the places, the tone, the time, the character, the feel of a background, the history, because so much of it is so expositional you're discovering it as you're learning it. Somewhere down the road, you'll go back to all the exposition and you'll be able to compress it into a line or a few lines, and you'll chop a lot of that stuff down into much more concise and more cinematic material. In the beginning, I just write long. Actually, I just write. Let it come. See what happens. Then you find your movie.

When you have to make a choice, don't panic. Don't say, "Oh my God, if I go this way, this is going to happen. Or if I go that way, that's going to happen." Go this way, and if you end up at a dead end, go, "Okay." Then, never be afraid to just, if you have a computer, just take it out of the file, put it into an outtakes file, and go in another direction. If that keeps opening and flowing, that's the way you want to go. You mine your material. You go toward the gold and toward the gems waiting to be found. As you do that, you'll feel it.

When you have a real obstacle and you don't know what to do—it took me years to afford it, but I bought a lounge chair, and I go lounge in my chair with my problem. I sit down and say, "What do I do now? How do I resolve this?" Often, I lie down, and I just take a nap. Inevitably, within fifteen or twenty minutes of that nap, the idea comes. I wake up, and I run over to the computer, and I start writing. I wait for it to be delivered. You can't pull it out. You can't open up a flower like that. You put it in the sunlight; the flower opens. You take your mind and put it in the light of your own imagination or your higher resources, and you just be quiet. You just wait, and then suddenly it goes. You say, "Thank you," then you sit down, and you write, and you'll know very clearly that it wasn't you. It was given.

The Greeks called it the Muse. Call it whatever you want, but there is something that wants our stories to be told. That's all I can tell you. We want it to be told, but there is something above you that wants you to succeed. There's something that's waiting for good stories to be told, and it wants you to pull it off. All we are are those beings who have been willing to cooperate with that process.

For a lot of people, their biggest problem in life, in terms of the stories they write and the stories they live, is that they don't pay attention. So when you run into a wall with a story you're writing, you can lift it up and put it in the outtakes file. When you run into a wall with a story you're living, it's harder to do. You can chop off a part of your life and say, "Whoops." Then go in another direction. Most people feel, "I went this direction. This is how it's supposed to be. I spend forty years banging up against that wall trying to get through, and it'll never happen." Learning to let go of material in your storytelling teaches you how to let go of material in your living, which I think ultimately is equally, if not more, important.

LEW: It says in this article on you somebody gave me a few years back, "I come to a point in many scripts—that moment of total devastation where you realize that what you're writing is absolute garbage. That you have strayed from your path, and you are deluded to think that you were ever a writer in the first place. I have never known despair as total as this, as consuming or as predictable. How a writer overcomes this obstacle is in many ways what determines his successes or failures. It's a time of battle, of sacrifice, of 'killing your babies,' as some writer once said. It's a terrible and ultimately liberating struggle. If you get through it, it weds you to your material in a blood ceremony that makes it yours. It becomes your life." And then in the following paragraph you say, "So many thoughts rushed into me, I could barely breathe. After the flower opened, it was a kind of euphoria, a massive rush into me, I could barely breathe. I was so excited, I began racing the house, walking in powerful circles around the living room, around the dining table, and I couldn't stop my wife from watching me, et cetera." Your wife must have many stories.

BRUCE: I'm sure she does.

LEW: So does mine. But so that it is the yin and the yang of the whole matter and a variation of what you just said. I recommend on the first 434 day Alan Watt's book *The Wisdom of Insecurity*. Would there be another one in that arena you could recommend to us?

BRUCE: Only *The Writer's Journey*. There are no other books I tend to go to. I always believe every writer who writes books gets his ideas,

inside and wherever that writer went to, we can go to, so we don't
have to necessarily get it from another writer. Sometimes they help us
clarify ideas very quickly, but I think that when you get into the battle,
you have to go through in your writing process. Being instructed by
other people will never be as valuable as being instructed by your own
psyche in how to deal with the extraordinary trauma of getting it right,
of trying to be true to yourself and your mind. It's about living right,
as well as writing right. It's about trying to find out how to take the
right step. What do I do? And when you look at your material not
working.

I think you were reading a reference to *Jacob's Ladder*. I think what
happened in *Jacob's Ladder* is I realized it wasn't going anywhere or I
didn't understand where it was going, and then I had this revelation.
I was trying to tell a movie about a man who was dead, and we were
observing his experience in what is known in Tibetan terms as the Bardo
state, the state in between death and rebirth. I know not too many
people trying to make movies about *The Tibetan Book of the Dead*, but
I was very determined to use that material in a storytelling mode. And
it wasn't working. Then I had this revelation. There was another movie
that preceded me that had done this well: s movie called *An Occurrence
at Owl Creek Bridge* by Ambrose Bierce.

LEW: I believe it was a USC student film.

BRUCE: I believe it was also French made. Was it Chris Marker?

STUDENT: Yes.

BRUCE: That's it, and then they put it on *The Twilight Zone*. It's a movie
about a man who, as he is being hung, has the rope snap, and he has
this incredible journey of rushing back to his wife, escaping all these
pursuers. As he's rushing toward his wife, he suddenly has these sort
of strange feelings around his neck, and as he's about to hug his wife,
the rope cinches around his neck, and he's dead. It's so powerful, so
emotional. I then realized, "I'm telling the feature-length version of that
movie." At that moment, I realized what my movie was. I knew what it
was about. The euphoria I described was so enormous, I literally could
not sit down. I surged around the house saying, "I know it! I got it!" To
get your script, to get what you're doing while you're doing it, and to be
empowered by that is the greatest thing in the world.

LEW: That's what the French call the reason for being. In the script you're working on with Jerry Zucker right now, let me ask you this: I was told not too long ago—well, soon after I came to town—that love stories are so difficult to tell because there are so few obstacles today. Do you have an obstacle? Race and class used to be big obstacles. Obstacles are hard to come up with today. That's why most of our love stories are about the halt, the lame, and the blind.

BRUCE: Well, we have been struggling. We came up with an obstacle today, in fact. We've had it for a few days, pretty mild obstacle, but what Jerry was saying was that the obstacle is not the problem. He said that a true love story is about pain and healing—somebody in pain and somebody healing. We felt our problem was not the obstacle so much as delineating the pain and delineating the healing, how they flow throughout the course of the movie, how one is rejected over and over and resisted, and then finally healing comes.

Love stories are tricky. I had no idea how tricky. Sidney Pollack says a love story has to have another story along with it. It can't just be the love story because it can't bear the weight of just being a love story. You have to have a—I don't know the right word—a plot story you're telling around which a love story has to occur.

One of the best love stories for me is *African Queen*. For them, it was going down the river and blowing up the ship. This is what motivates the movie plot. But while that's happening, there's this extraordinary coming together of two very different people. It's a wonderful, delicious, perfect love story. I look at that a lot, and I look at the wonderful *Moonstruck*, another of the great filmed love stories. What conflict, what an obstacle. She's engaged to marry his brother. Pretty powerful stuff. When you have these issues, then you really have something. By having two people who you want to be in love, you have to create these obstacles, which is what we have now done in this story.

LEW: Questions please.

STUDENT: I'm really curious about your meditation process. Do you have a certain time during the day and a certain amount of time you need to take?

BRUCE: When I came back from India thirty years ago, having looked for a meditation teacher, having lived in a lot of groups, not with a great many people, I had not found anybody I trusted in terms of technique.

I had all these Tibetan carpets that I was going to try to sell for the monks who I had lived with in Kathmandu. They were quite impoverished. I took the carpets to a store a block away from where I lived before I began this trip. The man who ran the store was a New York City businessman, and he asked what I was doing in India. I said that I had gone to find a teacher. He said, "Did you find one?" I said, "No." He says, "I can teach you everything you want to know." It was one of those moments of absolute, total hubris on one level, but it didn't come across that way. It was a complete state of fact. I knew exactly at that moment he was right.

I started studying with this man, and he taught me a process of meditation unbelievably powerful and dynamic. It has become the core centerpiece of my life. The voice I heard, Rudy, this was his name, has been dead many years, but the voice I heard when I turned down that movie was Rudy's voice saying, "You schmuck, get to work here." I studied with him for the last seven years that he was alive, and then I continued my studies in other centers around the country and then began teaching it on my own.

I have found that teaching has become as beneficial as studying because you learn more clearly as a teacher than as a student. But it's a practice—I don't know if you can give it a name—it deals with energy centers. I don't know if you know about these things—they're called chakras, an Eastern vision of the psyche, centers that govern aspects of our being—and in most people, they are either opened or closed at varying points and at varying dimensions. When you begin to experience these places in yourself—there are seven of them—you find you have a diagnostic tool to see where you are functioning well and where you're not. For example, this would be called the third eye. The third eye is the place of wisdom for penetrating insight. If it's really open, you begin to see deeply into life, and you also begin to understand you can turn it inward and see deeply into yourself. It's organic; it's like a tree; it reaches in and out. By opening this eye, you begin to have a broad mind as opposed to a narrow mind. If you begin to open up other centers—like you have one in your heart—you start to feel deeply into life.

You can experience love and emotion and empathy and connection for other people and for yourself. I've come into contact with enough people to know they're pretty wonderful at loving other people but pretty awful at loving themselves. They are very shallow in their capacity to experience love because they have no roots to support it. I started studying this process thirty years ago and have maintained a daily practice and discipline that has proven to be the essence of my life. It's what allows me to continue to grow and explore the universe and myself in a deeply satisfying way.

There are a lot of meditation forms. My sense is any one you pick will be the one you need and the one that will help. There are millions of places to go. There are so many forms. Find one. Or if you don't want to, just sit still. Sit still for twenty minutes a day. I sit for forty-five minutes to an hour in the morning, and I sit for about a half-hour at night before I go to bed. But the key is not to get up from that like you just went to church, and now you're going to go out and play.

LEW: You meditate every morning?

BRUCE: Every morning when I get up. Discipline is everything. If you don't have discipline, you'll always find a reason not to swim, and if I didn't have a discipline for swimming, I would have a reason every morning not to go. I would find a reason because I don't always like it. I love swimming, but getting through to that pool can be a hard job, but I do it because it's my discipline. I write every day. I sit down at my computer every day. It doesn't matter what I write. If you don't have discipline, you'll always find a reason not to do it. Always.

LEW: I don't think anyone here who had been to my house has ever mentioned why the Bible is by our front door. But when we go out into the madding crowd, to use a spin on a Thomas Hardy title, Pamela and I like to mentally carry a verse of scripture with us because that car oftentimes becomes a meditative chapel for America today, for better or for worse.

BRUCE: If you understand the flow of traffic as the flow of a river, sometimes it's rapid and sometimes it's really a slow ride. But if you can get into the glide mode and not always feel the need for rapids and that much stimulation, you can actually handle the freeway.

STUDENT: Bruce, when you're working with Jerry, say on a project like this, do you sit around and talk for hours? I say that not jokingly but because I have a partner I work with, and sometimes I say, "Gee, are we being productive?" I mean, it's interesting, but we spend so much time just talking.

BRUCE: You have to produce something each time. We do talk a lot. We spend eight hours a day with each other. We do have cards on the board, so we have something to relate to. We sit and talk and get into what we're looking for. You often have to work like that. I have all these friends who wanted to be in the film business from film school, NYU back in '64 to '65. They maintain this incredible determination to get famous and to get into making movies. A couple of them did. Brian De Palma and Martin Scorsese. These guys went right for it, and they made it. I have a lot of friends who are still like this, and they're not even close. They're completely rigid in their desire to get there. My life started like that, then it just went off in all these other directions all over those places. Yet it ended up getting where I had to go. It got there because I let go of the need to do that.

When you're sitting with your friends or your cohort working on a script and it starts to go like this, trust it because if you have a sense of the goal, if you know where you're trying to go, trust will help you get there. Trust often, and get there much more directly. So it's time to meander. The stuff that comes up, the stuff that opens up inside you, can be remarkable and feed your process.

LEW: Kind of like the first half of the Willa Cather quote and many before musing, "The journey is all; the end is nothing."

STUDENT: I think one of the many, many reasons why *Ghost* was so successful is that it made people feel good about the afterlife, but also the love story really worked. Maybe you can talk a little about love stories and obstacles. Actually, they had a really big obstacle: They were separated by worlds. But it really worked for me.

BRUCE: Everything that works in *Ghost* comes to me after the fact. I have no idea how *Ghost* works. I carried out the writing of it, and then Jerry and I reconceptualized elements of it, but the fact the film came together successfully is sort of out of all of our hands. We all got out of the way somehow. Everybody involved, except for maybe Demi; she kind of got out of the way, forgive me, Demi.

STUDENT: Early on in the script, when you're by yourself, the love story was not effortless?

BRUCE: I don't think I understood the extraordinary sense of longing to reconnect with someone who has passed on. It just seemed like a good story idea. I just wanted to tell a story about a ghost from the side of a ghost. I was very compelled by that idea. I was very compelled by the experience of watching Hamlet and the opening scene that has the ghost of his father on the parapet saying, "Revenge my death." I thought, "Wow." Bringing that into twentieth-century America is a good story idea.

I had two elements; the love story was kind of like a third, and the idea dawned on me because I had heard on television about a man who had left home and had not said, "I love you," to his wife. The wife cried, "He said I love you every time he ever left the house. This is the one time he didn't, and just this one time, and he was killed." She has been haunted for years and years by the fact that he didn't say it just that one time. That really touched me. I thought, "Boy oh boy, how we need to say 'I love you' to people regularly." I made a movie about a man who couldn't say "I love you." All he could say was "Ditto." What happens was not only couldn't he say "I love you," while he was alive; now he had to say "I love you" from the other side. So the whole movie is how does he get back to do that.

When the Whoopie Goldberg character came into play, I suddenly understood the medium, literally and figuratively, that I could use to have him communicate. When I made her a false medium, she became a much more interesting character. Then I had a movie that has strong rooting interest because every woman in the audience, I think, wants to be told by someone that they were loved by someone in real life. I don't mean to be sexist, but there was this really strong yearning for that completion to happen: for Sam to come back and for Molly to actually hear it. I think that it was so universally satisfying for people that it allowed for a very strong response and a big turnout, which was completely unexpected by us. We had no idea whatsoever it would do that. Having written that love story, I think people look to me and say, "Well, you can write love stories," while here I am telling you very publicly, I'm suffering like mad through a writing this current love story. So I don't know how to write love stories at all.

Lew: Did you cry when you saw the film?

Bruce: You know when I cried? It was about a month ago. I woke up one Saturday morning. I was at home and turned on the television, just flipping channels, and *Ghost* had just come on. The funny thing about *Ghost*—and I think this is a mark of a good film, and I don't mean to pat myself on the back—but it doesn't have any bathroom breaks. There is no time to get up and say, "I'm going to run to the bathroom and come back." You have to keep going through the film. I started watching it as if seeing it for the first time. I just really watched it. By the end, I was sobbing away. I got so moved by this movie. It was wonderful because for once I got to really see my own film.

STUDENT: It's so watchable because every time it's on HBO, I catch ten minutes, and then I find myself watching the rest of it.

BRUCE: It happens in good film. *Terminator 1* is such a wonderful piece of structure and storytelling. I can start looking at any point in that movie and can't turn it off.

STUDENT: *Predator* for me, for some reason.

BRUCE: They suck you in. And that's what good movies should do.

STUDENT: I love in this article you talked about the first draft of *Jacob's Ladder* being written not even in screenplay format. Was that unique to *Jacob's Ladder*, or do you still turn out first drafts not even written in screenplay format?

BRUCE: I don't know about screenplay format. We didn't have all these books, and nobody had ever sent me a screenplay. I first wrote it almost like a novel. I had dialogue and character in between, but everything else was very novelistic, and as I wrote it I became very compelled by the writerly aspect. I really cared about the words. I wasn't trying to find Ron Bass's shorthand for screenwriting. I was trying to evoke the feeling and emotion and place and character. So it had a very novelistic feel. I'm told that many people in Hollywood who read and who are so dismissive of the screenwriting form usually never read descriptive passages and just go straight for the dialogue. I think, for me, they read everything else, and I think that's why mine was suddenly so compelling to people because it was a literary experience, not just a film script. Now I don't do that. Now I write "interior" and "exterior" and everything else. I still care a lot about the descriptive passages, and I hope people spend the time reading them.

They're very important; ergo I think you still have to do the best writing you can do. For the first one, you've got to sell it to either to the studio or the producer, and you've generally got to sell them with a story first. Then you have to sell your actor, and in Hollywood these days, you have to write with stars in mind, not specific people necessarily but knowing a movie won't get made if it doesn't attract a star. Now, knowing that, it doesn't mean you shouldn't write a movie with no stars in mind and with completely abstract kinds of characters that nobody would want to play, if that's what your heart tells you to do. But if you want to get a movie made in a big Hollywood sense, of course, you have to have really engrossing characters. Harrison Ford has to look at it and say, "I want to do that." That's how it gets made. It's a very simple thing. But then, once your draft is written for these people, then you have to start writing for the director, and the director is going to have you write a very different draft. Then, when Harrison Ford really commits to the movie, he's going to want a draft that does certain things for Harrison Ford. You keep changing the nature of the screenplay; the descriptions start to get simpler and simpler and less and less detailed. But up to that point, you should write the most visual, descriptive version of the movie you can, without being so heavy-handed that they start to feel they can't see the movie.

Nobody wants to hear what the character is thinking, for example. That's a real cheat. It's interesting what happens when you put in a movie that the character is thinking this so the reader will think, "Oh, I know what's going on." But if the director doesn't capture what that is, then there is something missing. It's crucial because capturing what they're thinking is hard to do on film. That's why you have to externalize so much when you write a screenplay, so the person gets a clear sense of what is happening.

LEW: One more question.

STUDENT: When you're writing for hire, I get a sense they've tried to milk multiple drafts out of you, and you tried to resist that. If you're hired to write a first draft essentially and then a revision or polish, do you not show anything to the producer until you've completed the first draft? Or what did you do, particularly in your beginning days, if the producer wanted to see the first act or the first fifty pages?

BRUCE: In *Deadly Friend*, the producer wanted and I offered to show him each act as I did it. It's not always wise because they can start wanting millions of changes before you've begun to go onto the next segment, and that can really block your process. It's not a good idea. But some people want that. So I did it for him, and luckily he was thrilled by it, saying, "I love it. I love it. Just keep working." That doesn't always happen. Jerry and I started doing that on the twelfth draft of this movie, you know? Let me just give it to you scene by scene because it was finally about him. It wasn't about whether I liked it. It didn't matter if I liked it because if Jerry didn't, it wouldn't go forward. So I was really tailoring everything to him.

It's not satisfying as a writer, but it is a process you sometimes have to get into. Until you establish a certain level of authority and power in the business, which means you've written a film that's made money, until that point, you are the victim of a process. They can do whatever they want. You can say, "No." but they may not like you for that "No." But do you care? I wrote a movie for De Niro. They wanted another series of drafts for him, and I said, "I completed my contract. Good luck." I just walked, and I felt great. It felt wonderful. There was no reason to continue because they wanted endless shifts and changes. If they wanted to make the movie, there it was. If they wanted it corrected in shooting, I'd have been happy to do it. But to give them a few more months of my life, I can't do it. But you work with Jerry or Spielberg, it's very hard to say no because the power plays on a whole other level.

LEW: Finally, I would like to go back to doing things worth doing, what's it about, doing things that have something to do with your existence. Phil Alden Robinson once said, "This movie you imagined and was the product of so many people, working so hard for so long, a movie against all odds turned out pretty good, that movie that bears your name will outlive you. You will have succeeded in leaving something behind with the power to touch people. Something that says, 'I was here. I tried, and this is what I did when I was here.'"

BRUCE: Can you imagine leaving *Field of Dreams* behind? What a great film.

LEW: Or *Jacob's Ladder*. Or *Ghost*.

BRUCE: It's a wonderful thing to be able to write a movie that gets made, that you can walk away from and say you're grateful it turned out well enough you can put it on your résumé.

LEW: I'm always fascinated with Hitchcock. I knew him a bit when I was young. He would say, "That's icebox talk." What he meant in the overall was that some of the ambiguities in the movie continue while going to the icebox, getting a sandwich, materials, and knife before you go to bed. Icebox talks. I'm appalled with movies we often see which we dismiss before we even get to the theater's exit light. Is there a higher privilege than leaving a memorable film behind?

BRUCE: I have to say one more thing, and believe me, this is my last story. A couple of years ago, three years, I guess, I was walking out of *Jurassic Park* with my son. I was in a total funk. I sat down with my boy at this little yogurt place right by Universal, and he said, "What's wrong dad?" I said, "Just once in my life, I want to know what it feels like to have the biggest hit of the summer." He just looked at me and said, "'Dad, you did have the biggest hit of the summer." I'd completely forgotten. *Ghost* had faded away in the onslaught of *Jurassic Park*. In truth, these things don't stick. It's wonderful to have it, but it all fades away ultimately. You don't take your résumé to heaven, as far as I can tell. What I've really come to understand is that if you don't love the process, then don't do it because that's all that stays with you.

LEW: Bruce Joel Rubin, for myself, our 434 class here, and I'm confident the readers of *Naked Screenwriting*, you've left much behind, to which we say, "More, more." Thank you so.

3

William Goldman

Bill Goldman and yours truly have crossed paths personally and professionally since 1969. Professionally, in '69, when I was a story executive at Walt Disney Studios and Bill got the shocking price of $600,000 for the original screenplay of *Butch Cassidy and the Sundance Kid*. Wails emanated from every studio corridor, including mine, at the time: "That price will destroy the industry! Madness! Madness!" or "The inmates are taking over the asylum! Writers are getting more than directors or stars!" were just a few of the edicts from the producer's studio. Of course, that reaction had a happy screenwriter ending: *Butch Cassidy and the Sundance Kid* being such a huge financial and critical success. It made heaps of money, and Bill won his first Oscar, followed by *All the President's Men* and *Misery*, and his accolades go on and on.

Personally, we've shared agents (which is often far more intimate in Hollywood than sharing bodily fluids), been on the same panels, and exchanged phone calls in correspondence, as Bill proudly lives in New York. Due to his coastal preferences, Rita Augustine, one of my beloved research associates, and I could not get William Goldman to UCLA for a 434 gathering, so the next best thing was to get him over the phone. So, I end this transcontinental dialogue with the truncation of a six-year-prior phone call with Bill, in which I excitedly reported that a statue was being planned for the foyer of the new Writers Guild building, and he would be the honored subject. "You apparently told a roomful of studio suits that you were too old and too smart and too rich to take this shit anymore . . . and you stomped out of a 'notes' meeting," I recall telling Bill, and he replied, "For God's sake, Lew. First of

59

all, in our profession you never say 'you're too old.' Second of all, I'm not any smarter than anyone but certainly too smart to say that. Thirdly, no one is ever too rich. When that meeting was breaking up, I may have jokingly said, 'I don't know why I take this shit from you guys.' I may have thrown in 'too smart and rich,' but I was kidding for Christ's sake—kidding!"

That's my photographic memory of our phone conversation. You'll see what Bill Goldman says six years later about that piece of Hollywood lore. Rashomon redux, probably for both of us. Oh, and close your eyes if you're offended by F-bombs.

Lew: You have been an influence in many people's lives. I go around the world—literally, I just set up a workshop in Zimbabwe yesterday and one week in Poland the day before—and they know moi and Bill Goldman. It's amazing how influential we are, and we don't even know it, and it's okay, isn't it?

Bill: One of the awful things is that since I started, screenwriting has become the center of our culture. It's awful.

Lew: Horrendous. Horrendous.

Bill: Or at least movies are. Do you want to start?

Lew: Absolutely. I just had Francis in my class. Have you ever met him?

Bill: I only talked to him once on the phone about twenty-five years ago. I was desperate to write the screenplay for *The Great Gatsby*. I didn't get the job. Coppola did. I wanted to read the screenplay. I got hold of it. It's one of the best screenplays I have ever, ever read. It's just brilliant. Don't ask me what he did; I can't tell you. But I remember thinking, "He solved all the problems in the book, and it's fabulous." I went to see the movie, and of course it was the *Godzilla* of its year. It was a super, hype, giant egg movie. For me, it was awful, especially since I had read this great script.

I realized then how fragile movies are. They had hired a now-dead, sadly, but very English director. The English, as you know, have their class sickness. Five seconds after "Hello," they know what your daddy did because of your voice. The director decided that Gatsby's parties, which were the height of the social season and what everyone would want to go to, were tacky, crass, and lower class. So, he made the parties awful, and that reflected on Gatsby, who gave the parties. That decision reflected on everything else, to make a very mediocre movie with two actors that were brilliantly cast, I thought. Redford and Mia Farrow were perfect, but that one choice permeates so much.

One of the things in a movie is that we are all at each other's mercy. I can fuck you up, and you can fuck me up. For a movie to be wonderful, we all have to somehow, even though we rarely meet each other, have to have the same goal in sight. I often wonder what would've happened if a director of equivalence—I don't even mean a great director but a just decent American director—would have been given *Gatsby*. It would have been one of the great movies because it certainly was one of the greatest scripts.

LEW: I think the fragility of movies has so much to do with the spine, as you have very articulately said in a variety of interviews, as well as in your *Adventures in the Screen Trade*. By the by, I am doing an author appearance thing at a bookstore tonight, and I always say, "Bill Goldman's book *Adventures in the Screen Trade* is the best book written about Hollywood screenwriting wonder of wonders." There is excellent information there, even beyond the war stories. Although you didn't mean it to be a textbook, there are absolutely pertinent lessons to learn, when you talk about structure and spine. Even some years later, you still feel that way, don't you?

BILL: Oh yeah. I'm writing a long piece on the Oscar nominations for *Premiere*. And my favorite will be, by far, *Something about Mary*. I would give it the Oscar immediately. I mean that. But when you look at some of these other movies, like *Saving Private Ryan* and others, films which have such remarkable ingredients essentially, what fucks them up is story. It's just incredible to me.

I'll give you an example of a movie I liked: *The Truman Show*. It was a wonderful piece of work and inventive and different and funny and touching. Then three-quarters of the way in, he makes a dummy of himself and escapes. I'm sitting there thinking, "Well, I could do that, or you could do that." This is the most watched guy in the history of the planet, and I'm thinking, "Isn't some yoyo in Brazil going to be watching that and going to say, 'Wait a minute. Why has this guy been taking these things behind the corner, and wouldn't they get phone calls?'" Of course they would. It's an inconceivable act, and it blows the shit out of the movie. For that reason, I don't think it will win, and it shouldn't win. It's a lot better for me to think, in *Saving Private Ryan*, they just fucked up the story. Story is the hardest single thing there is. Whatever your rules are, you can't break them. Don't screw up your storytelling. Should I talk about *Life Is Beautiful* and how they fucked it up?

LEW: Before we get to *Life Is Beautiful*, I have come to believe that the most important thing in screenwriting is understanding the spine, to use your phrase, understanding what the movie is about. What the movie is about is not what the story is about, correct?

BILL: Right.

LEW: And they didn't know what *The Truman Show* was really about. Billy Wilder knew what his movies were about. By the way, I was recently teaching a workshop at the University of Oklahoma, and they asked me what film I wanted to show to illuminate what I believed. I showed *Butch and Sundance*. And, God, Bill, one of the nicest things a writer can hear is "It still works."

BILL: Does it? I haven't seen it for so long. I've wondered.

LEW: It still works. I don't think storytelling changes. Audiences don't get sick of certain things and go on to something else.

BILL: Also, I say if you can't get George Hill or David Lean, it's always a crapshoot. They give you the script you wrote. Anyway, back to *Life Is Beautiful*. It's quite controversial because some people who are smart love it. Some people hate it. My idea of story is only mine. You may want to tell a story this way, and I may say, "No, no. You've got to begin in the ballroom." You'll say, "No, no. I want to begin in the maternity ward." All of that is how we individually tell our stories. I had a huge problem with *Life Is Beautiful*.

LEW: Go on.

BILL: I did not believe the boy and the father could be in those circumstances, for that length of time, and nobody else said, "Will you shut the fuck up with that bullshit about the tank and that kid. We're all going to die here. I can't stand it. Be quiet!" Or somebody else says to the kid, "He's telling you the truth. You know my kid was going to win that darn tank last month, but he cried, and he blew the whole thing." You can't ignore it! They're in terrible circumstances. This is a loud-mouth guy. I didn't believe it would go unnoticed, and it went on and on. There were good things in the movie, and there were wonderful things in the movie, but you can never ignore the rest of the world. I was shocked and moved at the way they killed him. Just around the corner and bang. I thought, "Oh my God, is that how you do it?"

LEW: So, then, talk to us about the suspension of disbelief. For you, you could not suspend your disbelief. If that believability cord is broken, it's over.

BILL: Here's what I'm saying. Very often I don't say what I mean the first time. *The Truman Show*—I'm saying I understand that it's not realistic. There is this giant television and blah, blah, blah. Within that limitation and because he is the most watched person in the world, he can have no secrets in that way.

What I'm saying in *Life Is Beautiful*, even though it's a fantasy, it's still Jewish people suffering concentration camps and all that madness. There are all of these miserable men who know they're going to die, and in the middle of them is this sweet madman blabbing on to his son. There's not another kid in the barracks. He never tries to take the kid to anywhere and tries to make it only their secret, yet he's blabbing in the middle of everybody. I simply stopped believing. It begins when he starts giving instructions. Remember, there's someone who comes in with orders for the barracks, and he jumps up and does the scam. I thought, "Wouldn't somebody understand what he's talking about? This is life and death here. I don't want to fuck up. I don't want the guys beating me." Basically, I was moved, but I stopped believing. I also had a personal thing. I understand it's not as commercial, but I wish to Christ he wouldn't have saved the mother at the end. I would have been more moved if the boy is on the tank, saying, "This is the gift my father gave me." But that's not right or wrong for a writer to do. That's a choice. What I'm saying is, right or wrong, well, you can't have that kind of fuss going on. We've all been in groups of men in the army, at camp, in a meeting, and self-preservation behavior is common to us.

LEW: For you, then, the logic of human behavior got in the way of the fantasy? How about nobody ever heard him say "Rosebud" in *Citizen Kane*?

BILL: Right.

LEW: But nobody cared.

BILL: That's correct.

LEW: The logic didn't get in the way of the fantasy there, but in *Life Is Beautiful*, the logic blew away the fantasy of the storytelling.

BILL: *Saving Private Ryan* is another example, and it's got great shooting by Steven Spielberg and a wonderful sequence near the start that is much better war shit than Oliver Stone's or Francis Coppola's or any other great war shooter. What's brilliant about it is the length. It's twenty-four minutes, and nobody else has ever dared do that. I thought that was a high-water mark. The movie mulls along, and it's a little operatic and phony, but then the squad goes off after Ryan. I thought those adventures were fabulous. The search scene, the scene with the village, the scene with the crazy pilot who's killed all the people and all that stuff, and then they get to Private Ryan, and Ryan says, "I don't want to go back. I want to stay with these guys here." Now, I say, "Okay, I guess I believe that." If you're given orders by your captain, you voice your comment. He's a young man, he's shaken, et cetera. Tom Hanks can't let him stay. He just can't let him stay.

Let's say you and I are kids and our father comes to us with great seriousness, "Bill and Lew, what you must do on earth is get Little Matt in the next house to school today." So we go over to Little Matt's house, and he says, "My best friend in the world is visiting me only today. I will not go to school." We decide we have only two choices. We have the choice of leaving him there with his friend, or we have the choice of staying with him all day. So, I'm saying, "Wait a minute. The third choice, which is the only choice, is getting the kid the fuck to school."

What really is painful about the phoniness, which is really all through the last hour of *Ryan*, wouldn't have been so easy not to have it? All you have to do is have Ryan say, "I will not go. Okay?" You have the same set. This is only some extra shooting I'm talking about here. Tom Hanks says, "I appreciate your sentiment. Pack up. We're getting out of here now." Right? The next shot, the squad is leaving the village. We're all set up—doesn't cost us anything, right? For the next shot, the squad is crossing the bridge, right? Then, the squad is entering the countryside, right? Cut to a Tom Hanks close-up staring. Cut to the distance, and the Germans are coming at them. Now, they must hurry back into the village. Everything else is exactly the same. Nobody had to be phony. See what I'm saying?

LEW: Absolutely.

BILL: It's inconceivable to me they did it the way they did it because that's when you stop believing. Oh, I'll tell you the worst thing in that fucking movie, all right? Toward the very end, Tom Hanks dies with one of the inconceivable lines of all time when he says, "Earn this," to the guys. I still don't know what that means. I know we're going to go back to the cemetery, okay? I know who's got to be at the cemetery. It's got to be Ed Burns, and I'll tell you why. Everyone in the squad is dead except Ed Burns and the translator, and the translator was not at the twenty-four-minute battle, so he can't recall that. So it has to be Ed Burns.

But you go back, and there's cute Matt Damon, and I thought, "You can't do that." You cannot have an intimate story told by someone who never saw it, who never heard about it. There was never a moment when Tom Hanks says, "Let me tell you about the landing we had. Guys are losing their legs and this and that, and it took twenty-four minutes, and blah, blah." It's an inconceivable mistake, and that blows the reality for me. In other words, you could have shifted points of view in that wonderful moment when they find Matt Damon. If the next part of the movie is told by Matt Damon, I don't mind that. But you cannot have improper storytelling, a story told by somebody who knows nothing about it.

LEW: Hear, hear!

BILL: Does the young lady who's listening agree with that?

RITA: Yeah, absolutely. I was just thinking about my script where I screwed that up and was going back, trying to fix it.

BILL: I'm just thinking this in the void. No one's heard this before. Are you okay with it?

RITA: I absolutely agree. I think to make a movie clearly about one thing is one of the techniques I seem to be discovering in my journey of figuring out how to write a screenplay.

LEW: Rita, by the way, is going to be a big, big writing star. She's very self-deprecating about it all, but she's a wonderful writer.

BILL: The only thing is, why aren't there more of you? Now the fact is, that this kind of talk I'm doing with you, is of no import because the movie got made and got phenomenal reviews. It was a big hit.

LEW: I encourage my students to go see *Something about Mary*. I went to go see *The Waterboy* last week. Watch those movies to see why they are doing so well. Why is *Saving Private Ryan* going to win an Oscar?

BILL: I liked *The Waterboy*. I thought it was a well-structured piece.

LEW: Yes, it was.

BILL: I thought it was very touching. I loved Kathy Bates because I always do. I thought, "It's not a movie that I would go to see if it had done $30 million," but I wanted to see the shrink think. And it's not dirty. I thought it would be dirty and raunchy. It isn't. It's just a strange, little, ridiculous tale, but it never set out to be realistic. Overall, I think this is the worst decade in movie history. I don't think there has ever been anything as awful as the '90s. I wrote a piece in the *Los Angeles Magazine* the year of *Jerry Maguire*, saying that it was the worst year in Hollywood history. Now, I think this year was way worse. Where are the American films that you can honorably say, "These are wonderful"?

LEW: The only pictures I like thus far are international: *Central Station* and *Waking Ned Divine*.

BILL: This is a personal admiration of mine. I just happen to love *Something about Mary*. This one, for me, is a wonderful romantic comedy. There are movies the Academy always ignores. It always ignores comedies.

LEW: Well, now, for me, the logic in *Something about Mary* is questionable. I cannot suspend my disbelief to imagine how that much semen could emanate from one penis that would cause her hair to swoop back and stay up for the next three reels.

BILL: I would argue you're right.

LEW: You often talk about the commercial aspect of moviemaking. But the ubiquitous "they" don't understand that seminal movies do not end happily ever after (i.e., *Butch and Sundance*, *Casablanca*, *Citizen Kane*), but there is a redemptive factor, obviously. How do you respond to that? "Let's kill the mother" in *Life Is Beautiful*, for instance. How do you persuade people to—

BILL: I'm not saying kill the mother. I'm just saying I wish she weren't there. I'll tell you the kind of logic that I would go with. Somebody said they didn't like the mother, and they didn't like *Life Is Beautiful* because they didn't believe the mother didn't lose weight. That's not what bothers me. I wish I weren't bothered by what I consider to be mistakes because if I weren't bothered by them, I would love a lot more movies. I want to love the movies. I want to go there and be thrilled.

I just remembered something in *Saving Private Ryan*. I was shocked when Tom Hanks went against orders and character by saying, "Let's just stay here and fight Nazis." It's just inconceivably bad. After this, every other emotional decision in the movie is based on that same operatic horseshit.

LEW: Okay, then why is it going to win an Oscar?

BILL: Because critics are tacky and awful and second rate, and they have an awful job. They have to see all this shit. I think when they see something the caliber of *Private Ryan*, which has fabulous things in it, that they say, "Wow." Hats in the air. I don't think *Private Ryan* is remotely as fine a movie as *The Thin Red Line*, but that has huge problems for me, too.

LEW: Maybe it gets us to Marshall McLuhan and the medium is the message. The movie doesn't have to be good, but to see Tim Allen get fat, it pays off in *Santa Clause*. Or seeing believable dinosaurs in *Jurassic Park* is another audience payoff. Is there something there? When the audience's expectations are paid off and that's commercially enough? The critics, the audiences don't get caught up in the storytelling aspect of movies, just the "ride."

BILL: I basically look at all projects with my artist hat and my hooker hat. When you're talking about something like screenwriting to people, in theory, who want to learn, you can't say to them, "Go write *Die Hard* in a spaceship." What you want people to do is write wonderful movies, whether they're war movies or comedies or anything. You want them to be properly done so an audience can be properly moved.

I've been saying for years that Hollywood exists in great part, now, for mouth breathers in Asia to Europe to the Middle East. The young men in all these countries who get off on violence. I just saw the preview of a Mel Gibson picture, and he does stuff in the movie that is physically beyond human endeavor, but that's what the audience thinks is okay today. Okay, hell, I don't know. I understand Schwarzenegger can do certain things, and I think Mel Gibson is a wonderful actor and all that.

But in the preview, he's walking in the open, shooting these two guns with deadly accuracy. Is that humanly possible? Is the world's greatest pistol expert capable of shooting two guns with such marksmanship? I don't know. But the audience today has been dumbed down, as my fellow writers, I am sure, have commented to you, and this sort of illogical logic is what we're left with. I think it's a very bad time. I think studio executives are not what they might be, but they may have terrible problems I know nothing about.

LEW: I know that in my professional career, *Die Hard* and Quentin Tarantino have been two major master's-degree-screenwriting curses that people want to try and imitate. Fortunately, we're through both tunnels. What do we get the most imitation of today, Rita?

RITA: Now we've got a lot of twenty-something college comedies.

LEW: The *Friends* kind of stuff.

BILL: My whole feeling is that if you're going to be a screenwriter, and I'm not sure that's a good idea, but if you're going to do it, you have to write about what you give a shit about.

LEW: Hear, hear!

BILL: Because otherwise, even if you sell something, it's not going to make you ultimately feel very good about yourself as a writer. Most of the time, the process we have now is set up not to make you feel very good about being a writer. Daily *Variety* editor Peter Bart, a very good observer, has a book coming out, which I'm desperate to read, about movies this last summer. He mentioned in passing, while we were chatting, that he was shocked how consistently better the scripts had been over the finished movie. This is the kind of thing, if you say to the general public, their eyes glaze over. They don't want to know we do anything.

One of the things about being a screenwriter is very few of the times do you get away with it. Callie Khouri got away with it with *Thelma and Louise*. Tarantino got away with it. Bob Towne got away with it with *Chinatown*. I got away with it in *Butch*. There are so many times when wonderful screenplays are totally ignored or are totally, for some reason, ego, whim, or otherwise, are altered. I basically am shocked at the executive process when I go in to work with a studio now.

I remember when I did *Maverick* for Warner Brothers. I'm working with Mel Gibson, who's an Academy Award–winning director, and Dick Donner, no fool—he did *Omen, Inside Moves*, right? Of course we're not doing *Battleship Potempkin*, for Christ's sake. It's *Maverick*. And three people from Warner Brothers sit quietly in the corner, taking notes. And I would get messages that said, "We feel the script could be better if it were funnier and more exciting." And I would say, "Fuck you! I think so, too. Tell me how to do that." That's the process now. That's the process. I think if I wanted to make movies better, if I were God, I would pass a law that made all studio executives know how to read and give usable notes on a screenplay.

LEW: I have said exactly that. I was running for board of directors of the Writers Guild a couple years ago, and I don't think people heard me. I wanted two things on my agenda: One was to do what we could to have the screenwriter classified as an artist instead of a fucking wordsmith, and the other was trying to get more education disseminated to studio executives so these fucking committees wouldn't turn a thoroughbred into a camel almost without exception.

BILL: And they're all going to, sooner or later, get fired, and they all know it. It's true. I don't know who started this committee shit, but it happened, and it's wildly detrimental to a movie.

LEW: People say, "Why aren't movies better?" And every time I use exactly that dialogue. We go in there and get three to six people telling him or her what to do. And nobody talks about taking anything out, which is one of the reasons why these drafts are about 180 pages long. Then there's the fragility, back to the beginning of our conversation, the fragility. One comment can destroy the core, as you well know. I'm sure you've done Writers Guild arbitrations where the instructions relate to the "core" of the story.

BILL: I wrote about this in a book many years ago. A friend of mine was doing an adaptation of a novel. The producer said, "We don't want you to change anything. We love it just as it is, with the exception of the main character, who was sixty-five. Let's just make him thirty-five." They didn't get how much everything changes. Nothing is the same. That's one of the many examples of how they fuck things up. It's really true. Nobody understands; ergo nobody cares.

Lew: Jerry Belson got coscreenwriting credit for almost one suggestion. Remember *Back to School* with Rodney Dangerfield? Jerry Belson has become a comedy script doctor out here of some renown—a few people know about him on the outside—but Jerry Belson made one suggestion. "Let's make Rodney rich." Made all the difference in the world, right? Remember, he could buy the college instead of being a blue-collar schlepper like his son.

Wait, wait, I promised people at the beginning of the book we wouldn't have war stories, but I guess our war stories do have to do with the actual screenwriting process. Talk to us about your process. How do you do it? How do you write a screenplay? How do you identify an idea with both hats on: your whore hat and your quality hat? How do you identify an idea that you want to spend X number of months of your life with, and how do you go through the process?

Bill: The truth is, when I'm offered a movie to adapt, not originals, I never ever wear my hooker's hat. I think that's the studio's problem. So, I'm not thinking about selling the movie or about whether it will work in Southeast Asia. All I'm thinking of is, "Can I, terrified, somehow feel I can make it work?" If I feel like I can make it play, then I'll probably say, "I'll do it." But I have to feel somehow that it's something I want very much to do and that it won't be *How to Stuff a Wild Bikini*. Not to mock that great epic, but that's not something I could write.

My work habits? What I do is read the novel again because I've read it once to say yes or no. Then I reread it five or six times, each time after the first with a different-colored pen. Every time I come to something, I—remember that I have no idea what the movie will be initially—but every time I come to something I think would be good in the movie, I mark it. So after I've read it over a period of months, a half a dozen or so times, and I look at the pages, and if there's no mark or one mark, I'm probably not going to put that in the movie. If there's half a dozen marks on other pages, I probably will. When I looked at a copy of Steven King's wonderful novel *Misery*, and I got some of her madness, or when he gets out of the house and gets back and she begins to torment him more, there's a red, a green, a blue mark. Things are circled. You just know that part is going to be in the movie. These are also certain themes I think would be interesting in the movie. I'm also, at this time, doing research beyond the book. This is all for me to build up my confidence. That's the thing that dogs everybody, at least me.

LEW: You, of all people, need confidence?

BILL: Yeah! Will you be able to do it? You know at some point you won't be able to do it. I've been doing this for a long time, but I've always felt I couldn't do it. In my thirty or forty years as a screenwriter, I live my life constantly being afraid I'll be found out. That's true.

LEW: Larry Gelbart says, "Every time I sit down in front of a keyboard, I wonder, 'Is this the time they're going to find me out?'"

BILL: Well, It's the same thing with me. I understand exactly what Larry has gone through so long. The minute you think you know what you're doing, it's over. I believe that.

LEW: I remember, when Kurosawa picked up his Lifetime Achievement Oscar and said with his wavering, eighty-nine-year-old voice, "I think I know a little about making films."

BILL: Absolutely. Here's the deal. He didn't know he was Kurosawa. He's a little Asian guy who's trying to get through the day like the rest of us. One of the nice things about *Shakespeare in Love* that Mark Norman got so well is that Shakespeare was just another "schlepper." Shakespeare did not know he was Shakespeare. That's why historical movies are so awful. Somebody says, "Well, so-and-so, this is Bill Shakespeare. Well, here's Julius Caesar." But the fact is, Prince Charles has friends who call him Charlie. He's inside his kilt.

LEW: Do you know you're William Goldman?

BILL: No!

LEW: Half of you is William Goldman. The other half is Bill Goldman?

BILL: I don't want to hear anything good. I never do because it's too scary. I really believe that when you interview young kids getting hot, and they talk on interviews and say things on television or whatever, and they talk about how wonderful they are, I think it's over for them. I really do. One of the good things about not living in Los Angeles is that I don't know any people in the movie business. I hate LA. I think it's very damaging. I think, as I've always thought, young writers have to go there. I think once you make your break—

LEW: Get out.

BILL: Get out. They can find you by phone or fax or e-mail or whatever. One of the good things is not being surrounded by people in the picture business. Knowing who's getting what and what's the deal and who's hot and who isn't makes you less able to write. When you're hot, whether you're a writer or a director or a star, everybody wants to fuck you. I don't necessarily mean sexually.

LEW: I understand.

BILL: I'm proud of a line I wrote once: "Stars have no friends. They have business associates and serfs." And I think that's true. It's true of producing stars, of directing stars. You begin to think, "Hey, I'm great. Tell me I'm great." I think once that happens, the quality of your work goes over a cliff.

I got a wonderful quote from cinematographer Gordon Willis when I was doing *Adventures in the Screen Trade*. He said his great skill is he's able to say, "That's not the direction you were going when you started. We were going north, and now we're not. You know that?" I think what happens out there is that most people want to be told they're great. I know it's true of writers and actors, and I think probably of others. I don't mean money people. The others are so insecure that we want to be told we're wonderful. The danger comes when you begin to surround yourself with only people who tell you you're wonderful because then you begin to believe it, and then your career is essentially over.

LEW: Let's go back to process. You've made your checks in the book. Now, do you do an outline? Do you step outline? Just a brief or one, two, three, four, or are you thorough and elaborate?

BILL: What I do when I am really going to do it, I do two words. I'll say, "Phone call, mail codes, bomb explodes, subway station." From step 1 to, I don't know, 28, 29, 30. Two words can mean a transition, or it can be a seven-page scene. It's basically, for me, fine.

One of the problems I have is, when you're writing movies, you enter the story as late as possible. You enter each scene as late as possible, but somehow, having said this, it's very tricky to decide where to begin. What's the beginning of the story? Once I have that, I can hang onto that. That's an anchor for me, and then you begin to plod along. The reason the beginning is so important is because if you will conceive of a piece of string going from the beginning to the end, the way it goes is going to affect everything that follows the beginning.

LEW: Now, that ties into Billy Wilder. I said, when I first came to Hollywood in the late 1950s, I'd say hello to a writer, and he or she would immediately say, "I can't get a third act. I can't get a third act." And Billy says, "Well, maybe if you can't get a third act, perhaps you really haven't got the first act."

BILL: Of course he's right. All your problems are ahead. They're always before what you think your problem is. I think the single hardest thing for us to do is the ending. I've only had one terrific ending in my life, and that was *Butch Cassidy*, and that was because of history. But I mean, it's so hard to have Billy Wilder's *Some Like It Hot* ending or *Nobody's Perfect*. It's so hard, but that's not the third act. That's the sit-around-the-computer last couple of minutes. It's very hard. I met Stanley Kubrick one decade ago, and he was talking about what was a good story. He said, "An original premise that builds interestingly to an unexpected climax." Well, that's hard. That's damned hard.

LEW: Does that tie into the Tennessee Williams line "Give them what they want, but not the way they expect it"?

BILL: That's right. Absolutely. Leonard Bernstein said, "Art should be expected and constantly surprising." It's the same thing. They surely knew each other.

LEW: Somebody asked Cocteau, "What can I do to be a wonderful writer?" Cocteau said, "Surprise me."

BILL: When I go to the movies, and I really love to go to the movies, I want to be just thrilled because it's what I've done for years. I'm not your ordinary fan. I know more that I should about the discipline. When I went to see this recent movie, and I've been in love with the actress for generations, the movie opens with my heroine getting on the people-moving escalator things in an airport. She's like a statue. She's immobile. She goes along, the credits roll, then she gets on another one, the same thing. Then the credits keep on rolling, and she's still standing like a statue. Then she's on a third ride, and she starts to run. Now, all I'm thinking at this point is, "Why is she running now?" Did I miss something on the first two escalators? People movers? Did something happen I haven't seen? Then I'm thinking, "People don't stand like statues on those airport walkways. They look around." All of a sudden, I'm not watching the story. You want to control the viewer's eyes. You don't want them thinking about why your heroine is running. Once you do that, it's very hard to get the audience back.

LEW: Back to your personal structure. You write a group of one or two or three words and? Once I asked you, four to eight years ago, how long it took you to write *Butch and Sundance*. You said you thought about it for eight years; then you sat down and wrote it in six weeks. It took you both eight years and six weeks. You write much like Faulkner, who says he's like a dog circling the backyard and the circle gets tighter and tighter until he stops and takes a shit, right?

BILL: The truth is even worse. I researched it for eight years, and I wrote it over Christmas vacation at Princeton University. So I think I wrote it in two and a half weeks.

LEW: So you really tapped into your subconscious? You think that's where our creativity is?

BILL: I had this story about two guys who didn't really know each other, but they thought they did, and suddenly they became famous. I had only written a couple movies, and I remember being terrified. I knew I had to do it fast because I tend to write that way when I know what I'm doing. I start slowly; then I pick up speed. Then for the last third of the script, I'll go as fast as I can. That's if I've structured it properly. If I've got the beginning correct.

I had a huge problem in *Butch and Sundance*, which was how to get them to South America, which is not a problem today. But in those days, it was a huge problem. No one had ever runaway like that, least of all in a western. The whole superposse chase is there only to get them to run away. That takes twenty-nine minutes in the movie. Another problem was I was just sick of them. All those years of trying to find out more about them. There wasn't much about them then. There weren't any books, really. The whole *Butch and Sundance* explosion happened after the movie came out. But it's hard.

On *Misery*, I had another huge problem. The novel begins with the audience knowing that the Kathy Bates character is already crazy. Rob Reiner and I decided that the minute you know she's crazy, the movie takes an alteration, but up until she's crazy, she could be a nice lady who is trying to save this guy who is going to die. We decide to delay the reality of her nuttiness as deep into the picture as we could, which presented a problem. Why, then, should the audience sit there? So I began the movie with Jimmy Caan finishing his last novel, getting ready to go, having the car fixed up, then having the storm, then going with all the health shit, and having Kathy be as cute as she could be because we are delaying the moment when he is in peril. I knew that was going to be the start, and I knew the end was going to be essentially what it was, that he was going to win. So what I had to figure out was how to, drop by drop, make it exciting that she's nuts. So I think the logic on that screenplay, although it was years ago, was that was what my spine was. My spine was that a guy was trapped and finds out that the woman who saved him is also very likely going to kill him. I remember thinking how awful her breath is, how terrible and disgusting she is, and how she's the fucking devil and all that. That was the logic of *Misery*. That was the spine: the gradual reveal of Kathy's madness and what does Jimmy Caan do about it?

LEW: Let me tie this into Frank Pierson. Frank was in my class, and I said, "Frank, I was told you broke the back of the *Dog Day Afternoon* story when you found out the poor son of a bitch, Al Pacino's character, lives for everyone but himself. He lives for his wife, his children, his homosexual lover." Frank said, "You're absolutely right, but I didn't break the back of the story. I broke the back of the character." Now, here, is that what you're talking about for the Kathy Bates character? You actually broke the back of her character? In the beginning of the movie, she was masking her madness; in the King piece, she was mad right up front.

BILL: Every assignment is different, and everybody uses different words. I tend to be, at least in movies, to deal more with story. For example, there is a section in the movie where Caan gets out of his room, goes to a scrapbook, and sees all the deaths at the hospital where she works, and then he realizes. Now, that's a section, if you wanted, you could see as a flashback. I'm not saying that's the way to do it, but there are all kinds of ways in telling things. You could see Jimmy Caan in New York at the start, talking at Ninety-Second Street. Or it could begin on the *Today Show*, pushing his latest novel. You could begin it any way you want to, and somebody would say, "Oh, that's what I want to see."

There was a movie of a novel of mine that I wrote called *Magic*, about a guy who is a nutty magician. The character of Fat, for the first third of the novel, you think is a person because he's kept a diary, but it's the magician's dummy. Fat is very worried that Corky, the magician, is doing Mr. Goodbar stuff, attacking women. Yet the conflict is that Corky seems like such a nice guy. You watch him grow up through the diary. An early director of the movie had no interest in magic or in madness. He was interested in the looking for Mr. Goodbar stuff. So, if he had directed the movie, he would've insisted—he was a very powerful director at the time—that the movie shouldn't really deal much with what for me was the heart of it. We saw two different stories. I'm not saying he's wrong or right. I'm saying there is no right as to what is a story and what isn't because we can do it any number of ways. Am I making any sense?

LEW: You keep referring to story, so actually in movies—

BILL: There are lots of words that mean *story*: *story*, *spine*, *structure*—all of these.

LEW: Movies, writing scripts, moves closer to oral storytelling than any other performance writing or any kind of writing.

BILL: Say that again.

LEW: *Time* magazine critic T. E. Kalem once said, "In theater the drama is thrust at the audience, but in movies the audience is thrust at the drama." I just think that movies can be the purest storytelling of any kind of art form. Do you have a take on that?

BILL: I've written novels. I've written plays. I've written all those movies. Each have their own rules. In a movie, you have no fucking time. There's no time at all. You better get on it and get on it fast because the camera will tell you everything. In a novel, if you're a wonderful stylist, you can write pages with me thinking about this phone call and with you getting ready for your phone call. I don't know who you really are. I only know who you say you are. Maybe you're not who you are, okay? You can't do that if your story is going to be a movie. Such introspection would send people out of the theater in five minutes. Nothing is dumber than a phone call. It would be intercut; you, then me, then you, then me. But the fact is, there's not time. You've also got to begin with the fucking phone ringing because that's when it gets going.

One of the great cliché scenes of all time is the teacher in class saying, "And here, class, we can see where Wordsworth—" and the bell rings. The class leaves, and the girl comes up and says, "I'm pregnant." That's the start of the scene. The bullshit about Wordsworth is nothing. All teaching scenes are like that because teaching scenes are essentially boring because it's just me talking. And what you want are things moving. Sometimes I read scripts by young writers and say, "Get on with it, get on with it."

LEW: Aristotle says, "The movie should be about one thing, and that is what the hero or heroine is trying to get." Does that make sense to you?

BILL: It's all true. I can also give you a movie where the hero or heroine don't get what they want. There's a great line by Aristotle, which in essence is "If it were easy, everyone would do it." What's incredible to me is I've been doing this for thirty-five years, and I will look at some of the shit I write, and I'll say, "How could you have written that? You know better." We're all trapped inside our own skin. I was just reading an article about Ron Bass, who is so successful, and I heard he has a whole group of writers he works with. And I thought, "What a fabulous idea! You're never alone."

LEW: He's in this book, of course. He says he has his own development staff so that he can hear script notes before he sends something to the studio. They don't help him write it—just feedback.

BILL: The awful thing for me about being a writer is the alone part, being trapped with my own inadequacies.

LEW: Do you have anybody that you trust who reads your material before the philistines attack?

BILL: I have four readers I trust a lot. That's crucial because you've got to have a reader that will tell you the truth because if people just say, "Oh, it's swell," you're going to find out soon enough from the studios or the directors or the producers that it isn't swell. One of the things I also believe in, which is, when you're a writer, you only get one shot at someone reading something professionally.

LEW: Hear, hear! Do I know that one.

BILL: You better be at your best. So often I will read a script, and the kid will say, "I can fix that. I can fix this. I can fix that." He or she didn't, and I'll never read it again the same virginal way. You've lost my objectivity. You only have one time, and a lot of times you are anxious and get your script out there too soon and blow your shot because no one is going to really read something twice.

LEW: Is the one-word or one-sentence, basic structure/outline you develop for original scripts as well as books?

BILL: For books, yeah, I guess I do.

LEW: And when you're in the script, do you assign yourself a certain number of pages a day?

BILL: I think when you start, you can never stop. I think you have to go every day, seven days a week. Whatever your rhythm is, a morning person or all day, whatever it is, once you start, you can't fuck with that rhythm. If you only write on weekends, you can't go surfing one weekend because then you begin to be beset by devils, saying, "Well, no one really gives a shit. It's not going to be any good, you know." And once that happens, you're stuck not to write. I do three pages a day when I start. And if I do three pages a day for five weeks, I will have a movie.

Gradually, as I get more confident, if I've structured it properly, I begin to hear how the people talk, and I get a writing style for the piece. I will then speed up. And so, in the second week, I hope to be doing five pages a day, and the last few days, I would hope to be doing eight or ten. So, I would say that a movie really takes me three weeks. When a studio hires me, I assume it's going to be six months between that day and delivery day. It's never the writing that consumes everybody's time. It's the thinking.

LEW: Yes, absolutely.

BILL: And it's the researching. For me it's constantly trying to build up your confidence so they're not going to find you out. So that this time is really going to be wonderful. All that bullshit stuff, you tell yourself to keep going.

LEW: What about rewriting? Let's say you're rewriting for yourself. One of the students asked Irving Ravetch and Harriet Frank Jr. about rewriting. Irving deferred to Harriet, and Harriet nodded for him to speak. Irving said, "Well, we like to get it right the first time." Do you generally feel you get it right the first time?

BILL: No, but I get a lot of it right, if I know what I'm doing. I suck at rewriting. I basically have always hated it. For novels especially, it's very close to what gets published the first time, and I've gone over it and over it and over it, of course, before I turn it in. In *All the President's Men*, I was writing a series of boy-girl scenes for Robert Redford that I knew would never be in the movie. What was hard about that was not that he was wrong, because he's very smart, but that I thought he was wrong for this story.

I was writing about two reporters trying to crack a case, and it didn't have time for any side issues. Essentially, newspaper stories are boring, and you don't want an audience to think. You just want to go and go and go. That was my thinking. I didn't believe in the scenes, so writing them was very hard. If you think you're writing something you don't believe, making it work is very hard. If you think you're writing something and it's a good idea, that's terrific and relatively fast and generally good.

LEW: Shane Black is one of our ex-students. Shane claims he got his style from reading *Butch Cassidy and the Sundance Kid.* I have always said *Butch and Sundance* is the worst script to copy because Bill Goldman was well known at that time and people would have wanted anything you wrote on toilet paper. Generally, everyone should write in master scenes and blah, blah, blah. Shane takes *Butch and Sundance*, and he mimics you for *Lethal Weapon* and does even more wiseass comments than you, if you'll pardon the expression. And he gets bought! Are you aware Shane did that?

BILL: Well, I'll tell you a wonderful Shane Black story. We were both trying to doctor *Last Action Hero.* We were sitting in my living room here. I think I was working on character, and Shane was working on big action sequences. That sounds so fucking nuts when you say it to people not in the business. Anyway—

LEW: Oh, and they brought Elaine May in to do a woman's scene for that movie.

BILL: And Shane is so successful. He's a terrific kid, and blah, blah, blah. He looks at me—I don't think he's even thirty yet—and he says, "Do you know why I envy you?" And I said, "I cannot think of one reason on earth." He said, "Because you got to write movies in the 1960s." And I went, "Huh. You're right." In those days, everything did not have to be this great, gigantic, operatic shit they do now.

The first movie I wrote was a hit with Paul Newman called *Harper.* It was just about a woman who hired someone to find her husband. She hired Lou Harper, who finds her husband, and he was a millionaire. Today, the studios would say, "He can't just be a millionaire. He has to be Bill Gates. And there's got to be a deep secret." Paul Newman would have had to have known Bill Gates in his background, all that shit they do, which is one of the reasons movies suck, you know. But the thing about the '60s, before *Jaws* changed everything, was that not everything had to be a blockbuster. *Jaws* is the most important movie of our time. That was extraordinarily brilliant direction by Steven Spielberg for Universal. Great piece of moviemaking. I love it. It's just marvelous. The money is what really happened. *Jaws* rocketed past everything so quickly, nothing has ever been the same. A national event.

LEW: That happened to me with Universal. At that time, I had a movie in place, a love story in an insane asylum. Sally Field wanted to play the girl, Mark Hamill, the boy. John Badham wanted to direct it. Universal turned it down because the upside wasn't high enough. It didn't have the chance to pull the *Jaws* dollar.

BILL: I understand. They claim they know what's going to work, but if they knew what was going to work, they wouldn't get fired. So it was. So it is.

LEW: I understand you did a strong amount of work on *Good Will Hunting*. Do you want to talk about that?

BILL: I can tell you exactly what I did with *Good Will Hunting*. It's one of those awful stories I have been trying to kill. It was originally a Castle Rock movie. I do a lot of work for Castle Rock. The two kids, Affleck and Damon, came in, and I spent the day with them. I did nothing. Now, the person who did help them out a lot was Rob Reiner. They had a great deal of CIA shit in their script. Spy shit. The government was trying to get Matt to do evil stuff against their enemies or something. Rob said, "Get rid of it. You don't need that. Go with the kid's brilliance. Go with the lower-class people of Boston." And they did. All I did say was that Rob was right. So I did nothing, but I can't stop the rumors.

LEW: Well, this book will take care of that partially, and then I'm sure you will do much more in your own way.

BILL: I would love to say, "Yes, I rewrote it," but I don't know a lot about kids in Boston.

LEW: Do you think the screenwriter should be considered an artist?

BILL: Well, that's one of those tricky questions. I don't know. This is my problem. I was born in 1931 and came of age in the '30s and '40s.

LEW: Me too.

BILL: And at that time, if you wanted to be in the arts and you were a writer, you wanted to write the great American novel or the great Broadway play. Now, there's no such thing as a great American novel, alas, and Broadway is essentially dead for American playwrights. When I was growing up, movies were a guilty pleasure, and I loved it. So it's very hard for me to take movies seriously. I also have great problems with group art. Yet I wrote *Butch Cassidy and the Sundance Kid*. I made it up. It did not exist except in some very arcane books no one knows about. I made it all happen and come to life, and bullshit, bullshit, bullshit.

I didn't know it then, but to help me, I had the best director I've ever worked with coming into his top form, George Roy Hill. I had Newman and Redford, phenomenal talent. I had Connie Hall, with that amazing cinematography, on and on. When I said, "I had," what I mean it wasn't "I"; it was all of us together. So am I an artist? Somebody young may say, "Fuck yes, of course I am." I have a great deal of trouble with that concept in movies. Now the two great screenwriters, for me, absolutely are Bergman and Wilder—both European.

LEW: And both consider themselves primarily writers, you know.

BILL: I would say they were artists, but it's very hard today. See, I can't imagine Billy Wilder dealing with this shit that probably everybody but George Lucas, Steven Spielberg, and James Cameron have to deal with. But James Cameron had to deal with plenty before *Titanic* opened.

LEW: Rita, you're representing yourself and our graduate student body. Any questions to throw at Bill before we jump off?

RITA: When you were talking about the rules and how important the rules are that you set up in your screenplay and that you stick to them, is there some way you go about testing those rules for yourself? Or, on occasion, do you get so close to the work, you don't even notice? Like we were talking about all these movies and how they set up certain rules and at some point they violate the logic of their world.

BILL: Well, generally it's my own sense of story that says, "You can't do that." Somebody else might say, "Oh, that's great." Tom Hanks says,

"Let's stay with Matt Damon, although we'll all get killed." I don't believe that for a New York minute. I think it's horseshit. I think they do it for horseshit reasons. It was a terrible thing. I think it began to totally unravel the movie and make it unreal, operatic, and awful. Now, it's going to win the Oscar for best picture, so what do I know? You see, I also wasn't nutty about *Schindler's List*, which you're not allowed to say in Southern California, but I'm not there.

LEW: I bet you liked *Searching for Bobby Fischer*.

BILL: I did.

LEW: By the same screenwriter.

BILL: Yeah, absolutely. I think it's wonderful.

LEW: *Schindler's List* came from a book. *Bobby Fischer* was an original.

BILL: The part that breaks your heart is when movies like *Bobby Fischer* don't do business. I want to tell you a great story. When I saw *Bobby Fischer*, I didn't know there was a huge chess-playing audience there. The moves in the chess match got applause. I mean, you're sitting there, and you see a guy going, "Pawn, pawn, pawn," and the theater going off. It was the most wonderful thing. I found afterwards that this huge chess club had gone to see the movie that day.

LEW: My publisher says people buy screenwriting books looking for the secret. Are there any secrets you believe in for screenwriting?

BILL: The only rule I believe in is you better give a shit.

LEW: Last question. The legend in Hollywood is there was one time when you were in a notes meeting with *The Maverick* script with, let's just say, an anonymous studio. Lore has it you finally up and said, "I'm too old and too smart and too rich to deal with this shit anymore."

BILL: No, it was for a movie I've never seen, got billing for, and shouldn't have: *Adventures of an Invisible Man*. It was a very fucked-up project. There was an argument between the star and the director, and I left. Then the director left. Later I had a meeting with the producer and the star. They wanted to make these changes that were, well, clearly something I couldn't do. I said, "I'm sorry. I'm too old and too smart and too rich to put up with this shit." And then I walked out. I didn't say it with great dramatic emphasis. I think I said it quietly and joking, sort of. I don't actually remember saying it. I guess I did. Whatever the case, I'm real pleased. I wish more screenwriters would do it.

LEW: That's a good go-out for you. For me, let me give you something you will like that not many people know about. I was once with Godard. We had some sort of a Franco-American thing here. And I said, "Monsieur Godard, did you once actually say, 'I believe in beginnings, middles, and ends but not necessarily in that order'?" He replied, "Oh, my boy. It was a joke. A cocktail joke." And I said, "For a cocktail joke, we writers have been hoisted on that petard for years." And when I told this story to a woman who was interviewing me in Paris, her eyes clouded, and she said, "You know, I know Monsieur Godard." I quickly replied, "I'm sorry. I hope I didn't offend you, but that's what he said." She said, "No, no, no. He is now a very lonely man living on the outskirts of Paris and so sorry for having fucked up an entire nation." That's my go-out. William "Bill" Goldman, many, many more years of being William and Bill.

BILL: Thank you so much, Lewis and Lew.

4

Julius Epstein

When I think of Julius Epstein, I cry. There are a handful of screenwriters of these interviews, who submitted their thoughts to my 434, that have gone on to their deserved and great rewards. While all of these are screenwriting legends to cinema and to the WGA, two have drained my tear ducts. They are Billy Wilder and Julie Epstein, pour moi. You are now going to hear from Julius Epstein, who refers to himself as E.T.'s Grandfather. My heart palpitates, I admire him so. My favorite movie of all time is his, Casablanca. I promised Julie in front of my 434 class, that we would not ask him what Humphrey Bogart wore to bed, or other frivolous nonsense. Well, 434 student, Veronica Ehrenreich came late to class and she immediately asked, "Mr. Epstein, tell me something about Casablanca." I replied, "Oh no, we are going to focus on the craft . . . but as long as Veronica brought it up . . . uh, would you like to respond?" His answer shocked us all! You will be given his response in the following 434 interview with Mr. Epstein. This time I didn't cry. We laughed, we learned and we admired.

> LEW: We are very pleased and even more honored to introduce Mr. Julius Epstein. When wonderful directors or screenwriters are introduced, an armful of credits are introduced, and he or she will seem close to being elevated to sainthood. We prefer to use W. C. Handy's line when some-one asked him, "Mr. Handy, what are the blues?" He said, "Baby, if you got to ask, you'll never know." So, we'll forgo Mr. Epstein's numerous credits because you can check your computer if you don't already know.

Today we're going to do something that may be very rare in the annals of people talking about screenwriting and having screenwriters come to their classes as guests. We ain't going to talk about his movies. We will not talk about *Casablanca*; *Reuben, Reuben*; *Pete 'n' Tillie*; *The Brothers Karamazov*; *Yankee Doodle Dandy*; and so forth. We're going to talk about writing. We would like to talk about writing from the perspective of the writer. We want to talk about writing from this standpoint of agony or joy or anything in between that you would prefer to call it.

I have here a quote from Mr. Arthur Laurents. I want to hear if Julius would agree with Mr. Laurents when he says, "Writers are the chosen people. They talk about how awful it is to be in the room alone, but I would not agree. They're not alone. They're in there with all of these wonderful creatures. I consider myself to be one of the chosen people." Does that make sense to you?

JULIUS: Well, considering my background, I'm twice chosen.

LEW: True.

JULIUS: I never found writing to be a lonely vocation. My only real collaboration was with my twin brother, and that wasn't really a collaboration.

A year ago, I was asked to go to Boston. A stranger at Harvard Medical School was doing a survey on collaboration, and they wanted to get my view. I told them I couldn't give them my view because my brother and I were twins, and I don't believe in psychics. I think that, ESP, all of it, nonsense. Yet, it was really just one person writing. My brother would have a thought, and I would finish it, or vice versa. Then he died in 1952, and in the thirty years since his death, I've tried to collaborate with Billy Wilder three times. We couldn't get a word on paper.

LEW: Did you have a good time?

JULIUS: No. If I have a terrible thought, I'll keep it to myself, but I'll do my part if someone else is in the room with that look of scorn on their face. However, my brother would say those terrible thoughts.

I did have one successful collaboration after my brother's death, and that was with Max Schulman on *House Calls*. We worked differently, though. It was his original. He first wrote a play, and it was not quite right, but I thought there was a movie in it. So I did my version as a movie. Then he came in and we would look at a scene, and he'd go in a room and write that scene, and I'd go into another and also write the scene. Then we would get back together and use two lines from one and two from another and sort of collage our scenes.

It's a different form of collaboration from when people sit and throw lines at each other. When I have two hours a day, it's really deceiving. As I've said, writers are really working all twenty-four hours a day. You always have a small piece of paper or legal pad and pencil with you at all times because you just never know when something good is going to hit you. But actually sitting in a room or pacing for two hours a day—see, I can stand myself alone for two hours every day. So that isn't bad. A lot of writers I know cannot work alone. Their excuse is loneliness. I think it's just an excuse. I think they need someone to bolster them and say, "Oh, that's good," or something else.

LEW: A lot of writers, Julius, say they sit in front of their typewriters or computers or their quills until the beads of blood form on their foreheads. I, in my approaching senility, believe that's a writer trying to get sympathy from people, like a child would from a mother or father. "There, there, son." I can't imagine how anybody would want to spend year after year in that kind of agony. Does this make sense to you?

JULIUS: I read that Balzac took two months to write one sentence or something like that. Yet Sidney Sheldon says he does fifty pages a day. Well, I believe that, having read it. I don't know why he procrastinated so long. Anyhow, point is, it's all very different for different writers.

Also, there's a difference between today and earlier days in writing, when we had the contract system and you were obligated to write continuously. I came to Hollywood in 1935, and I have the *New York Times* film directory, which goes up to 1969, and from 1935 they have listed five released pictures. The joke for those years is that pictures were not released; they escaped. About two years ago, I was in New York, and I spoke to some film students at the New York School for Social Research with Philip Glass. I had a bio, and from 1935, they had me listed for seven pictures, not just five. It turns out that two of those pictures were so bad that not only had I forgotten about them, but the *New York Times* had forgotten, too.

I bring this up because several weeks ago, there was an article about a hot new screenwriter, and the writer marveled that he had seven pictures in six years. They thought that was worthy of comment; however, under contract we'd done seven in one year. I work in a way which I've found no other writers work in this same way. Usually, a writer will write their stint for the day, and when they start to work the next day, they will read what they've written the day before and make corrections. Once I begin a screenplay, I never go back. I will never look at the previous day's work until it's all finished, which is usually seven to ten weeks or maybe three months. By this time, I have forgotten a lot of what I've written, so when I pick it up again and try to read it, a lot of times I say, "Did I really write that?" or "Oh, did I really do something so bad?" But it has a freshness and perspective that I wouldn't have had without that gap in time. Three months makes the necessary rewriting so obvious for me; I can see what's good, what's bad, and what has to go.

LEW: Tell us about your habits. Let's start with an idea. How do you recognize a good idea?

JULIUS: I go back to *Reuben, Reuben*. It was published, I think, in 1956. It was laying around for twenty-some years, and I've always been a great fan of Peter De Vries. I think he's one of the great, unappreciated writers of our time, and I had done a picture from his material before. We had a working relationship. I had just done *Pete 'n' Tillie*, so when his developers called, I had read everything he had written years ago. I had read *Reuben, Reuben*, and I didn't see anything in it as far as a movie. *Reuben, Reuben* was actually three different stories. The first one, I doubt anybody has seen the picture? Two people here saw the picture? Well, that makes twelve in whole the country. You remember there's a grandfather?

The first section of the novel *Reuben, Reuben* was all about the grandfather. The poet, Dylan Thomas, was barely mentioned in the first section. The second section was only eighty-five pages, and it was all about the poet, and there the grandfather was barely mentioned. The third section was about neither. It was about Geneva, the girl who married an Englishman and who is not in the picture at all. It was originally about their marriage. It was really three different stories stuck together. It wasn't until I read it again, it suddenly struck me that there was a movie in the poet. So I went to work, and I'm a veteran, as you know, of the so-called golden era of pictures, which was a big myth. It wasn't even the bronze era. Then you had to write a hundred-page treatment before you wrote the screenplay, which was a waste of time because when you start doing the screenplay, you find out you use very little of the hundred pages.

What I do now is what I call a step outline, which is one sentence each. Number 1: Those who saw *Reuben, Reuben* will recognize when I say, "Number 1," was his poetry reading. Number 2, back at the hotel, the wife shows up, and number 3 is the scene in restaurant. Number 4, the scene in New York with his ex-wife. Number 5 is the scene on the street where he meets Geneva. It's all one sentence, and it usually amounts to about twenty to twenty-five numbers. Then, after I get the scenes done, it doesn't always stay the same, but usually it's the same old, same old. Very little change.

I start to go by the numbers. I write the first sequence and don't look at it again. I'll go through the whole numbers until the last one, then I'll pick it up again and start to read it from the beginning. It's all, like I said before, new to me, good or bad. It becomes very clear to me what I have to do. Sometimes, put a match to it, which I have done.

Lew: Well, your step outline process makes us feel very good here in these 434 classes. That's exactly what we do. In my experience with those hundred-page things, you also tend to leave your fight in the dressing room.

Julius: Coincidentally, yesterday, there was a call from the Writers Guild. They have a collection in the library of every script that's been nominated, but they only had one of mine, despite six nominations. They cannot get a script from a studio; the studio will not give them a script. They said, "But you have the script." I said, "No. As soon as I get through a script, I throw it right out, all of it." I save nothing. I go to friends' homes, and they have fifty screenplays beautifully bound with leather.

Lew: And autographed by the stars. Why do you throw them out?

Julius: Because I'm so bored with it by the end. There's usually so much trouble and so much grief in making a movie that I don't want any visible evidence around.

Lew: You've produced a lot of your movies, right?

Julius: Right.

Lew: What is your motivation to produce?

Julius: Very simple: A movie is a collaborative effort. Writing, directing, producing, editing, music—any one of those elements can ruin a movie. If you can reduce the amount of elements, you reduce the chance of disruption. If you can be a writer/producer on the picture, you have two of the five elements. There are now people who write, produce, and direct their own picture. They've cut the odds down of destructive elements even further.

LEW: I find that as a producer, you're also on the committee. A writer is rarely on the committee.

Back to ideas, please. So you've read *Reuben, Reuben* two or three times, but what is it? A light bulb? A golden flash in the corner of your room? What causes you to say, "This is a good idea," or "This is a lousy idea"? Is it difficult to differentiate one from the other?

JULIUS: Well, the character is what got me. As I said, *Reuben, Reuben* originated with Peter De Vries. Dylan Thomas was once a houseguest of Peter De Vries, who had to throw him out. If you saw the movie, you know what he did to the women of the town. Well, it was all true in real life. Thomas went right through the women and right through all the liquor supplies in town, and it struck me as a wonderful character.

STUDENT: Was he always a Scotsman as opposed to a Welshman in the book? Was that your invention?

JULIUS: We changed that because of the actor, Tom Conti. He said, "I can't do that accent." The character attracted me. I thought it was dramatic, it was theatrical, it was entertaining. Last Tuesday, I was at AFI [American Film Institute], and there's always one student like this in every class. I've been to a lot of them. I've been to Stanford. I've been to Pittsburgh. I've been to Davidson. I've been every place.

LEW: And now UCLA.

JULIUS: I've been to UCLA before. There's always one student who gives you a hard time. They're the only people who point out the ending. There's no dog in the novel. There's no dog in the novel at all. The reason I changed the scene was because I felt it was a predictable ending. Then my son, a UCLA alumnus from theater arts, went on a trip and dumped his shepherd dog on us. The dog jumped on me one day, and the idea came to me. The ending of the picture, to explain to the others who haven't seen it, he decides to commit suicide. He's on the chair with a rope around his neck. He decides not to commit suicide. The dog, who was finally his only friend, comes in and leaps up on his master, knocks the chair from under him, and he dies. That was the end of the picture. A lot of people didn't like it, and the AFI student didn't like it, and he gave me a hard time. He said, "Now, what were you trying to say with the ending?" I said, "I've been writing for fifty-two years. I've never tried to say anything. All I try to do is entertain people." But he wouldn't let me.

Usually I say to a class when they ask, "What is your theme? What are you writing about?" I find one sentence covers every script, and I defy you to name any story it doesn't cover. You always say to them, "No man is an island." It gets you off the hook. It did get me off the hook, but I'm not through with the AFI boy. It didn't get me off the hook with him. I then said, "It struck me that no man is the master of his own fate. You can be rich and famous and happy. Then you can walk in the street and be hit by a truck, and that's the end of it all. The same of this poet who decided to be happy and not commit suicide. You're not the master of your own fate." The student then said, "Aha! Is that the Buddhist positive point of view?" And I said, "No, that's the Orthodox Jewish point of view." That stopped it.

LEW: I went to a television academy presentation last week. There was a young woman who goes around and tells producers what's wrong with their scripts. Oh, there was not a writer in the room, by the way, when this diagnostic thing takes place. She's sitting up there, explaining concepts, turning points, the arc of the story, and the place is filled with people furiously taking notes. Earlier, at the Writers Guild, they have her in, and the boardroom is overflowing. She talks about plot and plot and plot, plot, plot, and I'm sitting there, going crazy, because I believe that character is more important than plot. Plot comes out of character, don't you believe? Or do you?

JULIUS: The thing that interests me least is plot. There's very little plot in *Reuben, Reuben*, but if you have a good character or if you're fortunate enough to have a couple good characters, you're going to have a sale. And you're going to hold an audience's interest. Plotting stories mostly bores me. When they depend upon the plot, the characters are often weak. I'm never too concerned about the plot.

LEW: I have on my wall a Lillian Hellman quote: "Plot is what the author wants to do. Good plot is what the character wants to do." Tell us about what you do at the end of three months of script writing?

JULIUS: Breathe a sigh of relief.

LEW: Is that true? You climbed the mountain. Do you feel it's downhill from there? Do you do a lot of rewriting, a bit, or does it simply just depend on the individual script?

JULIUS: It varies. In *Pete 'n' Tillie*, not one word was rewritten. That one was sort of accidentally not rewritten because they decided they wanted Carol Burnett, and Carol only had a certain window of time in her television series hiatus. There was no time to fiddle with the script. Over my career, I've done a lot of rewriting, I've done very little rewriting, and I've done medium rewriting.

LEW: Jim Poe is a good friend of mine, and I asked him, "How come *Lilies of the Field* turned out so good?" He said, "We had six weeks to write it, three weeks to prepare it, three weeks to shoot. So we didn't give anybody any time to fuck it up." *Pete 'n' Tillie* was not unlike that experience.

JULIUS: I'd say the same.

LEW: Were you producing *Pete 'n' Tillie*?

JULIUS: Yeah, I was one of them.

LEW: You have a specific discipline? You say you work two hours a day? Do you use a tape recorder or longhand or type?

JULIUS: Longhand. Yellow legal pad.

LEW: I do not know of a successful writer who does not have discipline. Am I wrong on that?

JULIUS: In everything else I'm very undisciplined. With my work, I'm very disciplined. I get up. I used to jog, but now I do my walking. I have a long, long breakfast. I take about two and a half hours to read the sports section in the *LA Times*. I don't get to work until about 12:30 or 1:00 p.m. I work five days a week, and those are my disciplined hours. I write longhand. I'm a terrible typist, and I can never read my own writing. After I get through the sports section, I go into the room, sit down, and I start to work. I do my two hours. Sometimes it's one hour and forty-five minutes one day; sometimes it's two hours and fifteen minutes on a different day.

LEW: You don't have a page count you give yourself? Just the two-hour period?

JULIUS: Well, sometimes. My favorite writer was an Englishman. I can't think of his name. An old friend did his movies. He's an English novelist and very successful. He was under contract to Artists Group, and I always loved him, and I honor his memory. He said, "I do three pages a day." He talks about novel writing. He said, "It may take me fifteen minutes, and if the three pages are done, I shut down and that's it." Sometimes I'll go, "I've done enough." But it's usually about two hours, and usually my output is about three pages a day.

LEW: You don't have any superstitions, any favorite shirts, any coats, or special kind of coffee?

JULIUS: I have a lot of superstitions but none about writing.

LEW: So, you find yourself periodically pleased at something you've done? Do you rush in and exclaim to someone, "You've got to hear this!"?

JULIUS: For me, it's all terrible. I was at the point of throwing *Reuben, Reuben* away when my son put it under his arm and took it to Walter Shenson, the producer. He liked it. It's like seeing the first cut of a picture—it's the worst thing that can happen to anybody. I've never seen the first cut of anybody's film that was good. Like reading it the first time, it only seems terrible. You should really give it to somebody to read: your agent, somebody. I have to have an honest agent.

LEW: A wonderful man in your case: Benjamin.

JULIUS: Who says, "Let's forget this one. Let's sell this."

LEW: Let's talk about your selling side. Do you spend a lot of time selling?

JULIUS: I have to let the work be the salesman. I know a lot of people who are wonderful salesmen and terrible writers.

LEW: You don't pitch ideas?

JULIUS: I'm really bad at pitching because when you pitch, you're doing plot, aren't you? That's not my strong point. I can't say, "Oh, this is going to be a wonderful scene." I have to see it in writing. After fifty-some years in the business, they know who you are, and you don't have to sell as much. In the past fifteen years, with a few exceptions, I have initiated every project myself.

Reuben, Reuben and now *Happy at the Time*—the material sells itself. Well, I know, in all cases, I've optioned books. I've taken the risk myself. *Reuben, Reuben* took three years and was turned down by every studio in town. Then, when all of the studio executives were out, we went through new executives, and still, it got turned down again. So, it was finally made without a distribution deal, and we got the money from Taft. They were gutsy enough to risk it. We were shooting about four weeks in North Carolina, and we got a phone call saying that HBO would like to talk to us about *Reuben, Reuben*.

LEW: What is your highest pleasure and lowest despair over your fifty-some years as a writer?

JULIUS: The lowest moment is always the same, and that's the first cut, without exception. I would never see a first cut and say, "Oh, great." The moment of elation is when the picture comes out and people like it.

LEW: Do you have people come up to you on the streets and tell you how you've changed their lives or helped their lives in writing a screenplay?

JULIUS: In fifty-something years, I never had one person, until last week at Cedars Sinai Hospital. Oh and one very sad thing happened: It was a very long time ago; I guess it was 1939. I did *Four Daughters* with John Garfield, and he committed suicide, leaving a note that said, "I'm just like the character Garfield." Well, you can't do anything about that because you feel something else would have turned him on perhaps a year later. That was a sad experience.

LEW: I once had a similar thing on something more trivial, but still, *Batman*: A young boy leapt to his death in England from a skylight, wearing his cape.

JULIUS: I think I read about that.

LEW: That changed my life completely about writing scenes involving violence or possible imitations thereof. Tell me about favorite writers, and then tell me about favorite screenwriters, people that you quite admire.

JULIUS: I'm not going to talk about screenwriters. I have only one favorite screenwriter, and that's Woody Allen.

LEW: Good enough.

JULIUS: I won't talk about anyone else. There are a lot of good ones, but nobody's in his class. It's silly to talk about the rest of us. Oh, there was Dudley Nichols, Brackett, and Wilder.

LEW: I asked Jim Poe that question one time. He said John Paxson was really special.

JULIUS: Good, he's very good.

LEW: How about as far as novelists and literature?

JULIUS: Well, I've reduced my novel reading as the years have gone by. Favorite novelists: I love Peter De Vries. John Updike—I think he's one of our great writers. He's so simple. He's wonderful. Sometimes you got a short story in the *New Yorker* that you love as you read it, and you're very surprised when you get to the end of it to see the name John Updike. When I was in college, I was very impressed by a group of playwrights like Philip Barry, S. N. Behrman, Robert Sherwood. The first play my brother and I wrote was *Two Boys from Brooklyn*. We had a butler in there because Behrman wrote about butlers. That was my youthful influence.

LEW: Steinbeck, Hemingway—do those people get inside of your creative bloodstream?

JULIUS: I think Hemingway is a great writer with a great adolescent streak.

LEW: Did you start out wanting to be a writer?

JULIUS: I started out being a ghostwriter. If anybody has read the book *What Makes Sammy Run*, I'm Julian Blumberg in the book. Two people I know, one from college, came out here and sold a story. The producers told them to write it, and I knew they couldn't. I was just waiting for the call. Finally, a telegram came saying, "We offer you a job as our secretary. $25.00 a week, room and board. Hop a bus." I came out, wrote the screenplay, and it was made.

LEW: Did your writer brother, Philip, come out with you at that time?

JULIUS: No, but he came out to ghostwrite for the same people. After I asked him, I sat down and wrote a little story every night. Now, in those days, a little story meant ten, fifteen, twenty pages, sort of an outline. It took me nine months before I sold one, which became a picture called *Living on Velvet*. Philip and I then got a four-week contract at a hundred dollars a week, at which time they could fire us, and they owned the property. After one week, they called us in, gave us a contract, and we worked for them for seventeen and a half years on that contract.

LEW: You did a story every night. Was that part of your discipline as a young writer?

JULIUS: Well, I was very young then, and I practically wrote the same story every night.

LEW: What makes you angry in relation to writing?

JULIUS: What makes me angry is to pick up the trade papers and see that *Porky*, *Rambo*, and *The Money Pit* are at the top on the box-office list. What makes me angrier is to go through Westwood Village and see the college kids lined up to see those pictures. That is beyond my comprehension. Those movies are doing $200 million. The sleaze, the terrible things. That's what makes me angry.

LEW: Tell me about books on writing. We here don't suggest too many books because we think most of those "how to write motion picture and television" books are probably more counterproductive than productive.

JULIUS: I wouldn't recommend any books. You heard my four-year education in screenwriting as a ghostwriter. My first Sunday, they took me to the Paramount Theater on Fifth and Hill. There was a double feature playing. I remember one picture starred Bing Crosby. It was called *College Humor*, and the song in the picture was called "Down the Old Arch Road." They said, "That's a cut. That's a fade-out." I went home and wrote a screenplay.

LEW: John Steinbeck one time told me when I asked him, "What can I do to be a better writer?" He said, "Write."

JULIUS: Also, it's kind of like George Abbott. He does the same as writing a movie. That was the day of the three-act play. He said, "The first act, you get your protagonist up a tree. The second act, you throw rocks at him. And the third act, you get him out of the tree."

LEW: We say here, too, "Tell me about second acts." F. Scott Fitzgerald says that Americans don't have second acts. I never could interpret what he meant by that; however, I know we do, as writers, have the most trouble with the second act. Do you look at screenplays in terms of act 1, 2, and 3? Or what I say here is situation, complication, and conclusion?

JULIUS: I never think of that. I just do it and ask, "Is it good? Is it full?" Where I have trouble, however, is with endings.

LEW: The third act.

JULIUS: Several times, like *Reuben, Reuben*, when the dog jumped up on me, I got the idea for the ending. Then, it simplifies the whole thing. I didn't know where I was going. A lot of times, you write and hope that in the writing, a good ending will occur to you.

LEW: But is there a key? Larry Gelbart said that in doing *Tootsie*, he came up with the idea that the Dustin Hoffman character puts on a dress and becomes a better man for it. Frank Pierson says that he realized in *Dog Day Afternoon*, when he was struggling with that character, that the poor son of a bitch was living for everyone else but himself: for his lover, for his wife, and so forth. Then, everything fell into place. Could that have been true with you and the dog? Is that periodically true, that one thing will reverberate throughout what you've done?

JULIUS: Absolutely. That's why I say you carry a piece of paper and a pencil with you at all times because you never know what or when it's going to hit you. It varies. Sometimes, I've started with the whole thing laid out perfectly, and sometimes I have very little to start with and hope with the character that something will come out of it. There's no strict rule.

LEW: Do you break down your characters? Do you do a considerable character analysis before you start the picture?

JULIUS: No. If you have to do that, you don't know your character.

LEW: I mean, you do that in your head.

JULIUS: Yeah, of course. All I do is, as I told you before, the one, two, three, four—

LEW: Yes. Step outline. That's what we believe in a lot here. Tell me about Aristotle.

JULIUS: Never heard of him.

LEW: Tell me about Egri. You probably know Lajos Egri, who wrote *The Art of Dramatic Writing*?

JULIUS: No.

LEW: Aha. Any questions from anybody? Veronica?

VERONICA: Do you have a definitive genre in your mind when you start writing?

JULIUS: Well, I feel I do one genre the best. That is, I can't write young people. I like mature people. *Reuben, Reuben*: mature people. *House Calls*: mature people. I think I'm quite good at doing mature people, and I can write dialogue for mature people. The problems with mature people interest me. Marriage, divorce, children, and things like that. I could never do a *Rambo*. I could never do *Back to the Future*. I couldn't do any of that stuff. I couldn't do *E.T.* I can't. I'm not unlimited. I have my age group of characters.

LEW: When did you start limiting yourself?

JULIUS: As I got older. It's my statute of limitations, if you can call it that.

LEW: When you were working at Warner's, didn't you and your brother do different genres?

JULIUS: But we were very young then. We did everything. We didn't do them well at the time, but we did them.

LEW: More questions?

JULIUS: I would like to say that I had an eye operation on Monday. You all look hazy to me, but still very good.

STUDENT: When you were writing about relationships and things, do you take from your personal experience?

JULIUS: Yes, you can't close the door. There's always a little autobiography in your stories, and sometimes the experiences of your friends, your family, the things you know about.

LEW: Is your family proud of you being a writer? Your children? Your wife?

JULIUS: My father wanted me to be a lawyer. My father called law students, "Your honor." Of course afterwards, well, no one put obstacles in my path. I did take a bus to Hollywood.

STUDENT: How much assistance do you give the director in your script?

JULIUS: I must say, maybe I overdo it. Because I had an experience with a little script at Fox called *Take Care of My Little Girl*. There was one scene that was taken from my experience of cheating on an exam. The boy asked the girl to help him, and she refuses. He said, "What's the matter? Scruples?" The director had the boy say, "What's the matter, Scruples?" After that, between "What's the matter" and "Scruples," I always put a dash.

STUDENT: You don't write a lot of director's direction?

JULIUS: I don't, no.

STUDENT: Like camera angles?

JULIUS: Oh, no.

STUDENT: Or dots and dashes?

JULIUS: I used to put a lot of dashes when I felt a part was dramatic, but now I don't bother. They don't pay attention to that anyhow, and it's really a waste of time to put camera angles in the script.

STUDENT: But you have a visual idea of what you want? The angle for which you want the shot?

JULIUS: That is why the first cut is always dreadful because you visualize the action coming from this way, and they're coming in from another.

LEW: But when you're writing descriptions in your master shot, do you have an indication for the art director to think about, and do you help the actors out a little with some of the interpretation?

JULIUS: Well, sometimes, if a close-up is absolutely necessary, but normally I don't bother with that anymore. Sometimes I feel that there are certain lines that can be misconstrued by an actor or a director where you're tongue-in-cheek. I'll note that in the direction. But for the last few pictures, I'm always on the set. I'm a nuisance.

LEW: When you were starting out, were you also on the set a bit?

JULIUS: Actually, we were on the set so much, Warner Brothers used to throw us off all the time. I was on the set every moment with *Pete 'n' Tillie* and *Reuben, Reuben.* I don't know if you would agree with me on this, but I think the most horrid word in the English language is *improvisation.* You struggle, you sweat, you try to get a line right, and then the actor will delightfully change it.

I'll give you an example. It's not a great line or anything, and it was a terrible picture. You know the old cliché from *Forty-Second Street*: "You're going out there an understudy, and you're coming back a star"? Well, I had a picture where the girl had her father put up the money for the play, and she says, "I went out there a star, and I came back an understudy." This time I didn't care much about the picture, but I just wandered on the set one day, and there was this actress saying, "I went out there a star, and I came back all wiped out." We had this tremendous fight. I'll tell you privately the name of the actress later—she's one you very much know before she did the part. It was not the first read. It was the second read. She came with pages and pages and pages of dribble. She was from the actor-studio method. Pages and pages of dribble. She said, "I won't play the part." The studio wanted to placate her. I said, "Here's how you want to direct it: Let her play her scenes, but play them sitting down, no movement at all." Then the entire nine pages of dribble could be cut. That was what was done, and she won an Academy nomination for best supporting actress.

LEW: They took the scene out?

JULIUS: Of course.

LEW: Julius, I have three of Woody Allen's scripts at home, and if any movies ever looked like they were improvised, it would be his. Yet, every word is exactly on the page of Woody Allen's scripts.

JULIUS: That's why they're so damn good.

STUDENT: What do you think of the trend for special effects?

JULIUS: I think it's awful. My son says that Steven Spielberg unwittingly ruined the motion picture industry with his singular talent. But evidently, it's what you kids want. Maybe not you kids; I saw the lines in Westwood. I went to my college, in the central part of Pennsylvania; they're lined up for the same dribble and sleaze. I can't blame them for making those pictures. *Reuben, Reuben* has done much better at home than at the box office.

LEW: By the chair where you write, if you were to put on the wall things you should have inside of the script, what would some of them be?

JULIUS: I would have notes.

LEW: No, I'm talking about—well, Frank Capra once told me that he and Robert Riskin used to go back and look at scripts to see what scenes would be enhanced by rain.

JULIUS: I've written about seventy-five scripts, and I don't think I had one scene with rain in it. I guess I'm a dry writer.

LEW: Do you see certain techniques consciously in scripts? Or does it all come from your subconscious as you're doing your step outline?

JULIUS: It comes from somewhere but not from the subconscious because I know who the characters are, I know what the story is. My first draft, I call the "kitchen sink version" because everything goes in it, every thought of mine, including the kitchen sink. These first drafts, they're usually long. A four-hundred-page first draft is not unusual for me. I put any and everything into it. Remember, I said that I don't go back and read it from day to day. When I finally pick it up in ten weeks or three months, it's so apparent what has to come out. It makes it so much easier. Sometimes I say, "Oh this will never be in the next draft." Sometimes I'm surprised. Some of them stay in. I'm not too critical of myself on the first draft.

LEW: Does anyone else read the "kitchen sink" draft?

JULIUS: Just me.

STUDENT: So you have that typed?

JULIUS: I read my own handwriting.

LEW: When you finally get to the point of having it typed, do you let other people look at it before you give it to somebody who is meaningful to the script?

JULIUS: That's my strict rule. I don't let anybody read it except somebody who has to read it or my agent, who has to send it out. Last three years, I've worked with Walter Shenson and my son, who works with him. They read it, but I don't give it to my friends. I also don't give it to wives, anybody's wife.

LEW: Is that true when you were beginning?

JULIUS: I think I was always afraid to give it to other people.

LEW: What is the showing-draft time frame after you're done with the "kitchen sink" version of four hundred pages? One week? Two weeks?

JULIUS: The rewriting to me is quite fast. It's so apparent from my method of not rereading every day's work of what has to be done and what has to go out and what to be put in. I'm a slow first-draft man and pretty fast second draft and third and so on.

LEW: When you get it to the studios and to the producers and they ask for rewrites, are you fast at those rewrites, too?

JULIUS: If I agree with it. I've reached the point now, in my life, if I don't agree with it, I won't do it. The studios are full of assistant producers who feel they have to earn their living by giving you notes. I think a rebellion is growing because most of the time notes hurt a script, but many times rewriting helps. I found that out in our own experience. But every writer hates to rewrite, you know.

LEW: So you did a lot of rewriting on *Casablanca*?

JULIUS: We couldn't rewrite because we were shooting all the time. We were just two pages ahead of them. There was no time. I agree to rewriting if there's a scene that I'm absolutely not sure of, but I know is not worthless or bad. I will leave it in, and sometimes if we get together and the director and the actor or somebody says, "Oh, this is a bad scene," I'll take it out. I'm very reasonable about that. There are other scenes I'm positive about, and then I'm a tiger.

STUDENT: How do you get the beginning? I find it to be the hardest thing, the first ten minutes. I always end up shooting things I think are essential, and when I get down to cutting it, I'm so glad to throw them out because I didn't need them in the first place.

JULIUS: I should have brought this up as part of my technique or method of working. My first day, I write, "FADE IN: EXT. BROWNSTONE—DAY—NEW YORK. Couple walking down the steps." I'll get through with the description, and that's that first day's work. I do not do the dialogue until the next day. I don't want to do that. I felt that exhausted me. I hate writing directions in the script. What I try to do is, if I know I have two lines at the end of the scene, I do not put them in that day. Then I can start with those lines the next day.

LEW: Hemingway did that, too.

JULIUS: Yeah.

STUDENT: And you don't go back, and you don't read it? Some people start writing, and when they have their structure, they get ideas as they're writing. Did you ever end up with a different animal than you started with?

JULIUS: Sometimes with my twenty or thirty sequences, I'd get to sixteen or seventeen and say, "I don't need this." Other times, an idea for a new scene will come, and I'll put that in. It's rarely exactly as you've outlined it. If that scene is drastically different, then maybe you've started out with a very weak theme to begin with.

LEW: Two or three writers, I think they come from the Andy Warhol school of writing, like to sit down and put out stream-of-conscious writing, which I have always found to be caca writing. Do you agree?

JULIUS: That's that horrid word: *improvisation*. There's a marvelous director who has absolutely ruined himself because he believes that Robert Altman, Scorsese's *New York, New York*, I saw the scene between Minelli and De Niro. The dialogue was so awful. They say it's natural dialogue. I say that most natural dialogue is awful. You can't do that in novels, the stage, screen, bar mitzvahs, or anything. You can't use the natural way people talk. You think people talk like Woody Allen talks? They don't. That's what happens when you have improvisation. You're down to the lowest common denominator. A lot of students ask me how to write dialogue. I don't know about you, but I say you can teach a lot of things about screenwriting which are absolutely necessary, but I don't think dialogue can be taught. You either can write dialogue, or you can't write dialogue. If you can write dialogue, listen. Listen to people and plagiarize a lot, too.

LEW: How do you feel about Pinter's dialogue?

JULIUS: I think Pinter is a better screenwriter than he is a playwright. He's written some wonderful screenplays, and I think his dialogue is wonderful.

LEW: He told me once—now this is a trick, so to speak, that I've passed onto students—he said, "Good dialogue is dialogue that illuminates what people are not saying."

JULIUS: I'm going to use that.

LEW: Because when you see *Reuben, Reuben*, they were consistently saying one thing, but you could tell they were thinking another.

JULIUS: If I'm known for anything, if I had a strong point, which is debatable, it is dialogue. There's one case that happened to me on the set. Sometimes you have to write a line of dialogue because of the way the scene is being shot. The actor had a quarrel in the previous scene with a gardener. Now she comes in; they shoot the scene, she comes in the house; she walks upstairs, a great, long staircase, and she can't just walk up the staircase without something to say, so I had to have another line. I thought a moment, then had her say, "No woman has ever had any luck with a gardener since Lady Chatterley." This was on the set, spur of the moment. That line was quoted in the *New York Herald Tribune* review.

STUDENT: When you came here as a ghostwriter, did you write before that?

JULIUS: I was just a press agent in New York and often unemployed. It was 1933.

STUDENT: What do you do when you write yourself into a corner?

JULIUS: You write yourself out of it. That's the only way you can do it. There's no other answer. I will never, never say, "To hell with it. I'll leave this scene unfinished and go on to another scene and come back to it later." Maybe other people will do that, but I will never do it. Good or bad, I will finish that scene.

STUDENT: Julius, you said, that you don't often know what the ending of the picture is going to be. In *Reuben, Reuben*, you knew he was going to die, but you did not know how. Is that what you're saying?

JULIUS: I hesitated writing it for a couple of years before I went ahead and said, "Let's just try it, even though the ending was too predictable." I usually have a general idea of what the last scene could be, but you never know what's going to be effective until you get there. Endings are terrible. They're like the bane of writing for me.

STUDENT: I had a superior on a job who said that movies were about endings. Do you think that's accurate, or is that just a Hollywood statement?

JULIUS: That's a Hollywood statement, I think. I think 90 percent of the picture is good; you might get away with a soft ending. It's better to have a good ending. The classics, like, *The Front Page, Some Like It Hot,* have great endings, but you don't often get that.

LEW: Have you been influenced by Broadway over the years? You've done a couple of Broadway plays. Were they good experiences?

JULIUS: Extremely different from a movie. You find more egos involved on Broadway than you do in Hollywood.

LEW: Well, isn't the writer God on Broadway?

JULIUS: In practice. It doesn't work that way. In the Dramatists Guild, no word can be changed; no actor can be fired. Producers say, "Okay, the thing is off. What do you do?" or the director says, "Okay, I'm walking out." It's continuous, these battles. I always thought theater was more important than movies, but a movie ticket is cheap, and there's no play better than a good movie. I'm often disillusioned. I hate plays where the actor gets up and talks to the audience. I'm not here to listen to a talk. Words for a screenplay and words for a movie are still words, but you have more freedom in a screenplay because you can move characters so easily from scene to scene and place to place. I had four plays produced and managed to make only $250.

LEW: What are your favorite movies over the years?

JULIUS: I'm afraid most of them would be foreign pictures, like *Grand Illusions* and also *Murmurs of the Heart,* which was an absolute classic. I would need time to think, but not *Gone with the Wind.* Certainly not *Casablanca* or *Brief Encounter,* although I must say, I saw *Brief Encounter* about two years ago, and time is really a plot killer. Adultery wouldn't work as the heavy today. Now it's so cliché, it doesn't hold up. It was great movie then.

LEW: Did you enjoy writing love stories?

JULIUS: Not particularly.

LEW: Do you ever talk about your writing when you're in the process of writing?

JULIUS: My children always say, "What are you doing?" They resent it terribly. I say, "It's a job. I'm doing it."

LEW: James Thurber was at dinner, and his wife slams her hand down on the table as he's looking into the corner absently, and she yells, "Dammit, Thurber, stop writing!" Do you get this from your family on occasion?

JULIUS: Oh, nobody's near me when I'm writing.

STUDENT: Any principles you use in comedy?

JULIUS: No, I think it has to come naturally. I'm sure Woody Allen has no principles. Woody is just a very funny man, as close to a genius as you can get.

STUDENT: Do you feel comedy comes more out of character?

JULIUS: Oh, yes. If you have the characters and the characters have a sense of humor, the comedy will be there. You won't even have to plan the dialogue; it will just flow. If you're going to say, "I want something funny for this guy to say," boy, you're in trouble.

STUDENT: Can you say anything about *Casablanca*?

LEW: Oh, Veronica, you were late coming in. We weren't going to talk about *Casablanca* or any of Julius's pictures, but well, do you want to say anything about it to keep her happy, or should we let her be frustrated?

JULIUS: Slick shit. That's all I care to say. Well, maybe a little more. We were shooting *Arsenic and Old Lace*, and we thought Cary Grant was awful, bumbling and all that. We got up enough nerve to go up to Frank Capra and say, "Don't you think Grant is a little overboard?" Frank said, "He's not a little overboard. He's way overboard, but I always shoot a picture two or three times. I'll get him in the next go around." Two days later, Pearl Harbor. We had three weeks left on the schedule. Capra shot the three weeks in one week. Then he was commissioned a major to do a series called *Why We Fight*. He asked my brother and me and a few other writers—I think Jim Poe was one of them—to come to Washington and work on *Why We Fight*. Jack Warner said, "You can't go because we have this agreement with Selznick for Ingrid Bergman." She had a stop date. You go over the stop date, it costs a fortune every day.

Let me tell you how we got Ingrid Bergman. Warner said to us, "Selznick wants to hear the *Casablanca* story. We have no story, but go on and wing it." So we were there, and Selznick was at his desk, slurping soup. He never looked up from the soup. If I saw a picture of the back of Selznick's head, I'd know it. I started to talk, "It's about refugees, they're in Casablanca, et cetera." Then I realized I'm talking about a half an hour, and I haven't even mentioned the character of Ilsa. In the unproduced play, Ilsa was a tramp, a bum. She slept with Rick to get the letters of transit—an entirely different story. Anyhow, I haven't even mentioned her, and Selznick hasn't looked up once. Now the big hit picture of that year was *Algiers*, with Hedy Lamarr and Charles Boyer. Now, can I use the dirty word again here? I said, "It's going to be a lot of shit like *Algiers*." He looked up, nodded, and we then had Ingrid Bergman. There was a start clause that said if she started shooting after a certain date, it would cost a fortune. Warner said, "We haven't started yet, so you can't go with Capra because we have to start shooting at a certain date." "Well," we said, "we're going." And we went to Washington for four weeks.

They put Howard Koch on *Casablanca* then, and he started. When we came back, we went to the beginning and worked on the script, but at that point, they were shooting, but it had no ending. We tried everything that could be used, but we sat there saying, "Now what? Now what? Where do we go?" There was real panic in the studio. They had about seventy-five writers on contract, and at least seventy were trying to get an ending. My brother and I, one day, we were driving to the studio, I know the exact spot on Sunset Boulevard, just east of Beverly Glen. We were twins, remember. We looked at each other and said, "Round up the usual suspects." Then, round up the usual suspects for what? For murder? Who does the audience want to see murdered? They want to see the Nazi murdered. The audience, we know, would love the Claude Rains character murdered, and by the time we were in the studio, we had the entire ending. That's the truth.

LEW: Today, we would go in and say, "I want to talk to the director." Did Michael Curtiz have any involvement in accepting the ending?

JULIUS: We did seven movies with Curtiz. He never understood a word the actors said. But if you're Hungarian, you have to have talent. If you've seen the old pictures of that era, you would notice that most of them had a credit for a "dialogue director." We had a lot of foreign directors who didn't really know the language. The dialogue director would take a scene and rehearse with the actors, then turn them over to the director, who was busy lighting the scene and deciding where the camera should be. Curtiz never said one word to an actor, nor could he. He had no knowledge of the English language at all. It was the dialogue director, many of whom became directors afterwards.

LEW: How do you really feel about *Casablanca* today?

JULIUS: Well, I used the phrase already, but I'll temper it. It was a successful combination of shit and sugar.

LEW: Which one of your screenplays are you most reverent about?

JULIUS: Every place I go, I'm always asked that. I mention three pictures, but *Casablanca* is not one of them. One nobody has ever seen: *Light in the Piazza*. Several years ago, UCLA ran a series called Overlooked Films, and that was one. The other two are *Pete 'n' Tillie* and *Reuben, Reuben*.

LEW: Are you proud to be a writer?

JULIUS: Well, I only became a writer because I could never hold a nine-to-five job. Once, I lasted until lunchtime.

LEW: Is that true at Warner's? "Gee, I can't understand why the script doesn't work, Jack. We stayed until five."

JULIUS: No, you got it wrong.

LEW: That's the one I heard. Tell us.

JULIUS: We broke the system of writers having to work in the studio. Metro had 150 writers. As you know, writers work twenty-four hours a day. That little pad should even be on your nightstand because you're working all night. When you actually sit at a desk the next day, it varies. Our hours were two hours at the desk after working twenty-four hours. A couple of nights of no sleep until four in the morning, things like that. We felt it was silly to check in with the studio, punch a clock at nine in the morning, and punch out at five. It was just silly to be there eight hours for two hours of work. So we didn't bother coming in at nine in the morning. We came in for lunch because the writers' table was a lot of fun, so much fun that actors fought for an invitation to be accepted at the writers' table. The only actor we ever allowed at the table was Errol Flynn because Errol Flynn gave us detailed accounts of his previous night's activities. I'm proud to say we never allowed Ronald Reagan at the table, and we still wouldn't.

So we came in at one o'clock to have lunch, and one day we ran into—what I'm about to tell sounds like we were really brave and courageous. We weren't. As a matter of fact, we were trying to get out of our contracts by that time, and we would love to have been fired, but they didn't fire us. Anyhow, we ran into Warner, he says, "Look, railroad presidents get in at nine o'clock, bank presidents get in at nine o'clock, and you don't get in at nine o'clock." So we go back to our office. We had a half-finished script, and we sent the script to Warner with a note. "Dear J. L. Have the bank president finish this script." And we never heard from him about it.

About three weeks later, we ran into him again. He was in a terrible mood. He said, "You speak to your lawyers. Look at your contract. You're coming in at nine in the morning from now on." So we wrote a terrible scene and sent it up to his office. He says, "This is the worst scene I have ever read in all my years in this business." My brother, Phil, said, "How is that possible? It was written at nine o'clock." Warner said, "I want my money back." Phil said, "I would love to give you your money back, but I've just built a swimming pool. However, if you're ever in the neighborhood and feel like a swim."

We tried so hard to get fired, but we couldn't. One day, Phil had an appendicitis attack. In those days, you were laid up for quite a while after an appendicitis operation. We had to work at his home, and we finished a script in three weeks. Warner said, "How'd you do that so quickly?" We confessed we worked at home. Warner nodded then and said, "From now on, work wherever you want to work." That broke the "checking in at nine and checking out at five" nonsense. I feel like that was our major contribution for screenwriters.

LEW: I guess that was the prelude to when William Faulkner said, "May I write at home?" and Warner said yes, and Faulkner went back to Mississippi.

JULIUS: Faulkner was at the studio. I must say he was—I can't use the word *unfriendly* because he just disregarded everyone. If you said, "Hi," he wouldn't reply. He just disregarded you, but we found he was drunk most of the time.

LEW: Mary McCall tells a story when she was a secretary at Warner, before she became a wonderful writer, that everybody was carpooling at the time at Warner because of World War II and the gas rationing. In her car, it was Faulkner, Pep West, Steinbeck, and Dos Passos. Tell me about F. Scott Fitzgerald. Did you know him? He was the only famous novelist that I'm aware of who wanted desperately to become a screenwriter. He just wasn't successful. Why?

JULIUS: He couldn't write dialogue. If you're a novelist, to establish a quarrel between a couple—say, a married couple—all you have to say is they fought and they quarreled, et cetera. In a screenplay, you have to put every word of the quarrel. You see what I mean? There's a big difference. And there's a big difference between dialogue in a novel and screen dialogue. I read a play by Hemingway that was awful. He wrote the same style of dialogue, and it came out flat and stiff. Nobody would ever really say the words he wrote. There's such a big difference.

LEW: I said we wouldn't have war stories, and here we are ending with them. I asked you if you were proud being a writer. Jim Poe said that Sam Goldwyn, who never, ever swore, was talking to Ben Hecht, and Ben frustrated Goldwyn to such a point—

JULIUS: Good.

LEW: Goldwyn shook. He could not say the vile things that were in his mind, so he said, "You, you, you writer!" What can you leave us with at the conclusion of such a lovely hour and a half?

JULIUS: You mean advice?

LEW: Advice, encouragement, discouragement, pick a word.

JULIUS: There are maybe six million writers in the world. All writers are different. You're all different people. You write differently. You think differently. Thank God! I don't have any general rule, except to say, write. Don't be discouraged by rejections. You're going to get a lot of them. It took me nine months of writing a story every night before I sold one to get started in the business. It took me three years to get *Reuben, Reuben* done. Don't be discouraged, and always, I repeat this again, you're going to meet people who ask, "What are you trying to say? What's your theme?" Remember what I told you: No man is an island. You're absolutely safe with that one.

LEW: Thank you very much, dear Mr. Epstein, you, you writer.

5

Alexander Payne and Jim Taylor

There are three sets of partners in this tome: Billy Wilder and I. A. L. Diamond; Irving Ravetch and Harriet Frank Jr.; and, of course, Alexander Payne and Jim Taylor. Only one was a consecrated marriage, but all writing partnerships are almost marriages. My personal experience with collaborations has been tenuous. Many have involved disagreements and constant arguments, and I prefer to go to the mirror to get my criticism in.

However, these three have made it work and have done so with a lot of respect and admiration for each other. Alexander is a fellow UCLA graduate. Jim Taylor is NYU, so these two have connected despite an original coastal separation.

On a strong personal note, Alexander and moi are both from Nebraska and quite proud of our roots. We come from the ripe soil of Fred Astaire, Marlon Brando, Johnny Carson, Henry Fonda, Montgomery Clift, Nick Nolte, and many others. "So many come from Nebraska because every fall they burn the field!" For elaboration on that, ask any Nebraskan. Go Big Red!

LEW: How long do you guys spend writing together? Two or three hours?

JIM: More.

ALEXANDER: Well, it takes us six hours to get those two hours in.

JIM: But also, because we live in different cities, our time together is valuable, and we only write when we're sitting together, so now, I think we spend more hours. When we can actually grab the weeks together, we try to make the best use of them.

Lew: Where do you live?

Alexander: I live in Topanga Canyon.

Lew: And Jim lives in New York? So you don't write together literally. I know a couple of writing teams that have computers synced.

Alexander: What class is this?

Lew: This is 434. Did you never take a 434 while at UCLA?

Alexander: Correct. I did not.

Lew: You learned writing on the job then?

Alexander: Correct.

Lew: Actually, one of the first scripts you wrote beyond your thesis film was for Universal?

Alexander: That was the first draft of what later became *About Schmidt*. Jim, did you take a feature screenwriting class at NYU?

Jim: I guess. [*laughter*] I'm sure I did. But by the time I went to NYU, we had written our first draft of what became the first feature that Alexander directed, *Citizen Ruth*. I'd worked in the industry for a while, so I know we had a feature writing class, but I didn't write a feature script.

Lew: You had wonderful professors there, one who is no longer with us, the venerable Herndon, who wrote *Alice's Restaurant*.

Jim: No, I wasn't there when he was. I did teach Writing the Short Screenplay at NYU, which seemed reasonable, and there were people making those films. The only way I can think to do it is workshop.

Lew: It's like a story conference day 1, the idea all the way. Most people outline meticulously and know every particular scene.

Alexander: We don't write like that. In fact, we were discussing that the other day because we went to hear the cartoonist Chris Ware speak, who actually is from Omaha. It's just a blueprint for a movie. We're all about the movies.

JIM: But my big thing about going to NYU and you guys being here—I don't know if this is exactly true—but this is an art school. I mean, at least at NYU, it's an art school, and there's a reason for that because you can go and learn all it takes to make a movie in a couple weekends.

There's not really that much to know about loading a camera. In terms of knowledge, you being here and me at NYU was to develop my voice. It's like to be in a safe environment, and that to me is what the art school part of it is: that you are protected and you are trying to figure out who you are and what you have to say. It helps to be in that environment, talking to everyone else, getting suggestions from people.

ALEXANDER: And guest speakers.

LEW: And from the profs. When Robert Riskin took a blank ream of paper to Frank Capra and said, "Put the Capra touch on that."

ALEXANDER: I think he mailed it to him.

JIM: But if you get to the point where you're making a short film and screening it for all these people, and it's competent, if it's well crafted, but there's just no personality in it, then that's no use because it's about your voice and being able to use that to connect with people.

LEW: How do you identify the idea that you want to spend however many weeks on?

ALEXANDER: Years. That's a good question. You just know it. In fact, we spend most of our time looking for that idea. Like I think my brain is always on "What's a good film idea?" mode, permanently. I'm just always thinking, "That's a film idea." It actually almost becomes oppressive. Every book you read, like I always tell myself, "Okay, this book I'm going to read only because I want to read a book and not think of it like a movie." Otherwise, it's pathetic. Books you read, articles, relationships, everything is suggesting movie ideas.

But the thing about a movie idea, whether we come up with it, like our next thing, we're in the middle of two scripts right now. The first thing Jim's going to direct, and the next thing I'm going to direct. Both are original ideas. However, we have mostly done adaptations. We don't really care where the idea comes from, but certainly the gold is that flash of an idea of "Oh, that's a movie." I've had it fewer than ten times in my life. That's what carries you through the years of work. Then the rest of it is work.

I think it is equally as important to the viewer, that basically what's the movie about, and I'm not talking about in high concept terms but just in "What is the movie about?" It will see you, the filmmaker, not just screenwriting, but for six months say but through three years of having to deal with that stuff, through casting it, through preproduction, making it, editing it, promoting it. That I can still be discovering new elements that it can offer within that whole process. The whole process of making a film is one of constant discovery, not of execution. Every day you discover a new thing that it can be. It is a discovery, not a statement, and really the thing that inspires most is that it's a movie I would want to see. It's really rare to get that idea, though.

LEW: You said something I really believe deeply in, which is, "What's the movie really about?"

ALEXANDER: It's got to see me through two or three years of work and a viewer has to be able to forgive maybe a lousy piece of casting or a low budget. You know, lousy production values or kind of a boring section or a bad montage or bad music. Maybe the ending isn't great, but you'll still say, "That's a good movie," because what it was about was good. There was something going on.

LEW: Do you find out in the "Ahas," or does it come to you as you go along?

ALEXANDER: I don't really think or articulate things to myself like, "Oh, it's about, like, the spine of it. Really what it's saying is . . ." Maybe it's an aspect of intellectual laziness on my part. Or maybe I just trust that it's there, and I'm more interested in just what's the story and who are the characters. And again, it's all subjective. What strikes me as a good movie may not strike someone else.

LEW: Francis Ford Coppola says—

ALEXANDER: You are just a name dropper: Billy Wilder, Francis Coppola—

LEW: They were all interviewed for this book, along with you, and in many ways paved the way for all of today's American filmmakers. Besides, I'm older, I've been around, we're no longer in Nebraska, Toto. At any rate, Francis said, "God, I just came from the Chinese theater." This is way before your time. It was around the guitar shop on Sunset

Boulevard. It was the last gasp for a film. You paid fifty cents. He said, "I just figured out what *Finian's* is about! Holy cow, what a terrible thing to find out after you've made it."

ALEXANDER: That's like the Billy Wilder story. He'd say, "I had the Vine moment." He'd be driving home from work, back to Beverly Hills, on Melrose, then get to Vine, and right when he get to Vine, he'd remember what he should have done in that scene that day.

JIM: Yeah, I think it's more of a sense that it's always changing. We do talk about thematic things, but I always like the idea of seeing things out of the corner of your eye. When you're attacking things really directly, it's a little dangerous. Your dialogue can get really bad. It's almost like not outlining. You don't want to pin yourself down and say, "I'm making a movie specifically about this." I guess, when we say, "That's a good idea for a movie," it's not like, "A movie about man's inhumanity to man. That would be great." It's more about high concept; it's like a shark that terrorizes a small town, not themes at all. We try and not articulate it too much. We talk around the theme.

LEW: Frank Pierson broke the story and could write the script after he figured out the Al Pacino character motives in *Dog Day Afternoon*.

ALEXANDER: Oh, that type of stuff, yes, that's good.

LEW: He didn't know the story at all until he broke the back of the character.

ALEXANDER: Yes, that's important, but that's something else.

LEW: The Paul Giamatti character in *Sideways* was so wonderful. Did you really know who he was up front?

ALEXANDER: I wish we had something like that.

LEW: You didn't have to break the back of Paul Giamatti's character?

ALEXANDER: It would have helped a little bit.

JIM: There are breakthrough moments, and sometimes they are articulated that way, but sometimes they're not. *Sideways* was based on a book, and it's semiautobiographical, so the author was a little bit of an inspiration for us as well in that book. How did we get to know that character?

ALEXANDER: It would be helpful.

JIM: We transform him a little bit. It's sort of how we remember him from the book. Both *Election* and *Sideways* were books that had characters that were very compelling to us and essentially a story that was compelling, so we started pretty far down the road.

LEW: Are your characters identifiable to you when you go into them?

JIM: They have to be. Otherwise, you can't write a word. It's all about acting or knowing what would they say and how would they say it.

LEW: There's a wonderful thing about the *Sideways* characters. I could particularly get with the male characters. There's an Aristotle saying: "Superior drama is drama and comedy that allows the audience to discover themselves."

JIM: I think we actually had that sense because people would always ask us, "Which one's Alexander, and which one is Jim in that movie?" Ideally, they are a person split apart, a different facet, every character, somehow you imagine. No matter what their race or sex or anything, that you can see the humanity in them and connect with that. So it's a piece of you and everyone somehow.

LEW: Back to ideas: Have you gotten deeply into an idea that you had an "aha," then said, "Eh, that's not going to work." Deeply, I mean, after three or four weeks.

JIM: Sure, especially when we keep coming back to him.

ALEXANDER: But we never gave up on him. I'll tell you this: When we're selecting ideas, like reading a book, oh, man, that book could be a good movie. Or an idea, we try it out for a month or so. Maybe tell a couple of close people or talk about it, and some of them go away, but others stay.

LEW: Is that the most important part of the process, the idea?

ALEXANDER: Well, it's all important. But none of the rest of it can exist without that.

JIM: Yeah. I would change it to, like, impulse instead of idea. That's why I'm talking about voice or connecting with you. You may not know why; it's just something that's going to feed you, sustain you, long enough to make it to the end. It has to be creative and to inspire you.

LEW: When you accept this impulse, then you can go forward. About how long in the process do you get a general beginning, middle, and end before you go on? Like telling a joke for two minutes.

ALEXANDER: Sort of case by case. Like the one we're about to start, we have an idea, we know a little bit of the beginning, maybe a little bit of the middle, but really only distant, distant looks. I have zero—honestly we don't know what the story is, but we have an idea. We're going to probably just talk about it for a week or two. Then ideas will come out. Then maybe at a certain moment, a type of order will begin to develop, like kind of bubble up. It will remain vague. We really have to begin writing it. Like, okay, what's the first scene? Well, it might be good if we start here. Then we start writing. Then what might come next? That's sort of how we work.

JIM: We always—I mean, not always—but we often think we know the ending, and in every case we're wrong when we get there.

ALEXANDER: Film is fragile. It's based on fragile things. One tiny thing changes, and it's, you know, stepping on a butterfly.

LEW: Goldman, too, talks about how it's so fragile. Goldman is prone to be scatological, and he'd say, "These fucking idiots! They take something out and just destroy your piece."

JIM AND ALEXANDER: Uh huh.

JIM: Yeah, because if you don't understand it, and they think, "Who needs that line?" then they throw away that line.

LEW: There was kind of an irresistible impulse. Schrader wrote this script, and he's one who does meticulous charts. At least he did back in the day. This comes from a John Brady interview about twenty-five years ago, back when you were in film school. Brady wrote a book of writer interviews. He interviewed Chayefsky, Goldman. This book pays homage to that.

ALEXANDER: What's it called?

LEW: It's called *The Craft of Interviewing*. All of the heavyweights are in there. Okay, now you're into the process, into the writing. You have an idea in your minds. Do you start writing the script?

JIM: We talk a lot, make notes, and yeah, at some point, we go, "Well, I guess we should say exterior, interior or whatever," and start.

ALEXANDER: I get impatient. I get impatient to start writing.

JIM: Which is good. Working as a team, a big advantage is keeping each other working. Mostly Alexander keeps me working, but having a schedule and having to show up and all that.

LEW: Who does the typing?

JIM: We both. We hook up a couple of keyboards.

ALEXANDER: Tell them what we're doing right now.

JIM: Now we call it playing Battleship because we have eternal monitors. It's nice. So there's a monitor facing Alexander. It's his laptop, actually, on a box and an external keyboard hooked up to that. There's a keyboard that comes around and another monitor that faces me. This way we can sit across the table from each other and look at the same document. Right now we're rewriting a draft of something I had written. But if we're generating stuff, which we still are when we're doing this because we decide we need a new scene or something, usually we talk about it. I think Alexander will sketch something out, but one or the other of us will generate some stuff, and then immediately we'll start editing it. It's really in the rewriting where we'll kind of end up dumping what you laid down on the page in the first place. Well, at least we are revising everything.

LEW: Do you have a lot of appreciation for your first impression of something? Because obviously it's a visceral impression.

ALEXANDER: Of a scene we write?

LEW: No. Just basically, you're going through an idea, and then do you intellectualize it into the delete bin?

JIM: Well that's another thing about being partners. We can protect each other from throwing out stuff. Because we're both, you know, writers tend to hate what you've written, so it's good to have someone saying, "No, that's working."

ALEXANDER: I think the only way to be successful is to think constantly that what you are producing is bad.

JIM: Every single time, we say, "I'm going to write something. It's going to be terrible." It is kind of really is terrible, or it often is.

ALEXANDER: Until it's done.

JIM: And then you have to try and make it better.

ALEXANDER: But usually people, and I'm sure you see this among your students, will, like, write a draft and turn it in and think it's really good, but it's usually the worst.

JIM: I can't understand that.

LEW: I'll give you an analogy. They come to you like a cat with a dead bird and lay it at your feet and look at it with pride.

ALEXANDER: People will come and say, "It only took me ten days to write. It just came, and I wouldn't touch a word." And it's usually awful.

LEW: Did you guys feel like that when you were starting out?

JIM: Never.

ALEXANDER: We have this confidence but—

LEW: Now I say, "I'll fix that shit." It took me six or seven—actually, it most often happened in television.

JIM: Yeah, where you don't have a lot of time.

LEW: No time to be precious. You have to get it to the stage. How long does it take you on that process? A couple of months? Do you have a set time?

ALEXANDER: The first draft for us is almost like editing a good film that never finished. It's the same with the script. You can come in and always keep tinkering. I mean, the idea is to have the finished draft, yet we don't really think of it that way. You could always go in and say, "Oh, this could be better." I mean obviously, the more you work on it, the more places you think need constant changing. You can always be tinkering. The first draft for us is really the result of about—and this is speaking very, very generally—but it's the result of about three passes through it.

The first of just getting it down, and it may not even have an ending. A character may have been introduced that doesn't pay off or doesn't develop or anything, but you just get it down. And then you start rewriting, and maybe, hopefully, there are blossoms to open more. That might be a very long draft. Maybe 150 pages or something. You let yourself overwrite it a bit, let the text, let the dialogue contain more than the subtext. Maybe there is more on-the-nose dialogue than you would like, but you find, like, those characters: "Oh, we're stuck here. Oh, remember we introduced that guy before? What if he shows up?" That kind of thing. Then, finally, a third draft.

So within the first draft, there's editing, then really cleaning it up, seeking to always to bury the points within the dialogue, to put layers to the dialogue, and also, it's very important to keep all of it as economical as possible. We are on a constant word crunch. I hate reading scripts that are too fucking wordy. We're appalled if we find we're writing that way. The large part of what we do is we really keep our scripts as complete but as economical as possible. The read has to flow. I'm reading a script right now for a friend, a good friend. I honestly can't finish it. It's laborious.

(to LEW) I could never do what you do because you have to read so much stuff.

LEW: I was just telling them, "Pages can turn like stone tablets."

ALEXANDER: We've been talking about craft and how there's always—I'm sorry I'm spinning in different directions—but like, screenwriters expect you to remember all of their fucking characters. Like you're reading someone's script, and you get to page 40, and it goes, "Hank," and you wonder, "Which one is Hank?" And maybe you have to take the time and go back and look, but now you're out of the story. It's nice when the screenwriter goes, "Hank, the guy we met at the gas station earlier." It's nice to remind your reader, to keep it flowing. The most important thing in screenwriting is to keep the flow, keep them in the story, because then the movie flows. A script has to have some semblance of that flow, and you have to give an experience. It's not just about describing the movie. Yet, you don't overthink it and also write every detail down. That, too, pulls you out of the story.

JIM: Today I was writing something out and was having a little too much fun and wrote, "The character boards the express train to dreamland." So I went to the bathroom and came back and Alexander had changed it to, "Nods off." I knew when I wrote it, it didn't need that.

ALEXANDER: I did see that laugh.

JIM: But ultimately, you can't say, "That's funny. Let's keep that." We can't write for each other.

ALEXANDER: With rare exception.

JIM: Sometimes that stuff is there more for the reader, just to have a light reading experience. You can leave it, but don't do it throughout.

LEW: This is an end question I'll use right now. Do you have selling draft and shooting draft?

JIM: Yeah, we haven't done that. Actually, part of going to see this cartoonist talk, Chris Ware, that he's so brilliant at what he does in terms of storytelling on the page. I thought, "Oh, maybe we could learn something from this." I think that I'd like to do more of that. I like to figure out how to be more expressive because screenplays are just ugly.

ALEXANDER: Also, who decided that was the way to go?

JIM: Well, it's all about how many pages and how many minutes. I mean all that stuff has good reason for being there. I always hear people say, "If I get a script that's not in the proper format, I toss it in the garbage." I think, "That's pretty short-sighted. Why don't you at least read a few pages and see?" I think there's room to have a reading experience or an aesthetic evocative experience more so than "INT," "EXT," "DAY," "NIGHT." Maybe there are more ways to be clear and more expressive.

LEW: Larry Kasdan says, "I write ordinary language for the description with a judicious amount of colorful words." He wants to keep us awake because sometimes at twelve o'clock in the morning, that executive is going to nod off, and you've got to keep him interested. Your first draft, the getting-down-to draft, how long does this take you?

JIM: It's hard to say because we also take breaks, and we go do other things. It could be months, never years, but months, not weeks.

LEW: What about the first draft you show yourself?

JIM: I'd say four months, if we're working diligently. Maybe three months. Three or four days a week, four hours a day. That would be an average.

ALEXANDER: I have to say, we get together for eight hours, of which there may be four hours of work and four of noodling around.

JIM: Sometimes we go into what's called "night shift," where we work until things are working, and it is four o'clock in the morning. We know we're not going to get phone calls.

ALEXANDER: And when we've done script doctoring, and we have to write an entire script in a month or three weeks, then all rules are out.

JIM: We get a feeding tube.

ALEXANDER: But that's rare.

JIM: We should think about that feeding tube.

LEW: You surely don't like script doctoring a lot, do you? It's kind of like creative mechanics.

ALEXANDER: We only take jobs that we think we can do something with it. We've done it, one, two, three, four—maybe four times? Five times? Five times.

JIM: I did it once, as a job with my wife.

ALEXANDER: *Thirteen Going on Thirty.*

JIM: Hey, you're not allowed to say that.

LEW: Do you guys ever fight?

JIM: Not really, no. We might get testy, and we definitely argue, but I think that's different from fighting.

ALEXANDER: I don't think we've ever had a fight. Not about money or creative things in our partnership. I think that's very rare.

JIM: But I do want to make a point that we do argue. We might say, "I want to make a case for this," then, "No, no it should be this way." However, it never turns nuclear.

ALEXANDER: It's just a movie.

LEW: I have enough trouble getting along with the mirror, let alone another person.

JIM: I'd have to say, the advantage of partnership is we're just really lucky it works because a lot of friendships fail through this method.

LEW: There is nothing more sacred than the "project" in this town. Not marriage, not friendships, not children—project.

ALEXANDER: That's weird. However, it's true.

LEW: I've seen a lot of things blow up because of a project.

ALEXANDER: The idea of living for something larger than yourself, which, I guess, trumps other ideas.

LEW: I think that's probably it. That's one of the reasons I've been in the business forty years. We do lot of stuff on and off of the set. It's about personalities, except when it becomes personal, and most often it doesn't. I'm trying to say, when you're in the making of the movie, the movie being the best it can be becomes the most important thing in your world for that period of time.

Okay, now you turn the script in. You've taken anywhere from how many months?

ALEXANDER: Call it six. It's about six months when we show it.

LEW: And you wait. You get an immediate response, you feel good? And if you haven't heard for a few days, do you start to feel nervous?

JIM: People get wrapped up in the speculation of "What's going on?"

ALEXANDER: I take time to read script. I don't always get back to people immediately. On the other hand, we turned in *About Schmidt* to the producer on a Friday. Monday, Jack read it. Wednesday, we were at Nicholson's house.

JIM: With *Election* we got a very positive response to our first draft, and we were excited because Alexander had made *Citizen Ruth*, but it hadn't done all that well. This was just a job, so were we going to get to make this movie or not. It was very, very positive, and I still hear, "Just wait," and then when it hit the marketing department, they go, "Argh, it's a teen comedy with an adult point of view, and we don't know what to do." Their big thing is, "We don't know how to sell it." So that's what happened, and that took a while to sort itself out.

LEW: There was a story around town back when it was out that one of the studio executives wanted you to change the end, and Alexander said, "I can't do it." And the studio executive said, "Martin Scorsese sat in that

same fucking chair and said he could do whatever I asked him to do."
And Jim Taylor said, "Wait a minute. We'll rework it."

ALEXANDER: That's how the story goes?

LEW: That's how the story goes.

ALEXANDER: Jim Taylor wasn't at that meeting. [*laughter*]

LEW: You guys are a team whether you are or not.

ALEXANDER: That story isn't exactly right. What that studio executive
said was, because I was arguing with that studio executive over a line
which that studio executive was forcing on me, I said, "But that's not
what you said before. I haven't been operating under that at all." And
that studio executive said, "No one talks to me that way. Other people
have sat in that chair, not Brian De Palma, not Martin Scorsese." I got
yelled at.

LEW: A crowning day.

ALEXANDER: I didn't back down.

LEW: Okay, I want the class to be able to ask some questions.

DAVID: Thank you for coming.

ALEXANDER: What's your name?

DAVID: David.

ALEXANDER: Hi, David.

DAVID: You talk about the process of three, four months. How do you
know when it's done? Is it sort of like the idea: when you know it, you
know it?

JIM: Yeah, and I think that for the same reason that we feel like not being
overly determined what the structure is. It's in your bones. It's ready
when you know it's ready. That's important to remember, too, because
people can just breathe down your neck if it's not.

ALEXANDER: Well, in Hollywood, commercial filmmaking, they have a
big budget, and they even start building sets, either because of a release
date or the availability of the stars. But they don't always have a script
yet. So they overpay people like us to get a script going. Then usually

it's just a disaster. I learned this in film school—this is just in terms of directing—never begin to think about production, ever, until the script is done. Even in film schools, "Well I'm going to shoot on May fourth! I've already started casting." "Well, is your script done?" "No, but I'll be working on it while I'm in preproduction."

LEW: Somebody one time told me that the most important part of the whole process is the preproduction. Of course, writing the script is the preproduction.

ALEXANDER: That's the movie.

STUDENT: Talking about actors and how you gave Nicholson the script. Was he the first person you gave it to, so you had him in mind when you were writing?

ALEXANDER: Basically no because the guy's a literary character, a film character, encased in a script. We knew Jack would be the first actor to read it because of the studio's connection, and he could have said, "No." So we couldn't box ourselves into writing just for him, nor would I want to. I want the actor to come to the character. I never want the character to come to the actor.

JIM: But it would have been tough to make that movie without Jack.

STUDENT: So was that a concern when you were crafting the story, knowing that it was an older character and there would be difficulties in possibly selling it?

JIM: It was a job, so we weren't selling it.

ALEXANDER: Yeah, but still I wanted to make it. I don't want to write anything that I'm supposed to direct that isn't going to get made. I've had that luck since film school basically: write, direct, write, direct. Except for *About Schmidt*. That didn't get made originally. But no, I thought it would get made somehow. I mean, I don't care about the budget level, so you cut the budget and hire someone else.

ALEXANDER: A question? What's your name?

PAUL: My name's Paul.

ALEXANDER: Hello, Paul, and what's your name?

WES: Wes.

ALEXANDER: Hi, Wes.

WES: You're kind of legendary for getting *Sideways* made the way you wanted it to get made, so I was wondering if you could give me one of your methods on how to deal with the business side of it. What is the one thing you guys always keep in mind?

ALEXANDER: Well, I have an answer to that certainly, but *Sideways* really pertains more if you are also the director. If you are the writer with no idea who is going to direct it, it's a totally different ball game. But in terms of us writing something that one of us is going to direct, the key is to write it on spec. I can't stress how important this is. If you want to write a script that you later want to direct, and you think, "I'll pitch it and get paid to do it, get involved with this financing entity," that's a huge mistake because they now own what you write. They can sit on it. They can force you to cast some idiot you don't want to cast.

So the thing with *Sideways* is that we—the producer and I—we optioned the book. Jim and I wrote the script on spec. The producer and I put our hands in our own pockets and cast the movie. You know, 20,000 bucks between offices, casting, photocopying, and all that. Then we went to movie studios. You know, it's like packaging: "Here's the screenplay, the preferred cast, the director. Here's a budget. In or out?" That's the place at which the discussions begin. Oddly, this film with no big names, at least not at that time, no big movie stars, is very atypical for today's Hollywood. It corresponds perhaps to an earlier time. But that was my fastest financing experience.

STUDENT: What was it about *Sideways* that you so believed in?

ALEXANDER: I thought it would be a great movie and fun to make. I don't really understand your question. Did you like the movie?

STUDENT: I loved it.

ALEXANDER: Okay, good. Now what are you saying?

STUDENT: You really have to fight to get something made, is what I'm hearing, and you really have to believe in the project.

ALEXANDER: It's humanity and the wine and, you know, the women, and it was fun.

JIM: The basic answer is characters and the situations, we just liked. It clicked, and it's pretty distinct from reading our other stuff.

ALEXANDER: The books you mean.

JIM: Yes, there was a huge difference in the response to the material.

ALEXANDER: I read the book *Sideways*. Like *Election*, when it reached us, unpublished, not even galley formed, I said, "All right, let me read this one." I started it on my flight back from London to LA, and when I got off the plane, I ran—I didn't have a cell phone at the time—I ran to a pay phone and called my agent and said, "I've got it. Who sent me this book? Get them on the phone right away. I've got to make this movie." I was on fire with it. I made *About Schmidt* first. However, *Sideways* was always in my pocket.

LEW: Some things you just can't explain, your affinity. Next question, please.

STUDENT: Jim, you were talking about how *Citizen Ruth* didn't do what you guys thought. How did that influence your writing and directing or even your generation of ideas later on?

JIM: I don't think that lack of success affected us at all. We didn't think it was our fault. I guess that's arrogant, but I was proud of the movie, and regardless if people went to see it or not, I felt satisfied for myself, so it didn't seem like there was any reason to change what we were doing.

LEW: Do you feel a sense of progression in your movies that have been made, getting better, better, and better? Or is it getting harder, harder, and harder? Or both?

JIM: I don't know if it's getting better and better, but it's definitely nice to feel that sometimes we can write faster. Or we hope we can write faster, which is good. And part of that comes from the rewrite jobs. I hope we can look back and say we're maturing because, you know, poisonous people, their bottom just falls out of their creativity, and you might think, "Now I'm going to make the movie that really capitalized on all of the experience I have." That's the kind of arrogance I don't think you can have, like, "The next one's going to be great."

ALEXANDER: And even already in our short careers, I get this all the time: "Oh yeah, you did *Sideways*. That was good. Yeah, I like that one, but

About Schmidt is kind of depressing," but *Election*, I get props for *Election* constantly.

LEW: The infamous Francis thought it was the best movie of the year, and I believe he invited you up to Napa to sit under a merlot tree?

JIM: *Sideways*, we really loved it, but I thought people will think, "This is funny," and you know it would be the most successful at the box office. But I never thought it would be an award-winning film.

ALEXANDER: Me neither.

JIM: I thought, "Oh, this is funny."

ALEXANDER: A nice little film our friends will like. I was hanging out with the director of the Cannes Film Festival, and he said, "Well, you know, *Sideways*, will it be ready for us in May?" I said, "Number 1, it won't be ready. Number 2, I don't think you'd want it anyway. It's kind of slight. It's too small for you." Then it's turned down from Venice, and I thought, "You know, I was right. We just have this nice little film."

LEW: Did France end up loving it?

ALEXANDER: It wasn't a big hit in France.

LEW: Really? But they love Jerry Lewis?

ALEXANDER: This is what I get in France: "Oh, *Sideways*, a very interesting film."

LEW: Question? Ah, here's a Nebraska boy.

ALEXANDER: Where in Nebraska?

DARREN: Near, Norfolk. I have a question because you guys just seem to be real genre-ified.

ALEXANDER: What genre?

DARREN: Dark comedy.

ALEXANDER: Okay.

DARREN: Do you plan on breaking that and doing an action-adventure movie? I mean you did some rewriting on *Jurassic Park III*, right? Do you ever plan on doing that, like, "We're going to do a horror now"?

ALEXANDER: We think about a western. I've been on a scout for a good western idea for a while. Whenever I see *Rosemary's Baby*, I think it would be fun to make a horror movie.

JIM: Yeah, *Rosemary's Baby*.

ALEXANDER: Just, like, take it apart. What would that be?

JIM: No, but again, that would probably come from reading that book, and we hope our genre is just our own voice. I think, if we make the western, it will have—

ALEXANDER: It would have more in common with *Sideways* and *Election* than it would with *The Wild Bunch*.

JIM: I think it just has to be honest. So if we were drawn to doing something else, I think if we decided, like, an action-adventure, we'd have to try it. The *Jurassic Park* movie, we were hired, and I always thought, "That's an interesting premise." I wasn't necessarily drawn to the movies that much. I thought, and it's impossible because we have four weeks to write a script, but Bill Macy was going to be in it. We thought, "Oh, that would be interesting to write for him." So, it wasn't like, "Oh, let's do an action-adventure thing." It was more thematically interesting. You know, it's almost like *Frankenstein* is interesting.

ALEXANDER: And "They're paying how much?"

LEW: Yeah, there you go. Tony?

TONY: Alexander, you always said, something I think about every day, you said, "Hold onto your material as long as you can." I'm at the point now where I'm starting to get material out. What is there to be wary of?

ALEXANDER: I really wish I could answer that, Tony. It's really such a broad question.

LEW: W. C. Fields once said to a starlet on the Paramount lot, "Beware, my lovely. There's marauders behind every bush."

STUDENT: Do you direct to have more control of your writing?

ALEXANDER: Well, if you want to be a director. I don't think necessarily writers want to become directors.

LEW: Actually, we've gotten more directors out of the UCLA writing program. Okay, couple more questions?

ALEXANDER: Wait, one last thing with Tony. Is your question more about getting material out there and getting it sold? Or choosing who to sell it to?

TONY: I think I've been dealing with the second with a part. I have a manager, but I'm not sure he gets my voice.

ALEXANDER: First of all, I distrust managers. I don't know why anyone other than really needy actors needs a manager. I don't know why writers or directors need managers. I don't get it at all. You should have an agent or a lawyer. A manager is almost like an agent but no license. I don't get, and I'm not saying my opinion is definitive, but I personally don't get the need. But if you want success, you're going to want an agent who is a shark. With a manager, you've got two sharks swimming around you. Keep it at one.

LEW: Speaking of selling: You have had such good success with *About Schmidt*. Producer Harry Gittes is an old-time schmoozer. That must have been pretty helpful to you. People who know people over golf or poker can connect you?

JIM: Harry is really lovely and a great guy. His relationship with Jack Nicholson goes way back. They're loyal, and that was key.

LEW: I was just trying to figure out if he was a good salesman or not. I've known him off and on for many years.

ALEXANDER: He is. He's a fantastic guy.

JIM: He's got a lot of heart, so he's very genuine and passionate, and that comes through.

ALEXANDER: Now what do I tell him, the one who couldn't do it? He's still going to want to be attached as a producer. We're going through this on something we're involved in. People sometimes want credits for work that they didn't do.

LEW: One more, and we'll hear from Morgan because he probably has a good one.

ALEXANDER: Probably the best question.

STUDENT: How did you two find each other?

ALEXANDER: We were friends. Actually more acquaintances in the '80s, and then by the end of the '80s, I needed a roommate and found through friends that Jim needed a new place to live, so we became roommates. Our friendship and our collaboration grew from then. I don't think either of us got into filmmaking anticipating having a writing partner. It really caught us both by surprise.

LEW: Morgan, how old are you? Thirteen?

MORGAN: I'm twelve.

ALEXANDER: We said some bad words here today. I hope you're okay with that. What's your question, Morgan?

MORGAN: Like, generally, how long does it take you from idea until you start production?

ALEXANDER: Each time is slightly different, but about six months to get a script. Then it's typically about another four or, in a hard situation, six months until we start shooting. It depends on locking in someone who's going to pay for it. And then casting. Casting, finding locations, and all that.

JIM: Usually, the story you hear is, "Years and years."

ALEXANDER: Which is what it was with our first film. *Citizen Ruth* was years.

JIM: Yeah, perseverance is key. You have to be ready for many years.

LEW: My last question, I guess: You guys have had certain experiences in your movies. Back to name dropping, Billy Wilder was trying to find the last line in *Some Like It Hot*, and Billy says, "Mr. Diamond was at a typewriter. I'm watching my cigarette smoke go to the ceiling, and Mr. Diamond says, 'Nobody's perfect.' I said, 'It would do.'" They left it because they never had time to change it. Have you had that experience, where something was left in, and it became iconic?

ALEXANDER: You keep thinking you're going to think of something better, and you never do. You have to shoot a movie.

JIM: I think, "Don't they think I believe that story?" I think they said, "That's that good."

LEW: Dissolve to fifteen years later, and I asked Wilder, and he says, "Mr. Diamond said, 'Nobody's perfect.'" They're passing the line back and forth. I told Billy, "He gave it to you. Your writing partner said it was you." Billy looked up at the ceiling and said, "This is why I miss him so."

ALEXANDER: Oh, that is nice.

LEW: Isn't it sweet? Just reflective of good writing partnerships, sitting here in front of us. Very much appreciate you guys coming.

6

Alfred Uhry

Alfred is a phenomenal writer, with a range that stretches from playwriting, for which has won two Tony Awards; novel writing, for which he has a Pulitzer; and then screenwriting, for which, of course, he won an Oscar for *Driving Miss Daisy*. Being tied to New York, for both his family and his work, as he still does a great deal of playwriting and began as a lyricist to musicals, which he considers an integral part of his storytelling education, Mr. Uhry was kind enough to dialogue over the telephone and has wonderful ideas on character and all forms of storytelling, as you will soon see.

LEW: We're talking to Academy Award–winning screenwriters, and we're delighted to have you in that company and in this book, Mr. Uhry.

ALFRED: Delighted to be there.

LEW: It's ironic and nice that not too many of your fellow Oscar winners are brimming with war stories. They're mostly brimming with the concept of talking about the process, and the war stories only come in connection with the how each of you screenwrite, being a screenwriter, the work habits, and all of that. Let's talk about storytelling first. Do you consider your playwriting as well as your screenwriting predominantly storytelling?

ALFRED: I think of storytelling, for me, as coming up with character. Most of what I write or am asked to write or what I want to write is character driven. That said, though, my friend Richard Zanuck said, and I agree with him, the three most important elements in a movie is first story, then story, and then story, and that's true. But for me, I can only get a good story if I've got characters I believe in down to the ground. And since I've never been called upon to write a film about blowing up banks or terrorists, I don't know if that applies to everything.

LEW: How were you attracted to storytelling? Was it first the theater? You are unique among our Oscar winners, with the exception of Ted Tally, who started out in theater, as well as Horton Foote. They have moved away from it a bit, but your 1997 Tony Award is a clear indication that you are still active in theater.

ALFRED: As we speak, I have a musical, a preview, at Lincoln Center.

LEW: Wonderful.

ALFRED: Yeah, it's my heart. I'm a theater boy who writes movies.

LEW: I know a little about screenwriters, having been one since 1969 and chairing the department here, where about twelve of the twenty people we accept each year become professional screenwriters. Fortunately for us, a lot of people wander over from theater, and I love having these people that understand Pirandello and Ibsen and Strindberg more than Lucas and Spielberg, if I may be slightly pejorative. What was the background that got you into theater initially, and how did you get to movies?

ALFRED: I was born and raised in Atlanta, where there wasn't any theater, so I was initially a movie freak. As a little kid, I'd see a movie on Friday night, and then I'd see it again on Saturday afternoon. My mother would say, "But you already saw it." I'd say, "Yeah, I just want to see it again." In those days, they had the neighborhoods, and the second runs were also in the neighborhoods. I could walk or take the bus not too far to go to the movies. I think I lived for them. I loved movies. Still do. Still love movies of the 1940s, my earliest ones. Those black-and-white movies still knock me out. I saw *A Letter to Three Wives* the other day. My God, that's a good movie. They weren't writing down to people in those movies. So I really loved all kinds of movies before I loved theater.

Then, I got to New York somehow, and I saw the theater. It seemed to me more accessible. I sort of thought in the movies that actors make up everything as they went along. It never occurred to me that somebody wrote them. Until I was about a teenager, I was going to the movies, and

I thought, "Well, I'd have more of a chance of getting something on at a theater," which I still think is true for me. I always tell people who want to write, start out with a play. Anyone can get their friends to sit around and read a play. Who knows who's going to hear it, and what's going to happen. That's not the case with a movie. Then I went to Brown in Rhode Island, and I became interested in writing for the theater. I met a guy who wrote music, and I wanted to write lyrics. We were going to be Rogers and Hammerstein. That never happened, but I did come to New York out of that crucible.

LEW: Are you writing the lyrics for your musical?

ALFRED: No, it's too hard. It's a musical called *Parade*, directed by Harold Prince. So, we're big stuff.

LEW: Oh, you're in wonderful shape.

ALFRED: No, I'm not in wonderful shape, but I'm in good hands. We're having previews right now. So anyway, I started out as a lyric writer and was hired by the late Frank Loesser. I'm sure you pretty much know him.

LEW: Absolutely.

ALFRED: Frank paid me $50 a week. He had a music-publishing company. I wrote, and he published some of it. What it really was, was a master class. I wrote lyrics, and he critiqued them and taught me that every syllable counts. He likened it to sitting at a railroad crossing, watching a long freight train go by. He said, "You gotta realize it's only going to pass once, so you got to know it's a blue car, and you're going to know a coal car, and you're going to know it's a this and a that, and a caboose. You have to make each one, while it goes by quickly, as interesting as you can possibly make it with the most interesting words you can put into each car." That was hilarious to me, and even now, I try to apply that to everything I write. I think that I am a fairly sparse writer because of this lesson. When I write a film script, it's usually too short, so I have to go back and stick stuff in.

LEW: When I was a kid starting out at NBC, I was in music clearance, and I remember working with Frank Loesser and Rogers and Hammerstein a bit. They would come up and see if their music was on the network variety shows. That Frank Loesser was the lesser of two evils was a joke at that time, related to his then wife.

ALFRED: Or she was the evil of two Loessers, I also heard. He also taught me something that's really hard. He said if you have something you've written, pretend you didn't write it, and be as hard on it as you would be on someone you're jealous of or in competition with. It's hard to do it, but you can do it. You try and turn yourself off. Don't drool on every word. Be tough.

LEW: You'll be pleased to know that in Woody Allen's picture *Celebrity*, "Slow Boat to China" is a very prominent song on the soundtrack.

ALFRED: It's a great song, "Slow Boat to China." I think that Frank wrote the best comedy lyrics. Nobody is going to do better. Not yet, and the way his words fit to his music is really unbelievable.

LEW: I have often been overwhelmed by that concept that both Irving Berlin and Frank Loesser wrote lyrics and music. Oscar Hammerstein told me, "I hate Richard Rogers. I'll bring in lyrics I've worked on for a week or two or three, and Dick will sit down and have the music in ten minutes."

ALFRED: Remember Frank Loesser's lyric in *Guys and Dolls*? It goes, "Call it hell, call it heaven, it's a probable twelve to seven." To get *probable* in like that is pretty hard to do. Frank was a genius. He taught me so much I've been able to use in my screenwriting.

LEW: After starting on Broadway, when did you slide into motion pictures?

ALFRED: I came into movies in a very unusual way. I wrote *Driving Miss Daisy* as a play, having never written a film in my life. I didn't even know what a film script even looked like. I sold the play to David Brown, and I said to my agent, "Well, I might as well take a stab at writing screenplays. They'll probably fire me, but please try to sell it with the condition I can write the screenplay." So she did, and I that's when I realized: I had never even seen a screenplay. David Brown then sent me over a bunch of screenplays, and I couldn't really read them. It all looked like Russian to me. "EXT." and "O.S."? I didn't know what all that stuff was.

Around that time, I got a phone call from Sam Goldwyn, who also wanted to do *Driving Miss Daisy*, but it was a little too late. He asked me if I had time to work on a screenplay called *Mystic Pizza*. The script had been written, but they weren't happy with it, and they were about to start shooting. He wanted me to rewrite one scene. He said, "The only thing you can't do is change the structure. It's been all slated, so you can't put anything new in there." I didn't know what he was talking about exactly, but I rewrote the scene, and he said, "Would you write some more? Would you come up to Mystic, Connecticut?" So I went and sat at the Mystic Hilton and ended up writing three-quarters of the movie. It was an interesting job because it was all boarded to be shot, and I wasn't supposed to make up any new scenes. Well, I wouldn't have known how anyway. By the end, I was feeling very confident, so I wrote a camera movement and that did get into the picture. That was nice.

LEW: One of my ex-interns directed *Mystic Pizza*. It was his first big directing gig, Don Petrie.

ALFRED: Oh, he was great on it.

LEW: So that was interesting. The two of you in some ways were going down first roads together.

ALFRED: He was very helpful. So I did that, then *Driving Miss Daisy*. *Driving Miss Daisy* got extraordinarily lucky, and I was barraged with offers. I took a few of them. My problem has been the fact that I don't do this full time, but I like writing scripts, yet they just kind of float around for years. That's one of the dangers of screenwriting. In theater, you'll probably get it on one way or another. But with movies, you don't always.

I have a couple now I've done this year that I feel very strongly about, and they're actor driven, so I think they'll probably get made. Sally Field asked me to write a screenplay out of Eudora Welty's *The Optimist's Daughter*. It was already at Disney, so that, I would think, has a pretty good chance. Morgan Freeman asked me to adapt a novel he likes, which I did. I'm feeling pretty good about those.

LEW: Making the switch from writing theater to motion pictures, what are some of your thought processes?

ALFRED: Well, I quickly found you just can't retype a play and call it a movie. In a movie you need to say less because you're right there in the character's face all the time. You don't need to talk so much. With *Driving Miss Daisy*, it was a question of deciding what to pull out. I would say there is no scene that is the same as the play. They're all shorter.

I made a rule for myself that I wouldn't expand the story in any way beyond what the play had suggested. I had just seen the film of Willie

Russell's, *Educating Rita*, at that point, which was originally a two-character play. Somebody added all kinds of subplots and characters, and it really didn't need all that. I thought I would like to make it seem like *Driving Miss Daisy* never was a play. That was my objective.

LEW: Did you obsess a great deal about opening it up? Or were you liberated by the not-so-mere fact that you could?

ALFRED: I just went back to the story and wrote a movie about those people. When you write a play, you're the audience sitting in the theater, watching it. I think when you write a movie, you're exactly the same thing, so you have to be your own cameraman, costumer, set decorator. I imagine all that stuff when I write a film.

LEW: Probably a lot of that has to do with your viewer-osmotic training when you were young and all the movies you had watched.

ALFRED: Probably.

LEW: And that probably carried over to your playwriting, consciously or subconsciously?

ALFRED: I would imagine.

LEW: Was there a particular book, like Aristotle's *Poetics* or any other books, initially useful for you in writing performance drama?

ALFRED: You know what really did it for me? I was teaching basic Shakespeare to ninth-graders over and over and over again. I taught *Romeo and Juliet*, and then I taught *MacBeth*. The rotation was such that I taught that same thing several times a year for years. I really got into the mechanics of how Shakespeare did it because I was teaching so much. I noticed the kids especially and surprisingly liked *MacBeth*. For instance, the sleepwalking scene: It starts with a maid and a doctor saying, in effect, that Lady MacBeth is nuts, and she walks around in her sleep, and she talks to herself, and she's really nuts. Then she comes in, and she does exactly that. She walks in her sleep, she talks, she acts like she's really nuts. Then she leaves the stage, and they say, "My God, did you see her? She was walking in her sleep and talking, and she's acting really nuts." He does it three times. He set it up, he did it, and then he shows you what he did. That's clarity. I think clarity in a screenplay can't be overstated.

LEW: I took a college class where the teacher emphasized a speech technique of "Tell them what you're going to tell them, go ahead and tell them, and then tell them what you've told them." That's the simplicity of the whole matter.

ALFRED: Amen. I think a basic demand of screenwriting is to let them clearly know what you're going to do. I don't mean telling them the story. Let them feel like they're in good hands. You can't write a script with a lot of murky stuff in it. Make your story rules clear. In this movie, I'm going to stop every scene right before it ends because it's going to seem mysterious and weird. I'm never going to put an ending on a scene. Make that a rule. Or I'm going to have this character never finish a sentence. Make up little rules like that for yourself. Those work for me.

LEW: How do you identify an idea or a character that you want to spend however many weeks or months or years with? What's your process that makes you finally say, "Aha! This is the one!"

ALFRED: I usually have to work on something I have experienced or seen for myself. If I were to write a movie based on how Katharine Hepburn felt about Spencer Tracy, I would be in big trouble because I don't know. I can imagine a spinster falling in love with a golf pro because I have known some of each. I can go to those places. Basically, all your characters are some aspect of yourself.

LEW: I like to use the line in professing from Willa Cather: "I became an artist when I stopped admiring and began remembering."

ALFRED: That's a very good point.

LEW: You basically rape yourself at every possible turn. When you don't, you risk the consequences of superficial writing.

ALFRED: I also think there's some little Tweety Bird in here that rears up its head and takes me places I personally have never been, but I feel comfortable pretending. I've been married to the same woman for many, many years and haven't had a date with anybody else since I was nineteen. That doesn't mean that I can't write about that stuff.

LEW: Though we do often write about the misery of our friends, or so says one who has been married for twenty years. Tell us about how you develop story. Do you discover your characters first and then go with the story, or do you do both simultaneously?

ALFRED: Usually, I try to know where the story is going to take me first and where it will end, the very end of it. I like to know that if I can.

LEW: So you want the third act?

ALFRED: You know, I don't fully understand the act breaks in a movie. I just write them.

LEW: Well, the act break is just really screenwriter's shorthand for beginning, middle, and end, which goes back to Aristotle. Right?

ALFRED: If I have two people I want to develop, I'll have some incidents in mind along the way that probably come, along with thinking about who they are and what stories they come with because, as I've said, I try to use things I've known a little bit. Let's say it's a love story. I'll know I'm going to get them together or not get them together. I'll rely on myself a lot, and I imagine. I do that a lot. And when the people start talking to me, I write.

Years before I was into movies, or even before I was born, some old movie producer said, "Here's the way it goes. You've got Gary Cooper on the corner of Fifty-Seventh and Fifth Avenue, and you've got Joan Crawford on the corner of Broadway and Forty-Sixth Street. You know they're going to meet. You just don't know how or where." I read that once and thought, "Yeah, I understand that."

LEW: So you get them together at the end of the beginning or the end of the first act?

ALFRED: You sort of know where, and then you start thinking, "Okay, she's the kind that would be a dog walker. If you walk dogs in New York, you often see a very small female person walking eight or nine dogs on a leash." So where would that take me? You know what I mean?

LEW: I subscribe to the theory that in a love story you have to have an obstacle. In *Driving Miss Daisy*, you had some wonderful, wonderful obstacles. How did you see what Bill Goldman calls the spine of *Driving Miss Daisy*?

ALFRED: I thought it was a story of two people who needed each other, and they were able to say so.

LEW: Very much the spine of *Remains of the Day*, which was also quite a lovely piece. Okay, now you've got the idea. You've pretty well got the characters. Do you do any structuring or outline for yourself?

ALFRED: Definitely, but it's very hard. If I don't do some sort of outline, I get messed up. But I don't want it too much because if you describe your honeymoon in detail, by the time you get to doing it, you've already written it out.

LEW: But you have some general parameters you can refer to?

ALFRED: I like to have a general structure, then write and see what I get. That's what's scary but also exciting.

LEW: What's the structure look like on paper? Is it notes?

ALFRED: It's scribbles and arrows on lined paper. And it moves around. I do a lot of character writing first. He was this kind of guy, and he'd do this and that, and this is probably what he thought that day. Then I'll get an idea for the script. That'll eventually give me an idea for structure and whether it's a good idea.

LEW: Do you refer to those scribblings periodically when you're writing?

ALFRED: Oh, I change them regularly.

LEW: Julius Epstein—you know he's one of the *Casablanca* writers—he says he writes half a dozen to a dozen lines on the back of an envelope. He refers to that every night. He says it didn't do too bad for Abraham Lincoln. Do you assign yourself so many pages a day?

ALFRED: No, because I would feel terrible. I'm a slow starter, but when I get going, I get going. Toward the ending, I'm writing twenty, twenty-five, thirty pages a day. In the beginning, I'm almost writing nothing for six months. That's the way I work.

LEW: Like circling?

ALFRED: That's pretty much what it is. I don't find it particularly wonderful that way. It's nerve-racking, but it's just me.

LEW: Do you enjoy the process?

ALFRED: When it's going well.

LEW: Andre Gide said the journey is all; the end is nothing. But when it's going well, you enjoy the journey. So predominantly, you don't assign yourself any particular period of time to work on a piece of material?

ALFRED: Well, I do, only because I know the due date.

LEW: Are you like most writers? If you have three weeks, you take three weeks? If you have three months, it takes three months?

ALFRED: That's it.

LEW: Rewriting—when you get it finished, what do you do when you look back at it?

ALFRED: I'm a big rewriter, but I rewrite as I go, always as I go. Rhythms are very important to me, very important. I hear it a certain way. Then, I read it, and I'll hear it again, so I rewrite and rewrite and rewrite. With a play, you turn it in, and you get a reading. You hear it again. With a movie you don't get that. You get meetings at studios. I often find those disconcerting.

LEW: Do you read it aloud to yourself at a particular point?

ALFRED: No, no. I don't need to. I can hear it.

LEW: Inside your head?

ALFRED: Oh yes. I do like being able to work with a director, particularly one I trust. I've worked very much with Bruce Beresford.

LEW: What does he give you?

ALFRED: He'll just say, "Can it have a little bit more here? How does she feel about him? What about her grandmother? She was in the other scene. Shouldn't she be in this one?" He opens my head up.

LEW: When you're rewriting as you go along, do you rewrite the same day or the following day?

ALFRED: As I go along, both. As soon as I bring it up on the screen, I tend to rewrite it.

LEW: If you were to get another idea, you'll jump back and do some rewriting?

ALFRED: I do a lot of back and forth.

LEW: Then when you're done and you've rewritten along the way, do you have a process of rereading and redoing before showing it to people?

ALFRED: When I get done with a certain part, I feel like I can't do anymore, then I just go on. After going through, I always show it to my wife—always. She's a good critic.

LEW: What do you think about screenwriting as an art?

ALFRED: I think any writing is an art, but I think screenwriting is also a craft, and we are subservient to the director. We don't really control what the final film will be. I think if we're smart, we put as many stage directions as we can in the first draft so they can see what we mean. When you're in front of them, you try to make them understand exactly how you see it. My natural tendency is to put in zero stage directions, but for a film, I try to put in as many as I can without going too far, so the director knows what I mean but it's not distracting from the story.

LEW: Now, you don't put in angles or camera stuff in it but just basically stage directions?

ALFRED: If I really see it, I do. Nobody ever told me, don't.

LEW: Many playwrights have told me that they feel liberated when they're writing a motion picture, more dimensional.

ALFRED: Well, in the movies, you have much more drama. If I'm writing a play and I want my characters to go to the drugstore, who's going to be the druggist? You can't just have people pop up. In a movie, you have to be fluid.

LEW: You never found that to be intimidating, I must assume. Which one of the screenplays that David Brown gave you to read was the most meaningful?

ALFRED: None of them. I loved the movies but hated reading the screenplays. I would rather watch the movies.

LEW: So actually your predominant learning process in movies was actually doing, specifically, *Mystic Pizza*?

ALFRED: Yes, and oh, AMC because at that point, AMC was just coming along. They would run the same movies one afternoon and then the next night, two or three times. And I would see setups and payoffs in the old movies, and I would learn.

LEW: Isn't that true? Like *A Letter to Three Wives*—what tremendous craftsmanship that went into those movies in terms of plot, and they have the characters, too.

ALFRED: My favorite movie is *The Best Years of Our Lives*. I think it's got everything.

LEW: So, so true. So true.

ALFRED: When I watch it, I think I'm only going to watch a little bit, and then I just have to watch it all. The same with *The Godfather I* and *II*. You don't get any better. Yet those are very different movies. They're character-driven plot movies, which is what interests me. I always consider *The Godfather* to be very character driven. Those kinds of people are why those kinds of plots exist.

LEW: Let's hear from one of our ace 434 students, Rita Augustine. Rita will be one of the twelve out of twenty that will become professional screenwriters.

ALFRED: All right, Rita.

LEW: She's also a product of the East Coast, so that gives her a leg up in that concept.

ALFRED: A real person.

RITA: Thank you, I hope so, Mr. Uhry. I originally came to screenwriting from writing musicals. You mentioned the brevities from lyrical writing. Do you see other musical influences? Oh, you also mentioned rhythm as being very important in your screenwriting. Has all of this helped you in screenwriting?

ALFRED: I think rhythm is important to me in dialogue.

RITA: Do you ever listen to music when you write? Woody Allen mentions doing that.

ALFRED: No, I just sort of have to cloister myself. Often I turn on television in frustration, just to take a break. I don't really look at it. It's just sort of there.

RITA: When you're writing those twenty pages a day, do you do that predominantly in the morning?

ALFRED: I tend to be a morning person. But when it's going well toward the end, for me, from one to ten, the first several months is a zero. I rewrite the beginning over and over again. From the sixth month, I get up to maybe five o'clock. And the last two weeks are eight, nine, and ten o'clock. That's when I do everything, really.

RITA: Do you find it fun to write, or is it painful? Especially when you get into those long hauls, toward the end?

ALFRED: Oh, that part is the fun of it all. The hard part is sitting there with nothing coming out. I'm thinking, "Okay, this time, they're going to realize I have no abilities."

LEW: When you're sitting there with nothing coming, are there any particular tricks you use? Do you get up and walk around the block?

ALFRED: Actually, I found a way to get out of it. I'll think, "Why am I stuck? What would these people really say? In real life, what would they really say? 'I'm cold'? 'I'm hungry'? 'I've got to go to the bathroom'? 'I'm thirsty'? 'Fuck you'?" Something. Usually, you can kick yourself off a story by thinking, "Oh, he shouldn't be there now. He should come in within a few minutes, and she should be talking to her grandmother." That will usually get you going. Works for me, anyway.

LEW: Is it sometimes you're doing more circling because of the multiplicity of choices or the absence of choices?

ALFRED: It's the multiplicity, I think.

LEW: I agree. I think, "Which way am I going to go?" Then I wait until one surfaces over another.

ALFRED: But again, if the character is strong enough, he or she will lead you by the nose.

LEW: Isn't that true? We always get into major trouble when we look to our own intellect and devices to get us out of a story corner rather than the character.

ALFRED: In my current play, I was writing toward the end, when something happened that I couldn't believe. I believed it, but I thought, "My God." Then I thought, "Oh, yes, that's reality. It just came out of her mouth." I was just, so—happy. I didn't know I was going to write that. I didn't know she was going to say that. She just said it, and it took me to the right places.

RITA: For you, are they the same characters when you write *Driving Miss Daisy* for the stage as they are for the movies?

ALFRED: It's a different way to tell the same story. They're in the same setting, but they're more dimensional in movies because they can walk downstairs, they can go outside, they can do so much more. You can get in close, see the pores of their skin, if you wish.

RITA: You were talking about your writing, that you tend to write short and then you go back and you fill in. What kinds of things do you do to fill it out? Where do you look to do that?

ALFRED: Although I say I write character, I start off writing my character just dealing with the plot. Then, I go back and put in, "You know, I'm the kind of guy who eats eggs on Thursday afternoon." That's the kind of thing I'll put in. Something about them. "I remember the time my mother took me to the oncologist to see my grandmother." Their back-story unfolds as the story unfolds.

RITA: You mentioned the influences of old movies. Can you write the same types of stories? Is it the same medium, or has it changed?

ALFRED: Well, it certainly seems they try to do that, don't they? We have *A Shop around the Corner* coming back. We've got *Death Takes a Holiday*. I don't think any of them come close though.

LEW: I was talking to Billy Wilder about *Sabrina*.

ALFRED: Oh boy, did they miss that one. I was called on to rewrite *Doddsworth*, and I did. Milos Forman was going to direct it for Harrison Ford. All the while I thought, "Well, Harrison Ford is a good actor and a wonderful movie star, but nobody is going to touch Walter Houston." I don't know if they are going to make it or not. I've rarely seen a remake that comes close. I like them when they're different.

   A Shop around the Corner sounds like a good idea to me. I don't know how it's going to turn out. I mean, how many basic plot twists in the world are there? That's why I work on character. There aren't many movies about a bunch of girls working at a pizza shop. There weren't that many about an old lady hiring a chauffeur, and they all came out of real events.

LEW: What was the real event for *Driving Miss Daisy*?

ALFRED: The real event is that my grandmother drove a car over a hill and smashed into somebody's garage, and we had to hire a driver for her.

LEW: My publisher says that people buy these various books with the idea of finding *the* secret. Is there a particular secret that you might have discovered?

ALFRED: The only secret I know about writing well is you have to write it so audiences know it's real, and that's not to say you can't write about Mozart or Socrates. Audiences know if a writer believes it way down to the marrow of his or her bones. I think also, the more specific you are, the wider audience you'll reach. I'll never understand that, but I know it's true.

LEW: I've never heard that. The more specific you are, the wider audience you'll reach. Well, that probably gets back to the idea of reality because you get the reality either experientially or through research.

ALFRED: Right. Then the audience can say, "Oh, yeah. I can understand how he felt." But I think that general writing, like soap opera writing, where they explain everything—"Don't you know the reason I went to Chicago is because Mary told me Karen said you love Billy and I wanted to prove you love me?"—people don't talk that way. People don't even know what they mean or feel half the time. They just talk. Take a movie like *The Godfather*. I don't know anything about that world, but I sure believed the world and language Puzo and Coppola created.

LEW: Once I was asked to write a movie about the mafia. We have twenty-nine hours of tapes that have been on a wiretap in Appalachia. So I listened to twenty-nine hours of tape, and all these mafiosi were trying to do James Cagney: "You stick the guys in cement shoes" or "You put the bird in his mouth by the East River." I said, "You can't do that. That's just silly. It's Warner Brothers 1940." Three years later, *The Godfather* opened, and the dialogue was just perfect.

ALFRED: They sure didn't talk like Jimmy Cagney.

LEW: Exactly. They talked like bankers, with the exception of a couple characters. I think the perception of reality is often more real to audiences than the actual reality.

ALFRED: Absolutely. It was about a family business. Most of us can relate to that. Coppola and Puzo found a way to tell the story that was believable. I also don't believe you personally have to have experiences for every single thing you write about. With certain actors, we love them, we believe them, we will watch them. If there's a movie we can feel. I'll give you an example that nobody thought could be wonderful as it was: *Dave.*

LEW: Very nice.

ALFRED: *Dave* seemed plausible. The character of Dave was interesting and, with Sigourney Weaver, made it work. If there's a secret, really believe in yourself. Really, really, really believe what you're doing.

LEW: Perhaps it's all believable unbelievability, like in *Peter Pan.* The audience comes into these darkened caves to look at these celluloid petroglyphs, and they sit there and let you cause them to suspend their day-to-day disbeliefs.

ALFRED: Yes, like *Men in Black*, which is really about those two guys being friends with each other and having wonderful adventures. It'll go all the way, the distance. It's amusingly written, and the tone is exactly right all the way through.

LEW: That's one of our ex-students, by the way, Ed Solomon, I say with pride.

ALFRED: He did a wonderful job.

LEW: Interestingly, *Men in Black* had clear, identifiable character traits, inside the comedy and the special effects, particularly with the Tommy Lee Jones character. If Ed Solomon didn't have those beats, I don't think he would have had much, but it gave the film something beyond superficial.

ALFRED: That's right. The fact that Tommy Lee Jones went back to his family all adds up. All that stuff stems from being character driven. I know *Men in Black* is an existent cartoon, but it didn't quite have as much depth as the movie because you actually cared about the two guys and their relationship with each other. For me, screenwriting boils down to telling the real truth the way you feel, by getting into yourself, opening up. If you' re going to write about Napoleon and Josephine, you're going to have to write about yourself and some romantic feeling you had for somebody, somewhere.

LEW: Well, Alfred you have been very, very illuminating. You've given us, as I said, a different perspective because of your background and because of your continuing on with theater simultaneously. There are very few of you around today. Ted Tally doesn't do it anymore. I don't think Horton Foote does it anymore. It really is down to Larry Gelbart and Neil Simon who are able to successfully go back and forth between movies and plays.

ALFRED: Wendy Wasserstein just did a movie.

LEW: She's going to start going back and forth? Excellent. Most people find it all to be very different gearshifts, but I don't get that from you.

ALFRED: I don't really. Maybe there's something wrong with me.

LEW: Au contraire. There's something right with you. Something wonderfully right, Alfred Uhry.

7

Oliver Stone

I confess to idolizing Oliver Stone! He is the screenwriter I try to be, a man who is dedicated to the "now" as well as marking the world by pulling the pants down on the thing called commensalism. Yet, he remains human, avant-garde, and pragmatic. Former UCLA student Shelley Anderson picked him up for this screenwriting course gathering. En route he mused, "I hope I do well." This man who turns studios upside down hopes he does well!? He was brave enough to take on some of the most important stories ever told, such as *Snowden, Nixon, Evita, Scarface, Born on the Fourth of July, JFK, Wall Street,* and *Platoon.*

You be the judge over the course of the next few pages. He is a master, one of a kind, a home run, a historian who is also making history. As Shelley Anderson drove him back after the class, he asked her, "Do you think I did all right?" Here is an artist, who in my opinion, has triumphed by always asking just this question. It's this self-awareness that likely contributes a large part to the successful creation of on-screen worlds that are so historical, thoughtful, philosophical, and predictive that one can immediately recognize Oliver Stone as the only possible auteur.

LEW: We're serving three masters today. The most important is the 434 class around the table. The secondary master is the people who read *Naked Screenwriting* to be as good as they can be in screenwriting and in life. Our next master is the video we're making to put it in the UCLA film archives. We've had people—well, to name drop, Billy Wilder

151

was here last year; Julius Epstein, who cowrote *Casablanca*; Eric Roth with *Forrest Gump*; Irving Ravetch and Harriet Frank Jr. with *Hud* and *Norma Rae*; Tom Schulman with *Dead Poets Society*; Bruce Joel Rubin— have you come to know Bruce?

OLIVER: No.

LEW: He was in Tibet for a year as a monk before he became a writer. Did *Ghost* and *Jacob's Ladder*, you know.

OLIVER: There are a lot of monks in Tibet. [*laughter*]

LEW: Ron Bass so informed us three weeks ago, and Oliver today. Ernie Lehmann was here last week. Frank Pierson is coming next week. Francis Coppola is in a holding pattern.

OLIVER: You're such a lucky class to be in Los Angeles. You get to meet more writers.

LEW: Hear, hear. The second master, *Naked Screenwriting*, will comprise all these various 434 class visits. All of you Academy Award–winning screenwriters bare your art, soul, craft, and secrets. We talk about process. Do you remember when George Plimpton and the cats got together for the *Paris Review*, and they compiled Writers at Work, which was a series of books where they interviewed Hemingway and Dos Passos, Steinbeck, Nabakov, Albee?

OLIVER: I'd love to see those.

LEW: They published eight volumes with at least eighty legendary writers. They solely talked about the process of writing, playwriting, as well as novels. Let's figure a way to get Oliver some copies, please.

OLIVER: I know Hemingway wrote standing up. It's interesting.

LEW: Because of his back problems. Thomas Wolfe wrote standing up and used the top of a refrigerator because he was six foot eight. He would take the finished pages, put them in a pickle barrel, and then his secretary would fish them out.

OLIVER: I never believe those stories. [*laughter*]

LEW: Hemingway first lined up and sharpened fifteen pencils. Then he said, if he's going deep-sea fishing the next day, instead of doing his self-prescribed 1,500 words a day, he would write 3,000 words so he wouldn't have guilt while fishing the next day. Those are the sort of things we're trying to do here. We're about process.

OLIVER: Hemingway said, "It is the ultimate grace man or a woman can have if he or she can write with a hangover." [*laughter*]

LEW: And Dorothy Parker said, "The definition of *gentleman* is a man who puts his weight on his elbows." [*no laughter*] Think about it, folks. Talk it out amongst yourselves. [*laughter*]

Okay now, enough. To introduce you, I'm tempted to repeat W. C. Handy when somebody asked him, "What are the blues, Mr. Handy?" and he said, "Baby, if you got to ask, you'll never know." So, I will simply say we're sitting on the day of February 12, two days before our beloved Valentines, whoever he or she may be, and no one has to ask, "Who is Oliver Stone?" *Seizure, Midnight Express, Scarface, Eight Million Ways to Die, Year of the Dragon, Salvador,* then *Platoon, Wall Street, Talk Radio, Born on the Fourth of July, The Doors, JFK, Heaven and Earth, Natural Born Killers,* and *Nixon.* Five nominations and three Academy Awards for out of that gathering: two for directing one for writing. [*applause*]

STUDENT: *U-turn.* You forgot *U-turn* as a writer.

OLIVER: I'm not credited as a writer. I did a bit of a backstage job.

LEW: One of my lines that invariably get a laugh in the twenty years I've been professing is, "You're taking notes. You're so respectful. Tell me I'm an establishment asshole. Tell me I'm full of shit. I can take it. I taught in the '60s." I want to communicate this personal bent because not any of the other writers here before have had your social revolutionary film spirit. None are referred to, as I'm sure you've possibly read, a "prolific delusionary entertainer," and here it says, "Oliver Stone, Hollywood's last angry man." Did you read that?

OLIVER: Yeah.

LEW: Isn't it a shame if that's true? [*laughter*]

LEW: When I read that, I remembered the line in *The Wild One* where the store proprietor, I think it was Keenan Wynn, comes out, looks at Marlon Brando on his motorcycle, and says, "What are you mad at?" And Marlon replies, "What do you got?"

OLIVER: That's a great line.

LEW: You don't think you're Hollywood's last angry man, do you?

OLIVER: No, my rebellion is through. It's a rebellion only about being myself and being free as much as I can. You know, I don't have enemies. I just have obstacles that get in my way. Sometimes they don't want you to be free, but then I always feel they're trying to repress me. It's that kind of thing. It's a rebel with a cause if you want.

I do believe that I want to make it a productive rebellion. I've seen a lot of rebellion that sometimes gets destructive. And certainly when I was a young man, when I was your age, I was once really on the edge of destruction. I lived my life very much like a razor. It was life or death. All was much clearer. You lived; you died. Survive or death.

The book I wrote is about survival really. At the end of it—well, it took me thirty years to really understand what the theme was about. It was about a nineteen-year-old trying to make it in the world. How do you survive? How do you live? Where do you start? I was confused. That was the anger, and my anger is obviously involved with my childhood. It's always been there. It's been strong in my work, but it's not the only note in the work, I think. If it is, then fine. I'll accept that.

LEW: From your book *A Child's Night Dream*, page 144: "He thought himself, 'This is a nineteen-year-old child.' He thought himself extraordinarily fortunate, therefore, in having seen a great deal of life, of having combined the sea and the land. A man not solely restricted to one modus operandi, he has had a finger in a few pots. Nevertheless, he knew that experience was not a solution. Rather, he had come to accept the fundamental discontent of our human nature, and he had vaguely realized that the best thing he could do in its terrifying face was to move, to move much. He had, to his satisfaction, combined movement with permanence, function with environment, life and art in a single existence."

Wow. I remember when I was writing a movie for Peter Guber back in the Neal Bogart *Casablanca* days, and Peter says, "Hey, I've really got something here. I got a nice script. Do you want to look at it?" And I read one of the drafts, *Midnight Express*. I finished it and said, "Holy fuck. This is really good." How old were you at the time? How many scripts had you written prior?

OLIVER: I was about thirty, thirty-one years old. I was about twelve, fourteen, fifteen scripts in. Do you want to talk about that process?

LEW: Yes, yes. Brian Price here sold a script last year to Universal, and *Variety* referred to Brian as an overnight success, that he was a first-time writer. In class I said, "How many scripts did you write before you became a first-time writer?" And what did you say when I asked that question? Ten?

BRIAN PRICE: Yeah, ten.

LEW: Brian had written ten. So here, Oliver, you were to me a first-time writer, but of course you were twelve or thirteen scripts in the process.

OLIVER: Yeah, and the book, too. I'd written a book that was sitting in a shoebox somewhere. I believe in screenplays, so I never deluded myself. But I always wanted to direct. You see the problem was I came out of film school with a hunger to direct, so the screenwriting was for the purpose of directing.

LEW: Much like Francis Ford Coppola because that's why Francis went to school here with that idea.

OLIVER: Or the tradeoff. Writing a script that was commercial for the screen, a western, or something that could be started by one of the stars, sell it, and then they'd always say they'd give you a chance to direct the second one. That was always the line. So I tried that method. I wrote scripts, so many different types of scripts. I wrote one script specifically for Charles Bronson. It was a western. I wanted to do a Sergio Leone western. I wrote it all out, a huge movie, and he never even read it. Bronson never even read it, you know. It was that kind of frustration. You'd get the script to them finally, but they'd never even read it. Lee Marvin didn't read it or whoever. It was always like, "Steve McQueen? You can't even get him to read." I think he actually charged $25,000 to read a script. [*laughter*] It was really frustrating.

LEW: Well, now, when you went to NYU, let me tie in to when you said you really had a goal to direct all along. Let me mention François Truffaut. I have a 1967 criticism he titled, *The Irrelevancy of the Screenwriter.* Then I have another quote in 1976 where he said that if he started all over again, he would start out as a screenwriter. How do you feel about screenwriting now that you've used it to open the directing doors?

OLIVER: Wow, you're jumping fast.

LEW: I'm saying that early in Truffaut's life, he said that screenwriting wasn't meaningful. Now you're sort of saying, not that it wasn't meaningful, but you're saying, "I used it basically as a door opener."

OLIVER: No. What I used it for was to be a writer-director. I wanted to be in a position where I could make a film, a filmmaker. The combination, that thing they call a filmmaker, that collaborative medium. Taking the word and the essential, the visual, and combining the two, that was the hardest thing to do. But that was the fun of movies coming off the novel. You have to realize, I grew up in schools in the East Coast, and I was very much from the literary tradition, and I'd read a lot, but I was not persuaded by the film medium. I enjoyed movies, but I never even believed for one second I'd be working in them at all. My life was somewhere else.

LEW: Did you respect the movies at that time?

OLIVER: Oh yeah. My dad took me to the good ones, and we talked about them afterwards. We always walked out of a Kubrick or a Lean movie. He'd say, "Kiddo, what did you think of the movie?" I'd say, "Oh, it was great." And he'd say, "But did you notice that this thing is wrong and that thing didn't make sense?" And I'd say, "What do you mean that doesn't make sense?" And we'd go into this chess-game argument of what made sense in a movie. My dad was logical. He always ended up saying, "Well, you know, we could have done it better." Without knowing it, he gave me my first encouragement for screenwriting.

LEW: What led you to NYU specifically?

OLIVER: Wholly other different motives. When I left the country for Vietnam, there wasn't any film education as such. It was not possible. See, I skipped my generation in a sense. I went over to the war. I came back three years later. I was twenty-two. They were sophomores. For the first time, I heard you can get a degree and actually go to the movies and sit there and get grades for that. It was a funny idea actually, and also the GI bill was paying for NYU. That was good and a good school for me because I wanted to stay in New York. So I did the subway school thing and got a degree after two and a half years.

I made three short films; that was the key. Most of the kids were not studying screenwriting. They were avoiding it, absolutely avoiding it. They didn't care for it. It was old, it was conservative, it was literary. And there were a couple of good classes, too. One professor gave me a couple of jobs at PBS, where he was a producer. That was when PBS actually had some money, and it was free to do what it wanted to do. It was an interesting time actually. They were doing some wild stuff.

I had a couple of other jobs. I drove a cab. I was P.A. on a sex movie. I made a low-budget horror film in Canada with a couple of young partners that was a movie unto itself. That failed. Married. My wife was working. I was struggling. Writing screenplays. I got a job at a sports company for about a year and a half, a well-paid job. I didn't do a bit of work. I was holed up in the back and kept the door, not locked, but open. I was working on screenplays in their office the whole time they were paying me. The boss would walk down the hall and check the rooms. He'd always come through and say, "How's it going?" I'd say, "Oh, great. Making a sale here." [*laughter*]

It was always things we're working on. It was always about things to happen. Never was anything actualized. We were also always about to shoot a film. The boss woke up and said, "What are we paying this guy for?"

LEW: I used to do that at CBS. In my case, they thought I was writing their stuff, and I was writing my stuff. I'm getting you into war stories. That's my fault. Tell us about your work habits then as opposed to now when you're into script.

OLIVER: Let me first address your other question about Truffaut. That was a good one. I would say the arc of my career is a little bit different. I really always emphasized heavily the screenwriter in my career. Of course, as you go on, you learn about different ways of doing things.

That's the truth about life. You understand there are other ways to approach the creature. It's not always the same. I admire good scripts and, to this day, I think the only way I can really monitor myself as a writer. Because as a director, you can't monitor yourself as much. What is good, what is bad? Some of the greatest films are huge excesses. The critics all tell you this is terrible, but they don't know. A hundred years from now maybe, you know. I don't know. There's something in film that has its own truth, but it's hard to find. As a writer, you can always say, "This movie needs work. This movie has a problem." I can define it on paper, but I can't do that as a director because it really doesn't start to happen for the director until he's in the editing room.

When he's in the room, along the way, after several weeks of peeling the onion, you begin to see the essences of these scenes. What occurs is really fascinating from your point of view as a writer. What occurs is, unconsciously and even consciously, the final rewrite is already taking place in your mind. Why did the writer write that? Why did I write that? Why did I say that line? What does it need? The scene is repeating itself four or five times. I didn't see it until now. It's not the same dialogue, but they're repeating the same attitude four or five times in the scene.

You start to see redundancies in the editing sometimes, and you'll rip out three of them or four of them, and you'll leave one in, and the scene is suddenly a moment instead of being a page, page and a half, or two. A lot of those tricks are going on. The deconstruction goes as far as taking structure and repositioning it. I've done that on two of my movies in editing. I've gone back and restructured the movie in editing because I abandoned the original structure. My alarm bells were going off, saying this is not right. It's not the right way. But this is the question of new rules forming, new strategies.

LEW: I've seen every one of your movies except *Natural Born Killers*. Would you mind telling us which one of the two you did the most restructuring in that final rewrite?

OLIVER: We did a lot of restructuring on actually three movies: *Heaven and Earth*, *Natural Born Killers*, and *Nixon*. And also on *U-turn*. Four. That's four. They do not resemble the original screenplays. The essences do but not the structure. It's bizarre, but there you are.

LEW: I was blown away by *Nixon*. The things you were reaching for there. I don't know whether I got "it," whatever "it" was in your mind, but it allowed me to get things from that time that I had only dreamt about. The only other movie close to *Nixon* was *Leola*. Did you see Leola, the Montreal movie?

OLIVER: I heard about it, yeah.

LEW: What was your process when you started?

OLIVER: In terms of scheduling and shifting, that was a good question because it changes. I've tried to work out a system, and it works for me to edit a movie and simultaneously write another one, two sessions in a day. I write in the morning or until, say, midafternoon, then go to the editing room late, which gives the editors time to talk about the stuff you talked about the previous day. Then I go in and spend three or four hours or sometimes one or two hours with the editors in a session collectively or sometimes apart in different rooms.

Also, critique-wise, there was a very good thing we did at NYU. We used to make each member of the class bid to make his film. In other words, you have to explain your story to the rest of the class. Some of them could be very hostile to your point of view. But it was a free marketplace of ideas. You had to convince the majority of the class to say yes to the film and the professor, too. In its pristine state, you're supposed to get the actors from the class, the editors from the class, the DP, and so forth, which I think was great. Then kids started to cheat. They'd bring in actors from the outside. They'd bring in money, so it got rigged a bit. Some of them were trying to make career films. They were trying to advance their careers through film school, and that sucked. They were trying to make big commercials that would get them signed by some agent. The best thing to do is to really try to develop narrative skills and also follow your heart, follow your imagination into the work, and use film school as a chance to exercise your deepest interests. Don't fake it in film school because you don't have a chance outside.

LEW: One of our professors, Dan Pyne, is a wonderful writer who wrote *Pacific Heights* and *White Sands*. Dan says, he came to school here and now teaches here: "This is your chance to be as good as you can be because once you get out here, you may have sad compromises." Do you agree?

OLIVER: Absolutely.

LEW: You said, by the way, "It sucks." Why do you say that in terms of trying to do the commercial film?

OLIVER: It distorts you. It puts you on another path to make your master happy. You're a slave. You're in bondage. Meanwhile, if you're working for yourself in film school, which is what you should be doing, explore yourself. You may not get that chance on the outside for a while or ever. You might be going into a situation where you're blocked for a while, but you must get back to it. I use that in my own example because I always felt like I would get back to film directing, and the writing was a pursuit of that excellence, a vigorous pursuit. It was hard. If I didn't turn out one or two scripts a year, I would be very unhappy with myself. That's while I was also doing a regular job.

LEW: When you were starting out, what was your process of developing the story, and then, how did you write the script, and how have both processes changed?

OLIVER: I always kept the demons inside myself thinking that that was probably the best part of myself. But I would write in different ways. Sometimes I would write wholly through plot, and characters would just exist inside the plot. I think some of the more interesting scripts followed much closer to a person but inside a plot structure that was interesting to me. The best script I wrote in that period was called *The Cover-Up*, a script that got the attention of Robert Bolt, the screenwriter of *Lawrence of Arabia* and *A Man for All Seasons*. It was a story based on Hearst, in which the kidnapping was a setup. The Black Cinque member is really a government plant in the script. There is some evidence of that, so I constructed this elaborate conspiracy actually very early in my writing life. People don't realize that. Bolt picked up on it and loved it because he was an old guy in the new world, English liberal, Whigs-and-Tory time. He helped me, got me an agent. I spent two weeks in a room like this with Bolt, talking about my script. Sometimes it would be very embarrassing because he would send me home like a schoolmaster. I'd do my homework, come in with new pages, and he would red-pencil and rewrite lines. But it was okay. I learned a lot.

LEW: Did you have a goal of writing a script in two or three weeks?

OLIVER: In the early days, I thought six weeks was a good time for a script because you get momentum, and you can best unify it. I hate to lose things like Bolt does, where he goes for a year and a half, and he just—well, you can get lost in these mazes.

LEW: Ernie Lehman talked last week about a year to write *North by Northwest*.

OLIVER: You're kidding.

LEW: Most of the people who come out of this class that become successful screenwriters—Randy Johnson, Neal Jimenez, Michael Werb, and Colleary—they're like, "God, I feel like I'm still in a 434," which is this class, because we have six to eight weeks to write the script after we develop the outline. So is that time frame still true today? When you're into script?

OLIVER: No, I'm more limited, and I don't have access to that free time I had before. It's a drag. I really miss it. I miss free time. If there's one thing I really miss in my life, it's just time to fuck off in the afternoon, go to a museum, talk to somebody, just do nothing. It's a wonderful feeling, and I really miss it.

LEW: Amen. I got the feeling, when people were talking about you, around the *Casablanca* or the Guber time, you would sit down and write a script in a twenty-four-, forty-eight-hour blast.

OLIVER: They confused me with Peter Guber, who I thought was on mega-amphetamines. [*laughter*]

LEW: We used to call Peter the electric Jew. We'd say to each other, "You have Peter for thirty seconds." At the thirty-first-second mark, he's gone.

Talk to us about process, Oliver, in terms of idea picking, when you go, "Aha! That's the one I want to spend time with." What is "aha" for you? How do you recognize that, "I want to do this idea."

OLIVER: What makes you write a movie. Yes. Well, you want to spend time with it. You have passion. You have a mental energy. It's a form of love. Love is action. It's like meeting a man or a woman. Why do you love him or her? It's because one eye was blue and the other was gray? I think with *Scarface*, it was. I hated the Paul Muni story, actually. I preferred Edward G. Robinson's *Little Caesar* because it was a harder-edged movie. They said, "We want to remake *Scarface*." Al saw it on TV the other night at four o'clock in the morning, and he thought it was a good role for him. Right? I'm like, "There are so many Italian pictures. I don't want to see another one."

Actually, Brian De Palma proved us wrong with *The Untouchables*, didn't he? So I said, "I hate that whole era. Forget it. I'm not going to do it." Then they came back—Sydney Lumet was the original director— they said, "What about doing it in Miami?" I said, "Wow. That's a whole other thing because there's an exciting social context going on with that story. It's going on right now." Miami was hot in 1980, pre–*Miami Vice*. And of course, having been involved in that world a little bit, it was a pleasure to get people into it. I had done a lot of research in South America when cocaine was cheaper and started flowing through Miami.

LEW: So passion is the hallmark.

OLIVER: Then I went cold turkey, completely cold turkey, and I swear I never hit the coke after that. Actually, I moved to Paris because I had to get rid of all the associations of cocaine, which is to say I didn't want to be around any friends that did it. All of my friends were doing it. Hollywood was awash in it in '79, '80. I got out of town, and that did me a lot of good, as I wrote *Scarface* in Paris in about an eight-, ten-week span. That is a screenplay I love. After all it's gone through, the structure ultimately stayed the same, all the way from the first to the thirteenth draft. It was the dialogue and some of the situations inside the scene structure that changed.

Frankly, it took a long time, about six to eight more months, as they insisted I stay on the set. That was one set I wanted to get off of, believe me. It just went on and on and on. It was a six-month movie. But listening to the dialogue, getting Al to give us stuff was worth it. He was a good improviser, and Marty Bregman was also helpful. Seeing it all the way through was quite something.

LEW: Now, structure. You had lots of material to work with, *The Untouchables*.

OLIVER: I didn't do *The Untouchables*.

LEW: I'm sorry, take 2. *Scarface*.

OLIVER: *Scarface* was the more respectable movie. [*laughter*] David Mamet's establishment; I'm not. [*laughter*]

LEW: Right. You have gotten movies from so many different worlds. *Salvador* and *Nixon*, for example. Every one of your movies does not come from the traditional original source, yet definitely they become original screenplays in their own historical way.

OLIVER: I'm one of the few people ever nominated twice in the same category for an original screenplay: *Platoon* and *Salvador*. Twice in the same category.

LEW: So in structuring your story, how do you do this? Do you have a legal pad, where you mark 1, 2, 3, 4?

OLIVER: *Platoon* grew out of my experience in Vietnam and wanting to put it on paper in some form. I wrote a screenplay when I got back in '69, which was the earliest form of *Platoon*, called *Break*. It was very Morrison-esque. It was too surreal for the market, and nobody would make it. They thought I was crazy and that I needed to go to a psychiatric unit or something. There was always a funny look in their eye. *Break* was one of my favorites, always. I never could do it in that form. It was born out of the late '60s, that mentality and those psychedelic elements of American society. *Break* eventually became *Platoon*, which was written very fast in the summer of '76, also with notes over periods of years.

LEW: Now did you put the notes in a step outline? For yourself?

OLIVER: Definitely. Not the ending, though, not the third act. I like to keep it loose because it's fun to feel it and find it as you go. If you pre-ordain the ending, it feels like you're playing God too much.

LEW: Once in a while, I'll say, "That third act. I don't think that's right, but don't worry about it, you'll get to it when you get to it. You have to get the first two acts right." When I first came to Hollywood and I said hello to a writer, he or she would say, "I can't get a third act!" When Billy Wilder was here, he said, "Well, if you cannot get the third act, perhaps you haven't got the first act."

OLIVER: I've had several lunches with Billy, and he always says, "Oliver, why can't you make your films shorter?" [*laughter*] He's tough, but he's great; Billy Wilder's great. You know, he had his share of setbacks and films that were not accepted and all that. He also had a hell of a writing partner, too: I. A. L. Diamond.

LEW: He also had a man by his side that constantly whispered in his ear: a film editor, Doane Harrison. He was sort of like a Jiminy Cricket to Billy, his Yoda. Do you have any Yodas?

OLIVER: I have many people I trust for that purpose, and I talk to them. I get alone with them, and I listen. Actors, too. That's later on, but in the initial stages, friends. But I don't give out pages like John Milius does. I know John very well. He writes three pages and then runs down the hall. [*laughter*] "Read it, read it, read it!" he screams. I'm very secretive. I like to put the pages away and let them sit there. I want to get the whole done first. Once you roll, I think you roll. When you go, you go. You do your research, you listen, you talk, but then you go. You have to be alone. You have to on your own. I think it's a wonderful freedom, too, by the way. It gives you a good and complete feeling for the movie.

LEW: Do you have a page count a day you work for when you're in a script? Three, four, five pages a day?

OLIVER: People lie to you when they say they never look at the pages. I think you always go for something.

LEW: Floyd Mutrux once said here when somebody asked him, "How many hours a day do you write?" He said, "It's not the hours. It's the pages." He had like five pages a day.

OLIVER: Floyd didn't write until the middle of the night as I remember, if then. [*laughter*]

LEW: Have you ever seen *Aloha, Bobby and Rose*? I love that movie. That was made in a Moviola, too. Do you miss Moviolas?

OLIVER: No. [*laughter*]

LEW: You work off of what?

OLIVER: Computers.

LEW: Remember, we used to have to wait a day or two before we'd get those cuts?

OLIVER: It was so dreadful cutting movies in those days. It was hard to make changes. You'd fight. That's why editing became such a fought-over thing. It's so much nicer on a computer, actually.

LEW: Back to pages: Do you have a literal page count?

OLIVER: If I do three pages, I'm disgusted with myself. If I do seven to nine, I'm pretty happy. I'm very happy if I hit eleven. I'm on a roll.

LEW: But you still don't run down the hall?

OLIVER: I don't even like to read it, actually, because when it's finished for the day, I like to walk away. Sometimes, I'd finish as late as eight or nine o'clock and then pick it up the next hour and see if I want to read it. But sometimes you can get caught. Like Bob Towne, I hear, looks at it the next day and says, "Oh, that's wrong." And then he goes back into it, and he spends another day, and then you know, it's a year. Forget it. Keep moving. I know what I want to say. I may not have said it right initially. You may scratch a few notes, change that, do that, but you keep moving forward. Get the spine. That's always my plan.

LEW: Keep on the roll. You can always fix it later.

OLIVER: Yeah.

LEW: From your book: "As I believe in the moments or days before your death, when you truly live outside of chronological time, it is then you remember the poem of your life. It's essence, rhythm, meaning, whatever, sometimes lonely, sometimes beautiful, always unique." This is the contemporary Oliver Stone who wrote these words. I want to impress upon all of my 434 class people about their uniqueness because that's the thing they have to ride with: their uniqueness. Forget about commerciality, but don't ever forget about exploiting your own uniqueness. Oliver, you are very aware of your own uniqueness. You were an only child I sense.

OLIVER: I was a lonely, autistic child. I was always alone as a child because my parents were away a lot, but also, I like people. I like friends, but frankly they were not always there. I didn't like noisy households because I grew up without one, so silence worked for me. I got into the world of privacy and imagination, and I really enjoyed it. I still do. Part of my biggest fear is that I get thrown into a prison with twelve guys in the same cell. [*laughter*]

Privacy is really nice and secrecy. It comes from the mushroom culture of the writers that have it. Writing is still a struggle. But the word *poem* is a very good word used for screenwriting. I think good scripts are like poems. They're filled with love, they're filled with passion, they're filled with a point of view above all, a vision, call it what you want. And people know it. They read a script, and I swear they know it. And that's the greatest thing of all. When you know it, you know it. No one can take that away from you. They can redraft it and fuck it up and make a lousy movie, but at the end of the day, you know that screenplay was good. I feel that way about *Eight Million Ways to Die*. It was a wonderful screenplay I wrote, the first draft, a New York City story. Poor Hall Ashby changed it into a completely different look. He sat across the table and told me he'd never been to New York City in his life. [*laughter*]

LEW: The poem. Get back to the poem, please.

OLIVER: *Eight Million Ways to Die* is a good script, but that movie sucks. [*laughter*]

LEW: I don't agree, by the way, with the "last angry man" description, but sometimes I feel like you're the last passionate man. Certainly all the people that have been in here—Ron Bass and all of his energy and his passion going and the rest—but they have a passion for doing projects, scripts, as opposed to passion for stories that have societal basis. And I admire you for it.

I'm frustrated how more people don't choose movies that espouse feelings for our human future, whether it's antiwar, for war, abortion. In my case, I wrote a movie about pedophilia because I realized this was a way to show the communication gap between adults and children today. Use movie storytelling to evoke passion. Why in hell don't we have more writers and directors doing that?

OLIVER: Because of the media police, that's why. I think that they're out there and on top of anybody who says anything. If a screenwriter says something in his script, it tends to be emasculated. If they don't get you at the studio level, they sure as hell get you when you come out. If they don't like what they hear, if you aren't telling them exactly what they're saying, they will cut you to shreds, and they will pick you out by name. They'll say this person wrote a lousy script, but this great actor and that great director somehow made this thing worthwhile, you know. They are vicious.

This concept of America, of conformity, I find, they review subjects. They don't review how the movie, how well it's made, or how badly it's made. They review the subject of the movie only, and they give you their thought on that particular cultural value. That's why we don't have any working-class people in movies. They're gone. It's because most of the people that look at movies don't even know blue collar anymore here nor there.

If you do a movie right now about fuckin' Chiapas, you'll get killed. You'll get killed. I mean, I went down there with one of your protégées, Marty Heebner, for one trip. I was nailed as a dilettante in the *New York Times* because I was trying to help the cause. That's the kind of mentality. You write something good about Chiapas. "Well, you're a white guy. What do you know? You got to be Mexican. You're rich. He's poor." I mean, they will shred you in a thousand different ways.

That's the media police. That's what's going on in this country. It's part of that Anglo mentality that's inhibiting and controlling the establishment of this country. It's disgusting, and it's a real problem, and so it turns kids off. How do kids get the strength within to write what they really feel? How do these guys and girls here know what they really feel? First of all, they've got to get in touch with their feelings, and second of all, they've got to have access to people who are outspoken. We need those Chayefskys who are as mad as hell. We need people saying what they mean. Sidney Lumet can make five hundred good movies, but if that guy ever says what he means, I'd like to be there. [*laughter*]

LEW: Questions, questions?

STUDENT: If you're not Oliver Stone and you're writing those movies, what do you need to do to get it made? Get an actor attached first? Most of our movies would be rejected.

OLIVER: I think if you wrote something of that nature, you're going to have a problem. And that's the problem. And I think you guys know it, and that's why you won't write anything about Chiapas or about a working-class stiff who wants to go on strike or has bad working conditions. "Who cares?" they're going to tell you. "Downer." "Boring." Don't buy into it. That's a hard one, though. Write one of those. And then you might feel a little softer and maybe try to do a comedy or something. Comedy films they love. And anything with a kiss. A sappy kiss they'll buy.

MARTY: Because Oliver brought up the trip to Chiapas, I remember I said something, too, on that trip, and I just want to hear what you think of it. I said that in order to tell great stories, you have to live the stories to tell.

OLIVER: Well, you don't have to be Ernest Hemingway. You can do it in your own living room. You can have your own life. You can create a life, too.

LEW: Can you create a life so you don't get behind the Bel Air gates actually or metaphorically and gain a working-class mentality?

OLIVER: I think the greatest enemy of creativity is actual luxury, not actual poverty. Luxury is very insidious, and it grows on you. You fall into comfort traps all the time. I flatter myself by saying, "No." I really feel I'm outside of Hollywood. I'm not a part of it. But perhaps I'm deluding myself in some ways. Staying honest with yourself is a lifelong task, not just as a writer, but as a human being. It's very tough.

LEW: Do you have certain devices you use? I mean, you used to go away to a museum, and now you don't have the time. Do you consciously do things to stay in touch with humanity, like Steinbeck's *Travels with Charlie*, schlepping across the United States with his dog?

OLIVER: I also travel a lot, and traveling helps me free myself. When I travel, I meet people left and right. I'm anonymous. I go a lot to Asia and a lot to Europe, mostly Asia, and I disappear in the crowd, and it's good. Research is also a good place. If you can get out into the field and do some research, you'll meet people on another level, and that is good.

LEW: Rob?

ROB: Knowing you wanted to direct as much as you wanted to write, did you find yourself writing differently than if you were a writer without the director dream? I mean, I'm like you. I want to write as a director. Did you find that your scripts were more slanted to directing more than scripts you read by other writers?

OLIVER: No, I studied the form. I went and looked at all the Epstein screenplays. James Agee's *The African Queen* was another model. I read the Fellini scripts *8½* and *Julieta* and *La Dolce Vita*. I really studied the form. I really thought it was fun. It was like going to architecture school. I had the instinct of a writer. I had a lot of passion for this book, so I didn't doubt the ability I had for the content. It was just a question now of play with, "How do you write the screenplay? Make the building? How do you structure the building?" Because that's what it is. It's architecture. The director is the engineer who puts it up, the head of the job, and the writer is the architect. He's the one who draws it.

STUDENT: At this point in your career, have you reached a certain level of power where you can get things done where maybe starting out you couldn't? Are there still projects you censor yourself on? Are there still things you'd like to do that you dare not?

OLIVER: Oh man, you're really off on that question. You've no idea. You see me in a way that's probably much larger than I am. My power is limited. I've never been a commercial director.

Certain movies I did made it through, but some didn't. There's more failure than success, believe me. It's always been hard for me. I've always had to make certain deals to make those movies. The moment they know you want to make a movie, they have you by the balls, you see.

The only way you can convince them to give you everything you want is to convince them that you don't give a shit about making the movie. [*laughter*]

LEW: Harriet Frank Jr. said that the sexiest word in Hollywood is *no*. These people don't need to know that because they're not yet at the point where they can say no.

OLIVER: I want to make the point that power is money in this business. Money is power. Or perception. Scorsese has power because of perception. Spielberg has power because he's delivered time and again. Barry Levinson and Barry Sonnenfeld is probably the hottest director right now. He's another Spielberg. Steve has done that. He's given back. Those are the type of directors that can get something done.

I took a hit, but I knew I would have to take one eventually because, I mean, well, I got away with *JFK*, which was a pretty outrageous statement at the time. Still is. I used the power of that success to make *Nixon*, essentially. But I took the hit because no one went to *Nixon* commercially. Then, when that was over, you see, they closed down on me pretty fast. I was developing something over at Disney with Joe Roth on Martin Luther King, and you could see, the moment *Nixon* flopped, the wind shifted. It's never overt. It was subtle, but it had shifted. And I got the message. And it would be very hard for me to do another type of movie like that right now. That's the way it works. Their memories are short, though, and that's the way the game is and always was.

STUDENT: If you had carte blanche and you could go make a $200 million movie and it could be about anything you wanted and you were even fairly sure it would do well, what would you do?

OLIVER: Oh wow. I'd probably have to think about that for a while. I could get into the story of my life.

STUDENT: For $200 million—

OLIVER: Well, probably Alexander the Great, if I could figure out how to do it. We've been working on that but didn't get the screenplay right. Noriega' s another one we worked on. We had a screenplay that was okay, and Pacino and I were rehearsing it around the table. We both agreed after one reading it had a problem; after two readings, we both rolled our eyes and said, "There's no way we can make this movie." We back out after $3 million into the movie. And I'm glad we did because it would've cost $15 million, and it would have missed. So it's better to lose the three.

LEW: Is screenwriting an art, or is it architecture as you said?

OLIVER: Architecture is an art, you know. They say it is, especially today. If you put your vision into, it becomes an art. If you don't, it isn't.

LEW: Are there secrets to screenwriting? Jane Campion, when I asked her that question, said that she really didn't quite understand the man with his charts in one of the screenwriting books. But she said that she got a great deal for her screenwriting life through Flannery O'Connor. Are there certain people that have been influential, certain readings in your own development?

OLIVER: Oh yes. Unfortunately, I've neglected fictional literature for a while. I'm on my case on that.

LEW: Did you get involved with Aristotle when you were starting out or Egri or any of those people?

OLIVER: I studied Aristotle in school, and I dipped back in once or twice. I'm not particularly literate anymore. The person who wrote that book is—well, was—very literate. That's part of the reason I went back last year to do more work on it because it was a pleasure to live in that world again and to read again.

LEW: Ecclesiastes, Solomon wrote, "I set my mind to know wisdom and to know madness and folly. I realize that this is also striving after the wind because in much wisdom, there is much grief, and increasing knowledge results in increasing pain."

OLIVER: Knowledge equals pain equals suffering.

LEW: It is so special to have you here for this 434 class because you say so much of what I believe as a writer, a professor, a man. Of course, being a child of the '60s, your being here is meaningful to me for that alone. And I also try to instill the passion. The passion. Forget about box office. The passion you've shown us today is so special because at the beginning of the quarter four weeks ago, I said, "We're going to learn from a variety of Oscar-winning screenwriters." And when I said, "Oliver Stone," around this table, I heard ten collective breaths catch in an "Oh. My. God." intake. That was exciting to me and I hope exciting to you.

To be able to get such gasps means these people have a clear touchstone with the passion you've conveyed to them in your films and now today.

You are much too fucking worthy of a meaningless "Goodbye and thank you," so we now give you a meaningful, "Goodbye and thank you, Oliver Stone." [*laughter and applause*]

8

Irving Ravetch and Harriet Frank Jr.

Irving and Harriet have a truly happy marriage, a beacon for all of us who work with collaborators. You can see it in their thoughtful responses and questions within this dialogue. They were married for forty-six years, and Harriet and Frank have gone to their reward, no doubt, still working together.

Rubin Carson, a comedy writer, and I were delighted to be invited to breakfast at Irving and Harriet's abode. Rib-busting dialogue ensued between the three of us, the frivolity of which often came from Irving. I was a laughing fool, but the laughing subdued once Harriet appeared. She is the leader that keeps one focused on the page.

Irving and Harriet penned dozens of iconic films, receiving Oscar nods for *Hud* and *Norma Rae*, as well as accolades for *The Long Hot Summer*, *Conrack*, and *The Reivers*. I am thrilled to have the opportunity to show Irving and Harriet off to you. More importantly, by my dime, their wisdom tops all in this treatise.

LEW: Irving Ravetch and Harriet Frank Jr.—a team. Very few people have teamed up for drama in this age. It has something to do with being married.

IRVING: Everything, Lew.

LEW: Let's start thusly: The 434 screenwriting warriors here are always trying to figure out what the movie is about—not what the story's about but what the movie is about. The story and the movie are practically always two separate things. At what point do you try and focus on what you're really trying to accomplish in your script?

HARRIET: I'll let my senior start.

IRVING: It's hard to generalize because each script is so special. Everything we both set out to do is very subjective. We're attracted very often by a character, so obviously that character must represent something, and something extremely important. We tend to minimize plot. Quite often, we are more interested in the complexity and ambiguity of characters who follow or drive adventure. We almost willy-nilly throw them into the plot because we think that would accommodate some kind of solution. Basically, we are interested in the character, which is another way of saying the meaning of the piece is who and what is that character.

LEW: Do you intellectualize the theme early on or never?

HARRIET: Never. It has very little to do with what we do.

IRVING: We have no intellect.

HARRIET: Irving speaks for himself here.

LEW: You did not start out on the stage but in American literature right here at UCLA.

IRVING: I wanted to be a playwright. I began at the age of eight.

HARRIET: I worked for money. I wanted to be a novelist and a short-story writer. I fell into writing through nepotism because my mother was an editor. When I graduated from college, I said, "What do I do next?" My mother said, "Guess what? I can get you $60 a week to be a screenwriter."

LEW: Was she a film editor or a story editor?

HARRIET: She was a story editor, and a very good one, working for Louis B. Mayer at MGM.

IRVING: Pardon me, let me tell about that because it may have some bearing. She was the storyteller when she worked at MGM. Her mother would come home, read books all weekend, extract the movie stories, and tell them to the board of eight or ten members on Mondays for an hour.

LEW: Like a reading hour for children at the library?

IRVING: And through extraction, they would make a movie.

HARRIET: She could find in a novel one of the stories to make a film. Very often, when producers would get into trouble with scripts or writers, they would come back and ask her to help. She was also not married to an idea of a very formalized structure. She was interested in an idea that would begin with an exciting leading character, like the film *Norma Rae*, which centered on a woman's life. Our attraction was to the character because she was a tough, irreverent, working-stiff kind of woman who was extorted, uneducated, and who would grab hold of somebody and turn them around.

The initial impact for us was *Hud*. The idea of the antihero with an attractive face came to us, but it was in the McMurtry novel. There has been critical comment that the story doesn't really power the movie the way it did in the *Hud* novel. Movies aren't necessarily powered by a story line as much as they were one time. They often are empowered more by the interaction of people.

IRVING: We consider *The Crying Game* to be one of the best movies ever because we thought it was original and exciting. We find it to be about tolerance, another form of love. *The Crying Game* doesn't seem like or a story or a plot to us. It's a story of a relationship between a man and a transvestite. Very, very unusual and very sparkling.

HARRIET: The great impact of that movie is that it became a story of all kinds of humanity and what happens when you're confronted with somebody who is a human being in a human situation. That would be a revolutionary: a black man at the beginning, then a transvestite comes in later in the story. We could reduce that to a plot line, but you noticed Neil Jordan rambled very widely. He told me it could have been two movies: one movie of a man's relationship with a transvestite, sort of everyman's touched by all sorts of circumstances, and this finally powered the movie more than the event did to me. The humanity of the man is really what you're left with in that movie. The feeling he was opting to make you feel that any human condition should be viewed powerfully. He got to be very big because of it. That's our particular thought. Another movie we liked very much this year was *Flirting*, a Canadian movie. Has anyone seen that?

There's another wonderful film by a young actor, writer, which I recommend to all. It's called—

IRVING: *Midnight Clear.*

HARRIET: *Midnight Clear.*

IRVING: Nobody has seen that?

HARRIET: And it could have been a very conventional war story, but because you were so invested in the characters, it became something else.

IRVING: There was no plot in it at all, but it was a marvelous, sensitive look at a platoon in action during the First World War. Can you imagine? I mean, what could be more stereotypical than that? It's terrific.

I want to say a little bit on intellectualizing. We work a lot with Marty Ritt, the director, who has been one of the founders of the Group Theater. So his is a historical figure, as well as a wonderful man and great director. He wished when he made a movie that the only people who saw it were children, and they would raise their faces to you, and there would only be wonder and awe. There's not intellect inhibiting them or moving them or stopping them or influencing them at all. It is all emotion. Marty felt that was what drama was all about. Your best chance at making something or doing something important is to have emotion or power. Those are two elements that a really important script or movie has to have. Children gave him that feeling.

LEW: That ties in with some French cinema. People try and say we are better screenwriters in America, but it is true that we are not confined by intellect. I've said to the class that Billy Sunday, who you know to be the forerunner of Billy Graham, said, "You can have their heads. I want their hearts."

HARRIET: Which is not to say there haven't been some brilliant movies that are totally intellectual.

IRVING: One of the sexiest things we agree we've seen for pure sexuality was a man sitting beside a woman in bed and just talking about sex for twenty minutes. It's thrilling!

LEW: How important is sensuality in cinema?

IRVING: That's what it's all about!

HARRIET: Well, I think sex is the thing that rivets an audience the most. More than machine-gun fire. The tension generated can be a wide range of emotion. It can be intellectual companionship. It can be sensual. But in theater, I think when you get the most rapt attention is when sex comes through some kind of relationship.

LEW: Is violence, psychological violence, something you think about?

HARRIET: When you ask about violence, I think the most thrilling moments in the movie have to do with the war between the sexes. It's just keeping the kitchen knives out of it, as far as I'm concerned.

IRVING: What is your question about violence?

LEW: I hypothesize that there are two primary colors a writer has to work with: sex and violence. It's clearly true in Shakespearean and Greek theater. If you don't have one or the other or both, there's no movie.

IRVING: Well, the word *violence* has become debased. We all use corpses in movies, but if you change that word to *conflict*, I don't think you could make a movie without it. I hate to make rules. No rules. I take that back, but most drama means conflict.

LEW: So you will not write a scene without conflict?

HARRIET: Better not try.

LEW: I love the simplicity of Aristotle. Beginning, middle, and end. This, for me, is the bible for performance and drama. But just as there's a beginning, middle, and end to stories, characters, and plots, I have always hypothesized that you have to have a classic sense of beginning, middle, and end in every scene. Do you agree? And if so, do you do it consciously?

HARRIET: I think it's impossible to formulate a formula. I think it's again like actors, who do things intuitively. An actor will intuitively find what they want and go for it. I think writers do the same. I'm not sure you cut out a conscious pattern.

IRVING: I'll go further. We have never asked each other how to do a beginning, middle, and end.

LEW: For a story or a scene?

IRVING: Either.

HARRIET: And we have had our heads hammered to the floor.

IRVING: We have trusted our intuitions to have the thing develop, to have the momentum, to have it emulate, and to have it be a conglomerate. I must tell you at the same time, we don't write scripts that we aren't wildly, wildly enthusiastic about.

LEW: *Long Hot Summer*. You rewrote a script Faulkner tried to write. What did you bring to it?

HARRIET: We were very irreverent. The novel *Long Hot Summer* was as brilliant as all of Faulkner. I mean, I consider him America's finest writer. What we brought to it was a kind of screenplay structure, bless his heart, he never had followed before. We were not reverent about the book, and I think when you come across a classic that is offered to you and you have to make a film out of it, without vulgarizing or destroying it, you have to have a certain degree of irreverence. It's not written in concrete, so we took the villain of the piece and turned him into a hero.

IRVING: We're talking about *The Hamlet* incident.

HARRIET: And he never objected. You are confronted with a piece of material that had a lot of robust Americana, which we love. It had possibilities, which he didn't have. There are all kinds of signposts in that novel, things you can take and turn on an ear if you were a fairly arrogant American screenwriter, which is exactly what we did. I think you have to proceed that way.

When you are adapting a book, you have to be very audacious and not be afraid. I wouldn't take a Cather story and flip it around too much. There are certain things that are very elegant in their own form and shouldn't be messed around with and vulgarized or changed or taken liberties with. Once a book is purchased for a movie, the author who sells that book has in effect taken their hands off of it. Whether they loathe what you do or love what you do, there are certain freedoms that generally follow. You can do whatever you think necessary.

IRVING: To clarify a little, *Barn Burning* is a Faulkner story by itself. We got the rights to *Barn Burning* in order to provide the background to Ben Quick in *Long Hot Summer*. This is why we initially find him on the road as a nomad. Then we also took Faulkner's *The Hamlet* and really stood it on its head; very little of *The Hamlet* remained. New screenwriters will be happy to think about this. We got a nice check for residuals today from Germany.

LEW: When you say *irreverent*, what is the criteria to being irreverent?

HARRIET: For instance, *The Hamlet* was a story about a man who had an obsession with a cow, not material Twentieth Century Fox would wish to make a movie about.

IRVING: That's maybe not true because I've heard Joe Eszterhas, who has made millions and millions on screenplays, just wrote one about a man falling in love with a cow. It's the president of the United States.

LEW: Did you see *Basic Instinct*?

IRVING: Ice-pick movie?

HARRIET: I had problems, let me tell you. I am about up to here with violence. I have made serious withdrawals from violence, and if you sat down and compiled a list of the one hundred greatest movies ever made, I don't think you'd find these types of things there. People will see *Wuthering Heights* for centuries; same goes for *Pride and Prejudice*.

IRVING: Tell them why you hate violence.

HARRIET: Everyone hates it.

IRVING: I like it.

HARRIET: You wonder how we collaborate. Many times it's gratuitous, it's exploitative, and it doesn't serve any higher moral purpose. If you were talking about *Crime and Punishment*, that's something else. That has a big resounding wall you can identify, and those movies are really about greater inner conflicts that arise out of this violence. The ice-pick stuff—it's just not contributing.

LEW: Two or three people in this room today will be contributing. They will become professional screenwriters. What can you say to inspire people to walk out of this classroom and reach for something other than a key to their Mercedes?

HARRIET: Work out of conviction. That's all that I can tell you. The sexiest word in Hollywood is *no*, and if you say that to someone, you're going to be more alluring than if you say, "This is the greatest thing since cornflakes." Only work out of conviction, meaning only write a script you're very interested in. If you think a slam-bang thriller is the greatest experience of your life, go for it. If you want to make a contribution to the understanding of the human condition, do it. But never do something glitzy or slick just because you think it will make a buck because you will never make a buck if the personal passion isn't there. Reach as far as you can to the original, and only do what you believe in. That's the whole smorgasbord. It has got to be something that you make an artist's commitment to do. Anything else, and it will most definitely not get you a Mercedes.

I can assure you that every studio head thinks they are as good of a writer as Jane Austen. She writes out of vain conviction: "I can do it, I believe in it, and I love it." If she had written to simply get a Mercedes, she wouldn't have gotten a skateboard. That writer who wrote *The Crying Game* wasn't sitting in a room somewhere, thinking about how much it would make them. It was a burning passion that brought that movie to paper. Anything less than this is a waste of time personally, financially, creatively, and emotionally. Period.

STUDENT: You stated you came from a short-story and novel background. When you transitioned into screenwriting, did you find the same flow you found in novel and short-story writing? Did you ever feel that screenwriting wasn't as valid?

HARRIET: Don't ever be afraid to transition because it's not as silly as you think. You're not in command of the world in the same way as you are as a novelist, but you'll find it's a wonderful medium once you learn how to have this medium at your command. You can make things happen in a screenplay that you cannot make happen on a printed page. I would say they are equals in terms of using your gift. If you're a good novelist, you will, undoubtedly make a good screenwriter because the same storytelling gifts and talents are operative through its different form. You're not as in command as when you're a novelist. That's totally your world, and you can move people around with complete autonomy, whereas in screenwriting it may be more collaborative. Well, it's always collaborative, with concessions for certain elements. But certainly don't be afraid to move from novels to screenwriting because it isn't that difficult.

STUDENT: So, all of the interior, exterior, description—it doesn't break your flow?

HARRIET: Well, if you were taking it from a novel you wrote and it's dramatic, it would be a direct transition. Very often, if it's very interestingly written and we're adapting, we will lift entire chunks of dialogue directly into the screenplay from a novel. The screenplay isn't so different; it's dialogue without the narrative prose. Be bold. Don't be afraid of it. It's not really so different.

LEW: Irving, give your take on the morality of being a screenwriter. We've heard Harriet. Do you have any additional information?

IRVING: Yes, I regretfully have to disagree. If you're a craftsman, you can do anything. For many, many years before television was mainstream or even present, movies were the only game in town. Writers were under contract to seven or eight major studios. Their job was to show up and punch a time clock. Literally, punch a time clock at nine a.m. and were then handed an idea, and had to write a script. Out of that came—well, you had Julius Epstein here, didn't you?

LEW: Yes.

IRVING: Was he honest with you?

LEW: We had a talk about punching time cards. He and Philip went in one day, and Jack Warner came up to them and told them that their script was terrible. Julius said, "I don't understand, Jack. We came in at 9:00 a.m. every day."

IRVING: Right. I have a feeling—this may be a bad example—but *Casablanca* has achieved a tremendous cult popularity throughout the world. At the time he may not have liked it very much and had a lot of trouble with it, and it didn't work. I think they looked at each other and said, "This is crap. What are we doing?" See, this is an ace craftsman who can make a living.

HARRIET: I'm not talking about starving.

IRVING: Well, in a sense you were.

HARRIET: No, if you are in a library and you say, "I'm now going to sit down and write a screenplay, which my agent is going to take to fifty-two people, and I know exactly where this is going to go," I think that's a recipe for failure. I think with an attitude of "This is my screenplay, and I'm not going to send this baby out into the world until it's ready," you have a much better chance of success.

IRVING: How do you explain the fact that when you were under contract with—

HARRIET: These kids aren't going to be under contract.

IRVING: How do some great movies get made?

HARRIET: Times are different. First place, they'll all go home and write. They all have written screenplays, which they are now going to send out into the marketplace, and they will become projects. Nobody hands a screenwriter material anymore. Everything is a package. They're going to write a screenplay, and their agent is going to say, "This is great for Jack Nicholson," and it's going to go to Jack Nicholson, and he's going to read it, and God willing, you're going to sell it for a lot of money and have a Mercedes.

IRVING: Yes, they can be saying, "Here's something I really, really believe in or something I can do a fabulous job with. On the other hand, here's an idea that is pretty commercial, and it's a piece of crap, I know, but I feel we can lick it and make a lot of it."

HARRIET: Well, my dear, you can do both. I concede to my collaborator.

LEW: Actually, we have a professor here, Dan Pyne, who wrote *Pacific Heights* and *White Sands*. He also came out of our program eight years ago. Dan informed students here, "This is your best opportunity to be free. You may go out into the world and do things you're asked to do, and it may be something you're not particularly thrilled to write about, so this is your opportunity to be as good and as free as you can be."

HARRIET: You bet! That's why we're here!

IRVING: And the money.

LEW: This is truly an idealistic setting we offer here. Harriet, you use the word *art*. Irving uses the word *craft*. Where do art and craft begin and end? Or do you each have different interpretations on screenwriting?

HARRIET: Well, I'm not sure craft comes any other way but by doing it, you know? You get to be a fine actor by acting. You get to be a writer by writing. You learn in the process, taught by your excellent teacher here. But art? What is art? Art is doing your craft to your exquisite best. Then it becomes art. You can learn the alphabet and do it, but if you're well read, and this is a point I would like to make to all writers and screenwriters and every kind of writer: The best way to learn to be a writer of any kind, it requires you to read the best writers. The more widely read you are, the more you'll know about art. You may absorb intuitively. I'm not sure if there's a formula but to be well read is the primary tool of your trade.

LEW: When you all are writing, do you defer to Irving's craft?

HARRIET: Defer?

LEW: Does he defer to your art?

HARRIET: Collaboration is a very special thing.

IRVING: There is absolutely no ego.

LEW: Do you have fun?

HARRIET: Oh, yeah.

IRVING: We enjoy it. We love it.

HARRIET: Even when he says it's lousy.

IRVING: Even until this day, we love it.

LEW: So, the idea of being a writer before a keyboard, where beads of sweat stream down your face—this isn't something you associate with at all?

IRVING: No.

HARRIET: If you feel like that, then you shouldn't be writing that.

IRVING: I know one or two guys that say writing is anguish. One writer, a very successful writer, says writing for him is like having words driving out of the ends of his fingers. Isn't that a terrible image?

LEW: Is he trying to get someone to nurture him?

IRVING: No, it was truly a painful process for him.

LEW: He's trying to get sympathy. He's got to love it. Otherwise, you cannot come out with anything good.

STUDENT: What if you're encouraged to write something special that happened to you, and the minute you start thinking about it, you get an assignment? Do you feel like a frog every minute that you're writing that assignment?

HARRIET: I think the best friends of writers are writers. The best learning tools of writers are writers. When you read first-class literature of the world, you see how you move from yourself to outside of yourself. That's how you learn to do well. It's like learning language. If you focus entirely on yourself, you're going to struggle. If you want to get outside of yourself, you have to study how the great ones do it. There's no other way. You read something by Shakespeare, by Shaw, by Austen or Chekhov or Faulkner, and you will see what the creative imagination is capable of doing. You learn to do it by seeing how they do it. If you're a painter, it's a different matter. A writer had to extend him- or herself the way a writer extends in the company of writers. That's all I can say. I don't think there are any other tricks other than to subconsciously absorb the gifts and tricks and passion and vision and everything else that a great writer presents.

LEW: Would you write something that has happened to you in real life? Would you personalize stories as I have done? I didn't research it; I lived it. You really want it to be similar to a personal source of inspiration, or as Faulkner says, "If it is irrelevant to reality, it is irreverent to the drama."

IRVING: Very good advice.

STUDENT: How do you go about collaborating?

HARRIET: Well, first you marry him.

IRVING: Not necessarily.

HARRIET: A collaboration is a very strange thing. Irving put his finger on it earlier. The bottom line of collaboration is lack of ego. You don't want to bully each other. You have to see each other's strengths and mend each other's weaknesses. You do that in a tolerant way. It's the only way collaboration works. We do a line-for-line collaboration. Many collaborating writers will pick scenes and exchange them and polish them with each other's work. We do a line-for-line collaboration, which means we speak the dialogue out loud.

IRVING: I'm at the typewriter, and she paces. We have long preparation discussion before typing and pacing. We really examine the characters, so we know them very, very well. Then we begin to work out the story. We make a little step outline of thirty for forty scenes, so we know how they run and how they accumulate. Then I sit at the typewriter, she paces, and then as she says it out loud, we throw it back out into the air. You know, first line of the piece. "That's no good. Next." We try again. Each of us throws out something until both of us say, "Ah, that's it. Write it down."

HARRIET: And in the end, we aren't sure who wrote it.

IRVING: But the flow that you talked about begins magically and, if we're lucky, out of that process.

HARRIET: They're the characters' voices, really.

STUDENT: The first couple of times you collaborated, was it difficult to get over all of the little instructions that you put into the script?

HARRIET: May I tell you all, and don't let your feelings get hurt, the instructions are disregarded completely. The dialogue is another matter. If you're writing a scene for a novel, and John meets Jane, and they have dialogue, you have to hear the dialogue. Once you have established the place, the people speak to each other in the same way that they do a novel. What is missing from it is the editorial idea that builds in a novel. You support that with the interior first-person monologue. In a screenplay, you are directing thought to the exterior monologue. But it's the same kind of talk. I could have a conversation with you right now that I could put into a novel, and you could take it and put it into your screenplay.

STUDENT: Is it gratifying for you when you don't have interior monologue?

HARRIET: Well, if you're asking me if riches to riches is exciting, there are virtues to both. It's a lot of fun to see a thing come alive on-screen. But everything—the camera, the actors, everything—is in view for the piece of work. It's wonderful to be God and to have a whole world you're moving around as a novelist, which is private and does not have a director or actor looking over your shoulder and saying, "I don't like that line." As a screenwriter, you're more of a schlepper or at the mercy of multiple cooks.

LEW: I think the most important thing is the idea and the characters. The second-most important and difficult step is the outline. The least important and difficult thing is the actual script. Although this is the most time consuming, it's the easiest part. Is the first draft especially important to you two? I mean, if you have gotten the outline in place, do you write it fast to deal with your subconscious and intuition? Do you have a lot of improving to do after this draft?

IRVING: We do a lot of thinking and talking. You want to hear something very strange?

LEW: Always.

IRVING: We have written for forty years, and this means a lot of scripts. For us, it takes ten weeks, all of it, always ten weeks. I can think of one script we did in six.

LEW: Do you have an actual page count goal each day?

IRVING: No, it just works out that way.

STUDENT: Do you mean for the first draft?

RUBIN CARSON: They go to the store and buy 120 pages. I've seen them. I lived with them. They get up at 10:00 a.m. and go to make their purchase.

HARRIET: I beg your pardon, it's 8:30 a.m.

RUBIN: I've never seen them work nights. I've never seen them work weekends. They do it up, and they deliver it and get millions of dollars.

IRVING: We've worked nights. We've worked weekends. We have a funny bias against rewriting. We don't like to do it.

HARRIET: Well, we rewrite for ourselves.

IRVING: We rewrite as we go. We'll do a scene, and if we don't like it, we do it again, so we're rewriting as we go.

LEW: When you say you'll do it again, do you mean you'll come at it from another direction?

HARRIET: Hopefully but not always.

IRVING: In fact, if it's a rewritten script, quite a few times. But not the whole script; just piece by piece.

STUDENT: You mentioned you've had scripts where you love the characters, but when you hand the script in, they say it's not dramatic enough. What do you interpret this to mean? What do you try and do to make it more dramatic?

IRVING: In one case, the script really had no conflict. It had two talking heads for the entire 120 pages.

HARRIET: One hundred fifty pages.

IRVING: Well, we invented a new character. There was a man and a woman, falling in love, having an affair, and finally making a commitment to one another. So we changed it to have the woman divorced, and we brought in her ex-husband to create the conflict. We had three people going at each other, pretty hot and heavy. Immediate and big conflict.

LEW: Throughout the entire story?

HARRIET: He came in on page 30 or so.

LEW: That's always one of my crafty things. When the scene just sits and yawns at you, I very often bring in a third character for that particular scene. What are some of the tricks of the trade that you have discovered and utilized? Oh, another for instance, when Bill Walsh said, "At the end of *Old Yeller*, let's kill the dog. We can bring the puppies out from under the porch." That line has become industry shorthand.

HARRIET: Well, if you have an impasse, my mother was a very good editor, and she used to remind me to turn around. If you're heading for a happy or predictable ending and you know the audience will be well ahead of you, turn it around. If you are heading to a final scene of predictable falling in love, don't have them say it.

You have that in *Norma Rae*, for example. We got lots of very strange responses about why he doesn't kiss her. We were determined to have the conflict between them from the outside. It wasn't necessary between the two people. We were not going to succumb to conventional falling into each other's arms in order to physically express an emotion. So then you could head to that scene and write it straight on with, the "I love you." Or you can simply say, "You're not going to fall for that same old manner of wrapping it up."

The key to *The Crying Game* was that he set up conflict that got resolved in a surprising way. Everybody thought he was going to shoot him in the back; he didn't. He went to meet the girl, and the girl was not a girl. It resolved itself but in a different way. Keep turning everything on their ear, it's a tool that may help you when you feel a story or scene doesn't have enough life.

IRVING: I think the best example in our own work was in *Long Hot Summer*. In *The Hamlet*, there's a character who, in my opinion, is the most vicious, evil, horrifying, disgusting character in American literature. I challenge you to find someone worse. We made him into Paul Newman, a romantic hero.

STUDENT: You were saying the characters are the core of your story. I understand that. I'm struggling more with structure. Do you see the screenplay in terms of the entire story, or do you say each scene must do something? Even though you may not consciously think of structure, it's obvious you understand it because by page whatever, if something hasn't started, something is very wrong.

HARRIET: You do, but I would say this. First, before you put pen to paper, you conceive the architecture of that piece, the structure. It's very dangerous, although lots of very good writers say, "Fade in," and begin to see where they go. Most create structure first, the architecture, which you mustn't view as extremely rigid because you will run into icebergs and discrepancies and roadblocks that will surprise even you. See the script in its entirety before you begin. Then each scene really does move the story along and even mold the story. Once the characters are thoroughly conceived, you'll find the scenes you like will push an audience from scene to scene to scene. You will get the movement you are talking about. You will also get the event because it will have a certain inevitability.

IRVING: And obviously the little step outline enables you to see the whole movie. You see, if it lacks events or drama, something is not happening soon enough. They are not being plunged into conflict early on. This helps to see where it might be weak or needs help.

STUDENT: What, in your mind, makes a good character?

HARRIET: They're no different from characters in life. You walk into a supermarket, and you see a woman with a little boy, and she gives the boy a smack. You say to yourself, "That woman!" Or you sit down at a lunch table, and the man next to you says, "I'm divorcing my wife." Everything that makes people live, and movie in life also makes them live and move on-screen. There's no such thing as a blind person on the screen that is not recognizable in life. There's no division.

IRVING: Beyond that, what would make you fall in love with a man?

HARRIET: Precisely. The same things that would make you fall in love with an actor on-screen.

IRVING: I prefer foreign movies to American movies because American movies, God knows, have really been responsible for the whole form, if it is an art form. There's a vitality and masculinity and a power in American films that no other country has yet achieved. The Clark Gables and the Spencer Tracys—it's very male dominated. But it's also very plot driven, which, you've gathered by now, is something we don't particularly admire.

We love, and have all of our lives, Italian and French cinema because they tend not to drive their viewer as fast and as hard as American cinema. We've been told again and again by various producers, "Drive your film. Get rid of extraneous excess." Well, we like the movies that pause and recognize the human things. The weaknesses and ambiguities. The ambivalence, too.

HARRIET: Monopoly.

IRVING: Yes, human things make people more interesting.

HARRIET: When you talk about what makes a good character, you should see this very good French film called *La Vie*. It's about a woman who is suddenly widowed. You live next door to this woman. Everything you see about her is true to life. Every woman sits and says, "Am I going to be able to pay my rent this month?" or "Now my brother-in-law is going to come over and make a pass at me. What am I going to do about that?" All is recognizable in the people you know.

IRVING: I would like to populate our world with people, as opposed to symbols.

HARRIET: These manufactured robots of what an audience already expects of a type. When a movie really grips and embraces you, you will always see the people you know in life.

STUDENT: You aren't creating a new vocabulary of emotions with characters.

HARRIET: What movies do you laugh and shed a tear in?

STUDENT: But it's not always the same laughter; it's not always the same tear.

HARRIET: Oh, course not. Not all of your friends are alike, are they? One of them is stubborn, and you love her for that. One is a heel, and you won't go near him. All that is the same spectrum you would put in a novel or put in a play or you would put into poetry or could put on the screen. There's no difference.

And where movies really fail, when they become mechanistic figures of the avenger, and that's fine for its genre. But if you're talking about a movie that really has vitality, it does from life. If Lew Hunter, who is an experienced teacher, says to you, "Look, this is a weakness I sense in your work. Let's talk about how we can shore it up," you listen with respect because he is imminently qualified to say that to you. If a very gifted director says, "This is a very interesting script, but there is a failure of emotion in the third act, and I want to talk to you," you'd be a fool not to listen and have an exchange about it.

STUDENT: Most of the people I've met unfortunately haven't been gifted.

HARRIET: There, you have said goodbye to the ungifted. Defend it where you can with the gifted.

LEW: Harriet used a phrase I have never heard before: "The sexiest word in Hollywood is *no*."

HARRIET: When I was a young writer, I worked for fifty bucks a week. This was under the minimum, and when a producer said to me, "This screenplay is not working." I would say calmly, as calmly as I would be able, "Why not?" And I would listen. I would make changes I could make, but when I got to the place where I couldn't out of conviction, I said, "I'm not the writer for this job." Believe me, I was looking for another job.

IRVING: Well, how do you account for your first credit, *Silver River?* One of the worst westerns ever seen?

STUDENT: When you make a script from a novel, what are the steps you use to pull your main story from the book?

HARRIET: Well, you hope you have a lot of help from the novel writer, and generally you do because something about it will grab you cinematically, and you'll say there is a good western in this book or there's a good love story. Sometimes, as I say, you'll turn it upside down, but a good novelist will generally present you with a stunning character or an off-the-wall situation or an interesting conflict or a thrilling setting or something that will make you say, "I can run with that."

STUDENT: So, you are saying that the best thing is to read it and immediately identify your favorite parts of the book and then say, "Okay, everything else will revolve around them."

HARRIET: Yes, that will happen: the thing that moves you emotionally and makes you excited or makes you laugh or makes you anything. Generally, if you're working from a book with a good writer, lots of things the good writer will suggest to you. There are wonderful books that cannot be adapted to the screen. On the other hand, some screenwriters are very clever about extracting elements from a good book. They find all sorts of critical scenes or say, "That's a good character, but suppose I made it a man." Or "Suppose it's a woman." You know, turn things around and around and around.

LEW: I think there's more tricks to the trade that we didn't quite exhaust sufficiently. Like, *The Hamlet* you mentioned turning on its ear. Anymore, dialogue where perhaps a character can ask another something in this obligatory scene becomes one that you have to obliterate to disguise the exposition.

IRVING: Well, you have to be very, very clever because those are the scenes that will stand out, and stand out badly.

HARRIET: If a scene feels that way, it shouldn't be there.

IRVING: But some have to be there, so you must be very clever.

HARRIET: I would say my best defense is again the character. The eccentricity, the wit, the passion of the character. You can get away with a lot and hide a lot in your character.

LEW: I say, when you are in a corner, look to your characters to get out. Don't look at your story. Also, rejoice when that happens. That is often when the wonderful things will come to mind.

HARRIET: I think that's true.

STUDENT: I am really attracted to what you were saying about character and finding your way through the story. One of the problems I've always had is that I love the characters, and I really struggle to get them into the situation.

HARRIET: I think your characters are your best friends in terms of both powering the movie and making it recognizable to you so that you are recreating the life that you know, and for the novelist, don't be afraid to make that leap. The tricks of the trade, I believe, you have more up your sleeve than you think you do.

STUDENT: What are some of the things that have helped you to get better?

HARRIET: Well, one that Irving pointed out, a very good director once said, "There was no conflict. The script was static and didn't move through a landscape." We had worked with him so long that it rang a bell. We went back and said he was absolutely right. I mean, what is this person up against? Why haven't we dramatized what he is up against? The was very illuminating. A good director will be a great help to you in that regard. The director is usually your best friend, your closest, most intimate collaborator because he or she is going to put it on the screen.

IRVING: The most helpful thing that was ever said to us, I think, was the same director said, "What is it about? Why make this? What's the point?" This is the bottom line. It must have meaning and be about something. Hopefully, something important.

HARRIET: You're not only going to get it from the producer and the director. You will also get it from the actors who think they can write better than you do. You're going to do have those pressures on you all of the time. Sometimes, though, an actor will be your best friend and say, "Why doesn't," or a director will say, "That can't happen." I know I sound very arrogant about scriptwriting because the reality is that making movies is a very collaborative medium.

LEW: Irving and Harriet have been honored with almost every award screenwriters can get, most importantly, the Laurel Award for lifetime achievement from the Writers Guild. There's a critic in Israel who likes to refer to screenplays as literature. I vehemently disagree with this, yet if there is an exception, the top major contributors to literature of the screen would be Irving and Harriet. We are delighted and honored that you came today.

HARRIET: Good luck to you all!

IRVING: Amen.

9

Tom Schulman

I am grateful to Tom Schulman for giving my grandson Adam the material that allows him to leap onto the nearest chair, table, sofa, or wherever there may be elevation. From that position or from some reawakened part of his mind, this allows him to proclaim the immortal *Dead Poets Society* mantra: "Oh captain, my captain!"

If this puzzles you, see the movie! The end result will be a story that will always stay in both your mind and heart and perhaps even change how you view the importance of the pursuit of the creative. This dialogue with Tom will give you a great deal of information about the frustrations of the "business." A friend of mine used to tell me the only business that matters is that which produces money. Of course, I responded with how much I loved "show business."

I want you to pay close attention to the last page of our time with Tom as you, too, will be reminded of the universal human condition and the naked-ness of screenwriting.

LEW: Written by Tom Schulman: *Dead Poets Society*. Wonderful Oscar, wonderful, wonderful. *Honey, I Shrunk the Kids*. The range here is interesting. *Second Sight. What about Bob?*

TOM: The idea came from Laura Ziskin and Alvin Sargent. Laura is a producer, and Alvin, a well-known, wonderful, famous Hollywood writer. Alvin got the idea from this Woody Allen line: "In August, everybody in New York gets a little mad because that's when shrinks go on vacation."

LEW: More Tom Schulman. *Medicine Man*. *8 Heads in a Duffel Bag*. *Dead Poets Society* was the first movie you got made?

TOM: *Second Sight* was actually before *Dead Poets Society* but released afterwards. Actually, it escaped.

LEW: *8 Heads in a Duffel Bag* is the first movie you've directed. I asked Billy Wilder when he was here, "Do you consider yourself a director or a writer?" He said, "Oh, a writer, of course. The directing is simply a way to continue the writing but in obviously a different form."

TOM: Anything Billy Wilder says works for me. When people ask me, "What do you do?" I say I'm a writer. I can't even bring myself to say director. He's right. Directing is writing in another form.

LEW: So, even working with the editor, ergo at the end of the picture, describe this.

TOM: Rewriting, totally.

LEW: Do you remember as a beginning writer when you said, "They're right. It's just blah, blah." Or whatever?

TOM: After the second friend read it, the first friend said, "Oh, this isn't working. I'm bored." I would shrug off the comments. When the second friend read it and would say, "This isn't working. I'm bored." Then I realized I'd better start rewriting and working on these things.

LEW: You actually bottomed out early in the process. It takes some people quite a while to get to that level of saying, "Oh my gosh. It's just simply words that can be changed." Now, if *Second Sight* was your first movie, tell me how many scripts you'd written?

One of our students, Brian Price, sold something about four months ago to Hal Lieberman, who is now at Universal, and Brian is a so-called first-time screenwriter. So, in class, I asked Brian, "How many scripts did you write to become a first-time screenwriter?" His reply was, "Ten." So Tom Schulman, how many scripts had you written prior to *Second Sight* being made?

TOM: If you count cowriting, six.

LEW: Did you grow up with the concept of becoming a writer?

TOM: It never even occurred to me to be a writer or get into film. I became interested in movies before I was interested in writing. I was actually interested in directing. Essentially, I started trying to use writing as a means to direct. Then I fell in love with the process.

LEW: Did you like the process in the beginning? As I understand, you directed *8 Heads in a Duffel Bag* very early in your career.

TOM: That's a hard question. I liked it sometimes. It was like being in jail for a year and a half. Every minute of every day is organized for you by someone else. They're helping you do something you want to do. They're making your movie, but once the process is in motion, you're up at six. You're there. I remember every day of the shoot I was driving out to Palmdale. It was 115 degrees every day in the middle of summer. And for some reason, no matter what time of the day I went there, three vans with Sierra Backpacking signs would go by on the way up to the mountains, and I'm just like, "God, I would do anything to get in one of those vans. Anything." I realized that it would be a year before I could get into one of those.

You sacrifice a lot whenever a movie gets made, particularly on a low budget. You get on the set every day, and you realize there are going to be problems, and they're not going to let you come back if you don't make your day, whether the star is late or it rains in the middle of the desert or some union hassle happens. Every day something like that happens. You say to yourself every morning when you wake up, "What am I going to lose today? What's going to be sacrificed?" You plan eighteen shots, and you get twelve, so something gets lost. It's demoralizing. Compromise. Compromise.

LEW: Julius Epstein was beside us, and he said that after every screening, because in the last half of his career he produced everything he wrote, he said after the first screening of the director's cut, he would immediately go and throw up. And I said, "Oh, you mean you'd already written it?" He said, "That's it. That's it." Now, obviously throwing up on the set is hardly something that would cause you to be considered less than a great leader.

TOM: Right. Right.

LEW: But let me ask if you ever get surprised that things actually turned out better than you had imagined when you were behind a blank screen?

TOM: Oh, yes. Usually the surprises came in rehearsals. Then you go out on the set and think, "Are the actors going to be able to get to that same place in the performance?" Occasionally, some wonderful stuff happens, even better than you got in rehearsals. The surprises are what makes it worth it all. Partly, anyway.

LEW: I've thought, "Oh my God. That actor is so fucking brilliant. Why didn't I write that in the script?"

TOM: I love actors who come up with great ideas, and sometimes they'll hammer you with something, and you'll go, "Oh, I see what they're getting at." You let them try it, and it's great. Just let them keep bringing stuff to the script.

LEW: When you're writing something early on, in terms of getting reactions, do you let people read it or have a table reading of the script to see how it sounds with people whose opinions you respect?

TOM: I did it with *8 Heads* but only after it was cast, not to hear how it worked as a script. And I did it with a script called *Holy Man*. It's useful. You can really see right away where the dead weight is and where to cut things out and where it's working.

LEW: When do you have the light bulb that pops on your head and say, "That's what I want to do. That's a good idea"? Does that come in an instant, or is that something that you mull a bit?

TOM: Both ways. There comes a moment when you're gradually compelled to write something. But with *8 Heads in a Duffel Bag*, it hit me like a lightning bolt. I was sitting, watching TV, and all of a sudden, I went, "Oh my God." I went straight to my computer and started writing. I just had a blast for three days. Others, I work on for years. I chew on ideas. I put them in drawers. I don't even think about them. Then one day, I wake up, and some other idea comes to me about that story, and I say, "That's what this thing's about. This is what this story needs." And I'm again drawn to the computer to start working.

LEW: How long did it take you to write the first draft of *Dead Poets Society*?

TOM: I wrote a draft of it a year before I wrote what became the movie. I try to write quickly mainly because I'm so anxious the story's not going to work. I just want to get it out there, so at least I can feel that sense of relief it's at least got a beginning, middle, and an end. I wrote the first draft of *Dead Poets* in a few weeks and read it and thought, "This is worthless." Basically, I threw it away. I put it in a drawer and never looked at it again until a year later, when I got that "Aha! Now I know what this is about!"

I sat down; back then I had a much more complicated note-taking system than I do now. I didn't have cards, but I would write ideas down and put them in a drawer. Then, when I was finally able to write, I would put the whole thing across the floor of the room like a giant outline, millions of notes all over the floor, and I'd walk around, repositioning, taking this note here and moving it over there, and I'd paste them in a book. The whole script would be about 180-page book with these strips of ideas. And then finally it was almost like the thing had written itself. I could just start on page 1, and it would take about two or three weeks to write the script.

LEW: We worked on two outlines before you came, Tom. It seems like my every other word was ragging on the students. "What's it about? What's it really, really about?" To use a line from fellow professor, Howard Suber, "What the story is about is generally not what the movie is about." Now, you put it away for a year, and then you say, "Aha! Now I know what it's about." How did you get to that, and what was "that"?

TOM: With *Dead Poets Society*, I think I made two mistakes in the first draft. One is the kids. I think I had the teacher. I knew what I wanted him to say, but I'd written kids who sort of weren't up to his level and didn't know what his message was. I had to go back and think, "Wait a minute. Who do I know in my life? Who are these kids really? Who can be affected by this?"

I basically recast all of those kids in the next draft, and I had been kind of toying with this notion of a trial or a student court to put that teacher up for the crime of his student's suicide. I had written this long, sort of trial, really. It would take place in the school. It would decide if this teacher was guilty. I realized, "Wait a minute. This is nonsense. For one thing, this doesn't happen, and for another thing, all that matters is whether these kids believe in him or not because they have been affected by him." I suddenly realized they stood up just as he had asked them to stand on top of their desks earlier in the movie. That would be it. I had the ending. I realized that was what the movie was about, the moment of the film.

LEW: The movie is about—say that again.

TOM: The theme of the movie is not just standing up for someone you believe in, but it's "Seize the day." Have the courage to act on your own beliefs. I think his whole philosophy was about creativity versus tradition. So to the extent they could express to him, they had gotten what he intended by standing up on their desks as opposed to watching him in a trial or testifying on his behalf. I used that as the ending of the movie, as a dramatic way of expressing the theme.

LEW: I love what you said earlier about the fact that the kids weren't up to him. They weren't open to what he had to give them because—isn't there a line, "and the teacher will come," in the last half?

SHELLEY: "When the student is ready, the teacher will appear."

LEW: "When the student is ready, the teacher will appear." Great. So this before us, Tom Schulman, is a collection of students. And we have a relationship to what your movie's about. And before us all are these small storyteller figures I put out in all of my 434 classes. They come from all around the world; some are gifts from some of my best and brightest; they are our storytelling deities. Are we in the oral tradition of storytelling, those of us who write movies?

TOM: Absolutely.

LEW: More than theater?

TOM: I think it's all the same really. We're just telling stories in different ways. Children's books, movies, television, although obviously, television and film are different.

LEW: Thornton Wilder says, "A dramatist is one who believes that the pure event and action involving human beings is more arresting than any comment that can be made upon it." I guess that's why I wound up writing screenplays because I didn't imagine that anything I had to say was more important that what could be shown.

TOM: I think we're defined by what we do, not what we say, at least as far as character is concerned. So I think, although what we say, hopefully, is consistent with what we do, our actions still speak louder than our words.

It's how people behave in a given circumstance that's more interesting to me than what they say. It also gets me off the hook for bad dialogue.

LEW: You're excited about being a screenwriter, aren't you?

TOM: It's a love-hate thing, you know.

LEW: What's love, and what's hate?

TOM: Hate is the anxiety of each time wondering whether the magic is going to happen or not. Whether I'm able to dig down to find something that keeps me excited while I'm doing it. Then hopefully it excites other people when they read it. But there's always fear of failure. Fear that whatever it is, the muse or whatever, is gone.

I had a little statue I kept over my computer when I was writing *Dead Poets Society*, and in the middle of shooting the movie, I gave it to Peter Weir, the director. I was exhausted. I don't know why, but I just said, "Here. Take this. It'll help you." And then I started thinking, "Oh my God, I need that thing back. How am I going to write from now on?" This sort of superstitious thing often hits me.

LEW: Well, it isn't superstition if you think in terms of writing for the Old Testament. Those cats never took name credit. They believed it all came from God. They were conduits, mediums. It wasn't until the New Testament, Matthew, Mark, they wanted credits.

TOM: Right, right.

LEW: They really felt they were instruments of God. And sometimes, don't you look at something and think, "This is better than I could ever really do as a mortal. Something happened here"?

TOM: I look back at half the stuff I've written and go, "I don't even recognize it as my own." I've dug through my old drawers, sometimes just to find old stories and say, "What is that? Who wrote this?" I mean literally, "Who wrote this?" I don't even remember this story. And my wife will say, "Oh no. Remember you telling me about it?" I don't remember a thing about it. I read it, and it's like someone else wrote it. It's bizarre, and it's usually bad. Then, back in the drawer.

LEW: Do you periodically find something that isn't bad and think, "My God. How could such a young child have put together these wonderful words?"

TOM: I'm still looking.

LEW: Don't you look back at some of the stuff you wrote early on and think, "Now, I've become more seasoned and become, I suppose, more cynical, more aware, and more dimensional. But God, there was freshness there"? Do you notice that?

TOM: I'm usually embarrassed by all that stuff, and I wish I had the chance to rewrite it.

LEW: Do you ever look at something and say, "That scene's perfect. I don't have to go back to that one"? Or do you ever see anything that's great?

TOM: I like some scenes, you know. I think the actors sometimes bring a life to something that I just never quite thought would be there. But I think part of what I must do is be critical of myself. Every day I look at a scene again, again, and again. I'm constantly trying to tweak and improve it, so I'm never really satisfied with it. I'm proud of them, but at the same time, I wish I could get in there and fix them some more. I watched the movie I just made yesterday and went, "I've blown three characters. Missed them altogether." Then I think, "If only I had a chance to go back and do it again."

LEW: What's the joyful part about screenwriting?

TOM: I think the exhilaration that comes when ideas from above fuse the work. You write something, and for at least the five or ten minutes you're writing, you're not there. Something is happening through you and to you. It's like a drug.

LEW: William Mastrosimone, who wrote *Extremities*, talks about writing fast, not for any practical reason, but because it taps into his subconscious. That's when the creativity comes. Do you agree with that?

TOM: Yes, it's amazing to be writing a character you know you've made up. They're people you know. Then, all of a sudden, this character thinks of something to do, and you think, "Where's this coming from?" And it gets me walking around my table, my office, very, very excited. It's exhilarating, but it doesn't happen very often.

LEW: Let's talk about process. I think there are three stages: the idea, the structure, and the actual script. The idea is the most important?

TOM: Definitely the idea is the most important thing. But you don't always think of the idea first. Somebody said, "We write to find out what we think." And that's a lot of what I'm doing. I sit down. I'm just messing around with some characters, some situation. All of a sudden, I find the idea that is sort of at the core. I go back and say, "Oh, now I know what this story is supposed to be about."

LEW: I remember Francis Coppola once told me he saw *Finian's Rainbow* at the final run, just before the video stores of today, and only then sadly learned what the movie should have been about.

Okay, you have the idea, a pretty good sense of what the movie's about. Tell us your structure process. Probably I should say, then and now. Do you build stories today differently than you did early on?

TOM: I think I'm a little, unfortunately, more conscious of structure now than I was back when I was writing *Dead Poets Society* because there's so much written about structure. We're inundated with so many books and theories. You can't pick up a magazine without seeing somebody's screenwriting class and the three-act structure ad nauseam, so you think about those things whether you want to or not. But, generally speaking, I try not to get anal about page 50 and page 30 and page 60, even though I know what's supposed to happen on each of those pages.

On one of my scripts, the director came and said, "What do you think the second-act break is?" And I said, "Well, it's where this happens." And he asked me what page that was, and I told him it was on page 93. He said, "It's three pages late. We're going to have to take out a scene." I said, "Just because it's three pages late?" He said, "Yeah." And I said, "We can't get this crazy about structure." But we ended up taking out a scene right then and there.

LEW: Jeffrey Katzenberg, when he was running Disney, used to have Bob McKee come in to lecture his people. One morning, I was basically attacked by a young student talking about "turning points." I said, "I've been involved in hundreds of hours of programming in TV and motion pictures, and I've never heard the phrase 'turning points' once in a story meeting from a professional writer." Maybe from executives who would regurgitate that stuff.

Jane Campion—you know, *The Piano?*—she said, "Well, I couldn't quite figure out that man with his charts and so forth." That was ten to twelve years ago with the Australian film school. She was talking about

Syd Field. "I got so much out of Flannery O'Connor." Are you familiar with Flannery O'Connor?

Tom: Oh yeah.

Lew: The twists and turns are all there, but still it has the Aristotelian beginning, middle, and end.

Tom: Before that stuff hit the market, I just did it naturally. I never thought about the structure, except that the story had to keep moving. I don't think I could have even said, "Movies are a three-act structure." I never thought about it. I just did it.

Lew: Where'd you get your training?

Tom: I basically got my training at a place called the Actors and Directors Lab, headed by Jack Garfin, who taught acting. I studied acting to be a director. It was a tremendous help, really, for writing. Understanding the process actors go through has a lot to do with what directors say to actors. They have a lot to do with what writers do because they're interpreting writers' work.

Lew: I would submit that, for us to have never have had anything to do with working in front of an audience, to put words into mouths of people, is "chutzpah."

Tom: A lot of my friends who are working screenwriters started out trying to be actors. That's why actors working on a set are so good at inventing words to go in our movies. They'll often come up with wonderful ideas.

Lew: So then you also say, "We writers can get into directing if we write some material."

Tom: I tried to direct a few plays. I enjoyed it, and people came, but nobody offered me a job directing movies, so I thought I'd better come up with a property that the studio would say, "Okay, you own this. We're desperate to make it. Therefore, you can direct it." How naïve.

Lew: *Second Sight* wasn't the first thing that sold?

Tom: The first thing that sold was the first thing I wrote. Unbelievable luck. It didn't get made for five or six years. It was an action piece called *Sins of the Father* with Brian Dennehy. I never saw it.

Lew: Never?

Tom: I read the script after they got done with it.

Lew: Was there anything in there that was yours?

Tom: Nothing. Nothing. *Second Sight* also had one line of dialogue that was mine, and that was it.

Lew: Did you get a "Story by" credit?

Tom: I think I did.

Lew: How does your heart feel after that? Or do you simply cut if off?

Tom: It all does damage. You become more cynical and more jaded as time goes on. But you have to get used to it. I've gotten to the point where I hear I've sold something, and I go, "Great." Then, when I hear it's going into production, I go, "I'm sorry to hear that." Usually what "they" do to our work is disappointing. It's rare that I meet writers who go, "They did better than what I wrote," or "They realized my movie." Usually they do damage to it. That's the plague of the writer, I think.

Lew: In motion pictures.

Tom: And television.

Lew: But in television, the writers control television—well, certainly in series.

Tom: Yes, yes.

Lew: Not in television movies. I spoke before the board of directors nominating committee of the Writers Guild, and I went on about how we should start claiming the role of the artists and how I think we should stop whining about how we've been fucked over by people in studios like children and start assuming the power that we, in fact, have. I think the whole board was appalled at what I'd just said. I ran for the writers' branch of the Television Academy on the same platform and found it's an idea yet to come for us. We should say, "Goddamn it! We're the writers!"

Tom: We say, "Goddamn it!" a lot.

Lew: But I want to be considered a primary artist in this process. On that sour note, let's go to questions from students, about us.

JAMIE: Looking at your body of work, it looks like there's a noticeable variety. Do you strive to avoid being typecast as a certain type of writer?

TOM: I don't think I try. It's really like analysis for me. Over the years, I've gone through different types of analysis. Each thing I've written is sort of representative of what I might have been going through at that time. Some things I will have no idea what they're about, but others are clear to me. I do think when studios offer me things that are similar to what I've done before, I resist it unless I find myself in love with that particular project because then you're in a career track you may never get out of.

I'm working on a few things right now, and they're all different from each other. One's a comedy, the other's a drama, and the other is kind of a horror movie, which I've never done before. I've written one, but I've never had one made.

SHELLEY: I really liked what you said about having ideas and sticking them in a drawer and pulling everything out when it was time to write. When did you know it was time to write? How many months of slipping papers into drawers until you said, "Okay, I have enough slips of paper now. I'm going to make it into a story"?

TOM: I resist writing every day, so once I feel guilty enough about a particular idea and think I really do have enough for a beginning, middle, and end, I know what to do next. Or I start to feel lazy after I know what I need to do. I go, "All right. I guess I need to do this." I start bringing out the slips of paper to see if it inspires me again, and if it does, it usually happens without a lot of fuss. But if I start forcing myself to the computer every day and beating myself up, unless I'm being paid for it and have to make it work, I put it back in the drawer and try not to think about it. I think these things have a way of persuading us without us having to do a lot if they're working.

LEW: When you talk about a beginning, a middle, and an end, what form of structure? Do you write out a beat sheet, or do you write it out in prose, keep notes, or is it just all in your head?

TOM: It's all of the above. I have it in every state, and it's kind of a mess. There's an outline, and then ten days later, I'll sit down and say, "I'm going to outline this." So I write an outline, then look it over and realize I'd done it ten days before. And then I'll just have ideas or a line of dialogue, and I don't even know where it belongs, so I'll put it in the computer or stick it in the drawer.

Later I go, "Oh, now I know where that line goes." Then I'll realize I'd written that same line fifteen times, you know. It's an odd kind of dreamlike process. I'm very compulsive about it, but at the same time, if it happens over years, it can be messy and long.

STEPHANIE: Once you have these ideas, does getting the character come easily, or is that something you struggle with once you feel you know the story?

TOM: I think I usually start with character. I have some character who needs something, and that's floating around in my mind first. Out of that need comes an action or a character or a conflict of some sort, and the story starts to grow from there. Occasionally, I get ideas like, "Wouldn't it be great if I wrote a story about blowing up the Brooklyn Bridge?" or something stupid like that but not very often. *Second Sight* was the closest I think I ever came to that level, the idea of a psychic detective agency. I didn't have any characters, but I had that idea. Otherwise, it's character first. And usually I know it's a good story if character problems yield interesting things that start to happen based on what that character needs to do.

STEPHANIE: It seems that you couldn't have done that in *Dead Poets Society* without knowing who that main character was.

TOM: Right.

LEW: Did you know who he was right up front?

TOM: I had three teachers who were really big influences in my life. That guy is sort of an amalgamation of those teachers.

LEW: What were those teachers teaching?

TOM: One taught English, and the other two, acting. I know where some scenes in the movie came from. They're sort of metaphorical. There's a scene where the student is called up to the front of the room and sort of forced to make up a poem. That's essentially an acting exercise. One of these teachers calls a student up who is too shy to speak and pulls his pants down and asks him to sing the lines of the play he was supposed to be doing. That's how that scene came about.

LEW: Were you ever able to share your homage with those teachers?

TOM: Yes.

LEW: That must have been wildly pleasing to them.

TOM: I think so. They sort of all looked at the movie and thought, "It sort of seems like me, and it sort of doesn't." They were all also a little perplexed.

LEW: Do you have a mentor, a Yoda? You know how Joseph Campbell talks about that everyone has a Yoda who they can go to? Do you have someone in your life you will go to who will tell you things that nobody else could ever tell you?

TOM: Not still alive.

LEW: Sorry. Do you still go to that person spiritually?

TOM: Often.

JAMIE: Going back to *Dead Poets Society* and character: You had a real clear sense of many of the children and their, to use the term, their arcs. I'm just curious, the main character, the Robin Williams character, is very clear. Everyone can relate to him. But what is his character development, character arc?

TOM: He's not the main character. Todd, at least for me, was the main character. Todd is the shy kid who is the first to stand up at the end. So the kids change, and the teacher is tested. He goes, and he doubts and loses faith, but in the end, he goes away with his faith restored in himself and what he believes in that lesson. He doesn't change in the sense that he starts as one thing and ends up as something else. He's a catalyst.

JAMIE: In development, was that something that was discussed?

TOM: Constantly.

JAMIE: And you fought over it?

TOM: Not really fought over it, just lots of discussion. I got lucky. I wrote the script, and it took two years for it to sell and lucky it even sold at all. The studio fought off any attempts by actors to make any changes to those roles.

LEW: Was Peter Weir helpful in that fight, too?

TOM: By the time Peter got involved, Robin Williams was already aboard, so those fights had been fought.

LEW: What's your life like when you're into a script? Do you assign yourself so many pages a day or a week, or do you do it by hours? What's your process?

TOM: It varies. I used to say, "If I can do twenty pages a day on that first draft, that's what I need to do." Now, I try to get through the first draft in three to four days—not because it's going to be any good but because of the fact that I'm so anxious about the fact that it may not work. By the time I'm writing it, I've put months, if not years, of thought into these things. The thought that it may not get there is just terrifying. I type as fast as I can.

LEW: I asked Bill Goldman how long it took him to write *Butch Cassidy and the Sundance Kid*. He said, "I thought about it for eight years and wrote it in six weeks. It took me eight years or six weeks." Obviously, it takes both. But in your case, you're far less than six weeks.

TOM: You don't want to be around me during those three days.

LEW: How does your wife put up with you?

TOM: I'm gone. I go down to my office to write.

LEW: Is your office on your home property?

TOM: No, it's an outside office. I could write at home, but people don't like to be around me because I'm so absorbed in my writing. I will bark at anything and anybody. I usually just go down to my office and write from seven in the morning until ten or eleven at night. Then I'll lie down on the floor and get up and do it again the next day. If you make it uncomfortable enough for you, you'll finish. Then, I can take a sigh of relief and immediately start to worry about all the things that weren't working in the draft and start rewriting.

LEW: When you're done with your first draft, do you consider, in a sense, that you're on top of the mountain, going down?

TOM: At the foothills, looking up after the first draft. It's rare that the first draft—

LEW: No, on a psychological level. Obviously when you write the first draft you must feel, mustn't you, that "It's going to work. I can make it work."

TOM: Sort of. I remember when I was writing *Dead Poets Society*, this teacher is making all these speeches about "stand up for who you are," and I'm falling asleep as I was writing it. It was the most bizarre experience. You just think to yourself, "This must be dreadful, but I'm going to get through it and see what happens." And those speeches hardly changed from the first draft. I can't explain it. I had no fun. I wasn't infused with the message of the teacher in that way. When I first thought of the boys looking at the pictures of the kids who had been there a hundred years before, the first time I thought, "Oh my God. This feels powerful." But once I got to writing, it was actually without emotion.

LAURIE: You still sleep on the floor?

TOM: No. Carol Corman, who was one of my three teachers, used to say, "Go to work like a grocer. Get there early in the morning. It's a craft, not an art." I think he's right about that. So I've very disciplined about rewriting. I go to work at nine in the morning.

LEW: So, it becomes, to some degree, like creative mechanics?

TOM: Oh, very mechanical.

LEW: In the rewriting process.

TOM: Well, in the writing process, too.

LEW: Now your mind is kicking in. The first time, your emotions; the second, your left brain?

TOM: Yes, when you're rewriting, you may look at a whole scene and go, "There's no conflict. Nothing. It's dead." And if you can't cut it, you have to get inspired. If you're writing a comedy, you may get a scene that's suddenly just not funny. By that time, maybe the studio has read it, and they're going, "Fix these five scenes. We want ten jokes by tomorrow." And you're going, "Where's that going to come from?"

LEW: Is conflict the most important thing?

TOM: Conflict is the most important thing.

LEW: In practically everything? In every scene as well as the overall movie?

TOM: Exactly. Every scene is like a little minimovie. It's got a beginning, middle, and end. It's got a conflict and a resolution. I don't spend a lot of time thinking about where that is in a particular scene unless I'm desperate.

LEW: I use the phrase "It's a nonscene." There's no conflict.

TOM: Right. Right.

SHELLEY: When Eric Roth was here, he said, for the past twenty years, he's been taking studio assignments, *Forrest Gump* included. It seems like you have a mixture of studio assignments and original ideas. Which do you prefer?

TOM: I prefer originals. I've taken studio assignments. *Honey, I Shrunk the Kids* was a studio assignment. *What about Bob?* was in some respects a studio assignment, although to me, they're sort of all voluntary. I read them, and if I feel excited, I'll get involved. I'd rather not take someone's money until I know I can deliver something. But overall, it's more comfortable writing specs.

LEW: Do you have a love child all the time? Let's say you're writing something that somebody's paying you for, but you have something on the side that you—

TOM: Always. Always. Always.

LEW: Why?

TOM: I think that, particularly, when I'm doing something for somebody else, it's like being in analysis, but you're pretending to be somebody else, whereas your own deeper demons are always a little more interesting to you, a little more compelling. Whether they would be to the rest of the world or not is really not relevant.

LEW: I'm used to working in television, where pages have to be on the set by seven o'clock in the morning. However, in motion pictures, sometimes you wait a couple of weeks to go to a script meeting. So what are you going to do for two weeks? You could rail on your wife or take your kids wherever, but right there is your in-progress love child.

TOM: Amen.

JESSICA: It's obvious Hollywood is a combination of art or, as you said, craft and business. I'm wondering when you're working on these love-child scripts, how much thought goes into your thinking process about the viability of the idea in the marketplace?

TOM: Unfortunately, more than I would like. I censor my ideas based on whether I think they have any hope of getting made. And all you really need to get something made is an actor of some stature who will commit to the part. So, if you can delude yourself into thinking that you've got a part in there that will attract a bankable or a marquee-value star, then you've got an excuse to write it. For the most part, if I have an interesting character in the middle of my movie, I'll go ahead and do it. But you can't help but think, "God, should I write this story set in the rainforest?" You think, "Has anybody else done that?"

On *Dead Poets Society*, I had two meetings where I had people who said to me, "I just wanted to meet someone who would be stupid enough to waste all this time writing something that takes place in a boys' school. Have you ever seen a movie that takes place in a boys' school that was either good or successful? No. So what are you doing this for?" "You're right, but you don't get it? It's about more than that." And they went, "No. It's not about more than that. Out."

JESSICA: But was it about that, or you knew you had a character Robin Williams would love to play?

TOM: Oh no. I didn't even think about Robin Williams.

JESSICA: Or any top actor?

TOM: At that point, I had written several pieces, including *Second Sight*, that were in some ways commercial stabs, and I just wasn't happy with them. I wasn't happy with where my career was going and I thought, "This thing has been plaguing me for several years now. I have nothing to lose at this point. I'm going to write a script I want to write and see."

LEW: Like *Medicine Man*? How was that journey. Was that an original?

TOM: My wife went to Costa Rica, and she sort of brought back all the rainforest, and both of us were pretty desperate to find a way to help save the rainforest; I tried to get Disney to do it. I think I pitched to them a sort of rudimentary idea of doing a story down in the rainforest of a guy desperate to save it. They passed. Then, I started thinking harder about it, and slowly the elements started coming together, and then one day I thought, "Oh, I get it." And then I wrote it. But it was basically passed on by the studios for reasons like, "Why would we want to do a story about the rainforest?" I kind of got into their cynical mood, and I'd say, "Did you vote?" Yeah. "You're the only one in this room who voted." But I guess I showed more in the screenplay than it did in the final movie, although I haven't seen the final movie. That movie was on a mission to bring light to the audience what was happening in the Brazilian rainforests and to get people to stop it somehow.

LEW: You haven't seen the movie?

TOM: I read the rewrite, and I just was so upset, and I had such a bad experience with some of the people involved that I didn't go to the premiere. My agent called and said, "You know, it's just awful. Don't go. Don't see it." Right after that, my attorney called: "I didn't see you there." I said, "That's right. I wasn't there." He said, "Did your agent Jack call?" I said yes. And he asked, "What did he say?" And I told him, and he said, "I knew he'd lily-white it."

HOWARD SUBER: The first draft was wonderful.

TOM: Thanks.

LEW: And Howard did read the first draft. Howard, any questions?

HOWARD: Could you just continue on with what you're talking about when Sean Connery got attached?

TOM: It's interesting. The first person to get attached was John McTiernan, the director. We had some great meetings. He was really excited about the material, wanted to do something different than *Die Hard*, and was a bright guy. I came away from my first meeting thinking, "Wow. This guy can pull it off." Sean Connery got involved, and I really got the feeling that one day Connery and McTiernan were sitting with each other and said, "We're making a movie. This is a kind of liberal movie about guys trying to save the rainforest. What are we doing this for? This is wrong. Fuck the rainforest." And the next day, they came in, and McTiernan said, "Fuck the rainforest." And I said, "Why?" And he said, "Because this is a cause. The hell with that, you know. It's got to be a story."

And Connery started talking, "My character, he's kind of pining away in the woods for his wife who left him. What's that about?" I said, "Well, it was his wife. He was madly in love with her. She went away. She stole his research. She left him there the past couple of years, and he's upset." And he goes, "Wouldn't he just get somebody else?" "Well, I mean, I guess he could, but if he takes that attitude, there goes the love story, you know." And he goes, "So be it." And I said, "Guys, what's left? We lose our passion for saving the rainforest. We get rid of the love story. What are we doing out there?" And they said, "Well, if you can't figure it out, we'll find somebody who can." And I said, "So be it." So they brought in another writer.

About a month later, they called me back and said, "Will you do this? Will you fix it? Read it, and tell us what you'd do." So I read it. I said, "There are five ideas in here that I like. I'm going to reintegrate those ideas into my original draft. That's what I would do. That's what I still believe in." They said, "Okay, do it." So I did it and got a call from the director's secretary, saying, "Did you happen to save this by any chance?" And I said yes. She said, "Could you send it over?" And I said, "Does John want to talk about his reaction to the draft?" She said, "I think you just got it." Okay. So I sent it over, and that was the last I heard from them. So we went into arbitration with the guild, and I read the other writer's draft, and I thought, "Oh, God. This is sad."

LEW: Now tell us a good story.

TOM: Yeah. I don't have many good stories.

LEW: I guess everybody in this room, except for Matt, who may be a closet writer, and Kurt, who I know is a closet writer, I would say probably over half of these people will be professional writers within the next five to ten years, tops, but hopefully five.

TOM: *Dead Poets Society* was a good story.

LEW: And, getting made, continued to be a good story?

TOM: Good story getting made. It was fun thinking of it, fun writing it, fun doing it. The studio was incredibly supportive. The first preview was not a disaster but a mess. Two hours and fifteen minutes—long for a comedy. And they just said, "You know what to do. Go to it." They never got in the way editorially or any other way, so it was an exciting experience.

LEW: Sometimes some people have a good experience, and somehow or another, they never connect up again. How come you and Peter Weir never connected up again?

TOM: We've tried. I've wanted to direct even before I met Peter, and he knew that, and he said—when I first met him—he said, "Why haven't you thought of directing this?" I said, "I have thought of it. It's just that no one else has." And he said, "Well, it doesn't bother me. I'd like you on the set. If you want to watch and ask questions, feel free because I'd like to help you in that way." So we've talked about it.

One time we got together and talked about doing something, but I just said, "Peter, anything I'm going to get excited about writing, I'm going to want to direct." I think I asked him to direct *Medicine Man*. I showed it to him, and he just said, "I did my rainforest thing with *The Mosquito Coast*. You have no idea what torture it is to go down there."

LEW: What you're working on now, are you going to direct it next?

TOM: *Dancing Man* is sort of popping up again.

LEW: How long ago did you write *Dancing Man*?

TOM: In '93 or '94.

LEW: It's fascinating how certain things we writers do won't die.

TOM: It's the thing I've written I love the most. I didn't quite realize how expensive it was going to be when I did it. It just seemed like it's half of a really expensive movie and half of a medium-budget movie so together ought to add up to a doable thing, but it's out there.

KURT: How much of a collaborative effort was there when you did *Honey, I Shrunk the Kids*? There's a lot of effects. Was that from you?

TOM: It was a rewrite. By the time I got there, they had a lot of the special effects sequences storyboarded, so it was, "Well, here we've got these kids, and there's a bee in there, so this has to be done. But we need a good excuse to get this kid on the bee. Whatever you want to do, but just get him there." The adventures in the yard were fairly logical in terms of their build, so it wasn't so difficult to write to them, and what I think was missing in the first draft was that these particular events were not tests for the characters. So there was not conflict with their inner story, so that was a challenge: to create these characters who could be tested by these adventures and grow from their experience.

KURT: It's tough when you don't know the limits with the effects. As you're writing, you're not sure, "This is a great idea, but can they do it?"

TOM: Well, I think if you can think of it, they can do it nowadays.

SHELLEY: The late Hal Ashby always watched *The Conformist* before he started a movie. Do you have any movies that have really influenced your work?

TOM: Huh, another friend of mine also watches that before every film. For me, no.

SHELLEY: Any things that really influenced you early on?

LEW: Books, any books?

TOM: Faulkner, Joseph Conrad, and *Heart of Darkness*. All of them sort of typical high school and college influences. The movie *Blow-Up*. Oh, *The Graduate*. Between *Blow-Up* and *The Graduate*, I was hooked on making movies.

LEW: *Dr. Strangelove* must have meant something to you.

TOM: *Strangelove* was amazing. Bergman, too. I was a philosophy major in college, and one course we got to watch all of Bergman's films and talk about how they expressed existential themes. That was exciting to see that movies could actually have ideas and express them through drama and visuals. When I grew up, it was that era of European directors—Bergman, Fellini, Godard. Godard was kind of a negative influence because I just never understood him, and I would be outraged when I came out of the theaters.

LEW: I was teaching in Copenhagen at the National Film School, and they said, "You always use European films as examples." I replied, "Well, remember Howard Suber and Jorge Preloran. We'd run down to the Los Feliz arthouse on Hillhurst just to see all those wonderful European film artists." But I now despair. Another friend of mine, Lenny Bruce, used to say, "There's nothing sadder than an old hipster."

TOM: Guilty.

LEW: I despair that these students don't have the ongoing joy of, "Oh God. How could Antonioni have done that? And Visconti, Kurosawa." What takes their place? Is there hope? Do you see anything in your shuffling around. I suppose with all of the independents, in terms of academy nominations, they reflect hope in terms of thought introduced into movies.

TOM: But the next day, you read about the glut of independent films and how they're mashing each other out of the market because they're merging with the majors. And now we're a special-effects-driven business in Hollywood. I got into movies because I was interested in characters and ideas and examining the human experience. Movies don't seem interested in that, and the audience also doesn't seem interested.

LEW: We may be getting some hope like this. Scott Rosenberg is directing a picture now. You've finished your first picture. The writers, inmates are taking over the asylum. We're finding that in our screenwriting program here at UCLA, twelve of our twenty become professional screenwriters. About three or four of those every year start directing. I think there'll be more and more of the writer/director, with the writer being in the first position. Would you share that feeling?

TOM: That the writer would be in the first position?

LEW: I'm talking about the writer being a hyphenate, and he or she will be like yourself or Billy Wilder, who considers himself a writer who directed—not necessarily to protect it but to keep going with the vision. Were you on set for a lot of your pictures?

TOM: I was on set a lot for *Dead Poets Society*. I was bouncing back to town, doing rewrites for *What about Bob?* Not on set for anything else. Actually, I didn't want to be. *Honey, I Shrunk the Kids* was shot in Mexico. I made them put in my contract I wouldn't have to go.

LEW: Would you like a writer on the set if you were directing something that was not your own material?

TOM: Absolutely. Absolutely. God, yes. I think part of what a director does is sort of bring as much talent to the process as possible, and the writer, you hope, is the talent.

LEW: How did the writer relate to the director in *8 Heads in a Duffel Bag*?

TOM: The director was angry at the writer a lot.

JAMIE: One of the golden rules we're taught is, don't tell; show. I often have to check myself because I do tend to tell too much. Is that something that has been a recurring concern in your own writing?

TOM: I'm a little bit of a contrarian anytime I hear rules floating out there in the world. I think if I'm doing the opposite but doing it effectively, then my work is going to stand out. It's going to be a little different. I wouldn't do it just for that reason, but if it's getting in the way of your own voice, this kind of internal thing of, "I'm telling too much." Constantly, you're cutting out stuff you like. However, I do find myself getting dialogue heavy and exposition heavy and writing five or six scenes I don't even need. I think, one day it occurs to me that I can cut five scenes out for greater effect than if I left them in, and I think, "Okay," and I cut.

LEW: But you had lots of dialogue in *Dead Poets Society* and an actor who pulled it off. I'm sure some part of you felt you'd probably cut half of it along the line, but you decided to see what happened. Then, at the other end of the rainbow, the dialogue held, didn't it?

TOM: It seemed to. I had speeches that were two pages long, my God. But I knew at the time that people were going to look at it and go, "This is an amateur," but I read the scenes and thought, "This works."

AMIE: How many pages was that script?

TOM: Well, never turn in a script above 129 pages, you know, because they see that, and that's the first remark you'll get: "It's too long." So I squeezed it down. I remember going back to the set about halfway through the movie, and they were shooting nights. Peter Weir walked up to me and said, "They just sent your script to something called Barbara's Place. They typed it out and found it's 162 pages long. You're going to have to cut forty pages." I said, "Peter, we're halfway through shooting. What do you mean? We've only got seventy pages left." And he said, "I know. Just cut it, and let me know what it's going to be." He walked away. I watched him, and he went over, sat down, and fell asleep. And I thought, "Okay, I get it. He's the walking dead." But my scripts tend to be too long, you know. Always.

Lew: Ah Barbara's Place. I did one, and it came in at 135 pages. "Barbara could you readjust something and get it down to 120?" It came in at 119. It was the same fucking script. Once in a while, I'll slip in a few A and B and C pages, you know, to bring it down.

Tom: Right.

Lew: They flip to that last page, right? Relief if it's 110. Furrowed brow if it's over 129.

Tom: Right, I had a first AD on my movies who was the military organizer of all time. She had *8 Heads* printed out exactly the way it should have been. Every continued; every period; every dot, dot, dot was there. I'd say, "Bonita. They're killing me already. They want me to cut it down." She'd say, "You're just fucking yourself. Don't do it." She kept making it longer. But she was right, you know. She said, "Two and a half pages a day. That's the most you're going to do. I'm telling you." She was right, you know.

Lew: Another reason for not having the script long is that it engages nonwriters in the creative process.

Tom: You don't want to do that. However, every script I write, the first draft is about 180 to 200 pages. You'd think I'm going to put a bullet to my head. It just gets out of control. Sloppy. I think, "All right, all I have to do is take one and a half pages out of every ten, and I'm there." So I chop away. You get ruthless about cutting. Pretty soon you forget about anything you care about. You just tell the story as simply as you can, and what's left is your movie.

Matt: Tom, talk a little about the editing, your involvement in that process. Did you find scenes you thought were going a specific way in your mind changed in the editing process, and you're almost rewriting?

Tom: This is an actor who's wondering, "Where's my line?" In the editing process, you want to tell the story as economically as possible. To me it's a matter of cutting all the crap in between the good stuff. You think, "God, scene A works, scene C works, but scene B is terrible. I've blown it. What am I going to do? Can I cut it out altogether? Is there some way I can bridge A and C, using only a part of B? Can I cut? How late can I come in on the scene and still tell the story?"

The first cut of *8 Heads* was two and a half hours. The editor called and said, "We're in good shape. It's two and a half hours long." I said, "Oh God. It's supposed to be ninety-five minutes long. We're dead." And you go at it with a meat axe, and it gets better. The decisions were all made in the most ruthless frame of mind. If a line didn't work, get rid of it. If we don't need it to tell the story, get rid of it.

LEW: A final question: Do you have any children?

TOM: Yes.

LEW: What if any one of your children came up to you and said, "Daddy, I'd like to be a screenwriter."

TOM: Oh, I'd feel so bad. I guess I'm talking to you 434-ers here. I was pretty naïve when I was starting. I've heard how successful this program is, so anything I can say doesn't really apply to you. You're all going to be working soon. But the odds are really—I mean, it takes so much luck.

It's a rewarding profession in many ways. I don't like what's going on in movies now. But there is some kind of deep personal reward that comes from teaching through what we do. I think that's what screenwriters are, is teachers. Our themes we're saying in our scripts are something we're teaching, theoretically, to a very big audience. And there's a lot of personal reward you feel when you come across things necessary for the world to know and when you're able to communicate through story and get that story out. That is the excitement of it. You may lose lines of dialogue or whole scenes to a director who just doesn't like this, doesn't like that. But if the basic theme comes through, if you're getting what you've tried to say out there, it's as exhilarating and wonderful as anything except sex that I know.

LEW: Perfect. Tom Schulman, you have again seized the day.

10

Ted Tally

Ted Tally is a nice man. How could such a nice man develop Hannibal Lecter, one of the seminally evil human beings in the history of cinema? The question is answered in smoothing out our phone dialogue and not being seduced by his velvet voice, a voice not so different than Anthony Hopkin's seductive, velvet timbre in his Oscar-winning portrayal in *The Silence of the Lambs*.

In working with the transcribed words of Ted and myself, I very clearly see Ted Tally is extraordinarily intelligent. Educated at Yale, he's gently forceful and articulately passionate, not dissimilar to his interpretation of Mr. Lecter and his bountiful filmography. Like Alfred Uhry and the upcoming Horton Foote, Ted Tally began his career in theater and subsequently toggled between the camera and the proscenium arches. These three Oscar-winning screenwriters are particularly unique, as the other award winners hail from backgrounds involving journalism, fiction, or film school.

Ted Tally's particular uniqueness, even beyond the theater origins, is his principal work today: his ability to bring book adaptations to the big screen, a specialty occasionally but not majorly shared by our other *Naked Screenwriter* artists. With Ted, adaptations are primarily by choice. He loves them.

I know of no other resource that so succinctly elaborates the special parameters of adapting fiction novels to the language of film than in the dialogue with Ted that is forthcoming. A lengthy phone discussion with a master, perhaps *the* master, reveal Ted Tally's guidelines, his wisdom, and his passion. Learn and enjoy, old and young, experienced and beginner.

TED: Hello?

LEW: Ted Tally?

TED: This is Ted.

LEW: Hooray! This is Lew Hunter.

TED: Oh, hi, Dr. Hunter. How are you?

LEW: I'm fine. Please call me Lew, if I may call you Ted?

TED: Please.

LEW: The doctor: I'm reminded of how once Paul Whitman got a doctorate in something and challenging his new title, his trumpet player said, "I bet you can't cure the clap." Also, I cannot cure the clap. I'm delighted to be visiting with you. This is an experiment for us. I have had a handful of Oscar winners come to my 434 screenwriting class to talk about their own process in becoming successful screenwriters, not in becoming rich or famous, but in becoming great writers.

TED: Yes.

LEW: Which is, I don't know if you're familiar with a wonderful series of books that George Plimpton and the cats put together for the *Paris Review* called Writers at Work.

TED: I've seen some of that, yes.

LEW: It was very empowering to me when I was starting out as a writer many moons ago. I was at Northwestern at the time—this would have been in the '50s—and there were eight of them, and they talked to Hemingway and Katherine Anne Porter and Dos Passos and Steinbeck. It was such a wonderful thing to realize, "My God, these are regular human beings."

TED: I always enjoy reading books about writers and how they write. I remember reading John Gardner's book.

LEW: Oh, isn't that a wonderful book? I have on the phone, also, Rita Augustine, who is my right and left hand. She is here, number 1, helping me, but also she is really one of our top students here in our graduate screenwriting program at UCLA. We've turned out some greats, such as Francis Ford Coppola, David Koepp, Colin Higgins, Alex Cox, Scott

Rosenberg. It's a long compendium. Well, Rita, just jump in any time you want to.

RITA: Okay.

LEW: Don't be timid.

TED: Hi, Rita.

RITA: Hi, Ted.

LEW: The book thus will include yourself, Francis Coppola, Bruce Rubin, Julius Epstein, Oliver Stone, Irving Ravetch and Harriet Frank Jr., Tom Schulman, Billy Wilder, Eric Roth, Ernie Lehman, Frank Pierson, David Ward, and Ron Bass.

TED: You could just skip everybody else and say Billy Wilder.

RITA: Exactly.

LEW: You know, somebody asked me the other day, as to my favorite screenwriter, and without a pause, I said, "Billy Wilder."

TED: Oh, me, too.

LEW: Chayefsky was another kind of writer, but oh God, was he wonderful!

TED: He's great.

LEW: We're going to do a few by phone: yourself, Robert Benton, and Ruth for certain. I think Woody Allen's the only one who will probably successfully spurn us.

TED: Well, I'm honored to be in that company.

LEW: I'm so delighted to have you in that company. I realized that this book would show the reader that while we're all heading for the same ocean, we're all in different rivers because we all have such a different method in how we go about writing a great screenplay. I would like to ask you about screenwriting and how it relates to storytelling. Is it storytelling? Is that your take on what screenwriting is?

TED: Yes, it is storytelling. You know, like any other form of writing, it begins with being a reader. If you love reading stories, then it's a natural progression to want to tell stories. My background very much has been theater, as it happened, and not in film. I came late to movies, except as a fan of them; that was early on. Narrative storytelling, I think, is largely the same no matter whether it's theater or novels or movies or even short stories. It's just a love of narratives for me.

LEW: You came to it by being a reader. Did you also become interested in theater as a result of your upbringing? Maybe a member of your family?

TED: There were no writers in my family, but there were teachers. My parents were teachers.

LEW: Did they encourage your writing?

TED: Absolutely. Yes. They encouraged reading, and they encouraged writing, and they were thrilled with all of my stumbling, youthful efforts. Overpraised them. It made me think that it was something I could do without people laughing at me. I also had very, very good teachers who really encouraged writing. They stressed the importance of daily themes and weekly themes and coherent short essays, and they just made us write a lot.

LEW: Was this high school or college?

TED: Junior high school.

LEW: Oh, my lord, back that early?

TED: I grew up in North Carolina. I just happened to be lucky enough to have a series of outstanding English teachers.

LEW: Ah, North Carolina, and so many wonderful Southern writers. Was that meaningful to you?

TED: Not so much the Southern writers because I'm sure I was just reading people like Alexandre Dumas, Robert Louis Stevenson. However, I very much benefited from the sort of old-fashioned Southern storytelling, the verbal storytelling tradition. I had a couple of grandparents who were great, great yarn spinners, my mother's mother in particular. I will never forget. She was a farmer, a farmer's wife, and when we were kids, she would gather us around at night, and we would say, "Tell us a story. Tell us a story." And she would make up a story on the spot. She would just spin it out. It would come out as one of these kind of country tales she had heard. Other times there were witches and haunts and things involved. She would say, "Well, once upon a time, there was this old man and this old woman who lived alone in a farmhouse." She would go on for maybe twenty-five minutes and would wrap it up with this stirring conclusion.

LEW: Oh, that's wonderful. I do the same thing with my kids. I'd say, "Give me a good guy, and give me a bad guy, but don't tell me anything else, and I'll tell you a story without a book." I had never heard of anyone else doing that.

TED: We never interrupted the story to ask questions. She would just go by what she saw in our faces. It was a real theatrical performance from this rather uneducated woman. She was such a great storyteller.

LEW: When you went into theater and you transitioned into movies, did you find yourself liberated or awed by becoming a motion picture writer?

TED: Well, I guess a little bit of both. I had some success in theater, so when I first started writing movies and television scripts, it was more with one hand tied behind my back. I had gone to drama school, and I was having plays produced in New York, and I thought of theater and movies as something that were a bit foreign and exotic. It seemed like something that really happened on another planet. People who made movies were these exotic creatures who lived in a far-off place and had all kinds of technical skills that I never would have. They had expensive equipment and big budgets. I didn't see how I could ever actually be involved in the making of a movie, so it became just a way of making money while I pursued my real career, which was theater.

However, I soon reached a point of frustration with my theater career where I realized I had better start taking it seriously. I realized there's a whole lot to learn here, and I started focusing full time on screenplays. It was liberating because I had been working in Off-Broadway theater, where if you're going to add a chair to the set, the prices go over budget. Getting from one scene to the next could be a major crisis, too, with the set changes, for one, so it's liberating to just be able to snap my fingers and be in a different country. I can ride a cavalry charge if it's called for. It's very liberating to the imagination.

LEW: One of my students did some Off-Broadway stuff, but before he became one of our students, he felt the quickest definition for him was that theater is for the ear, while motion picture if for the eye. Does this definition resonate with you?

TED: I think if you're good at writing theater, you're paying a lot of attention to the eye, as well.

LEW: Yes.

TED: If you're writing good movies, you're paying a lot of attention to the ear. I think the two are much closer than they're often considered to be. The first time I was ever hired to write a screenplay, I had never even seen one. I was hired by the late British director Lindsay Anderson.

LEW: Oh, my stars. The best.

TED: He wanted me to write a screenplay for him because he had seen a play of mine. I said, "Lindsay, I'm very flattered, but I don't even know what a screenplay looks like. I love movies, but I don't know about camera angles and all of that kind of stuff." He said, "Oh, forget all of that stuff. It's nonsense. Just write it like it's a play but one where you don't have to wait for set changes. Don't give too much description, and don't worry about all of that camera nonsense."

LEW: Had you ever seen Lindsay Anderson's work before?

TED: I'd seen *If . . .* and *O Lucky Man!*

LEW: What about *O Dreamland?*

TED: I don't know that one.

LEW: That's a documentary he did. He went to a carnival. It's fabulous if you get a chance to see it.

TED: I think that's fantastic. *In Celebration*. David Storey. He was very good at filming the plays he worked on. My apprenticeship in movie writing was with him. A year, sort of back and forth between New York and London and Los Angeles, working on a script he supervised, which was never made. It was a historical epic set in India, and he wanted to do a sort of John Ford movie in the place where he was born. So for me, I was going from Off-Broadway productions with four characters in one room to literally writing battle scenes. Yeah, that was very liberating.

LEW: My God, you were in historical India. That was a wonderful opportunity. Have you ever tried to get something going that you consider to be extant rather than extinct? I hate the word *trunk*, you know, for a writer. I think it's such a pejorative term, that the word *extant* is much more appropriate.

TED: I tried to turn one or two of my old plays into movies, but they didn't go very far. I think most things I have that are in a trunk are in there for a good reason.

LEW: Tell me about your work habits. Do you write in the morning, afternoon, evening, that sort of thing?

TED: I write in the morning. I get up, and usually I take my children to school; sometimes my wife does. I have an office about five miles from my house, so I drive to work afterwards. I've found that working at home has too many distractions. It just felt more professional to get out of the house. I usually start at eight o'clock in the morning. I work until about noon. The best work I always do in the morning, when I'm freshest and my concentration is high. I find that afternoon work is better to just review some of the work from morning and revise it a little or just to clear my mind and read or do correspondence, whatever.

LEW: Do you assign yourself so many pages a day?

TED: I try to do two pages a day. It's hard. I have to write four pages to get the two that I'm happy with. There are plenty of days when two pages turn into one. You know, where you just go down a blind alley, and then you have to come back. I try to average two a day, which is ten a week, which would mean finishing a script in three months. However, real life has a way of intruding on this timeline at times.

LEW: You do this five days a week?

TED: Five days a week, no weekends. I don't carry it home with me, either. When I'm at home, I'm a full-time husband and dad.

LEW: You don't share your scenes with your wife?

TED: No, no, no. In fact, she doesn't even always read the finished script.

LEW: Oh, you, too.

TED: I wouldn't want to inflict that on anybody. I mean, why should she read some rewrite of some monster movie or something?

LEW: I used to come rushing in, "Oh honey, listen to this. Isn't it wonderful?" I don't do that anymore. Probably the jadedness of old age, too.

TED: In my playwriting days, I used to do that. It's more of a job now. It's more of a craft. I feel really good about the craftsmanship of screenwriting. I'm happier to think of myself as a carpenter than an artist with a capital *A*.

LEW: Do you consider screenwriting an art? Should we be referred to as artists?

TED: I suppose it's an art. It's a communal art in the end. That's what it is. Making movies is a communal art. No screenplay is ever written in a vacuum. Eventually you're revising it under the input of other people. So is it an art? Yes. I still think of it as more of a craft, however. I once said, "You know, I feel like just a carpenter here," when I got into this habit, which I still am, of doing strictly adaptations, and a friend replied, "A carpenter can make a park bench or a Chippendale cabinet. There's nothing wrong with just being a craftsman."

LEW: Let's talk about the process. In terms of your adaptations or an original idea, how do you identify the "Aha! This is the one I want to work on"?

TED: That's a great question. I guess the answer changes from book to book. I guess it always comes down to the main character or the two main characters of the story. I have to feel moved by them. I have to follow their journey. You sort of have to fall in love with the book at some level. If it sort of gets under your skin, if you feel a little jealous, wishing you had written it yourself, if it lets you maybe put on a new hat, you know it's going to work. One of the great things about adaptations is feeling that. For instance, I did an adaptation of Cormac McCarthy's book *All the Pretty Horses*.

LEW: Oh, yes.

TED: I love westerns, but I had never written a western. I would have trouble sitting down and convincing myself that anybody would want to watch a western. However, I love them. When the chance came to do an adaptation of a western, I leapt because it's a chance to be a sort of writer I have never been before. That's one of those good things about adaptations. I have to fall in love with the characters, basically.

RITA: You talk about steep affection for the book. Does this get in the way sometimes, maybe when you're trying to pick and choose what goes to script?

TED: No, because I can be objective. It's not my book, and in a sense, with every book that you adapt, you're having a lover's quarrel. In a sense, you're not even a writer. I mean, you are, but you're also an editor and a critic.

RITA: Right.

TED: And what you choose to emphasize in a book and what you leave out is a sort of critique of the book. That's why I tend to distance a bit from the writers who have written these books. You can love and respect a book and still see things that will improve it. I mean, somebody once said the three greatest human drives are sex, food, and rewriting other people's work. If you're an adaptational screenwriter, that's the ultimate blue pencil.

LEW: I would guess that your beginning in theater would be the most useful to you in adapting books because so many people who adapt books start out in screenplay writing. I'm so blown away by people in my class who have a theater background. We always have a handful of students who came from playwriting, and it changes the atmosphere when we have two or three people who know Pirandello and Shakespeare, as opposed to people who grew up with Spielberg and Lucas.

TED: Everything in my writing grows out of theater, even though I haven't written a play for, gosh, a decade. However, while I was doing it, I was doing it very intensively, and it began in high school. Everything in my writing still grows out of that but not so much out of the literary tradition of drama as out of the practical experience of working onstage.

LEW: Had you done acting?

TED: I'd done some acting. I'd done some directing. I've done a little bit of designing. I think I'd done about everything you can do in a theater. The practical experience of working as an actor, just watching actors work scenes that I had written, meant learning how to reshape those scenes for actors' voices and learning the kinds of physical things that actors need to help them play a scene. That was the most valuable experience that I can remember. Because of my theater background, I feel able to play all of the parts in a story as I'm writing it, imaginatively.

LEW: At some point do you read aloud to yourself?

TED: No, it's just sort of a voice in my head.

LEW: Ah, I walked into a tennis club one time and saw a writer over by the pool. Oh! That's Neil Simon. Oh! He's reading his script aloud to himself. Way to go, Neil! That's how I do it!

TED: They come and take you away if you do that in public, you know.

LEW: It was the Beverly Hills Tennis Club. They're all candidates for Bellevue, anyway.

TED: I read it aloud sometimes in my head, but I'm still using the same sort of ear for dialogue that I used in the theater.

LEW: Francis was talking about periodically getting a group of actors together and doing a table reading as he's working on a project.

TED: I have done that, too. I've had the experience with two or three screenplays, and that's really useful. Far more useful to hear real actors read it aloud than for me to read it.

LEW: Tell me about the development of the story now. You have identified the character and obviously the basic story area of those characters, whether it's an adaptation or an original screenplay. How do you construct your story? How do you build your outline?

TED: With screen adaptations, I'm given a story, so it's a matter of interpretation, selection, arrangement, and rearrangement. It's always first, middle, and last, a matter of compression. A certain amount of invention is necessary, too, because no book just automatically pops onto the screen. If you reduce 400 pages to 110, you just can't do that with an axe and scissors. You also need to create new scenes, new transitions, maybe even new characters, and certainly a lot of dialogue. You start by looking for the spine of the story. You start by trying to eliminate unimportant subplots, unimportant characters.

If you're doing adaptations, you just have so much compression to do. The first thing you have to do is find the central spine of events, and then you have to try and see the story through the protagonist's eyes because it will begin to eliminate things that aren't that important.

I always work from a treatment, even if there's a book sitting there, and it's just a book, I can't write directly from that. I have to make my own sort of bible to work from, which is usually about thirty pages long. It's either a paragraph outline about the movie or by scene as I imagine it.

LEW: Do you let other people read it?

TED: Yes, I let the studio look at it, as well. If there's a director involved from the beginning, I would let him see it. It's not a secret. It's primarily meant for me to see, however. It's not polished in a sort of Hollywood, salesmanship way. It assumes tremendous knowledge of the underlying material. It's shorthand but in paragraphs.

I try to imagine every scene or sequence of the movie, one after another, in order. It might actually say something like, "Act 1, scene 4," and list the pages of the book attributed to each section, with changes and additions. It will also roughly describe the action and how it's like the book and how it's different from the book and what it will emphasize in the movie. I just sort of create that road map until I'm satisfied, and that's the most difficult part of the actual screenplay. Only once I've completed this will I begin on the first draft of the script. Of course, what inevitably happens is you end up departing from that treatment, sometimes quite a lot, but it's the map that gets you started on your journey, even if you take some detours.

LEW: Arthur Miller said that he figures out what his play is about, and then he types it in a short sentence or paragraph and tapes it to the front of his typewriter. This way, everything that goes through his typewriter is carrying his central theme. Do you try and figure out the theme from the beginning, somewhere along the line, or not at all?

TED: I try to know it at the beginning, but in my experience, you never really do. Now, when it's an original screenplay as opposed to theater plays, then no, it wouldn't be possible. That's similar to the example Anne Lamott gives in her wonderful book *Bird by Bird*.

LEW: Yes!

TED: She talks about how it's like driving a car at night. You can only see as far as the headlights reach, trying to work from the beginning, toward the end of an original work. I never know what my original work is about until the end, and by then it's often too late. With an adaptation, it's different. If you don't know what it's about specifically before you start, then something is really wrong.

LEW: Yeah, yeah.

TED: Nevertheless, it can surprise you, I'm not sure I realized until way, way into the process that *The Silence of the Lambs* is really about a young woman orphaned in the world, searching for a new kind of father, wanting to fill a void because her father had died. I'm not sure I realized how much Crawford and Anthony's characters were about two different kinds of fathers: one good, one evil. Often, the deeper meaning of things eludes you, no matter how well you think you understand it intellectually. Your heart discovers this when your head is looking a different direction.

LEW: I've had directors say, "Do you know what you've done?" and I'll say, "I think so," and they'll state it, and I'll reply, "Oh gosh, you're right! That's really what this move is about."

TED: I think that's what keeps us writing. We're pulling from our subconscious and surprising ourselves with what may be brewing there, and this is even true in adaptations. You can do an adaptation and continuously be surprised or astonished at the deeper meaning of the work. You can always discover things that you missed, even after three or four readings of the book.

LEW: Francis Coppola and I went to school together here at UCLA. He was coming in as I was going out. I saw him one time, and he said, "I finally figured out what they were saying in *Finian's Rainbow*." As a screenwriting professor, I've always focused on asking writers what their movie is really about. I really think that if they aren't at a place to answer that question, then they aren't at a place to write an incredibly good piece.

TED: I guess that's true. You have to at least think you know what your writing is about. However, maybe it's about more than you realize. Maybe it's about more than what one person or many people will take from it. Sometimes, it skews away from what you originally thought it was about, that someone has to tell you what it's about or what it's about to them, and suddenly you see more meanings. Whatever those meanings are, it has to be something that engages you deeply and passionately.

LEW: Earlier you used the word *acts*, which is really just a screenwriter's way of saying "beginning, middle, and end."

TED: I've done three acts, and I've done four.

LEW: Oh my. Now that's what I need to know about because obviously I'm inclined to Aristotle's *Poetics*.

TED: I'll normally do three. However, I have done two, and I've also done four. It really depends on where the major beats really feel like they fall. Also, I'll do four if the book is particularly long.

LEW: Well, I just made the assumption that for writers and for most people, three acts is writer's shorthand for "beginning, middle, and end." If you're going to do two acts, would you have an Aristotelian relationship there?

TED: Ah, yes.

LEW: What do you call the first act and the second act if you're going to do two?

TED: Well, there's still the beginning, middle, and end but not necessarily in that order.

LEW: Just a sidebar: I'm on faculty at the Sorbonne in Paris, and I met Godard once, and I said, "You believe in beginnings, middles, and ends but not necessarily in that order?" and he replied, "Oh God, it was just a little cocktail joke." I mentioned this to a journalist woman at Sorbonne, and she said, "I know Mr. Godard. He's living on the outskirts of Paris, really quite lonely. He's so sorry that he's fucked up the entire nation." Well, Ted, I'm telling you and the critical studies people: They hear that, and there's nothing they can say.

TED: That's hilarious.

LEW: I mean, it's bad enough that he said it's just a cocktail joke, but when they say he fucked an entire nation with auteur theory, that's heavy. Let me ask you, you will write, and you will rewrite and get your words down to an outline. I do not know a screenwriter who does not think this is the most difficult part of the process.

TED: I think it's the most difficult and probably also the most important. Nonwriters often think a script is just dialogue, but writers well know that this part is the easiest. Getting the structure down is the most difficult, and in terms of the craft, it must come first. The structure is there to serve the character, and the dialogue is there to serve them, as well. It's finally about how much we care about them as writers and how much we can make the audience care about them. Everything comes down to character, and the character of the writer will always break through a little bit.

LEW: I make the same point to my students. We may remember the story for a few months or years, but a good character stays with us for a lifetime, whether that be Clarice or Hannibal Lecter or Charles Foster or Rick Blaine or fill in the blank.

TED: In terms of the actual craft of screenwriting, the hardest part of all is to have the story be logical, to not only have its own internal logic but also to have some looseness, some rough edges, some messiness to it, to have it resemble life and be believable. Logic fights against the kinds of surprises that are deeply satisfying in a story. This is especially true if you're writing a thriller or an action movie because this form demands a certain number of surprises. Yet, they can't feel like they were thrown in there just to be surprises. These are maybe the hardest thing of all for screenwriters to figure out. They are, at least, for me.

LEW: Jean Cocteau was once asked, "What can I do to be a wonderful writer?" And he replied, "Étonnez-moi," which means, "Astonish me." And I rarely hear people talk about this. However, if there is one problem that exists inside a well-made picture, it is the lack of surprise.

TED: Well, it's hard. I mean, you can be rational and intelligent and logical, and I'm quite a logic maven, myself, in storytelling. I don't like things that strain credibility. But in the end, you can't make a story out of just cold logic. There have to be flashes of lightning in the dark, and they have to come out of some unconscious space. It's hard to make great surprises in storytelling. They don't usually come about by some logical process.

LEW: I'm always amused at the last scene of *Citizen Kane*. We all hear him say, "Rosebud," but who else hears him say it? We just accept that these are his last words in an empty room.

TED: It's true. No one hears him. Everyone rushes into the room after he says it.

LEW: The nurse appears after.

TED: I've never thought about that.

LEW: No one does. We're too rapt in the character and the story. It's the same with *Casablanca*. Why did those two visas become so inviolate? Because from what we know of the S.S. officers, they rip them up and throw them in the wastebasket.

TED: *Casablanca* was one of the greatest movies ever made, and I'm sure it's rife with that kind of bull.

LEW: You're so right, and while I was interviewing Julius Epstein for this book, a student asked in class, "Mr. Epstein, tell us about *Casablanca*." And I said, "No, no, no. I promised Julius Epstein no *Casablanca* questions today." But Julius replied, "Lew, you used a scatological word a while back. Can I use one?" and I said, "Oh, of course!" He said, "Slick shit."

TED: That's funny.

LEW: Okay, now in the process of developing the story or the structure of the story, do you give yourself any particular time frame? One week? Three weeks? One month?

TED: Well, I guess this is the outline phase, and it usually takes about three or four weeks. It really depends on the length and the complexity of the book. Of course, sometimes, the bigger the book, the easier it is to write a screenplay from it. A shorter book that's beautifully and densely written can be very difficult to turn into a screenplay. Bob Benton said to me once that he thinks we've got it all backwards trying to turn novels into screenplays, that really the most natural source for screenplays would be short stories.

LEW: Coppola says the same thing.

TED: A short story can be enhanced in a movie, and a novel is really being reduced.

LEW: I don't know about you, but in my own screenwriting, I'm more comfortable on the shorter side rather than the longer.

TED: I'm always at page 140 by the end.

LEW: Of course you will be because a novel adaptation means so much removing.

TED: Yes, but on the other hand, a book can come with a sweep and grandeur that's rare in a short story. Books can offer a lot of extra things to a movie, but the compression is a constant source of headache.

LEW: Now you go into script, and you do it at a rate of two pages a day.

TED: Yes, but somehow it still takes four months. I don't know why that extra month. I guess I'm doing a lot of laundry these days or something. It's always a full extra month with the first draft.

LEW: Is the first draft for yourself? Or is it the draft that you're ready to show people?

TED: I work very slowly and meticulously as I go, so it may look like someone else's fourth draft. I'm actually sick of it by the time I turn it in. I work so hard on that first draft because I always think that it's just a brutal fact of the industry that the first impression is so crucial. A lot of times, although they won't tell you this directly, the first draft is either headed immediately to production, or it's doomed.

LEW: Right.

TED: Now necessarily, an original script is going to go through longer birthing pains. Maybe a reader would be more tolerant of some flaws in an original script. I don't know, but I feel like you better try to nail it in the first draft. Then the changes that come thereafter are relatively minor. They shouldn't be addressing the skeleton of the piece.

LEW: This reminds me of Irving Ravetch and Harriet Frank Jr., who are also being interviewed for this book. One of our students asked about rewriting, and Harriet kind of gave Irving a quiet nod, as if to go ahead and say what she was thinking. Irving leaned forward and said, "We like to get it right the first time." I know very well that Irving and Harriet are two-page-a-day people, as well. So that revising as you go along is good, and it's not often talked about.

TED: It depends on the particular writer, I think, with an original script. There's a lot to be said for just hurrying it out, as well. The two-week writer is just letting it pour out, and they're writing to discover more about writing, in a way. I don't want to get all hung up and constipated on just perfecting each and every scene. But with an adaptation, you're starting so far ahead of the game in terms of the plot and characters that

I think, yes, it's appropriate to make it as polished as you can in the first draft.

LEW: You mentioned *Bird by Bird*. The next book my publisher wants me to do is a *Bird by Bird* for screenwriting, this book. So being a screenwriter, where do you want to talk about the soul of screenwriting, the interior process that goes on? Give us a little input as to your thoughts on the *Bird by Bird*, Anne Lamont/soul of screenwriting?

TED: I don't really know how to do that. This is getting into really hard-to-explain sort of territory. I like the fact that there's something about the kind of directness and vulgarity to the types of movies that I respond to. I spent seven years at Yale, including graduate school. There's something to be said about movies in life holding no more or less importance than they ought to.

Now, living in Los Angeles, it may not be that way or feel that way for you. That's one reason I don't live in Los Angeles. I live in a normal sort of community, where people like movies and people talk about movies, but it isn't more or less important than other aspects of their daily lives. I like that. I don't like the idea of art as a shining marble temple on a hill, where only a few people are allowed inside, only if they have the right education or the right amount of money. I like the fact that so many movies are dopey or coarse, and a few movies are masterpieces. I guess the big tent of movies is exciting to me.

As I've said before, adaptations are exciting because you get to put on different hats. For a few months, you're a different writer than maybe you've ever been before and that you may never get to be again. For example, this year, I had the opportunity to adapt a science fiction movie. I don't know much about science fiction, I don't read it, but I had a lot of fun and learned a lot by doing it.

LEW: Do you feel your guise is more chameleon when you're writing adaptations?

TED: Yes, it's definitely a chameleon, and it also depends on whether you're drawn to it or not.

LEW: How did you get drawn into adaptations? Because almost everyone I've interviewed, their predominant thrust has been original screenplays. Some have done adaptations, but none have made it their specialty.

TED: I don't know. I wrote original plays, and I initially wrote original screenplays that didn't get made. Probably, like everything in my career, it was a sort of meandering, fortuitous thing. I've never been very good at planning out these things. The first movie I did that was made was called *White Palace*, and it was an adaptation, and soon *The Silence of the Lambs* got sent to me. One thing leads to another, and pretty soon you're looking at a stack of ten to fifteen books. If you're as lazy as I am, you realize, "Hey, I wrote a better thriller than I could think of myself. This guy wrote a better western, or this writer a better this." I couldn't compete. I couldn't have made up this plot, but I could utilize tools to make this plot even better. I knew how to tweak this and shift that. Well, here's something I can change. Before you know it, this kind of thinking has taken over.

LEW: Now, in my experience as a screenwriter, every once in a while, an actor brings so much more to a character or role that I'm astounded. Did you feel this with Anthony Hopkins in his portrayal of Hannibal Lecter?

TED: Definitely.

LEW: I should imagine, as a writer, you must have been absolutely euphoric when you saw his performance.

TED: I was euphoric even during the table reading.

LEW: You saw it coming?

TED: I said to the director, Jonathan Demme, it would be very helpful if I could hear this read out loud. It was a bit of a pain for him. He had to fly people in, find times to get them all together, because this was months before shooting. He said, "You know what? It's a useful tool. Let's do it." So, we just sat around a table and heard the actors read it aloud. It was astonishing because it was already right there. I mean, Jodie Foster and Anthony Hopkins, they had just met, there in front of our eyes, ten minutes before they sat down and started reading. There was just, like, stunned silence. They're two such intelligent people. They just knew how to bring these characters to life. There's no form of writing that happens more vividly than in theater and film, where it passes into your hands and into a larger community, and a single line can have five colors where you were hoping for two.

LEW: Well said.

TED: It's through the nuances of the actors' performances that those sub-tleties come back into the story, except that now, they're implied instead of directly stated. In the book we're going to go inside a character's head, and these thoughts and feelings are going to be directly stated. Let's hope that they're very skillfully stated; however, they remain explicit. In a screenplay it all gets pared down to the bone, and you just see the char-acter's name: Clarice Starling. Next you see a line of dialogue, whereas in the performance you see Jodie's expression, fear and hope in her eyes, a tremble, all of the inner subtleties that she brings to the character. The internal confusion and torment are there, just as they were in the book; however, now it's being shown rather than stated. Perhaps this is even richer for an audience.

LEW: One of the most frustrating experiences in my life—I've adapted about six things in my career—is creating strong dialogue for the char-acters during the adaptation. For example, I adapted Willa Cather's *My Antonia* into a miniseries, and while I consider it a brilliant book, the dialogue isn't as strong as the internal descriptions. I've observed the same phenomena with Fitzgerald and Hemingway; their strengths as writers seem to be in the character observations rather than the character dialogue.

I once asked Julius Epstein, why Fitzgerald, who really wanted to write for the screen, was less successful as a screenwriter, and he said, "He couldn't write dialogue." Do you find yourself writing new dialogue for many of these books?

TED: When there's good dialogue in a book, I use it. Other places, I'm mimicking the same style or just adding something on my own.

But you bring up an interesting point because as we were discussing earlier, it really is all about character, and in a character this is displayed only in dialogue or action. One has to know what actors need and what will stumble in their mouths and what speech will soar and what props they'll need to get through the scene. To think about it literally, they're going to have to get up that morning, go to their trailer, go through makeup and hair, have their coffee, and then go to set and act out the scene in front of a bunch of sleepy, hungover crew members. It's six o'clock in the morning on some freezing Pennsylvania hillside, and maybe no on wants to be there. It's, therefore, your job as a screenwriter to not just be thinking about the needs of your screenplay but also to be serving the actors so well that everyone is excited about what's happening in each scene.

LEW: Very good.

TED: And you better know every actor, like every character, has their own enlightened self-interest.

LEW: Yeah.

TED: You better not try and make a character do something dumb just because your plot called for it. You have to stay sensitive to the needs of the actors if you want them to bring your character to life. I don't just mean the leads either. I mean each and every supporting character, as well. This is the sharp difference between novel writing and the kind of writing we do.

LEW: Every screenwriter in this book has thus far emphasized a specific aspect that they consider carefully when writing a screenplay. It's what makes these interviews so interesting because each writer has their own specific emphasis. You emphasize the actor more than any other screenwriter that has contributed to this, and I can't tell you how much I agree with that because I have also been producing throughout my career, and I have been sitting there in those readings. Those readings suffer a good deal if the actor doesn't understand what the scene or the line is really about, and you're calling attention to this.

TED: Yes, I'm saying it's often the writer's role to make certain that the script is written so that each and every actor does understand the scene and each and every line.

LEW: Exactly.

TED: Of course, that's why, I mean, the one thing I really miss in going from theater to movies is the extended rehearsal. I've only had rehearsal on one movie of mine, and most directors don't like to do it because they would rather have the spontaneity. A lot of movie actors probably don't want to do it, either. But the ones with a theater background are always happy to rehearse because they know the value. I miss that because actors will let you know more or less in a hurry when something isn't working. Sometimes they don't let you know by complaining. They try their very, very best, but if you consistently see that it's not working, that's a huge value to the writer.

LEW: And often the communication is nonverbal, too. Perhaps they aren't even quite able to verbalize what's not working, but everyone can see it. You know, you're one of the least cynical people whom I have ever talked to. Perhaps that's because you're not in the contiguous Los Angeles area code.

TED: I'm deeply cynical about the business of moviemaking and about Hollywood studios, but I've developed this sort of schizophrenic ability to divorce what I do at the computer from what happens after I send off the script. I try to do the best I can with what is in my control. I try my best to ignore what's not under my control, which is about 95 percent of moviemaking.

LEW: Sounds like the serenity of Alcoholics Anonymous. Give me the courage to change what I can and the wisdom to—

TED: Screenwriters Anonymous.

LEW: It's commendable that you can do this because in my own pejorative thinking, writers who go around whining about how they've been fucked over by so many studios and producers aren't helping themselves.

TED: Yes, it's so tired, and we're ridiculously well paid.

LEW: Exactly.

TED: You can't take the money and then whine about what you didn't get.

LEW: Hear, hear.

TED: What I want to hear screenwriters say is not how some writer fucked up their line or some director, their scene, but rather, "Hey, that actor made that scene so much better," or, "Thank God that editor cut that horrible scene I couldn't fully resolve."

LEW: Do you know the actress Melinda Dillon?

TED: Yes.

LEW: She did a movie of mine, and oh boy, did she give things to lines without changing a word. She thought of more things that I ever dreamt of for that part.

TED: A truly communal art form.

LEW: Yes.

TED: And either your ego can accept that, or you should be writing poetry or something different because once you accept that, it brings a bounty, too. I think for every time somebody makes you look bad in this business, there's one or two times that they will make you look better than you thought you were. That's the trade-off. Either you accept that, or you don't.

LEW: Rita, speak for yourself or from the student perspective. Do you have questions or something you would like to add?

RITA: Do you really think there's a sort of advantage to being outside of the Hollywood loop? I grew up in Pennsylvania, and I have lots of affection for my hometown; however, people say that if you want to write for movies, you need to move to Los Angeles. Do you disagree?

TED: I grew up in North Carolina, and I've spent my whole life in the east. I went to school in New England, and I'm very much an East Coast kind of person. I love being in Los Angeles when I do go out to visit, but stuff is right in your face there. There are the billboards, and the premieres, the newspapers, the coffeehouse talk is about it. I would find it very hard to do what I do when I know that every Starbucks barista is also working on a screenplay during their breaks.

RITA: Exactly what I was wondering. In school here, we are a bit away from it all; however, it's hard to go out into it and be influenced by what you're being bombarded with. You lose some of the purity of what you're trying to do.

TED: It makes me feel really self-conscious when I'm in Los Angeles too long. I live in an area where everything is corporate, and people work for companies like Johnson & Johnson, or there's a schoolteacher or this plumbing contractor. I sort of like that. It gives you exposure to other walks of life and other realities. When I lived in Manhattan, I lived in a building that was filled with actors and directors and writers. You couldn't go down the elevator without people telling you about their production deal or their new pilot or whatever. I just find that this can be very claustrophobic, and I was glad to go back to what I called "real life." It was liberating, and it helped a good deal with developing real-life characters.

RITA: I can see that.

TED: Although, as it turns out, I've discovered three other screenwriters who live within a ten-mile radius. They're really solid, professional screenwriters, too.

LEW: Well, we screenwriters have been liberated by the fact, actually in point of fact, I'm retiring from UCLA soon, and I'm going back to the "real life" of Nebraska. I have a home in a small town in Nebraska. People say, "Oh God, won't you feel like you're out of it?" And I reply, "Out of it? I have a computer, and the internet. It's going to be fabulous."

TED: And you've got FedEx.

LEW: Thank God for FedEx.

TED: And airplanes.

LEW: And I can be in Paris from Omaha, Nebraska, at noon tomorrow, if it were necessary.

TED: I think writers are uniquely fortunate in this. I mean, a director or an actor, they have to go to set or go for auditions. A director has to do whatever horrible things they have you do to get the jobs. If you're a writer and you've got a tangible product that you can just send, then you can live anywhere and make it work in the movies.

RITA: Wow.

TED: Now, television is probably different. You have to press the flesh and take meetings.

LEW: I see from your credits that you did one piece for television.

TED: I did one TV movie, and that was a good experience. It's the first thing I had made.

RITA: I got one more sort of nascent question that I'd like to ask since you've been through so many adaptations. Are there specific pitfalls that you've learned to avoid?

TED: Yes, many.

RITA: I mean, it was very interesting to hear you talk about the point of view of your protagonist.

TED: The most important pitfall for me is to not make the mistake of thinking that you're a lot better than the person who wrote the book. Some poor schmuck has been sitting there, alone, for ten years writing this book, and this is the best ending that he or she was able to come up with after talking to just about everyone that they know. This was the ending that the arithmetic of this book led to. Don't assume that you can come up with a better ending than that and think that it will leap into your head in a flash. One of the main pitfalls to avoid is agreeing to adapt a book with a weak ending. Only do it if you instantly have a better idea.

RITA: That's interesting.

TED: You'll stumble around and chase your tail, and you and the director and the producer will realize that you're $45 million into the picture, and three years have gone by, and no one ever did solve that ending problem, did they?

LEW: In my book-adaptation experience, I feel I'm too reverential to the original author. Do you suffer from this?

TED: No, I'm not overly accepting of the original.

LEW: Perhaps that's the difference between a Yale background and mine at Northwestern?

TED: I began as reverential, but after a lot of adaptations, you're a hardened professional. You figure, "Oh, what the hell. They got their check, and the original will always be there." So my attitude is like what I said earlier about screenwriters: Be grateful for the money, but recognize that it's now a communal art form.

I've had very good relationships with some of the authors, but eh, the smartest of them, Tom Harris, said to me one time, "You know, you have to do what you have to do. The book and the movie each have their own agenda. They're not the same." He went on to say, "I don't want to look over your shoulder, and I don't want you to worry about what I think. It doesn't matter. It's becoming something else now." That's the right attitude, I think, if you're willing to sell a book to the studios. You can't really control the process, no matter how hard you try. You might as well get out of the way and hope for the best.

LEW: There are volumes of screenwriting books out there now, so let me back up a little bit. Was there one particular book that was of great benefit to you? Maybe Aristotle or Egri?

TED: Well, it was all of the different books, but for me, I don't actually remember reading a particular primer on playwriting or screenwriting. For me, it was the books on writing fiction, the John Gardner and the *Paris Review* stuff.

LEW: What about when you were a student at Yale?

TED: I read about fiction writing there, yes.

LEW: But you didn't read the Baker book? Or the John Howard Lawson book? Because Baker came out of Yale.

TED: No, but I had a great high school textbook by Maynard Mack. When I arrived at Yale, the next year, Mack was still teaching there. He wrote a wonderful book called *Character and Conflict*. He was the editor of it. It was a group of plays, and he wrote the introductions to them and discussed them and sort of broke them down. It was one of my senior-year-of-high-school textbooks. It was invaluable. I mean, my copy just fell apart from all of the dog-ears and use.

LEW: You were a theater major at Yale?

TED: Yes, I was.

LEW: Did you specialize in playwriting?

TED: I guess you could say I did. I mean it was more of an English major there. It was technically a drama major, but it was, in effect, a sort of English literature major and also dramatic arts. I went on to the drama school, where I got an MFA in playwriting.

LEW: Now, then, finally, back to secrets. My publisher said that people pick up these books to see if they can find a useful secret.

TED: Would that there were. And if there were, we would like to give it away for the reduced price of $22.95 after twenty-five years of bloody struggle. The secret is the same adage that these kids have heard a million times: Talent matters, but perseverance matters more. It is, after all, a craft. There is never a single day of writing that is wasted. You're getting better every time you sit down and work on it. You have to write your way into a better writer.

LEW: Are you becoming a better writer, or do you find yourself becoming a different writer? Do you look at the earlier Ted Tally and wonder, "Gee, he was really good or really different"?

TED: I don't know. I'm certainly less idealistic. I'm sure on some level there's sort of less of a passion in a pure sense, but you know, you make up for it because you've become craftier and more cunning.

LEW: I guess the reason I asked this question is because I'm so disheartened when some writers seem to peak and then disappear. You wonder if they were at a time in their lives when that was as good as they could get, or if they lost their passion or interest or just their perseverance, as you just stated.

TED: Some writers are so great in that moment, there's no better to be had.

LEW: Then it goes back to, should we be judged by our best things as opposed to anything less?

TED: Yes, we should.

LEW: Then you look at Frank Pierson, who was so affluent and strong in every screenplay—

TED: Pierson. Incredible writer. But how many of those are there? How many Billy Wilders are there?

LEW: There you go.

TED: How many Robert Townes are there?

LEW: Townes, too. After *Chinatown*, he didn't get any better.

TED: He didn't need to.

LEW: It reminds me of that line from another contributor to this book, in Tom Schulman's *Dead Poets Society*: "The powerful play goes on, and you may contribute a verse."

TED: Everybody would like to be judged by their best work. You've also got to pay the rent. I'm a great believer in the realities of the business, and this business is not for the faint of heart. This is a blood sport.

LEW: I one time said to Louis Armstrong, "Louis, you're such an unbelievable horn player. Why do you also sing?" and he replied, "I've got to pay the rent, baby."

TED: That's great. Nothing wrong with that.

LEW: No, not at all.

TED: You know, if Shakespeare were alive today, believe me, he would be writing movies.

LEW: Wouldn't he, though?

TED: Or television.

LEW: It's unbelievable to me that so many people thought he was a whore back then.

TED: He wasn't a whore; he was a hack. He was just a really, really good one. If he were alive today, he'd be saying, "You mean I can reach an audience of five million versus two hundred?"

LEW: Did you ever hear the Molière phrase "Being a writer is like being a hooker. You start off doing it for yourself and then for a few friends, then you figure, 'What the hell? I might as well be paid for it'"?

TED: That's hilarious. And very true.

LEW: We're at this point—and dear Rita, she's just starting—if we see each other five years from now, please ask me what Rita's doing, and I'll tell you, but I'm sure I won't have to.

TED: I won't have to ask, I'm sure.

LEW: She is a wonderful writer.

TED: I always look for the writer's credit before any other credit.

LEW: Oh, me, too.

TED: Only writers do that.

LEW: Only writers, but can you imagine the thrill of it? I went down to the AMC, and seven of the ten movies were by former students.

TED: Oh, that's great.

LEW: I'm telling you, that is just to die.

TED: You must be doing something right, or it's an amazing coincidence.

LEW: I'm not sure that it's either. We have hundreds of applicants, and we narrow it down to about two dozen for our program. We really try and make good selections, and you're right, it's not just the talent that we're looking at but also how much have they already written? It tells us something about perseverance right away.

TED: Talent definitely helps, too.

LEW: Yes, and as you've stated, it can develop further with constant reading and writing. Any rate, dear Ted, thank you so much.

TED: Thank you.

LEW: You've been our virginal experience. We've never done it on the phone. This has its own value. Rita's been to about half a dozen others, and each have their own value because over the phone you're not with a group of other people.

TED: It's always a reassuring and very warming thing to meet young writers.

LEW: Right on, Ted, and write on!

11

Ruth Prawer Jhabvala

Ruth Prawer Jhabvala I wanted for this book as much, if not more than, any other Academy Award–winning screenwriter. Women used to be a quality and often-favored staple in screenwriting. A few names who will resonate with film ancients, buffs, and scholars include Frances Marion, Marguerite Roberts, Frances Goodrich, Leigh Brackett, Sally Benson, our own Harriet Frank Jr., Mary C. McCall Jr., Phoebe Ephron (yes, Nora's mother), Anita Loos, Isobel Lennart, Ruth Gordon, Helen Deutsch, Dorothy Parker, Zoe Akins, Betty Comden, Virginia Van Upp, Catherine Turney, Lenore Coffee, Jay Presson Allen, Eleanor Perry, Joan Harrison, Bess Meredyth, and many more I could exhume, but I'm sure the point is taken and hopefully well made.

It was said, snottily, that many women used husbands as a near shill so that she could write screenplays. "The real talent is the wife" was a common whisper. I certainly want to except our Harriet Frank Jr. from that scurrilous conjecture. Or maybe I should really except our dear Irving Ravetch, okay, Harriet?

Today many women are the show runners of television shows; unfortunately, however, cinema has not been overwhelmed by women writers with the career stature and body of quality work represented by our two-time Academy Award winner of true class, Ruth Prawer Jhabvala. Often pairing with Merchant Ivory Productions, Ruth is responsible for such unforgettable adaptations as *The Golden Bowl*, *The Bostonians*, and *The Remains of the Day*, winning her two Academy Awards for the adaptations of E. M. Forster's *Howard's End* and *A Room with a View*.

Ms. Jhabvala (a.k.a., Ruth) had a background of short-story and novel writing, which made her unique to the Academy for Screenwriting. Nearly every screenwriter wishes to give novel writing a go, while many novelists long to write screenplays. Ms. Jhabvala wished and did. Did she ever!

LEW: I am so thrilled to have you on the line, as is my dear research associate, Rita Augustine. I'd like to visit with you, Ruth, about the process of screenwriting. This book is totally focused on how each screenwriter does it. As Bill Goldman says, "The horror of it all is that we all do it so differently," and I responded, "Bill that's the joy and importance of it, too. It's your own uniqueness that brings the screenplay to life, whether you're a student or an Oscar-winning screenwriter." Would you agree with that?

RUTH: Yes, of course. I suppose everybody does do it a little bit differently.

LEW: Would you classify yourself rather than as a screenwriter as a storyteller?

RUTH: Well, I started off as a novelist and a short-story writer, and I think I've remained one throughout the years. And since you talk about approach to screenwriting, mine has been extremely literary, which I suppose is almost heretical.

LEW: When I started teaching, I came to the realization that this field is really just about storytelling, and we're using the medium of film. How do you respond to storytelling as it relates to motion pictures?

RUTH: Well, when I started off, I wanted to tell a story about characters in certain situations. That's how I approached my novels and short stories, which I was writing long before I even thought about screenplays. I think I've stayed true to this.

LEW: How were you persuaded to do "performance writing," if you will, as opposed to novel or short-story writing?

RUTH: Purely accidentally. Merchant Ivory read one of my books and asked if I'd be interested in writing a screenplay. I'd never written a screenplay, and they'd never made a film, so we tried it out. Well, it wasn't a success, but then we went on to another, and after that we never stopped.

LEW: Did you look to any particular source when you were switching gears from novels and short stories into screenplays?

RUTH: None whatsoever, absolutely none. I'd hardly seen any films in India. No new films came there. I think the only time I'd seen films was in England, during my time there.

LEW: Well, now, I believe India has quite the thriving movie industry.

RUTH: Yes, but I didn't see those either. Even Satyajit Ray was extremely hard to see in India. His films would be playing in Delhi, where I lived, only on Sunday mornings, and they were in Bengali, which I didn't understand.

LEW: Satyajit Ray was one of my idols when I was a student at UCLA. Was he appreciated in India?

RUTH: I think not in those years. There was just no cinema for him. He was always appreciated in his native Calcutta, but the rest of India was sort of saturated with cinema from Bombay.

LEW: Did you get to know him as time went on?

RUTH: Yes, we did. He worked with us and was very kind to us. He even wrote the music for one of our films, which was *Shakespeare Wallah*. He also helped us with the editing of the first one we did. We were really just amateurs, but he really helped us out. He even gave us his editor and sat with us for weeks in the cutting room.

LEW: Tell us about your work habits. How do you get to the keyboard or pencil or pen or quill or what have you?

RUTH: It hasn't really changed. I still write every single day. I always write in the mornings. I used to write mornings and afternoons, but I don't seem to be able to do that any longer. In the afternoons, I do corrections or copying drafts or something like that. The real work, now, only comes in the mornings.

LEW: Five days a week or seven?

RUTH: Seven, except when I'm traveling.

One strange thing, when I'm writing fiction, I never think of it again once I've finished writing. I like to believe it is germinating in my subconscious. However, when I'm writing a screenplay, I consciously think of it all day long. Even in the middle of the night, it may come to me where I can compress some of it or where a better line of dialogue might be placed.

LEW: Do you utilize computer or other means?

RUTH: I always write in longhand first. I used to put it on a typewriter, but I never learned how to type properly. I used to type with two fingers, but my typewriter isn't made anymore, so now I use a computer like I used to type on the typewriter.

LEW: But always first in longhand?

RUTH: Yes.

LEW: Is that a habit, or is there something spiritual connected to that? Neil Simon said he likes to write in longhand because he can feel it spill out of his brain, down into his arm, and on into his fingertips.

RUTH: There is that feeling, yes. Also, there's some satisfaction from including some drawings and doodles, as well.

LEW: I sort of feel the same way. People told me that once I went to computer, I would never go back to the typewriter; however, I like that tactile feel to it all. The idea is to not stare all day at a phosphor screen.

RUTH: It's just a machine between you and whatever you're doing.

LEW: Now, let's go into the actual process. What is your litmus test for what you're going to choose to spend all of your time working on when you have several options?

RUTH: With Merchant Ivory films, this is not a decision for me. If I have an original idea, I'd prefer to write it as a story or novel. I have written quite a number of original scripts, but they were usually dreamt up with James Ivory, who always does the Merchant Ivory films.

As for adaptation, there were some books that I've always felt were perfect for James, such as the E. M. Forster or the Henry James. As far as choice of screenplay, my own predilections don't come first. Because I always work with the same director, I always consider what would suit us both. What particularly suits me are novels and stories.

LEW: Let me ask you this—Rita has already heard me talk about this in class—do you consider writing as more of a feminine act, whereas directing and producing is more of a masculine act? I've always regarded writing and editing, in some ways, as trying to please other people. How do you regard this?

RUTH: You're talking about attitudes?

LEW: Precisely. It isn't literal. Some men can be quite feminine vis-à-vis writing and editing, and there are some feminist men who are more feministic than many self-proclaimed feminists I know. There seems to be something very nurturing and giving to these trades.

RUTH: Precisely. Even as a novelist, you're never really free or in complete charge.

LEW: Right.

RUTH: So I suppose you're kind of a spouse or partner as an editor or writer.

LEW: Let's talk about structure. Do you use a longhand outline? Of course, a good share of your screenwriting works have been adaptations. Do you use scene cards? What is your process?

RUTH: Well, let's talk about original screenplays first, yes?

LEW: Okay.

RUTH: I do make an outline, but I abandon it at some point. I rarely really stick to it if it doesn't take on a life of its own. If things happen that I didn't know about, it wasn't worth it in the first place.

LEW: So generally, you don't think it's worth it in the first place?

RUTH: No. Writing an outline is almost like writing a formula. As with fiction writing, the thing has to take on a life of its own.

LEW: What about adaptations?

RUTH: With adaptations, I read the book three times, and then I put it aside. I try to work out the structure, as far as how the movie should go, on my own. It's not always how it is in the book. It's a different rhythm with a different emphasis, so I work on that without the book in front of me.

LEW: Do you write it in outline form?

RUTH: Yes, I do, and I stick to it much more than I do an original screenplay. The thing is, the outcome of the story is already there in an adaptation. Sometimes the outline works; sometimes it doesn't work.

LEW: Do you ascribe that to any sort of mental blockage?

RUTH: No, no. Sometimes I'm just not in tune with the material, or it's the wrong type of material for me.

LEW: Ted Geisel, who is also Dr. Seuss, said that he goes in at nine o'clock in the morning, and he won't let himself come out until five o'clock at night. So some of his pieces, such as *The Cat in the Hat*, came out of sheer boredom. I can't imagine that's totally true, but it's a nice anecdote to highlight the importance of perseverance.

So you really just give yourself assignments or times to write. I'm fond of quoting the Old Testament and pointing out that those writers didn't give themselves credit because they considered themselves conduits rather than original writers.

RUTH: Yes, that's exactly how it works.

LEW: When you turn a script in, does it generally relate to the time frame given by the people around you?

RUTH: No, we don't work with a time frame, exactly. I'm usually far ahead of them because they're finishing a film while I'm moving onto another. Nowadays, I do like to ask for the year. *The Golden Bowl* was on and off for three years.

LEW: Since you have such a close relationship with Merchant Ivory, they probably don't give you the kind of pressure that studios and such give most writers.

RUTH: No, they don't. I'm on my own, as it were.

LEW: Oh! That's heaven! And you know it, don't you?

On the subject of rewriting, some people say that scripts aren't written but that they are rewritten. How do you feel about that?

RUTH: I think it's true. I do the first draft fast—very fast. Then I begin the process of going over it, adding to it, expanding it. I'll then put it aside to clear my mind and then pick it up again. It goes on and on, and by the time I'm ready to show it to Merchant Ivory, it has gone through about seven drafts. Then they come and say what they like or, more often, what they don't like, but it's only Merchant Ivory, nobody else, and by the time we are ready to show it to anyone else, it's complete.

LEW: Do you look forward to their thoughts and suggestions and input?

RUTH: Yes, I think I do because by that time I've been alone with it for so long. I'm glad to have some input.

LEW: You're one of the rare screenwriters who does not mind input, then. I've actually had two directors in my life where I loved to hear what they had to say because so often they were in tune with making it better. Other people were philistines, but you've never had that experience, have you?

RUTH: I've been lucky, working with Merchant Ivory every time.

LEW: The rewriting, for the most part, it's all you?

RUTH: I do it on my own, then they make suggestions, then we do some more, until finally we have a script that we can send to actors. Once they're on set, there isn't much rewriting, but I come in at some point and look at the dailies and realize I can save some money somewhere, and I remove things that really aren't needed.

LEW: Do you go to set often?

RUTH: No, no, no. Maybe once.

LEW: Is this your own choice?

RUTH: Absolutely, yes.

LEW: But periodically, you've been asked to look at dailies?

RUTH: Well, usually only once, and it's usually on my way to India, and once I've done it, I just stay in India.

LEW: They encourage you to look at the first cut?

RUTH: Absolutely, yes. The first cut is extremely important to all of us. It's usually terribly long, and we have to cut it down. I certainly work at that stage. I do quite a bit of cutting and reordering and just generally messing around with it. I try and compress as much as I can so that the scene still holds the essence of what it needs to convey.

LEW: Do you consciously write a bit long to have a bit to work with as part of this process?

RUTH: No, not really, but they do seem to come out long. I don't know why. Even at the script stage, I compress as much as I possibly can. I try and never make an actor say a superfluous word.

LEW: Sometimes you take certain things out or readjust things a bit, and maybe this is quite important to do in the writing part of a plot-driven film; however, in my experience, movies you've adapted, such as *The Remains of the Day* or *A Room with a View*, these are the evolution of characters. Does that change the rewriting a bit, where you can spend more time in the editing room to get what you want?

RUTH: Yes, quite a bit. Sometimes it happens that the actors have not come out as well as one has hoped, and then we can throw emphasis on the other. One can always improve performance in the editing room.

LEW: Isn't that true! That's something nobody's said. In theater we only have rehearsal, while in cinema we have the editing room. And people talk about writing actor-proof pictures, but the reality is, a lot of performances are cut together. Do you find that the editing room allows you to go beyond the boundaries you anticipated of their characters?

RUTH: Oh, absolutely, and it's almost what one expects. If they don't do that, if they don't sort of take off on their own, if they don't add another dimension to what is written, then the whole thing falls down. So we've always had absolutely marvelous actors.

LEW: Haven't you, though? Have you been involved with writing with them?

RUTH: Not really, no.

LEW: Many times there is an adversarial relationship between writer and director, but this isn't your case.

RUTH: No.

LEW: Because you have so much confidence in your director?

RUTH: Yes, yes, I just leave it to him. Once the script is completed, then it's really his completely, until we get to the editing room. I might come in and shift everything around, but even still, someone might just go and put it all back.

LEW: Tell me about art as it relates to screenwriting. Would you consider screenwriting an art?

RUTH: I suppose yes, it's part art. It's not an independent one, however. It's one that everyone contributes to, and that's when it takes on a life of its own.

LEW: It's fortunate that has not been frustrating for you because you have written quite a lot of prose, where collaboration is not important. What would you term the difference between novel writing and performance writing?

RUTH: In novels, of course, you do the whole thing. I mean, novels really are an art form because you're the actor, the director, and the writer. You have do to the scenery. You have to get every character's intonation correct. You have to do the whole thing. Certainly, novel writing is more demanding. I think it's more difficult.

LEW: Aha! Many novel writers have told me that they find screenwriting more difficult, and when I ask why, they say, "Because you have to stick to the story. You can't go off for fifteen pages on the flora and the fauna." Thornton Wilder once said to me that the difference between performance writing and novel writing is that in performance writing, the act itself is the most important thing, while in novel writing, the writer feels it's the commentary on the act. Would you agree with this?

RUTH: No, I'm not that kind of writer. Even in novels I try and show rather than say. I try and make the characters reveal themselves. Also, I don't have that much description or commentary in my books or stories.

LEW: Have you found that being a woman screenwriter has been a disadvantage or an advantage, or has it made no difference at all?

RUTH: No difference, I think.

LEW: Rita, do you have some questions?

RITA: Have you found when you're writing screenplays that certain things really just don't work? Perhaps they work on the page, as they might in a novel, but they don't work once it goes to production? What sort of things go through your head as to how to adapt a story to make it better from a book to film?

RUTH: This is very much true, absolutely. I found out early on that some things work on the page that won't work on the screen. I used to love to have my characters walking and talking. Now, I don't know if it's my fault, but our walking-and-talking scenes were terrible. I've seen it work in other people's films but somehow not in ours. I can tell you one example: In *Howard's End* there is the notion that people must connect, that different kinds of human beings must connect, so I wrote a scene where they're sitting on a hillside, talking about it, talking about the need to connect. It didn't work out.

LEW: I use the term *show, don't tell.* I'll put the phrase more nicely, but Humphrey Bogart once said, "If you're giving me a scene with talking heads, put two camels behind me, fornicating, so at least the audience has something to look at." When you use the phrase *doesn't work*, what would be an example of working versus not working? Is it an emotional connection, an intellectual connection, or some combination?

RUTH: No, it just means when something comes alive. It doesn't remain dead. It remains alive and vital and thus works.

LEW: Almost an aesthetic feeling.

RITA: You appear to have so much freedom in the pieces you've chosen to work on. Is there something you keep going back to that you feel is a thematic constant to you in these pieces?

RUTH: They're all, as we've said, character driven. They aren't plot driven. Always the action is within the intellect and emotions of the characters. Everything I do, both in novels and screenplays, is fueled by this. It's always about people showing emotions while contained inside civilized behavior.

LEW: I was going to say, it's civility, but underneath lies so much sensuality, passion, and rage.

RUTH: Yes, that's what we like.

LEW: That's probably the sensibility of your youth, in your own cultural background, correct?

RUTH: Yes, it's also the sort of literature that I grew up with.

LEW: Do you spend a lot of time researching? In terms of originals and adaptations? Or is most of it already there in an adaptation?

RUTH: It depends. With Henry James, I'd already read a lot of Henry James. I'd read his novels, his letters, biographies, autobiography.

LEW: Is there a point where you say, "Enough," because you realize you could spend the rest of your life researching?

RUTH: Yes, and that's when I really just get going.

RITA: When you research for period pieces, for example, does it ever worry you that you may be missing something? That there's something critical that you may not understand about that time period, or do you feel confident?

RUTH: No, not really. You don't feel confident, but on the other hand, in a way it's one's own interpretation of the time. It can never really be an authentic thing. One's self is always mixed up in it.

LEW: Ruth, my last question is about the word *secrets*. Every aspiring screenwriter hopes to find something amongst the world of successful screenwriters that will give them a glimpse into their secret for success. Do you feel there are any particular secrets to screenwriting?

RUTH: No, never. There are no secrets. You just have to keep building up your scenes, building up your characters. You have to make the story work. It takes a lot of time, and it isn't easy. It's not a secret, and it's more of a craft than an art. Have you found any secrets that you give to writers?

LEW: My secret is just to tell writers to write. It's exactly what you said: You only get better with writing.

RUTH: Yes, exactly! Just do it over and over. It really is something that can improve.

LEW: I don't believe in writer's block. I think a true writer, when he or she gets stuck, it's due to the array of choices. This is when you get up and walk around the block or stare at the tile because writers just write. It's what defines and separates them. Some people will spend their entire lives talking about their idea of the greatest screenplay, but until they bang out a first draft, it means nothing. It's like the play *La Ronde*: The beginning is the end. We should be writing on and on and never let it end.

RUTH: That's right! Writing for the rest of your life—that's the only secret.

12

Ernest Lehman

In the gestation period of this book, I made a battlefield decision. I would include three career screenwriters who have not won an Academy Award but who have contributed significantly to the craft and have, in some way, shaped cinema. The husband-and-wife team Irving Ravetch and Harriet Frank Jr. as well as Ernest Lehman were my chosen troika, as all three had won every other significant screenwriting award. Ernie has earned nine Writers Guild of America Awards (more than any other screenwriter), two Golden Globe Awards, and four Oscar nods for such iconic classics as *North by Northwest*, *Sabrina*, *Who's Afraid of Virginia Woolf?* and *Westside Story*. In 2001, Ernie was showcased at the Academy Awards ceremony and was the first screenwriter to receive an honorary Academy Award. Huzzah, and about time!

Ernest Lehman presented himself to our 434 screenwriting gathering with style, wit, passion, wisdom, and eyes periodically sparkling with mischief as he recalled certain moments that were important to him in his career as a screenwriter, moments that truly represented the way it was with the great and those who thought they were great. Men and women screenwriters who suffered fools also helped morph these screenwriters into sophisticated, educated, tall children putting miscreant deeds over on mom and dad. These men and women, on both sides of the desk, often found themselves working in a system where entertainment, not box-office commerce, was the most desired goal, men and women who wrote many significant visual moments and words for a celluloid time when actors and directors received credit for the "making up" or "creating" rather than the writer.

The opening scenes of *The Sound of Music* are read in every 434 by yours truly. The goatherds, the passing birds, the valley vistas, the glorious mountains with Maria on the highest peak—none of these meticulously crafted scenes were credited to the true screenwriter: Ernest Lehman.

Here comes more reel-ality, style, wit, passion, wisdom, and mischief from the seminal screenwriter, Ernie Lehman.

LEW: Ernie Lehman, we are here, with these 434 screenwriting warriors, to talk about developing screenplays. We want to talk about the beginning, middle, and endings. Could you give us a reaction about screenwriting as it relates to storytelling? Is it storytelling? Is it that simple?

ERNEST: It is storytelling, but it isn't simple. Obviously, we have a beginning, middle, and end. Sometimes the beginning of the movie can be the beginning of the story. Other times, the beginning can be halfway into the story, meaning you come in on something when it's at its height or depth and have it go to new heights or depths and then resolve it. I don't like to generalize, but I can give examples. *The Sweet Smell of Success* is a movie that begins in the middle of everything. When I cowrote the screenplay and the novelette, we started with tremendous difficulties. That is the way the movie opens.

LEW: There are two books for anybody who wants further information on what Ernie is saying. One is John Brady's *The Craft of the Screenwriter*, and the other is *Screenwriters on Screenwriting* by Joel Engel.

ERNEST: I prefer my interview with Joel Engel, but they're both good.

LEW: There's this great question asked by John Brady, which asks for the required ingredients by act. You reply, "In the first act, who are the people, and what is the situation of the whole story? The second act progresses that situation to a point of high conflict, and the third act is how conflicts and problems are solved. That's putting it simply, but I think that's the way it should be." Do you still hold to this?

ERNEST: In a general way.

LEW: It's pretty Aristotelian.

ERNEST: It's pretty obvious.

LEW: Was Aristotle meaningful to you when you were starting out?

ERNEST: No, not at all. I never took anything from that book. I think what I know, I know from seeing a lot of movies when I was a kid.

LEW: Which movies were affecting you?

ERNEST: Seeing movies when you're six years old and up until you're twenty-five, you can say, "Oh, that movie is influencing me," but when you become a screenwriter, you have all of these unconscious parallels in your memory, and without knowing it, you could be copying something you saw forty years earlier. I guess, that isn't helpful to these 434 ladies and gentlemen.

LEW: It is, actually, because you're suggesting that maybe they're influenced by what they saw as adolescents but not consciously. It's a biological rhythm beyond movies, and even before movies, writers were influenced by the stories they had heard or were told. We've been told stories since sitting on our grandmother's knee.

You know, Jane Campion was here, and when I asked her about books, she admitted that she had acquired a great deal of her writing ability from reading short stories by Flannery O'Connor. What about you? Was there any fiction that was affective to you in becoming a storyteller?

ERNEST: God, I've read so much, I don't think I could point to one author. Well, Irwin Shaw, he comes to mind. John O'Hara, too. Even earlier than that were all of the famous so-called mystery writers and novelists, most of them women. I wrote lots and lots of short stories before I came to Hollywood.

LEW: That was really your entry into Hollywood. Or was it through journalism?

ERNEST: It wasn't journalism. It was my short stories and novelettes, like the comedian in *Sweet Smell of Success*, were instrumental in my being brought out by Paramount. Writing short stories, you have the setup of the situation, and you follow it in a way that the reader doesn't stop wanting to know what's going to happen. A short story is a very difficult form. A movie ought to be on a richer, deeper plane, and it begins with exposition that should never seem like exposition. Never let the audience know you are trying to give them information. Let them figure things out by the nature of the scene.

I am someone who doesn't want to miss a frame of a movie. I get nervous if I find something I must have missed. It's kind of disturbing, and I blame it on the screenwriter. *LA Confidential* was like that, and yet it struck me as being very intelligently written without calling attention to the writing. Now *Good Will Hunting* was also very intelligently written, but I was aware of the writing and the speeches.

LEW: Tell us about your work habits.

ERNEST: I constantly look back at what I've written, and I wonder why in the hell I did something. I can't believe that I spent ten months on *North by Northwest.* I just don't know why it took so much effort and time. My impression is that I'll do anything to avoid the typewriter. I wander around a lot, seemingly doing nothing, but my mind is working hard to solve some ridiculous little script situation. My sons grew up with a father who paced the kitchen at night.

LEW: Faulkner says a dog circles the backyard, and the circle gets tighter and tighter, until the dog finally sits down at the typewriter. Do you use a typewriter?

ERNEST: I use a word processor but obviously not until it was invented.

LEW: Pencil? Pen? Legal pad?

ERNEST: Yeah, a lot of illegal writing on that.

LEW: Is most of your writing done at night? Is that your prime time?

ERNEST: It depends. If I'm working on a movie, then it's around the clock. Writers are not good sleepers.

LEW: Did you work on the lot?

ERNEST: In the early days, I had an office at MGM.

LEW: You have a number of original screenplays that have been made into movies. What, in terms of the idea, do you say, "This is the one I want to do"? What causes you to choose one idea over another?

ERNEST: I wrote *North by Northwest* because I had quite the movie. I was supposedly doing the movie with Hitchcock, and I made up *North by Northwest* as I went along with things, so it wasn't originally an idea for a movie. I have several ideas today that I keep saying I want to do, but I don't do them. I have maybe fourteen pages written on one and the first ten on the other. I have a complete script that I'm meeting with a producer about next week. He likes the script, but I finished it over a year ago, and I think it's miserable.

LEW: *North by Northwest* was an original screenplay. You had the opportunity to write that one because that one picture fell out with Hitchcock?

ERNEST: It didn't fall out. I quit. I said, "I don't know how to do this picture, Hitch. Maybe you do." After three weeks of that kind of talk, I arrived at his house and said, "I'm sorry, Hitch. You, you'll have to get a new writer." He said, "Don't be silly. We'll do something else." I said, "What will we tell the front office?" and he replies, "We won't tell them." That's how *North by Northwest* got written over a laborious ten months.

LEW: Talk to us about developing story. Did you develop stories one way for yourself and another for Mr. Hitchcock?

ERNEST: It's terribly mechanical when you talk about it, but some creativity must go on. I don't know what exactly, but it does. Hitch said, "I always wanted to do a chase scene across the face of Mount Rushmore." I replied, "Wow, that sounds like a great idea." All of these notes are at the University of Texas now if anybody wants to see them. I thought, "Well, who is chasing whom across the faces of Mount Rushmore? How'd they get there? What's going on in this scene?" This is how we started. We wanted to end it with the chase. I made a list of protagonists I would consider: a Madison Avenue advertising executive, Ted Husing–type sports announcer, a radio show host. I had a list. It was all very mechanical. Where do you we start? New York and then work our way northwest.

LEW: Talk about the difference in developing originals versus adaptations.

ERNEST: If I'm adapting something—by the way, that's a term we no longer use in the Writers Guild. It used to be adaptation; now it is regarded as a screenplay based on a novel title or whatever written form it had. If you have something to start with, you are trying to see the three acts. I did a movie based on an eight-hundred-page novel by John O'Hara called *From the Terrace*. That followed the character from early childhood through middle age. I had to figure out where the three acts were going to land so that I could figure out where to pick the character up and where to leave him. I did the same thing with *Somebody Up There Likes Me*.

LEW: My favorite of yours.

ERNEST: I went to the Soviet Union by invitation, and I was allowed to take one screenplay, and I took that one.

LEW: That was from a book?

ERNEST: His autobiography.

LEW: Rocky Graziano. Paul Newman played him.

ERNEST: I get out on his winning the championship. That's how I ended because I knew the next time out, he was going to lose the championship, and a few years later, he was going to become a retired-prizefighter-turned-television-star, and he was well known in television when he wrote his autobiography. So, I figured, "Here's where I start, and here's where I get out."

LEW: When you are developing the three acts, the getting in and getting out, do you spend a bit of time figuring out what the movie is really about? Let me give you an example: Frank Pierson told me that on *Dog Day Afternoon* he finally broke the back of the story when he understood that Al Pacino's character was living for everyone except for himself. The poor son of a bitch lived for his wife, his children, his homosexual lover, but not for himself, and that was his key.

ERNEST: By the way, that's my favorite Frank Pierson movie. Terrific suspense.

LEW: Mine, too. It was basically an original story inspired from a little newspaper article. Some guy held up a bank, and he wanted to be to taken to the airport so he could flee the country. From this idea, he built the character up, but he still couldn't quite figure it out. Then he saw it, his raison d'être. It's like the fight in *Raging Bull*. Scorsese told me that the reason for being is a throwaway line in there, when a character said, "That poor son of a bitch would be a loser, even if he won a championship." Do themes come to you deliberately?

ERNEST: No, I suspect Frank's thoughts about *Dog Day Afternoon* helped him to write it, but his thought about what he was saying and what gave him the touchstone to what he was doing I doubt served the audience. In fact, much of the audience would be as surprised as I am to find out there is a deeper theme to the picture. I was impressed by the immediacy and the tension. It was just a terrific movie.

LEW: How do you outline? Do you do cards? A formal written outline?

ERNEST: I'm not formal. I used to do cards, and I put each scene on a card, and I would put them on a cork board and step back and see the first act had twenty-four cards, the second act had three, and the last act, thirteen. Obviously, the first act was way too long. I used to do that when I was new to Hollywood. In time, I figured out that if I had to solve the entire movie up-front, I'd never get to writing it.

In fact, you can talk movies to death. I have all of the tapes of my sitting with Hitchcock on his last movie, *Family Plot*. We talked for three months. It was based on a novel, yet we just sat in a room talking, sometimes about the movie, sometimes not. You can go on forever until finally you wonder, "How can I get out of this damn thing?" because you don't see a movie. Once you sit down and you have a legal pad or the typewriter and you grind out a page or two, it's a good day. That's the way I seem to have worked. Now I will know the whole movie before I begin.

LEW: When you were talking with Hitchcock on *North by Northwest*, did you pretty well get the structure down before writing the script?

ERNEST: No. In fact, I was really scared. I had never written a movie like *North by Northwest*. I was all alone at MGM, as he was shooting *Vertigo* with Paramount. I tried to quit that picture, too. I didn't know what I was doing, but while Hitch was away, I wrote sixty-four pages without knowing what the sixty-fifth page would be. Generally, a vague setting up of drama that must have had ten acts in it by the time I got to page 64. I mailed that portion to Hitch, and he was very excited. I have this four-page handwritten letter at home, telling me about my own picture they already had cast, and he sent his people into preproduction when I had no ending whatsoever. It was terrifying. I had the same experience with Billy Wilder in *Sabrina*, except then the picture was shooting, and they had nothing to do unless we got home after dinner and wrote the next day's scene. I had a semi–nervous breakdown. Billy had all kinds of body ailments.

LEW: I understand you were ordered home by the doctor, and you had to sneak back to Billy's house, and when the doctor returned, you hid in another room.

ERNEST: No, Billy had to hide. I was ordered not to work. Then the doctor randomly appeared at the door and examined me and said, "It's okay.

You've recovered from this breakdown." And as the doctor was exiting the house, he said, "You can come out now, Mr. Wilder."

LEW: Ah, a much better story. Did you see the new *Sabrina*?

ERNEST: I heard it was good.

LEW: Have you heard about Billy Wilder seeing it? Sydney Pollack showed it for his reaction. Apparently, he was given a limo, and they took Billy to the Paramount lot. When Julia Ormond came on, Billy leaned to Pollack and said, "I had Audrey Hepburn." Then comes Harrison Ford, and he goes, "Humphrey Bogart," and then Greg Kinnear, "William Holden." After the picture, Billy stood up, adjusted himself, walked out to the limo, and went home. He didn't say another word.

ERNEST: That's not nice.

LEW: Billy's was perfect, though. No need for a remake. Now tell me about plays. Are there problems in terms of adapting them? You did *Who's Afraid of Virginia Woolf?*, *Westside Story*, and *The Sound of Music*.

ERNEST: And *The King and I*. All plays I had to make appear to be movies, among other things. I went to Salzburg, Austria, for *The Sound of Music* and spent weeks there looking for the places I thought would be ideal for certain scenes. I had the great advantage of the film medium. Whereas doing it on-stage meant being trapped in a living room for all twelve minutes of "Do Re Mi," I had all of Salzburg as my stage.

LEW: I mention *The Sound of Music* in my book here, and let's see what I have to say: "Ignore the sensuality of Shakespearean or Greek drama. *The Sound of Music* seems to not fit the mold. Nonsense, the Nazis are the overall threat."

ERNEST: Who said this?

LEW: I am having a colloquy with myself about the people who say that *The Sound of Music* is soft pap. My God, they ignore the fact that the Nazis are your heavy.

ERNEST: Well, they really weren't an integral part of it, but I think it's a hell of a good movie. I knew it was kicked around when it first opened as a stage musical. In fact, it's being revived again and again as a stage musical. *The Sound of Music* will live on for thousands of years. I still manage to cry a little, even though I see it about once a year. There's definitely nothing to be ashamed of in that film. I think Bob Wise did a fabulous job of making every frame of that film perfect. Eventually, he helped me to learn to take some guff.

I had a motto—I think I still have it: One of the secrets of success in this business is to be lucky enough to lose the right battles. Fortunately, I did lose them. The boys in *Who's Afraid of Virginia Woolf?*—the son—he existed in my first four screenplays. He had hung himself at the age of sixteen in the closet. I had a whole damn script like that. Mike Nichols battled me and battled me, and luckily, I lost.

Lew: Is the battling often helpful to the process?

Ernest: It's inevitable, whether it's helpful or not. Making movies is an example of antagonistic cooperation. You work against everyone else. Everyone has their own idea. Writing is not like mathematics; there is no one correct answer. Show me any picture, and I'm sure we could all find something to argue over and say it's wrong.

Lew: Do you agree with Irving Thalberg?

Ernest: I'm sure I don't.

Lew: Let's see: "The writer is the most important person in Hollywood. Just don't tell the sons of bitches."

Ernest: He probably didn't word it that cleverly.

Lew: I did help in the rewrite. By the way, did Hitchcock value writers?

Ernest: He valued us in our presence, but he had a lot of covert hostility. Like in the middle of a story conference one day—and compliments from Hitchcock were rare, if not nonexistent—he said, "Ernie, I figured out why *The Sound of Music* was such a success." And I thought, "Oh my God, Hitch is going to give me a compliment." I said, "What is it, Hitch?" and he replied, "They all went and saw it because they thought it was *Mary Poppins* because the woman comes to take care of a house full of children."

Lew: Disguising your exposition is so important because most lay it on with a trowel. Give us a few tricks of the trade.

Ernest: One of the best ways of getting exposition out is to make sure it's in a scene where characters are in conflict and one of the characters is being forced to say certain things that he ordinarily wouldn't say, and the other character is forced to say something else. Gradually, a scene full of conflict can reveal a lot to an audience without them realizing that plot information was being given to them. Another rule of exposition is, don't have a character tell another character something that the audience has already heard or witnessed previously in the picture. Don't let an audience be stuck with the same thing twice. That has been violated in a couple of instances.

LEW: There's a phrase that I don't hear new screenwriters use: "The audiences need to know."

ERNEST: I think you do it instinctively. Somehow, writers are daring enough to know that audiences won't immediately understand why these characters are doing what they are doing but that this is a more clever way of doing it. Do a scene where you know why the characters are doing something but the audience doesn't. Give them what they want but not in the way that they expect it. That's all right until just before they start resenting what they don't know. Then you go a little further into the movie and let them see it. It's a clever way of not being too obvious with your exposition.

LEW: You used two words about screenwriting in the Brady book that I have never heard before. They are *verbal music*. Verbal music. One of our students here, who also writes plays, referred to theater for the ear and motion pictures for the eye. Does that make some sort of sense to you?

ERNEST: It does, relatively speaking. Movies are more for the eyes.

LEW: So many things are communicated by visual inference. Questions, 434 warriors?

STUDENT: Could you please sum up, as a writer, some of the best things to be thinking about when you're working with a director?

ERNEST: What stage?

STUDENT: Getting ready to shoot. You have started to collaborate more, and some of those antagonistic—

ERNEST: I think even in an idealistic world, there's no way you can avoid feeling the resentment of somebody else telling you how to write. You can't tell the director how to direct or the actor how to act, but anybody can tell you what you ought to do with your script. You'll have resentment, but if you can, listen and kind of say, "Maybe I'll get a good suggestion." It's very tough. Writers are neurotic people. They get kicked around quite a bit, and in this community, people act like they don't exist.

Your question is how to best work with a director. Try not to hate him. He's not saying things just to ruin his own picture. He may have a point. I found you can be more influential and get things to happen if you are just a screenwriter, meaning since you have no real final power, no final say-so, people are not afraid of you. They know they can overrule you. The director can say, "I don't agree with him. He can talk for the next two weeks, but I have more authority than he does." Maybe a producer has greater authority than he does.

When I switched from writer to writer-producer and then to writer-producer-director, I found that I had a lot of trouble getting through to people because they saw me as someone with final authority who was a bigger threat to them. Anything I said got them very upset because they knew that if I really wanted it to happen, it could. So just be a writer.

LEW: But the writer isn't often on that committee that makes those important decisions that causes us to hate from afar. Stirling Silliphant called the directors traffic cops.

ERNEST: A clever exaggeration. We have a number of brilliant directors and brilliant writers. I don't know of any brilliant producers.

STUDENT: In the process of conceiving a project, does the meaning emerge from the story or as a result of the story?

ERNEST: Meaning? What do you mean?

STUDENT: Do you realize what the movie is about and then build a story around that, or does that come after the story has already congealed?

ERNEST: I am not much on themes. In fact, I am zero on themes. I won't even go to see theme pictures. I am interested mostly in what will hold an audience's attention and make them care about what's going to happen next.

LEW: Did you see the Billy Wilder retrospective?

ERNEST: I did see it.

LEW: How was it, working with Billy Wilder?

ERNEST: Billy found his diamond, Izzy Diamond, at a Writers Guild Awards dinner.

LEW: Izzy wrote eleven screenplays with Billy.

ERNEST: He met him the night we won best comedy for *Sabrina*. It was unique working with Billy. Izzy would sit at a typewriter, I was seated with a yellow pad, and Billy was pacing up and down. It's such an atypical experience. It doesn't shed any light on anything. Billy also lives dangerously. I mean, writing a screenplay as you go along, even the scenes you have to shoot the next day. This means that at four o'clock in the morning, you're walking up and down the streets of Beverly Hills trying to figure out what he says, and then what she says in response. That was my first on-set experience while working on a picture.

LEW: Joseph Campbell talks about heroes that have Yodas to go to, a wise source. In terms of Billy Wilder, I am told there was an editor who would whisper in his ear.

ERNEST: Yeah, Doane Harrison.

LEW: Doane Harrison is who he used to play off of? Have you had that sort in your life?

ERNEST: Actually, I had Doane Harrison in my life. Billy Wilder loaned Doane Harrison to me so that Mike Nichols would not be directing his first film ever without having Doane Harrison, who was a film editor. Billy used to listen to Doane, but he wasn't really a story consultant. He would tell Billy how to shoot it so there would be no unnecessary wastage of shooting time. They would cut in camera, and Doane was a great help to Mike. But Mike resented having that kind of help. Eventually, Doane Harrison made good on his constant threat to quit. He just couldn't take it.

LEW: You were producing also?

ERNEST: That was my first time ever.

LEW: A lot of Jack Warner stories came out of that?

ERNEST: I have written a journal of my making that movie.

LEW: Did you publish it?

ERNEST: I didn't. My agent wants to give it to Universal, and I'm sort of holding out. It's about 300,000 words, dictated every single day into a recorder as I drove home from the studio.

STUDENT: Have you ever worked with a writer whose work you were adapting?

ERNEST: No.

STUDENT: You didn't consult or talk to [playwright Edward] Albee at all?

ERNEST: No, and I didn't talk to Philip Roth on *Portnoy's Complaint*. I did go to Princeton University and spent an afternoon with John O'Hara at his request. Only once did he bring up the subject of the movie. We just rag chewed about everything else.

I did have one meeting with Edward Albee where I sat in a hotel room and felt, "Gee, if I were Edward Albee, I wouldn't want me to have his famous play in my hands." I felt it was ridiculous. I thought, "Why did he do this? Why did he sell that play to Warner Brothers?" We had some correspondence recently. I keep it in my scrapbook.

LEW: Jack Warner did not want to shoot the picture?

ERNEST: Well, he had other people he suggested to me, and I said to Warner, "I'll let you know when I make the decision." When I finally decided on Mike Nichols, I had to fly from Paris to Burbank to hear why that was a ridiculous idea. I was lucky enough to win that battle, and Mike did a brilliant job.

LEW: Wasn't it Jack Warner who referred to screenwriters as schmucks with the Underwoods, or was that Harry Cohen?

ERNEST: That's Harry Cohen, another paean of praise. Underwoods are typewriters, and the quote is actually unattributed.

STUDENT: You mentioned that you wrote *North by Northwest* because you quit something else?

ERNEST: *The Wreck of the* Mary Deare is what I quit.

STUDENT: Why?

ERNEST: Well, I was under contract at MGM, and I was working on something, I forget what, and the head of the studio at that time, Dore Schary, told me they had just made a deal with Alfred Hitchcock, who had never made a picture at MGM. They bought a novel for him called *The Wreck of* Mary Deare, and Hitchcock requested me as his screenwriter. I had met Hitch at Paramount, socially. We were introduced by a mutual friend. I said I would have to read the book first. It's hard to believe, but I read the book and turned it down. The reason was, I didn't know how to a make a movie out of it.

One day, my agent, Lew Wasserman, came to me. He was also Hitch's agent. He said, "Hitch is very angry and upset you turned him down. If I could arrange a luncheon meeting, would you have lunch with him?" I said, "Sure." I had lunch with Hitch at the Beverly Hills Hotel, the Polo Lounge. It was a very enjoyable lunch. I kept thinking, "Maybe he knew how to do the book," throughout the lunch, so I agreed to do it. As I mentioned earlier, I spent three weeks going to Hitch's home and soon realized that he didn't know how to make it into a movie, either. That's when I quit, and Hitch suggested we just do something else.

Then I traveled to all of the places that would be in *North by Northwest*. I went to Mount Rushmore and hired a forest ranger to help me climb it. I looked down about halfway and thought to myself, "What the hell is a screenwriter doing on Mount Rushmore?" so I just had the ranger take pictures of the top.

STUDENT: So you couldn't find the beginning, middle, and end of *The Wreck of* Mary Deare?

ERNEST: I couldn't find anything. The whole novel is an inquiry into what had happened with the ship floating up the English Channel with nobody onboard. That sounds like a great Hitchcock picture. You know what? MGM made the movie eventually, and it was a disaster.

LEW: Did Hitchcock tell you he wanted to shoot a car being built in Detroit?

ERNEST: Oh, sure. It's in my notes. It's the longest dolly shot in history. It starts with nothing, and then you follow an assembly line slowly, slowly, all the way to the fender, the engine, then the hood, and you follow it until it's a finished car that gets driven off of the assembly line with a dead body in the back seat. Hitch told me that, and I thought, "Wow, it sounds good." That is actually how it came to be in a northwesterly direction. We are going to start in New York, go to Detroit, and we have to aim for Rushmore. I was calling the project *In a Northwestern Direction*. The story department suggested *North by Northwest*.

STUDENT: How did you pick up the profession for the protagonist?

ERNEST: Madison Avenue advertising executives, you know, are given to a repartee and a certain manner of behavior that's cynical and speaks a certain way. Both Cary Grant and Jimmy Stewart were lurking in the wings, waiting to find out what their next picture was going to be with Hitch. That's the way it was in those days.

STUDENT: Seems there are fewer films where the characters have the charm and style they used to.

ERNEST: I must have wit and charm. I wanted to write this superficial, cynical, advertising guy who had been twice married and divorced. His life was so boring because he had a suffocating mother, and it was a Hitchcock picture. I had seen *To Catch a Thief* by John Michael Hayes, and I suspected that Hitch's popularity, which had been low, had risen again because Hayes had written a smart, sophisticated type of repartee. After my years as a writer, I find that comes natural to me.

LEW: Also, writers like Mr. Lehman grew up on Broadway, literature, and never went to film school, so they are distinctly individual. They admired the Algonquin Round Table wit and Oscar Wilde.

ERNEST: Yes, I grew up in that milieu in New York City. I had been going to the theater since I was eight years old.

STUDENT: You mentioned Cary Grant and Jimmy Stewart could have done *North by Northwest*. They would have been very different movies. Do you often write with a specific actor in mind?

ERNEST: Usually. It was a great advantage to know it was going to be Cary. If Jimmy Stewart had done it, as wonderful as he is, with his drawl, that picture would have been four hours long. I knew it would be Cary. These days a studio buys a script written with Sylvester Stallone in mind, and it ends up being Eddie Murphy.

LEW: Our UCLA *Face/Off* writers wrote for Sylvester Stallone and Arnold Schwarzenegger, and it ended up being Nicolas Cage and John Travolta.

STUDENT: Has it ever been that a story sort of bends around and out from the character that you want to write about?

ERNEST: No, I don't think that has happened. I have created characters and did so with all of the characters in *North by Northwest*. I don't know where they came from. Why did I make Martin Landau's character slightly gay? In those days, I don't know why I did it, but now it gets called to my attention.

STUDENT: You mentioned gallivanting around before starting *North by Northwest*. How important is it for the writer to have actually experienced or at least simulated the experience before writing?

ERNEST: Very important. It's so difficult to write about things you don't know or places you have never seen. If I hadn't visited the Long Island courthouse, I would have never known how to write it. The more you know, the easier it is to describe the location. For *Westside Story*, Bob Wise and I toured the streets of New York, driving a police car around, meeting with social workers who deal with gangs, doing a lot of research. In fact, we did so much research, Bob finally said, "What are we doing? We've got a whole plot to base this on." So we went back to California, but the more you know, the better you can write it.

LEW: Is screenwriting an art?

ERNEST: It's a craft, I think. Some excellent craftsman are also artists, and you get some pictures you can't even define. They're so wonderful.

LEW: For me, Jim Sheridan is a special writer. Those of us over fifty remember the Hacketts, Frances Marion, Preston Sturges, Billy Wilder. Once, there was only Syd Field. Now we have volumes dedicated to screenwriting. My publisher says these books do well because people want to know the secret. Do you feel there is a special secret?

ERNEST: I think you have to bear in mind when you write a screenplay, you also have to write a script that reads well. So much of that future project depends on the people reading your screenplay. You should have a well-written screenplay. Don't start off by saying, "Close up. Head of man." Write it so it engages people, so that they feel that they are reading a story, and occasionally drop in a little inner monologue that will never make it to screen. Be aware that it will be read by dozens and dozens of people. You can fool them into thinking it's better than it is by just writing well. Having said that, I have no other secret.

LEW: Are you proud to be a screenwriter? Do you wish you had stayed with writing fiction and short stories?

ERNEST: No, there's no market for short stories. I am sorry I never tried to write a play. Maybe I will. Most think sitting down to write a screenplay is impossible. You often recognize what an impossible thing it is to do as you push forward a little bit at a time. It's impossible, and that's why you can only do a little bit at a time. Don't think about how you have twenty more miles to get to the end. In fact, don't even think about the end. Make sure that each day, each page, is moving inexorably forward and well. You actually never stop feeling that it's impossible, and that's what keeps you going.

I used to think my secret was something to do with pen and typewriter every day to keep people from figuring out that I didn't know how to write. Who am I to proclaim myself a writer? Well, I'm the only one who knew that I don't know how to write a movie. Whatever I do is going to keep me from finding out that I don't know how to do this. It doesn't have to be the great American screenplay. It just has to be something people want to see. Who starts out trying to be great?

LEW: And Ernie Lehman, that's exactly the word I use to describe your seminal screenwriting career: great! Write on.

13

Eric Roth

Eric Roth comes to this book in the tried and not-so-true Hollywood way. He was born into the business and may have learned by watching. Leon Roth was one of the top motion picture executives, with United Artists being his most prestigious pit stop. Mother and wife Mimi Roth was a legendary story executive and reader, with practically all the major studios at one time or another under the spell of her prowess.

I did not know Eric as he grew, but both of his parents were professional friends in their individual guises. Mimi came into my writer's circle when I was a beginning screenwriter; Leon, when I was director of motion pictures for television at NBC in the '70s. Leon; Mimi; my beloved wife, Pamela; and moi came together as a unit for a screenwriting reconnaissance trip to Russia and her eastern satellite countries under the auspices of the Writers Guild of America in 1989, at the very end of the Cold War. There was much laughing and scratching and tossing back of vodkas after expansive toasts in these repressed regimes.

Leon and Mimi were not repressed, so they gave me a surprise when I called for Eric's phone number for this book and my 434 class. Leon said, "You know, Eric can't talk." Mimi vigorously agreed. I asked if he could respond to questions. They mused that might be possible. To confirm this unusual warning, I checked with one of Eric's professors when he was in UCLA's screenwriting program for confirmation. Sure enough, "Eric never said a word in any of my classes, then he would turn in a marvelous script. I would have him to my office, tell him it was marvelous, and he would inaudibly mumble something I interpreted to be a thanks. I would give him some notes, and he would mumble again and leave. A few weeks later, Eric would hand in his rewrite, and each time, what was marvelous would be transformed into something more marvelous." Suspecting that between the effervescent professor and Eric's gregarious parents, the then young man couldn't or didn't try to get a word in edgewise, sideways, or front- or backways, so he chose to do his communicating at the keyboard. *Forrest Gump* was his lightning, thunder, and rain in a bottle. More awards were to follow throughout this talented writer's lifetime.

Hollywood is not a small town; it's a closet. We crisscross back and forth in each other's lives, similar to a handful of worms, each dipped in a different color of wet paint and dropped in the middle of a white canvas rectangle that becomes Jackson Pollack–like. Eric, Leon, Mimi, myself, and our mutual friends have crisscrossed many, many times over thirty years, and we now vector in *Naked Screenwriting*, for the good, I believe, of any wannabe, gotta-be professional screenwriter or earnest movie buff who picks up this book.

Can Eric Roth talk? You will see and read. Oh, a final footnote: It was reported in *Variety* shortly after the explosion of *Forrest Gump* that Eric was signed by Disney to deliver a script a year over a ten-year period for $30 million. That about says it all.

LEW: I promised Eric we wouldn't ask him what Tom Hanks is really like, okay? Just like when you went to UCLA, Eric, we try to help each other get the best possible story in these 434 workshops. We have only eight people. Did you have eight in your day?

ERIC: It was pretty small. Seven or six. At that time, there were only about forty students in the graduate screenwriting program and zero women.

LEW: In terms of screenwriting, we're now about 50/50. I think we have about fifty-two total currently in screenwriting. We have hundreds of applications and pick about twenty people. Well, that was then and now. You've been a professional writer now for about—

ERIC: Twenty years.

LEW: Was it a good decision?

ERIC: Yes. Great decision.

LEW: Have you been tempted to become a producer, or have you been one?

ERIC: No, no, not producing or directing.

LEW: In other words, the war stories haven't pushed you into being a director?

ERIC: No.

LEW: Have you had good experiences?

ERIC: I've got to say, all in all, pretty good. I've had a couple of bad ones but more with studios than directors.

LEW: Is Aaron Spelling going to take out a full-page ad pretty soon?

ERIC: I don't know!

LEW: Aaron Spelling took out a quarter-page ad because Eric has a deal with Aaron for a pilot. He's congratulating Eric for *Forrest Gump* hitting the $280 million mark. Aaron says, "When it hits $300, I'll take out a full-page ad." But here, we talk about storytelling, not dollars. Beginnings, middles, and ends. No more complex, no less simple. Beginnings, middles, and ends. We want to talk a little about your own special process and what your habits are and so forth.

ERIC: I hope I'm not going to say things against what you teach.

LEW: No, no. That's perfectly fine. I can take it. I taught in the '60s.

ERIC: I write a little more by the seat of the pants than I think maybe I should, but it's more comfortable for me. I know the beginnings. I know generally the middles, and I definitely know the ends. So, the middle can sometimes change substantially, but I'll end up in the same place. I don't make step outlines, exactly. I outline maybe five or six scenes ahead. I divide the story into acts. I'll do usually three or four acts. Then each act, I'll break down mentally into X amount of scenes, depending on the structure of the piece. I'll have a pretty good idea of the characters and a good idea of the story and a better idea of what the theme of the piece is and what the piece is supposed to be about.

The script I'm writing now is maybe a little more indicative than *Forrest Gump* because it's so complex. It's for Coppola. It's the history of the CIA to a certain extent, at least the first thirty years. Thematically, I know what it's all about. I know the characters very well, and I know what the beginning is and the end and a pretty good idea of the middle. Well, I'm not strong about the middle.

LEW: Well, that sounds to me like structure when you're talking about three acts.

ERIC: Well, it's not as structured as doing a formal step outline or 3 × 5 cards.

LEW: I encourage people to step outline basically for a class talking paper. But like Julius Epstein says, the back on an envelope will do for him.

ERIC: Well, I'll do that, too. But I know guys like Waldo Salt are very organized. Waldo would make 3 × 5 cards and sometimes mix and match them.

LEW: And Paul Schrader. He knows what every page is going to be like in his outline before he starts a script. It sounds like leaving your fight in the dressing room to me.

ERIC: Amen. I couldn't write that way. There are good people who do.

LEW: Now, I always say that three acts are just writer's shorthand for beginning, middle, and end. You threw me when you said four acts. What would the fourth act be?

ERIC: I'm not sure it breaks down so consistently into three acts for me. I guess it should, but I guess I was thinking more, and—forgive me if I get sort of anal—if you're willing to write a 120-page script, 40-40-40 or 30-30-30, and you've got another 10 or 15 pages left over, then one act is a little long somewhere.

LEW: I'm going to do something I wasn't so sure I was going to do, but here goes, says he bravely. I've talked to these 434 warriors about *Forrest Gump* in terms of breaking down the acts. I want you to say what you want to say after I lay out the structure. The first act is when mom, Sally Field, sends him to school, and he's going out into the world. "We're not strangers," says the driver, et cetera, and he gets on the bus. I've been saying that center-point area that some of us screenwriting educators like to talk about is when his pal Bubba dies.

ERIC: That's kind of close.

LEW: The third act begins, as I see it, when the woman says, "Wait a minute. You want to go three blocks down the street," and then he gets off the bus to begin the beginning of the end.

ERIC: I don't know why, that might have been the fourth act. I thought the third act began when he decided to run and when he was running, and that ends the third act. The fourth act, if there are four acts, would be from that point on, where he finds her again. But I think you're fairly close.

LEW: Beyond beginning, middle, and ends, I think that something always happens in good movies around page 30. When Forrest, as a boy, goes out into the world.

ERIC: That's right.

LEW: And in this case, the character takes a quarter-turn when he goes into the army, and then there's more overt action. I think that can generically be applied to most seminal pictures.

ERIC: I think so. The one I'm writing now, I'm too long on my first act. I'm at thirty-five pages, and I need to be closer to twenty, where I reveal the situation.

LEW: *Forrest* was a great experience?

ERIC: Great experience.

LEW: I was telling our gang here last week, a woman producer, Wendy Finerman, hung with that project for ten years and finally made it happen with the Eric Roth script. She just had those teeth gritted and her ears pinned back, as we say in Nebraska. Whether it's *Rain Man* or *Casablanca* or *Forrest Gump*, generally there's one person with each film who just won't give up. If you decree that all the Oscars have to be returned to the Motion Picture Academy if the picture was in development for more than five years, almost all of them would have to be shipped back. You didn't write that script ten years ago.

ERIC: No, no. I came on *Forrest* two years ago or so. It all was fairly quick, and it wrote itself. It was one of those lucky things.

LEW: Did you do a rewrite of someone else's screenplay?

ERIC: Well, to be honest, I never looked at the other screenplay. I didn't want their influence. And I just skimmed the book. I'm not trying to be arrogant. The movie was so successful, but the book, to me, was unreadable. There was something in there that I thought was pretty magical, and it gave me some hints of what I wanted to do. It also gave me courage to start breaking time and breaking rules.

LEW: What was magical?

ERIC: I think seeing the world through the eyes and soul of this fictional person.

LEW: I think we all have our own interpretations of watching everything, but my interpretation of Forrest is that he is metaphorical for America's loss of innocence.

ERIC: I had sort of lost my own innocence also. My kids and all and just growing up.

LEW: I think one of the reasons beyond the quality of the picture, and God knows the quality is self-evident, is that Americans are still trying to deal with such a complex life so young. My God, children have to know about school shootings when they're five years old. Everybody, to a person who has read the book, has said to me, you brought magic to the screenplay.

ERIC: One of the advantages for me was that the book had been around a long time. I said, "Fuck, I'm going to go for it." If the worst happens, it would be another ten years, so I just threw the book out in essence. You won't find any of the book left, except certain structural things. I think it's a bit bold normally to go down those lines.

LEW: Did you have Tom Hanks in mind?

ERIC: No, no. They went first to Penny Marshall, and she wasn't sure. She sort of waffled, and then it became an interagency thing with CAA.

LEW: Who was your agent?

ERIC: Jane Sindell.

LEW: Jane Sindell is head of the literary department at CAA. I don't mean this on a pejorative level, but she tells the CAA heads whether a book or script is good because obviously they carry all the scripts and books home to read and often don't have time to read. She's also a very special person.

ERIC: I think so, too.

LEW: She's honest.

ERIC: Maybe a little too honest.

LEW: There's a woman at William Morris who handled people like Tennessee Williams years ago. Authors liked her because she was honest and motherly and just good to have around for groundlings. Questions, 434-ites?

STUDENT: You were talking about working, structure-wise, and you brought up the idea of certain themes that follow certain sequences. Do you have in mind where to do this sequence and that sequence and where the two connect? And does your theme come out of that?

ERIC: No. I try to connect everything, and I don't think I do it consciously. But in some way, the themes of scripts just emerge naturally. In other words, your message, if it's well done, will get across. I'm kind of obtuse with *Forrest Gump*. The director, I think, pushed me to go for good and for real. He would tell me to say what you mean. Sometimes I don't. I'm not saying I'm trying to be clever. I'm not as specific in my dialogue as maybe I should be.

STUDENT: Where do you draw the line with saying what you mean and holding enough back?

ERIC: I think your first task is to communicate your ideas and sentiments to an audience. It should be clear. That doesn't mean it can't be clever, well done, or intelligent. But above all, you should be clear. Otherwise, you'll be the only one who can understand it. The one I'm doing now is interesting. It's a complicated piece of material because the nature of the main character is suspicious and lives within his own wilderness of mirrors. And that's what the CIA is. The guy eventually loses it. It's hard but important to make sure I'm being clear.

When I was starting out, I wrote this script, and Frank Perry told me it was on-the-nose bullshit. That so petrified me, and I spent the rest of my writing career saying to myself, "What do you mean by this line?" The words *on the nose* are like saying it's worse than bad.

LEW: *Soft* is another negative word. Getting back to theme: You used the word *theme*.

ERIC: Maybe I used the wrong word.

LEW: No, it's exactly the right word. I keep ragging on people, including myself. When I go to the mirror on my scripts, I ask, "What's the movie about? What's it really about?" Is it true for you that sometimes you don't really quite figure what a movie is about until a bit into the process?

ERIC: I think I know what it's about, but sometimes I can't quite get there. Like this one I'm on with Francis, I know I have a great script, but I'm not there yet. I can just feel it's not right.

LEW: Last night we had Michael Werb here who wrote *Mask*. Have you seen *Mask*?

ERIC: Yes.

LEW: Michael wrote the movie that just missed on the thematic level. The idea of just putting a mask on should say something. Then, fellow writer Michael Colleary talked a lot about how things were taken out, everything that related to the theme, because of special effects and all those horrible things apparently you didn't have to go through in *Forrest Gump*.

ERIC: No, but I have experienced it all.

LEW: We've all had experiences, oh Eric, as you came out of these UCLA 434 classes. The idea that two of the most successful pictures have come out of our program is better than great.

STUDENT: Can you tell, in *Gump*, the parts you thought were terrific and parts you don't like?

ERIC: I liked probably 99 percent of the movie. Bob Zemeckis did some things a little less artfully than I wished he had. But on the other hand, I think he's more comedic than I am. I don't want to speak for him, but Bob's design is to entertain, then along the way give the audience an emotional and dramatic movie. I think this was a first for him. I mean, he's usually done cartoon things.

Specifically, what I didn't like was, well, I never was wild about the way he portrayed some of the antiwar stuff. I don't mind the humor, but, well, we came at that from different points of view. I think the end result was just supposed to be Forrest's point of view, so I figured that was fine. I'll tell you one thing where he was totally right. I had originally written *Forrest* with a lot of animation. You were going to see through the eyes of this guy. But it was totally unnecessary.

LEW: Animation like we saw in *The World According to Garp*?

ERIC: Similar to that, except this would be sort of quoting from an idiot's point of view. One thing I had throughout was when he saw a woman he loves, or at least at dramatic moments, she always had angel's wings, which is how he first imagined her. It was a bad idea.

STUDENT: In the book, he sums up the war in pretty negative terms. When he makes his statement in the movie, it's cut off. Was that your idea?

ERIC: That was intentional. We tried to come up with an either tremendous, dramatic speech about the war, which we started not believing that he could give this character something really funny. I went to some people I knew, comedians like Billy Crystal. They came up with this one line that sort of summed it up, but it wasn't about the war. No one could do that. As we started talking about it, I said, "Maybe the best thing is that we don't know what he said." And so we did that.

STUDENT: It was very different from the book and, I thought, more successful.

ERIC: Thanks.

STUDENT: This is a little bit more personal. I'm comfortable with story structure and the technical details of storytelling. I'm interested in how screenwriters achieve art or the feeling of being an artist.

ERIC: That's a good question. I guess, I don't know who's the judge. I think screenwriting is a craft.

LEW: I think the art happens when you come in from wherever your writing cubicle is, and you say to your significant other, "Holy fuck! Look at this!"

ERIC: Yeah.

LEW: How did it come and from where? You know, in the Old Testament, the writers didn't name the testaments because they thought their writing came from God.

ERIC: I'm amused if you think God is art. A lot of people attribute God in *Forrest Gump*. There's no God in there—well, maybe some nicely expressed things. I'm kind of creative, but I'm no Mozart. When you write a scene and you feel this is as good as you can do it and it's really well constructed and it's about what's going on.

STUDENT: I think I get fired up about scenes right now, but I think my test would be if I could bring myself to tears. That's what I was going to ask you because I cried in your movie.

ERIC: That's nice. Thank you.

STUDENT: When you were watching it, did you ever cry during a scene, or have you ever cried while watching a movie?

ERIC: When I was writing it, I cried. Maybe not when I'm sitting at the computer, but while I'm taking a walk in the morning or something and I'm thinking about it. It may not be specifically about the scene. It may be more of the emotion I was feeling at the moment, you know. Writing *Forrest Gump*, it was embarrassing because I would be walking down the beach, crying to this thing.

It's so corny, the song, but somehow, I like to write to interior music. I find a piece I can keep coming back to in my head that sounds like the movie. In the CIA one, I have a piece of Wagner music that I just think is provocative for this particular movie. Every time I come to it in my mind, it gives me a certain emotion and helps me write the scene and to stay with the soul of what it's all about. But art. I don't know.

LEW: Eric, here's the other half of the half that I dedicated my book to, my beloved wife, Pamela.

ERIC: Hi, how are you?

LEW: She's also a lover of your folks. I thought of my daughter Eileen while you were talking. She's a social worker. She said to me, after about her tenth year in the game, "Dad, I can't cry anymore, and I'm just terrified. When I first started, there were tears on my steering wheel going home at night." When I first started writing, I used to cry with my characters, particularly if somebody died. Now, I can't do it anymore.

ERIC: Yeah, really.

LEW: I feel like the comedians and comedy writers, you know. Have you ever been over to Nate and Al's on Saturday or Sunday mornings when the guys are spritzing each other?

ERIC: Yeah, nobody laughs.

LEW: Everybody is just bang, bang, but nothing. Maybe a sober "That's funny." I had a class last year that went over the next Sunday morning to get the nearest booth. They laughed. They got thrown out. Do you continually do sort of a sensitivity check? Like our mutual friend Rubin Carson goes to a shrink once a year, for like a lube job to see if the car is running. Right? Do you have a certain way to check yourself to see if you're losing something?

ERIC: I just keep reading a piece. I'm a detail-oriented person, so every day I go back to page 1 and start reading it over again to see if it's still working.

LEW: Every day you go back to the beginning?

ERIC: Every day. I do start skimming after a while, and I'm also very slow. Maybe I take too much time, and maybe I'm trying to be an artist then. But at some point—let's say act 1 is done—I won't really look at it much anymore. Then I skim.

LEW: Are you always slow?

ERIC: Always.

LEW: What does *slow* mean? If you've got basically the story parameters, how long does it take you to do the first draft?

ERIC: Eight or nine months. But I think, for good or bad, my first drafts are like most people's third drafts.

LEW: You're like our mutual friends, Irving and Harriet. I asked, "How do you feel about rewriting?" Irving says, "We get it right the first time."

ERIC: But take Zemeckis with *Forrest Gump*: we did the same thing every day. We sat down to work because he's a writer, too, and we'd start on page 1. At first I was a little annoyed, but there's a method to it because I think it was more for him to know the subject matter as well as I did.

LEW: So then you work on a few pages and then the next day go back to page 1?

ERIC: And start again and then would keep on going, asking, "Is this scene as good as we can do it?" and "Is this the best line?" It was interesting because as we got close to shooting, I wasn't really sure if he spiritually got the movie the same way I did, you know. And I thought, "That's life." But, when we got to our first day of rehearsal, he gave us sort of a talk about what he thought the movie really meant, and it was really forthcoming because he's kind of a reticent guy. I thought he understood better than I did. He really got it, and I could tell then that if the elements were right and the acting was as good as we thought it would be, it could be relayed to an audience really well.

LEW: When you say rehearsal, do you mean a table reading?

ERIC: Yeah, we did that for a week.

LEW: Did you make any changes?

ERIC: We cut out the obvious excess, then went back to square 1 as more bones of the scenes appear. Then we started evaluating and reevaluating. I think when we were done, we probably came full circle, except for the excesses with the animation and things.

STUDENT: The dialogue was the same?

ERIC: The dialogue stayed about 85 percent, maybe 90 percent, the same, except for certain things dictated by location or the actors being able to say things better or more in character.

LEW: Was that the only reading through the whole movie?

ERIC: Yes.

LEW: Was it exhilarating?

ERIC: I always love that the best.

LEW: Me, too.

ERIC: It was in an older theater hall in New York, and it really felt real.

LEW: When you have to interrupt during that first reading, you know you're in some degree of trouble.

ERIC: You can tell it starts falling apart pretty easily.

LEW: If you go right through, at the end, it's like, "Oh, my God." A lot of these 434 folks around here get more and more into taking an evening and persuading some friends to do a table reading on the whole bloody thing.

ERIC: I think that's great, except they're doing something a little bit dangerous in the movie business. Because so many things are expensive, they're doing table readings on a lot of scripts, and it's killing a lot of projects. They did it on one script over and over again. The actors think the director was stealing ideas from the table readings.

STUDENT: Do actors read the description as well as the dialogue?

ERIC: Usually the director, if it's a director who really knows what the movie is.

LEW: On my own scripts, I've always read my description. In my case, the director likes to sit back and listen. But Zemeckis did the reading for *Gump*?

ERIC: Yes, and Peter Yates on *Mr. Jones*.

STUDENT: I'm curious about your career process and what advice you have and what you've learned. Was it instantaneous success or a hard struggle?

ERIC: I'm not sure it was really a hard struggle, to be honest with you. Not because I'm so good. I think there's a certain amount of luck to be in the right place at the right time at certain times. There were some years I wasn't able to get some things made. Fortunately, I was getting paid. Also, it wasn't terribly fallow, as I had a movie every four or five years. At first, when I got an agent, I was able to get a job. And when I wrote a movie that got made, then there was another one that got made. Look, actually I wish I would have written *Butch Cassidy and the Sundance Kid*, right out of the box. Still, I was very lucky.

LEW: Well, I feel the harder I work, the luckier I become. But your parents being in the business, do you think that helped or hurt you?

ERIC: I had information, and my parents, though not particularly wealthy, I always had them. I never thought I was going to be homeless, you know. That was an advantage, obviously.

LEW: You mother has a wonderful story mind. Does she get involved with anything?

ERIC: Not really. I'm so embarrassed to show them my work, to be honest. I don't show them much. I don't know why. I'm not sure whether it's I don't trust their opinion or I do and don't want to know their opinion.

STUDENT: Do you have a good friend or group of friends you bounce your ideas off of? Anyone from school?

ERIC: I never did and never do.

LEW: One of your professors said you never talked.

ERIC: I was quiet. I'm sort of a loner, I guess.

LEW: You have children?

ERIC: Five.

LEW: Five?

ERIC: I guess maybe I'm not too much of a loner.

LEW: You were with William Morris, and now you're at CAA.

ERIC: I was with William Morris for seventeen years. It was like a divorce because I was really close with my agent, Ron Mardigian.

LEW: That's Irving and Harriet's agent. Ron was once my agent.

ERIC: A wonderful man, a wonderful agent. I think he's a unique man because he never had any other ambitions other than being a really good agent. He didn't want to be an executive. He would never sell you out that way.

LEW: So did CAA just offer you something great?

ERIC: No, it wasn't like that. It was time for a change. I felt William Morris didn't have a lot of the people I wished they had. I didn't feel my material was getting to people I wanted it to get to. Scripts would fail on their own merit, maybe lack of merit. At CAA, the second you write anything, everybody gets a script because they don't want to have—I'm just pulling a name out of the hat—the Sydney Pollacks say, "Why didn't I get to see that?" You get exposure. There's a huge advantage to that.

William Morris went through a major upheaval when Stan Kamen died. He wasn't business oriented. He was more protective, and he had everybody. You name any actor and every director, wouldn't you say that was true?

LEW: Absolutely.

ERIC: You had to go through Stan to get scripts to people. Ron gave my scripts to Stan.

STUDENT: Back to creative questions. When you are looking at page 30 and you're trying to think about your next scene, so you go through a certain process? Do you think about it a couple of days?

ERIC: I'll know the next scene, or I couldn't get to page 30. I'm not loose and easy. I'll know the next six scenes.

STUDENT: But in knowing what the next scene is, do you think about it for a few days?

ERIC: I think about it all the time.

STUDENT: Actually, I want to know how much you sold the screenplay for, but I'll ask—

ERIC: Which screenplay? I'll tell you.

STUDENT: *Forrest Gump.*

ERIC: It was an assignment. I was paid, I think, $250,000 for the whole thing. Maybe $300.

STUDENT: So when you see the success of the film, do you feel like that's enough, or do you ever in your mind start to calculate the hours?

ERIC: No. I'm also kind of pissed off at Paramount now because I have 5 percent of the net, and they say, "We'll see what happens." Don't sign for any net, ever. If you get one *Forrest Gump* in your life, you're really lucky.

LEW: Peter Guber said a number of years ago, "I have points in *The Deep.* They tell me it's made $149 million." At that time $149 million was a staggering sum of money. He says, "And they still haven't made money for my points." I don't ever think about net points in my deals.

ERIC: Initially, you think you're getting some great thing.

LEW: We have an ex-agent here and a current writer, and he's nodding, not off, but in agreement.

ERIC: It's a little early to see if they're going to be generous or not. I mean, that's what it's going to come down to, whether they're feeling generous.

LEW: Or they make so much they can't hide it all.

STUDENT: I'm sure your asking price just doubled.

ERIC: My rewrite price has gone up, and so have the weekly rewrite prices, and my next script, I'll ask for a big raise, so obviously the benefits are tremendous.

STUDENT: How many projects do you work on at a time?

ERIC: I can only work on one. The worst thing is to be slow and not get movies made. Then you're also in big trouble if you're quick and don't get them made.

STUDENT: But if you're slow and you turn in a very good product.

ERIC: A good product is in the eye of the beholder. At least if it attracts some talent, then they'll say it's worth your while. But if you're slow and nothing comes of it, it's certainly not to anyone's advantage.

LEW: Did you spec-write screenplays all the time when you started out?

ERIC: I spec-wrote a couple, but I was fortunate that after I won the Goldwyn Award here, I got an agent. I did a little love story set in Israel with a director and a very small independent company, and it got made. Then I decided to write a spec script called *Nickel Ride*, which you've probably never seen. It was a little lovely movie with Jason Miller at Fox.

STUDENT: Let's say you write scenes out of order—

ERIC: No, I don't. I've got to write in order.

LEW: I'm astounded that people periodically write out of order.

ERIC: My wife, who's in the business also, will say, "Why don't you just go ahead and then come back to it later?"

LEW: She's a producer.

ERIC: I had written a movie called *Mr. Jones*, an original screenplay. My wife and I had a major battle with the director. So later there was a phone call from the studios. We were sitting in our kitchen. She hung up and said, "You're fired." I said to the director, "Did you want to fire her or me?" She stayed on to try to protect whatever we thought was good about it.

STUDENT: Are there any studios you find extremely difficult to deal with?

ERIC: No, I'll tell you why. I try to not be as available for meetings and things. I mean, we moved up here recently about two months ago. I used to live down toward San Diego, so I wouldn't answer the phone. They can only tell you to go fuck yourself so many times. I've been in situations where I either creatively couldn't do it or I couldn't work with the person. So, I said, "Here's your money back." Life is too short. It's easy for me to say, you know, because I've been fairly successful, but I wouldn't recommend it often. I think you have to have some integrity with what you're doing.

What happens when you're slow is that you're going to blow some opportunities. I'm sort of at an interesting point right now. Coppola had told me he was definitely going to do this CIA project and I could take my time. So I'm taking my time. Then, he called the other day and said, "When can I see your script?" I said, "Well, it's not quite in shape." He said, "Well, I really want to read it because it will help me make some decisions."

LEW: He could go on and do something else if he doesn't like your script.

ERIC: And I'll still be writing, you know. But it will come back around. Either he will do it, or he'll get somebody else to do it. If it's no good, it doesn't make any difference.

STUDENT: Contractually, do they give you a time frame?

ERIC: Oh yeah. They can hold you up to it, but it's not to their advantage.

LEW: In seventeen years as an executive, I've never seen or held a writer to the time in a contract.

ERIC: Well, it does say in there six weeks.

LEW: Nobody will ever say, "Come on, come on, come on." They'll say it in more subtle ways than that.

ERIC: Well, they hound me to death.

LEW: Did you ever hear the legend about five or six years ago, when Bill Goldman said before he walked out of a Warner's meeting, "I'm too old, too smart, and too rich to take this shit"? We're all like, "My God, where are we going to put his bust?" I'm the lobby of the Writers Guild, so I called him up and said, "Bill, is this true?" He said, "Oh Jesus. That's such bullshit. I just stood up and gave that as a one-liner as I was walking out of the room."

ERIC: I think it was Lonnie Elder who threw something like a piece of office furniture at somebody's head.

STUDENT: I learned recently there will be some production companies out there that will require writers to hand in pages after a certain point. Is that your policy or not?

ERIC: I wouldn't do it. I don't care, unless your back is totally against the wall. I mean, I'm being a big shot, but if Francis finally asks for pages and I'm on page 30, I would never send them. But, if I had seventy or eighty pages, then I think, pushed to the wall, I would give them to him.

LEW: But you'll more often have people who are not really skilled at all that will want to read your pages as you go along. Then, call me, and let me talk you out of it.

ERIC: It becomes insidious because they may be subtle or they are blatant and say, "Are you sure we need to have this go like that?" or, "I was thinking, maybe the woman should be here." It's going to make you go nuts because you'll start doubting yourself and doubting what you're doing.

LEW: What you're hoping is that you'll have another Zemeckis or Coppola.

ERIC: Maybe this is my personality. My ego is not so huge that I don't think somebody else doesn't have a good idea. In most cases, it's been collaborative with the director, so they haven't felt threatened that way, and then maybe their vision is different, and you get a different discussion about things.

LEW: The best line I like in the process is a director saying, "I don't need that dialogue."

ERIC: Well, for me, I was doing *Onion Field*, and Stuart Rosenberg was supposed to direct it. We had a big battle about a scene. I just loved this fucking scene, and I was not going to give up until he said, "Leave it in the script, and I'm not going to shoot it." End of discussion.

STUDENT: You mentioned earlier about a defining image that informs you what the story is really about. Do you let that come up naturally, or do you consciously create that image?

ERIC: I try to do it as naturally as possible. Actually, that's the hardest part of writing. Writing a scene about what you want the movie to be yet not to in-your-face write about it. I think there's the difference between Ernie, the explainer, and good writing. It's the hardest. I wish I could do it well all of the time, but you can't.

LEW: I use a line that I either dreamed myself or heard from someone else. I think good dialogue is dialogue that illuminates what people are not saying.

ERIC: Exactly true. It's hard to do, especially when you've got exposition you've got to get in. When that's the case, I think you've got to get it out of character.

LEW: It gets back to knowing your theme. I say when you're in trouble and you're backed into a corner with a story and everything is dark around you, look to your characters to get you out of that corner. That's exactly what you're saying. You know your characters. You know your story, hopefully consciously but always subconsciously.

ERIC: I'm not probably as good of a storyteller that I would like to be. I have to let the characters tell the story.

LEW: Well, in my book and mind, screenwriters with that philosophy are damn fine storytellers and Eric Roth, you are a damn fine storyteller. Go, Forrest, go! Go, Eric, go!

14

Jean-Claude Carrière

I happily learned that Jean-Claude Carrière had won an Oscar for a live-action short he wrote with Pierre Étaix. I originally said to myself that his Oscar nominations for *The Discreet Charm of the Bourgeoisie*, *The Obscure Object of Desire*, *The Unbearable Lightness of Being*, and *Belle de Jour*, as well as having been Luis Buñuel's screenwriter of preference, would be enough to include this screenwriting giant. However, the Oscar win for *Heureux Anniversaire* meant his brilliance had touched the masses. Those of you who know Buñuel and Carrière also know that this needs zero legitimizing, for there is none better, dead or alive. Jean-Claude responded to my first handwritten note, assuring me, "We do know you in France and admire your work." This letter was immediately framed and hung on my award wall. Praise from Carrière is as equal to me as the Emmy nominations and awards from the Writers Guild of America. I agree with Larry Gelbart's introduction of Carrière at a 2001 WGA Love Feast: "Ladies and gentlemen, I give you the world's greatest working screenwriter."

I flew to France, and armed with a video camera; my wife, Pamela; and former students Maren Chumly and Fabien Michel, we were buzzed into the courtyard of Carrière's apartment building, our minds bursting with anticipation. Carrière's apartment is located in the Pigalle, an area between the ninth and eighteenth arrondissements of beautiful Paris. We walked across the cobblestones toward a twinkle-eyed, bearded man, who spread his arms with a hearty welcome.

We settled into his dining room, gratefully accepting flagons of Cabernet Sauvignon, as a gorgeous, mottled red cat climbed into my lap for the total comfort of moi and the beast. "She never does that except for beautiful women and also for writers." Jean-Claude nodded to Pamela and Maren, "You'll be having your turn." We were now giggling and totally at ease as we settled in to focus on the screenwriting techniques of the "world's greatest working screenwriter."

LEW: Bill Goldman said two things which are pertinent. He said, "I don't live in Los Angeles, where you people hide behind gated communities. I live in New York, and when I walk out onto the street, I'm in life." But he also said, "The horror of it all is that we all do it so differently." And I said, "That's also the joy of it all." Because as a professor, I teach your own uniqueness is the only thing that is unusual. Everything has been done before, generally speaking. We are interested in your uniqueness and how you write screenplays.

You have about seventy-five credits at least on an internet search, we found, so you have been truly a career screenwriter. I'm asking very good screenwriters basically the same five questions. I'm very, very familiar with your book. I read it again down in Croatia. I'm interested in how you feel about screenwriting as storytelling? Do you feel it's the closest thing to oral storytelling, or do you have another notion?

JEAN-CLAUDE: I think basically screenwriting is modern storytelling. I very often think of myself as a storyteller traditionally but using the means to my storytelling advantage. Basically, something is the same, and something is different, of course. The part which is the same is that we are using fictional characters that we sometimes invent or find in a book or a play or something else to tell a story. Then we give them scenes, one after the other. A fiction thing does not exist without scenes between characters and without an evolution between these scenes, which is storytelling.

This story is not necessarily a story with the traditional beginning and development, the final point with the punch line, or ending. It could be a much more impressionistic story. Cinema has invented, as you know very well at this point, even silence sometimes. So all these means, all these ways, are to be used, but it is still storytelling. Anyway, film must have a beginning and an end. You enter the theater, or you turn on your television set, and there is a beginning, and then the work ends. You have to put something in between. You can't leave the spectators at the end without telling them the full story.

LEW: All right.

JEAN-CLAUDE: When Chaplin walks away from the camera at the end of *City Lights*, it does not tell us, "Get on and find how my story ends." No, this says to us, "This story which I've been telling you is finished. I am going to walk into another story that maybe I will tell you some other time." You understand?

LEW: Yes.

JEAN-CLAUDE: That's what we call a Chaplin-esque ending. That's all we can allow ourselves. So my answer to your question is yes.

Now the main question about this to me is to choose the story that we are going to tell, that we are going to make into a film. There are thousands and thousands of possible stories in any newspaper, in anything between people. If you start, and we start to tell each other what we've been told yesterday, what we heard in a café, what we have dreamt, what we have read in some books. There are a lot of possible stories. Which one are we going to choose to spend more and more of our time working on? That's the main point, and sometimes I may be wrong. Sometimes we make the wrong choice, and then we realize that we are on a wrong track and that the story we have chosen is not rich enough to make a rich and beautiful film. So what should we do? We have already signed a contract. We are supposed to deliver, as you say in America—which is a beautiful word—to deliver a story, and we can.

So my first point, my first piece of advice, would be to never sign a contract before being sure that my story, I wouldn't say it's a good story, contains the possibility of development. I think sometimes weeks and weeks, whatever it is, from a book or a new story I've invented. I would never sign a contract on a very short and brief idea. On the contrary, I take a lot of notes. I try to build not a script, but let's say what we would call an outline, a treatment, for the building of the script before I sign the contract. It means that when I meet a producer and we agree to working on this film, I am already able to tell him more or less the building up of the film. That's my first rule, which was not the case at the beginning.

I have certain experiences, you know. At the beginning, you are fresh and young and excited because you want to make films. After a couple of weeks, either working alone or with the director, you realize this story is not as interesting as you thought it was, so what are we going to do? Make sure it's solid, a good story. It's very important.

LEW: Did you give money back at times?

JEAN-CLAUDE: I did sometimes. Yes. Absolutely.

LEW: Me, too. Was the take-back any good?

JEAN-CLAUDE: Not when the story had been offered to me by the producer, but when I had proposed the story myself, that is the idea, yes, I did. I did two or three times, yes.

LEW: Is there a certain way the moon is shaped or whatever when you say, "That's the one, I think, that I want to spend a good deal of time on"? About the script, you say, "Rich enough." Are there other criteria besides it being rich enough?

JEAN-CLAUDE: There are two conditions. One is that I like it. I am not accepting to make a film because somebody else has convinced me to tell the story. I have to like it immensely. I am going to spend part of my life alone with the story, so I'd better like it. And the second is I test it, and I tell the story, not as a film, but, like, for instance: "Oh, my mother told me this story. I'd like to hear your reaction." That depends on the films. I did this very much for *The Return of Martin Guerre*. I told it in slightly different ways to old people, to young people. I remember once I told people in a hotel, and I didn't know them, so just to see how they react to the simple storytelling.

The story of *Guerre* was very important to me because the story is a story of a man who goes away, who leaves and comes back nine years later, and he is not recognized by everybody. Some say, "Yes, it is Guerre." Some say, "It is not. It is another man." Today, that story would be impossible because of our documents, our passports, our photographs, you know. So my question was, is this story, which takes place in a small French village in the sixteenth century, acceptable for us? That's why I was testing it. Everybody liked the story. Nobody told me that it could not exist. The people who we are telling the story to are expecting us to relay a specific situation, and we could see that they are expecting a good story from their body language.

LEW: It's like a studio meeting.

JEAN-CLAUDE: Very small movements of the body sometimes tell you a lot.

LEW: And when you go to the lay audience, the actors are not good enough to lie, but they can lie with their body language.

JEAN-CLAUDE: Especially in *Martin Guerre*, there was a necessity for a flashback. The story starts when they are babies, and then the story lasts for forty years. So you need to condense some scenes. So at which moment does the flashback stop? All this, the way you tell the story, helps you a lot in beginning to build the tension of the story.

LEW: Aristotle says that superior drama and comedy is that which allows us to discover ourselves. You see in the story that the audience could discover themselves and see themselves coming back and saying, "This is me," and people not believing it.

JEAN-CLAUDE: That's going maybe a little bit too much into detail. But when I started working on the story of *Martin Guerre*, I met an American historian, Natalie Davis, who was teaching at Princeton University, an excellent storyteller who specialized in French sixteenth-century history, and she knew very well the story of *Guerre*. So our question from the point of view of the historian and my point of view—we did a book together afterwards—was what happened?

The man comes back and is welcomed by his wife. They already had a child together They know each other very well. The very first day he returns, she welcomes him as her husband. They had been separated for nine years, so she takes him to their bedroom, and the following day they wake up together. What Natalie Davis was saying, and I was saying, is that for a woman, it's impossible to be mistaken about her husband. She knew if he was or not her husband, it's impossible. So since at the end, he's not, then at the very beginning, she has cheated a little. Why? For which reason? The mystery is there, so our conclusions were absolutely the same. That secretly that was the lost story. The only answer Davis could get from her point of view and from my point of view was that this was a secret love story. She fell in love with this man when she saw him, and he fell for her. But they could not show that this love was a new one. They had to behave like an old couple.

So in America, when they make a remake of the story, with *Sommersby*, I talked with the screenwriters. It was extremely interesting. You have Richard Gere and Jodie Foster. In our version, you cannot have one scene with the two of them alone. It's impossible because immediately you know that he is not going to keep the secret when they are alone. So they go into the bedroom and close the door, and we stay outside. There is no one scene in the film where the two of them are alone. But when you have Richard Gere and Jodie Foster, two big stars, you need to have scenes between the two of them. It's an absolute obligation. So what they did was change the story very clearly indicating from the very beginning, from the very first shot, that it's not the same man, that he has killed the other one and has come back. So that for many different reasons sometimes, we can tell the same story in a very different way.

LEW: But it was not as successful or as good as the first story?

JEAN-CLAUDE: Right. There were other parameters. They had to put the story in the nineteenth century in the South with black characters. That was another problem.

LEW: The reason I ask that is that Bill Goldman says, in this book you're going to be in, that films are so fragile. You change one small thing sometimes, and the whole thing is gone. He said the best screenplay he's ever read was Francis Coppola's *The Great Gatsby*. Then in comes the English director. I believe he said "class-obsessed English director," and he said the director believed the whole movie was about the lowness of Gatsby's parties, which is not really the theme, and he made it the theme, and he said the movie was shattered for him. This might be the same for *Sommersby*.

JEAN-CLAUDE: A script is always very fragile.

LEW: You identify the movie, the idea. And you test it by telling stories around the idea and seeing the audience reaction. How do you develop it? Do you develop it in a sophisticated, prose-like outline?

JEAN-CLAUDE: Now we have to answer with the usual answer: It is developed. There is no universal rule. For instance, it depends very much on, is it an adaptation or not? Is it an original idea? When you adapt an original, it is already sort of structured. When I did the adaptation of *The Unbearable Lightness of Being*, there was already a certain structure of scenes in the book that you are not going to expect because it's a book. But you have already material, something to start from. When you are just by yourself and sometimes the producer, sometimes the director, that's enough story. You are so "free" that sometimes it's frightening. So, as I told you, first of all, I try to find a general structure but not too precise because I want to be surprised by myself from time to time.

The second important thing is, as soon as possible, I work with the director. That's, to me, essential. I've been used to it. I always make a point to have the director in front of me, even if he says that he is not an author, not a screenwriter, because he's the one who is going to make the film, because I can read on his face whether this idea that I am proposing pleases him or not. I have the feeling that I have to try to convince, and that if finally he does accept to do this scene of the film, he will do it without withdrawing, without shooting his own film, his own scene. That is the most difficult point: to work on the same film, the same scene, as the director; to try to identify myself through the director on one movement; to try to convince the director to come to me. In other words, there is the director, the screenwriter, and the film. The most important of the three is the film. That is my point of view all the time. It's not to win over the director or to be enslaved by the director, although some people can like it.

But no, the most important thing is the film. And it's very difficult being a man or woman, a human being, to cancel inside any kind of pride, of self-indulging, like "This is my idea." I can't understand that. But the director is the one who is going to make the film, so he'd better like it. The real challenge is to write a scene that the director wants to shoot immediately. That's one point.

The other point is to find a way to write the script which is going to be the best way to help the director and not only the director, but all the other technicians around. In other words, not to try to make a literary object of what's going to be anyway thrown away in the garbage can at the end of shooting. A script is a written object that looks like a book but with very few readers. So the script has to answer all the questions that the cameraman, the sound engineer, the set designer are going to ask, without giving a preference to one of them, in a very discreet way. But everything has to be there.

LEW: I'm jumping ahead a little, but since we're already there, are you on the set often when your movies are being shot?

JEAN-CLAUDE: When I'm asked to. But when I'm not asked to, it's a good sign, and everything's going smoothly. From time to time, I'm called because of the reasons that they say it's too long, or when the guy goes from the door to the window, it's too long, and the phrase has to be shorter. All these things, and also some actors can be whimsical and refuse to say this or that, even though they have accepted to say it when reading the script. So you have to be there, to come in. There is a narrow relationship between the screenwriter and the actors, and maybe not very often, but it happens, the director and the main actors are on very bad terms. Sometimes they don't even talk to each other. In that case, the screenwriter is going from one to the other as the go-between.

LEW: Again, I want to go back to the outlining aspect, but for the moment, since we're here, directing. You have directed?

JEAN-CLAUDE: Sure. Two or three short films.

LEW: Why have you never directed many of the scripts you've written?

JEAN-CLAUDE: Because I'm a writer.

LEW: You don't feel being a director is equal?

JEAN-CLAUDE: No, it's too long a road.

LEW: A fellow writer, Bill Walsh is his name, who wrote *Mary Poppins*, for instance, says, "You have to get up too early in the morning to walk to the set."

JEAN-CLAUDE: The main point is that screenwriting is about the third part of my life. I'm writing books, and I'm working on theater very much. I've been working with Peter Brook for twenty-six years.

LEW: You came from the theater before you went into motion pictures?

JEAN-CLAUDE: No, I came from another writing, anyway. Then the cinema, then theater. Actually, I have been working closely with Peter for twenty-six years now, and we've done things which I could not have done if I were a director. When you are a movie director, you can't do anything else but make a film. You have a sort of tag on your shoulder, that says, "Movie Director." And if you write a book, it will not be considered a book.

LEW: Are you still President of La Fémis, the French state film school?

JEAN-CLAUDE: No, for ten years I was. Now I'm retired.

LEW: Did it have a screenwriting program?

JEAN-CLAUDE: Yes, of course.

LEW: Back to the structure now: So do you involve the director as quickly as you can back when you're outlining and writing the treatment?

JEAN-CLAUDE: Yes. Giving him samples to write and discussing, talking about locations, actors, as soon as possible. You have to have the faces of the actors as soon as possible.

LEW: Directors must love working with you because I don't sense you to be adversarial.

JEAN-CLAUDE: Absolutely. When I was working with Milos Foreman, with Louis Malle, with Phil Kaufman on *Unbearable Likeness of Being*, we always found the locations together.

LEW: I love the story in here of going to Greenwich Village and going to different places with Milos.

JEAN-CLAUDE: I'm speaking a bit from the soul. Shall we proceed in order or not? Should we start at the very beginning or not? You understand?

LEW: Yes, yes.

JEAN-CLAUDE: I remember when I wrote the most difficult play in my life, an epic. I didn't start at the very beginning. There were some scenes which were compulsory, key scenes, so trying to find a tone, I start with these scenes. So it's exactly the same today. I didn't start at the beginning, and I won't end at the end.

But one thing I would like to say, which partially answers your questions, is when I write or when anybody writes, I think there is always a double movement. First of all, I am part of the film. I try to invent a film which I would love to watch. I am a spectator. I am entering a movie theater, I want to see this film, so what is it telling me, showing me? And I'm also out of the film. I try to imagine the film as if I was the best possible spectator.

LEW: Or when you were a little boy. You and I are about the same age. When I was a little boy, I used to watch films, and "My God, it's going to be over, and I don't want to get out of this world. I love this world. They're taking me out, and it's going to end. Oh, it ended." We don't do that anymore. Part of it is because the movies are shorter.

JEAN-CLAUDE: That's not enough. This attitude is very useful sometimes because sometimes you write things, and all of a sudden, you realize that you don't want to see this. You don't want to watch the scene. You are used to writing, so the main attitude is to get into the film, to take the place of this character, and to ask yourself, "What if I am in this situation? What should I do?" Identify yourself totally. Going in and going out of the film is my basic attitude. Very often I do it quite rightly, going inside and outside. But if you don't put yourself, as we say in French, into the "scheme" of your character, you miss something. Even if the character is a scoundrel, a young girl, anybody, you have to find at least part of this character inside of you. If you don't find it, it can't happen.

LEW: I think there's quite a relationship to being a superior screenwriter and being a tall child: that when we were small, we played imaginary games, and the nice thing about it is you don't have to go in because your mother never calls you for supper. But do you find the childlike qualities, and do you think screenwriters are maybe more feminine professionally?

JEAN-CLAUDE: They must be.

LEW: Screenwriters, editors, and cinematographers.

JEAN-CLAUDE: Yes, we all have a feminine side, I suppose. I very often have written especially onstage for women, and very often I have been told by very feminine actresses, they do not know where I find this, but it is there. I do not invent it.

LEW: I just happen to think that it is a giving profession. We help each other as writers. We nurture. We accept as opposed to directing, and acting is more thrusting; producing is more masculine.

JEAN-CLAUDE: I don't know who was saying, "You have to find the bastard inside of you." Don't worry. You'll find him.

LEW: Have you written a great many originals?

JEAN-CLAUDE: About half and half.

LEW: When you're developing an original as well as an adaptation, do you write a structured outline?

JEAN-CLAUDE: I don't like to write a very precise outline because I would feel imprisoned. I like to be surprised, but I need a certain outline, a certain structure which is not necessarily written. If I speak with the director, I tell him, and we know. But the more I grow old and the more my memory is weakening, so the more I write so I don't forget.

Very often it happens that the two of us are working together and improvising as usual, trying to act and trying to invent a scene. I say something, and if you're the director, then after a few minutes later, you tell me, "You said something before that was quite interesting and very good." I say, "Yes, it was the meaning, but not the form." And it's impossible to get it back. The improvisation came out in a certain way that you can never find again.

LEW: Fighters call it "leaving their fight in the dressing room."

JEAN-CLAUDE: Just to go back to being in close contact with life: I have nothing against people who are being screenwriters, close themselves, and invent their world. But I am not that type. I am always out meeting people, traveling a lot. I like to go to the places where the story is going to be shot, to know the actors. I like this.

LEW: Jean Cocteau said, "Surprise me. Surprise me." He used that word twice. So every now and then, I or whoever will write something and go rush to their wives or to their husbands and say, "Oh my God. Look what happened."

JEAN-CLAUDE: I like to be surprised, even astonished by myself. Some writers or directors like everything they find, everything they write. They are immediately satisfied, which paralyzes the work. You stop. But of course, there is something wrong here. But the other attitude is as wrong as this one, the one which consists of saying, "Look at that. What a piece of shit I have written today. Another stupid scene."

I remember once a very good French director who was looking very down, and I said, "What's wrong?" He said, "I am coming out of such a bad film." I asked, "Which one?" He said, "Mine." So it's very difficult between these two extremes. The person who is immediately seduced by himself or herself and the other who is never satisfied. That is why the presence of the director or another screenwriter can remedy this sometimes.

Just to give you a short example: When I started working with Buñuel the very first time, I had written two films. Buñuel was immensely famous already, so I was sitting right in front of him, and I wanted to know everything he was saying. So all the time, I was going, "Yes, yes. This is all wonderful." After two or three weeks of work, the producer came to Madrid—I was in Spain—and invited me to a dinner, just the two of us, which was very strange. Usually when we dine, it's the three of us. At the end of the dinner, he said right away, "Luis is very happy with you. He believes that you work very well, that you are very serious, and you write very good work, and you are nice, but you have to say no to him from time to time." That was a very good lesson. So I stopped, and it was not very easy. But that's what was waiting for me. Of course, he was expecting new ideas. I did bring them.

Lew: You have developed the outline, and now you're moving into script. What sort of work habits do you have when you're involved with the script?

Jean-Claude: The main problem for me is to go from literature to cinema and know that what I am writing is not a piece of literature, but it's going to be transformed to a film. I prefer to write scene after scene. "Interior dining room afternoon. Three ladies are sitting around a table. One of them, the youngest, is having a piece of cake. She's rubbing her hands." But without technical indications. That's one possibility, but if I am asked, I often write a shooting script with all the technical indications. I start by the way we've projected in the text, and we're writing a very precise script, quite unreadable, full of technical indications, drawings, so I can do it. That depends on the need of the director. Most of the time, the director does it himself.

Lew: Do you assign yourself so many pages a day when you're in the script after the outline? Or so many hours?

Jean-Claude: I'd love to. Hours, for sure. I'm a good worker. I'm not structured. When it comes to work, I love it, so you can demand me a lot. But that doesn't mean that I write three, five, six pages a day. Sometimes it goes very fast. You know, the moment you see the film, the characters escape your control, and they have a life by themselves, and you have the feeling that you are spying on them, and you are writing very quickly what they say. These moments, which are very rare, are always good.

Lew: Do you write in the morning, in the afternoon, or in the evening?

Jean-Claude: I prefer the afternoon. I don't know why. Usually more than three hours is significant. I can be very well concentrated for three and a half hours, and then for another one or two hours, I can do some work, like preparing the work for the following day, but not real writing. If I persist, if I insist and keep on writing, very often the following day, I can't solve this. Two hours and a half is perfect.

LEW: Do you go about two months to finish your screenplay?

JEAN-CLAUDE: A little more, between three and four months. But what I like very much is to get a first version of the script finished and then to let it sleep for two or three months and to write a play, travel, to direct a workshop, to work on theater, and then to go back to the script. I like it very much.

The Distinct Charm of the Bourgeoisie was written in five different versions in two years. Sometimes the problems that we have been incapable of solving appear all of a sudden very clearly because you have given time to your unconscious to do its part. If you're always conscious, intelligent, trying to write, you miss something. We all have an unconscious spot. Many of them don't give this side the possibility of working.

LEW: I teach that creativity really comes from the subconscious and the subconscious mind. Billy Wilder says, "As soon as we take out the rewrites, the improvements, we might have a good script." The improvements meaning "conscious" rewrites that start sabotaging what the unconscious mind has: the creativity. Do you feel that way also?

JEAN-CLAUDE: Yeah, of course. I know also that by working too much, we are getting used to a story. We know all the details very well. They are beginning to become boring for us. We get rid of things which would be very interesting for some others. At one point, you have to stop. It's very difficult though to stop correcting, stop changing.

LEW: Do you have a particular warning bell or caveat that says, "Stop"?

JEAN-CLAUDE: No. If you have one, I am going to buy it.

LEW: So rewriting varies upon the people involved, upon you?

JEAN-CLAUDE: Yes. There's some scripts I've written eight, ten, eleven times, and this is really the best. Some of them are written in two or three months, and you don't know what to change. *The Unbearable Likeness of Being*, many people told me it's impossible to make a film out of it. I had a feeling that it was possible. I think I wrote the first version in two months, with very few changes to the second version, so you never know.

Lew: As I get older—and I don't know whether I'm getting smarter or not; one never exactly knows, but one does become more informed— I'm so conscious and so keenly interested with what the story is really about. I use as an example Larry Gelbart. When he wrote *Tootsie*, he said that he finally understood that the Tootsie character put on a dress and became a better man for it. Arthur Miller actually types it out and puts it on his typewriter rather than his computer so that every time he writes, he has to look over the raison d'être in front of him.

Jean-Claude: That's what I was telling you about *Martin Guerre*. Very often, it's a human tendency to leave the main road and to go in some other path or on some other roads, and where is the film? So you have to go back. So this road was interesting. It happens all the time. It happens with you. It happens with the director, or someone who is offering you something which doesn't fit at all with the film. He likes him a lot, but this is not the film. We are telling another story, not this one. And it's impossible to marry them, to put them together. Of course, that's essential.

Lew: Aristotle says the movie or play or piece of drama should simply be about what the main character gets. Do you agree?

Jean-Claude: Yes. The hero could be one or a group. The word *get* is impossible to translate in French. It's very general.

Lew: Accomplish.

Jean-Claude: Accomplish or to know or sometimes to lose. *Get* is right, but the best way to translate would be *to do*.

Lew: David Mamet says that working in movies has taught him not to cheat, to stay with what the hero is trying to lose or trying to get, trying to accomplish, and to get off that mark is moving into novel territory. In novels you can go off for ten or fifteen pages and talk about the flora and the fauna and then come back, but not in screenwriting.

Jean-Claude: If you cheat, the audience will notice it immediately. But the question is, What about telling the story of a cheater who is a liar, somebody who is ambiguous? These characters are quite interesting, and you cannot simplify that without betraying them. The tension is always to make things too simple.

LEW: Einstein said to make things simple but not simpler. I've often felt that many problems with motion pictures and screenplays is that they were too complicated, and everything canceled each other out. There's a movie called *Children of Heaven* that was done in Iran that was the biggest movie of the year at the Rotterdam Film Festival. It was about a small brother, and he lost his shoes, so the sister gives him her shoes so that the father will not be angry. That's the focal point. Of course, *Jean de Florette* is about watering carnations or the simplest part of it. But you see what I'm saying?

JEAN-CLAUDE: Yes, there must be a profound simplicity to the story.

LEW: Our next question is about my publisher saying that people buy these books, expecting to find the secrets. Do you have any secrets? Because when I was growing up, everyone wanted to write the great American novel. Now, as I become older, everyone wants to write the great American screenplay. Truly, thousands of young people are writing screenplays today. Over here, the wave is just beginning. When people ask me about the secret, I tell them to read *The Poetics* because what you get out of there will be a secret to performance drama and comedy. But as far as secrets, do you have any?

JEAN-CLAUDE: It would be a mistake to talk about secrets.

LEW: Why?

JEAN-CLAUDE: The language of a film is secret. It belongs to a literary form, but it's a technical form. We have to learn to write in film language. That's the only thing. Don't write a script as if it's a novel. Think that what you are writing is going to be a film, that what you are writing is provisional, something that will not last.

LEW: That can be taught. When I taught at the Sorbonne, the first thing they told me was screenwriting could not be taught. I said, "Bullshit," because that would be to say that Monet did not need Manet and Dickens did not need Dostoevsky. It's a craft, of course. Talent helps, but writing and reading a lot helps more.

JEAN-CLAUDE: The only craft is that you have to know the film language. If you want to write a novel in Chinese, you'd better know Chinese. You have to absolutely, necessarily know how a film is made. That's the only secret. That's why so many novelists fail when they want to become screenwriters. Screenwriting is not the end of the literary convention. It is the beginning of the cinematic convention.

LEW: You wrote in your book, "Since we believe neurologists assert that the human brain, that prestigious organ, is also an idle blob which delights in simplifications and reductions, a dull prodigy ready to applaud at the first witty or noisy phrase it encounters. The pitfalls lying in wake for both author and actor are legion. Our brain likes to seduce itself, to outlive itself like a conjurer, astonished by its own skill and honestly assuming that he is a real miracle worker, even applauding himself at the end of his act. Our brain, our mind, if you prefer, is ever ready for self-worship, ever ready to adore whatever springs from its own depths."

Jumping over, you say, "Writing a story or a screenplay means injecting order into disorder; making a preliminary selection of sounds, actions, and words; discarding most of them; then stressing and reinforcing the material selected. It means violating reality, or at least what we perceive of reality, to rebuild itself in another way and finding the images within a given frame, selecting the real voices, emotions, and sometimes ideas." Your book was written twenty years ago. Do you still feel the same?

JEAN-CLAUDE: Absolutely. There is something artificial in a script. Life is disorder. Life is never dramatized. When someone tells you a story which happened to him or her, you can never directly put that story into a film. You have to treat the story, to dramatize, to put your development into it.

LEW: I'm fascinated with creating the illusion of reality. The last question: Can screenwriting be an art?

JEAN-CLAUDE: That depends on if the cinema is an art. If the cinema is an art, then screenwriting is an art. That's my only answer.

LEW: Do you ever miss working with Buñuel?

JEAN-CLAUDE: Yes. But he's still alive to me. I talk to him every day.

LEW: To me, you are truly a monument, and your cinema is an art. Thank you.

15

Frank Pierson

Frank Pierson is a giant, and I don't mean just to the screenwriting world. Frank stands a stately six foot two, with a short beard and perpetual smile. He was a two-term WGA president and of course widely known as the screenwriter who penned *Cool Hand Luke*, *Dog Day Afternoon*, *A Star Is Born*, and *Presumed Innocent*, and the list goes on and on. Frank is one of the most decent men I have ever known. He is revered by every Writers Guild of America colleague, not only for his capabilities, nor for just the sheer expanse of his writing career, but also for passing guild acts that created towering gains for the screenwriters as far as pay, protection, and industry stature.

I knew and loved Frank along with these colleagues. I remember one occasion when my dear wife, Pamela, and moi bumped into Frank and his sweetheart under a full moon in London's romantic Berkeley Square, both couples en route to see the Degas exhibition at the National Gallery in Trafalgar Square. One of my favorite memories of Frank is trading quips about our children. I asked him if his children liked him, and he quickly replied, "Oh, yes. They think I'm one of them!"

In this dialogue with Frank, you'll be taken into his mind and gain a better understanding of how deeply involved he becomes as he develops the psyche of each of his characters. You'll also get a glimpse at how he outfoxes the suits in order to get his story told the way he wants it told. We must be both crafty and amiable, a seemingly antagonistic pairing yet one that Frank mastered early and that played into his many, many successes, both in writing and in life. I hope you will find yourself thrilled to be inside the mind of such a giant.

LEW: What are the blues? Louis Armstrong said, "Baby, if you gotta ask, you'll never know." I'm just going to name some movie titles that most of you know, but now you're meeting the writer: *Cool Hand Luke, The Happening, The Anderson Tapes, Dog Day Afternoon, A Star Is Born, Presumed Innocent*—what's this, *Hand-Carved Coffins*?

FRANK: *Hand-Carved Coffins* is an adaptation of a Truman Capote story that's been around for years. Everyone wants to make it, but the producer who owns it, everyone hates him, and they won't work with him. They keep trying to buy it, but he won't sell, so that's a lesson to you all: Watch out for when you're hired to write. The minute you are hired, the United States copyright law says the employer is deemed to be the author of the work. After that flows everything else, namely that the company. Warner Brothers or whoever is hiring you owns the work and can do anything with it that they want. If they decide they don't want somebody else to make it, well, the studio head said I'd better get my head right about a piece because I keep trying to get it away from Warner Brothers to take it somewhere else. Anyone can say, "We don't want to make this picture, and we don't want anybody else to make it, either." So, then what?

LEW: Is there a political reason?

FRANK: I don't think so. I think he's scared somebody else might make it, and if it turns out to be a fairly successful movie or wins an Academy Award for somebody, then he looks like a fool. That's all.

LEW: I wonder how he felt about *Forrest Gump* since that was at Warner Brothers?

FRANK: He felt like hell. [*laughter*] He would rest his case, right?

LEW: Exactly. Zanuck one time was asked, "What if you had to flip-flop the pieces you turn down, that became pieces you accepted?" He said, "The success-to-failure ratio would probably be the same." Anyway, Frank's also been directing since—gosh, I remember when you were doing *The Neon Ceiling*. Is that the first piece you directed?

FRANK: Yeah, I'd directed some episodic television and a couple of series that I created, but I was their producer, and I assigned myself as the director.

LEW: Frank has been directing for a good number of years; however, we have him here today for his Academy Award nominations on *Cool Hand Luke* and *Cat Ballou* and his win for *Dog Day Afternoon.*

I quote you without authenticity, as I heard this from Billy Sackheim: "Good writers always look to their characters when they're in story trouble. Frank Pierson was dramatically stymied while developing *Dog Day Afternoon* from a real-life incident with a bumbling bank robber who took hostages when confronted by the police while his hold-up was in progress. Frank struggled and struggled with this small-time hood until the key came to him. The Al Pacino character was living for everyone except for himself. He lived for his wife, his homosexual lover, even his hostages in a scene where he ordered pizza for a pregnant woman, and he was asking her, 'Is it hot enough? Did they make it hot enough? We'll make them bring in some that's hotter.' Frank's character got him out of his story corner." Is that true?

FRANK: Mm-hmm. It's absolutely right. We were working with a real-life event, and we had been around and interviewed all the people who had participated: the police, the FBI people, the hostages, and the one person I was never able to meet was the guy who did the bank robbery himself. His real-life name was John. John would not talk to me. I had such a good idea of who all the other people were, and we got a sense of how they would behave and so on. His gay wife in particular was a wonderful character, hilariously funny, a drag queen without putting an obscene spin on it. He'd knock you out. He was very, very funny. Sort of a queen of the desert. But one person I was not able to meet with was John, our main character.

When I started the screenplay, he was doing twenty-five years to life in federal prison. he gave me permission to come, but when I got there, he'd sent down a message that he didn't want to see me. It turns out, that he was in a contract fight with Warner Brothers for the rights to his life story. The producers had gotten waivers for everyone else involved, which allowed them to be portrayed only in terms of the context of characters in the bank robbery but not using their real names and so long as we didn't portray anything sexual about them. Those kinds of waivers Warner Brothers bought, and we're talking 1972, so for $25, $50. The most they paid was $100 for Ernie, then already Liz Eden, who'd gotten his sex-change operation. I think they paid him $1,500 or something like that, but John was holding out for more, and he had an inexperienced lawyer who had no idea of what to ask for or how to structure a contract, so he kept waffling. In the meantime, John kept holding out and wouldn't talk to me. So I had no idea who he was or any sense of his speech rhythms or anything like that. Then finally we got an agreement via John. By the way, Warner Brothers paid John $7,500, and that was it. He gave the $7,500 to Ernie to use it to get his sex-change operation, so in a sense Warner Brothers paid for the sex-change operation, which was the purpose of the bank robbery in the first place. [*laughter*]

The question then became, How do I write this? How do I write this character who is the central cause of everything that happens in the screenplay? We had a chronology: This thing happened, and then that happened, and then that happened, and so on, and I could change those things around, reshuffle the cards, as it were, to have a better progression from the beginning of it to the end, but it made no sense without a character whose story I was writing. So if I could understand why was it that these people had their particular attitudes that they did toward him, and that was the major problem: not having met the guy and make up out of my own feelings about who he was. I was really relying only, as far as research was concerned, on what the hostages, his family, the various people that he'd met along the path of his life, the costumes, and so on.

It was also contradictory. It was as though everyone involved in this whole process was talking about a different person, so it was of no help, and as I say, a great deal of it was contradictory. One person would say, "He was a wonderful person, so helpful and kind." And someone else would say, "He was a liar because he would pretend to your face that he was so nice and kind and so on, and then he would turn like a snake. I got fired from my job because of things that John would do." Sorting out all of this contradictory material was despair. I just did not know how to write a scene with him in it. I did not know what the story was in terms of—and I hate the word, but it's the only useful one we have that means the same thing to everyone—the arc of the character in the story. What drove him? What made people respond to him the way they did?

I almost quit the project. I fiddled around with it for weeks and weeks and weeks and couldn't get anything out of it, until finally, out of desperation, I went through all of the research material to ask myself simple questions. This, by the way, is part of my working thing. I'm so stupid, I have to ask myself questions. I write them on the screen so it's up there on the computer, and then, when I have to answer them, "What, if anything, is the common denominator in all of this contradictory and confusing material?" It became clear that there was a single, common thread, and it wasn't what they were saying it was. It was the feelings they were expressing throughout.

The one thing that they all expressed was their own sense of betrayal. I'm so stupid, I write on my computer screen, "Betrayal. What does it mean?" So I go to the dictionary, and I look up the word *betrayal*. It means essentially "a promise has been made that is not fulfilled." And then I went back, and I looked at the history that he had with all those characters: with his wife, with his gay wife, with the people in the gay community that he associated with, even school friends, and people who had worked with him before, people that had been with him in Vietnam, even people who had worked with him when he was a very straitlaced guy and was working as a cashier in a bank and was a worker for Goldman-Sachs in 1964.

Sorting through all of that, I began to understand what it was and in what way he had betrayed them. With all of them, he was making a kind of promise that he was going to take care of them. Of course, he was always unable to do that. What began to form in my mind was a character—if you could describe it like this—it was as though he imagined that he was a wizard, a magician who had the gift of being able to fulfill the dreams and ambitions of all the people he came in contact with. Of course, what happens is you can't do that for other people; you can barely do it for yourself. So people bought this and accepted that this is the man that's going to make things happen for them. If it's a woman who's falling in love with him, then this is the man who's going to make her happy. Inevitably, he is not going to be able to do it, so in the end, the person feels betrayed. His parents felt betrayed because he was supposed to be this boy who was going to be successful in life. He promised them that, and he failed. In fact, he winds up a bank robber, worse than unsuccessful but also a criminal. It's the ultimate betrayal of everybody involved in his life.

If you look at Ernie, this was a man he'd met while cruising the gay bars at Greenwich Village. Ernie was sort of part drag queen, part God knows what. Ernie had one thing that he yearned for in his life, and that was that he'd be married and have a "normal" or an idyllic life. What did John do? He married him in a Catholic Church with a gay priest and so on. Wedding pictures and videos were on television showing the two of them getting married, with Ernie wearing a full-length, white satin dress, John in his Vietnam uniform with his medals of honor. It was very touching, and the party afterwards was terrific.

Then, of course, things didn't turn out the way Ernie wanted because once the party was over, life went on, just as it had before, and nothing was that much different. John couldn't make him happy. The very episode of robbing the bank came out of that because Ernie decided to talk to a shrink, and the shrink told him he was actually a woman trapped in a man's body, and that's why he needed an operation. So the very thing that's happening in the movie is that John robs a bank to get the money for Ernie's sex-change operation, and he also does it on Ernie's birthday.

Ernie by this time is in the hospital because he's swallowed everything in sight. The cops bring him down, and what is his reaction to all of this? Is he grateful? He says, "My God! What a birthday present! Fuck you, you've ruined my life! They're telling me I'm an accessory after the fact of you robbing a bank, and so your birthday present to me is I'm going to go to prison." John says, "No, you won't. I'll take care of it."

That's the kind of character he is. Well, certainly then, the character I wrote, you could put him in any kind of situation, and he'd take care of it. He's the guy that would come into this room, and he would look you straight into the eye in the most intense kind of way and say, "What can I do for you? What do you want?" And you'd tell him, and he'd say, "Well, I can help you with that." He's full of shit. He can't possibly do that. He's highly neurotic and an ineffectual failure, lower-middle class guy with no prospects, no friends, and no money. I don't know how anyone would do all these things for all these people to whom he's promised. Now, I know why he has the relationship he has with the cops and so on. You see him in the course of the film, scene after scene, telling the cops, "Listen, I'll take care of it. This is what you'll do, and this what I'll do," and it never ends. That is, until the FBI comes in.

The FBI aren't buying that shit. This cop, who is played by Charles Durning, plays into that whole scene, so I've got things to write. The actual process of writing the screenplay from that time on took only— let's see—I had that inspiration around the middle of October, and I finished it on New Year's Eve with my last bottle of coke. The drink. [*laughter*] The point is that until I got a hold and had a sense of how that character was with people and so on, it was impossible to write anything. I just could not do it. Then, once it happened, it came very easily.

LEW: Larry Gelbart talks about breaking the back of the story. Was that breaking the back of the story?

FRANK: No, that's not the way my mind works. The story, to me, is the plot, and the plot is easy. I don't give a damn. I mean, sometimes you have problems figuring out what happens next or what is the event that will dramatize this change in character. You'll have a moment when this young man in the course of your fictional story is looking in this girl's eyes. It's that moment where he's saying to himself, "This is the woman I want to marry." The problems associated with that have nothing to do with breaking the back of the plot. They have to do with what do we see as an audience that motivates him and explains why he's motivated to love her and to ask her to marry him. But what do we see on-screen? Do we write it in words, or do we trust the actors to convince us of these choices? You've got Helen Hunt in the scene, and you don't write any words; you just show it. Then what is the outcome of that? It's very hard because those life moments don't always show up visually.

LEW: Gelbart said he broke the back of *Tootsie* when he realized Dustin Hoffman put on a dress and became a better man for it. Tom Schulman said in *Dead Poets Society*, his moment came when he realized the boys were as smart as their teacher. Then, boom, twenty-four hours later, he had his script.

FRANK: Yeah, but you know something? People say a day, three days, a week. They attribute that to the writing of their script, but it's been gestating inside for a much longer period of time. The key is discovering what you need to let it all come pouring out.

You mentioned *The Happening* earlier. About three or four years ago, a couple of young girls brought out a book called *The Hundred Worst Pictures Ever Made*. *The Happening* has a whole chapter devoted to it. [*laughter*]

LEW: Oscar Hammerstein, after the success of *Oklahoma!* changed musical theater and on and on, but afterwards he put all of his failures in *Variety* as an advertisement. Did you know that?

FRANK: No.

LEW: He wrote out all of the titles of his failures, and at the bottom he wrote, "I've done it before, and I'll do it again." [*laughter*] Wasn't that sort of an interesting and unusual thing to do?

Let's do a chronological thing here. That moment where you go, "Ah, that's the movie I want to work on." How do you recognize it? Is there a no-bullshit detector, where you say, "This is it"?

FRANK: I don't know why that's a hard question to answer because so many answers come at once. In retrospect I understand it, why I chose *Luke*. It wasn't until I got a lot of other pictures, both not produced and produced, that I began to perceive what it was in myself that was attracted to the oppressed, misunderstood outsider who, in his own way, bucks the system and nine times out of ten, he loses. Those characters were so interesting to me. I know that now about myself, mostly because people pointed it out to me after three or four pictures out there, and someone says, "Hey, do you realize that you always do this?"

That's something that certain people do not understand, that things that are going on that are quite obvious to everybody around them. My wife and I were talking to Redford about this picture he's about to finish up called *The Horse Whisperer*, and Helene, my wife, had read the book, and I had not. I read the screenplay, but I won't talk about it. The agent was talking to us about the book and about the movie and so on. Helene said, "Why do you always have to make movies where you die in the end? You're this mythological character who dies in the end." He said, "I don't do that." Helene went through six pictures where this was the case. Redford was astonished. I understand that now he's had a substantial change from the original story, where the character will never clearly die at the end. [*laughter*] So after all the screenwriters he had working on that picture, one after the other, the only person whose story advice he really took, was maybe my wife's.

LEW: We have a professor here we all admire very much. Howard Suber says seminal movies do not end happily ever after but uniformly end with loss.

FRANK: The studios never, never understand that every time they try to make *A Star Is Born*, we have to go back and show them Selznick's memos because the hero has to die at the end because everybody wants John Howard to live. Well, Jesus, if he lives, then you don't have the one thing that makes the movie worth doing, which is the all-star going out and announcing herself as Mrs. Norman Maine, and it goes from *Luke* to *Dog Day Afternoon*. I have these arguments a lot, but you were asking how I recognize if the movie is something I want to do.

With *Luke*, and that was early in my career, and I was very pleased to be asked to do what was going to be a big movie with Paul Newman, so I said, "Great." Jack Lemmon had a whole lot of extra money, so they set up a tax-sheltered company, which required him to make that with other people, not just himself. He hired a very successful producer to come in and run the company. This producer looked around for directors that would be a good fit, and Stuart Rosenberg was really hot at that point.

The two of them went to Musso and Frank in Hollywood for lunch, a few drinks, and agreed to work together. Up the street from Musso's is a great bookstore called Pickwick, and it was part of the tradition of going there after going to Musso's and then mosey around Pickwick while the alcoholic fumes dispelled themselves. There was always a stack of nineteen-cent books there in the "Remainder" book bin, and Stuart sees a copy of *Cool Hand Luke*, picks it up, and says it has a great title. For nineteen cents they bought the book; for not much more, the book rights. Neither had even read the book at this point, but once they did, they said, "Jesus, what a great story." And that's when the movie idea began. [*laughter*]

At that point, they came to me and said, "Do you want it?" I liked them, I liked Lemmon, I liked the story, but I had no strong feelings for it at that point. I had to work my way into it. So, the answer was, maybe yes, maybe no. I found the story was something I could maybe get passionate about. This time I found passion in the expression of things that were not actually in the book but expressed some aspect of myself in order to get into the story. If there's a repeated dramatic beat in the picture, I used this to express why I could understand that it might happen and to build it.

Luke is a man in prison, resisting the tyranny of the system by simply doing what he's told. The guards might be harassing him or being petty or ridiculous, and he just abides because he doesn't give a shit. He drives the guards crazy with his silent, obedient rebellion. So, they begin to watch him more and more closely. He knows it. He's now more and more careful about everything. They lay traps for him, and they can't get him. At one point, it's the key thing that's misplaced in the structure of the book, is the one thing that triggers the central event of everything. That is, his mother died, and the response of the prison guards is to put him in isolation.

It's a terrible experience. Four days, they're telling him the reason is that when a man's mother dies, he's going to try and get home, so they put him in isolation to prevent him from trying to run to his mother's funeral. It's such a cruel response. They're saying to him, "Well, we have to do this because it's our job." Then I have him answer with a line that I put in all of my films. He says, "If a man's got to tough me up like this, let him do it because he hates my guts, not because it's his job." I love that. It's in all my stuff. Sometimes it gets thrown out, sometimes it stays. In any case, that's the critical event.

In the book, we never see the mother. We have no idea who she is or what have you. I felt it was important for an audience to respond to that kind of emotion, but when you're reading a book, it's different because you're in the character's head. You've made up those characters for yourself in a way. You've put faces on them. You hear a voice for them. It's all in your own head, too. It's one reason why when we love a book very much and we see the movie, no matter how well the movie is made, we never like it as much as the book. We had different rhythms or faces or ideas or feelings when we read it at key places.

However, for a movie audience, I felt it was very important to have a strong presence for Luke's mother in their own mind, so that when her death was announced and he hears it, it's something we know and have a response to. I felt it was not a casual scene. It needed to be a long scene. So I brought his mother into the story as he comes into the prison and that long scene between the two of them that plays out. It won an Academy nomination for the actress, Joan Patterson. It was quite a long scene, but it was also fully resolved. It has its own little story that was very important. Here is part of the process of the business that is purely technical, saying to myself, "The audience needs to have a character they can relate to later on." There is a reference to this character, and to then die, they have an emotional response and not just another piece of information. Now, we really wanted to see what Paul Newman would do with it.

In the course of writing it, I really had to sketch out who Luke's mother was, what she did, how she felt about him being in prison, what their relationship was like, what they would say as he's being brought into the prison. How do they talk to each other? What I did was I stuck my own mother in there. A lot of what she says are things my own mother actually said to us. I still remember the scene: My brothers and I were all sitting around the living room of the house. My mother was a chain smoker, and she always stepped through a doorway, lit a cigarette, and then she would take a puff and then speak. She came in one day and said, "You know, I wish people were more like dogs because there comes a day when the puppies are no longer puppies, and the mother no longer recognizes her own pups." She always timed it so that when she finished talking, she was out of the room. There was no standing up to her. So there were these moments of using material from my own emotional life in building a theme in *Cool Hand Luke*. It became more and more passionate as I got more into the writing because I was also digging into my own past. The first draft was just over two hundred pages.

LEW: Did you invent the egg scene?

FRANK: No, the egg was one of those things you read that made you know you wanted to make the picture. An amusement. Something that you know would make a great scene.

LEW: So you immediately liked the story, but you had to pull from your background to get into the characters. This was after *Cat Ballou*, right?

FRANK: No, I was the twelfth guy on the project. They had been trying to do *Cat Ballou* for years at Columbia Pictures. Harold Hecht originally bought it with Burt Lancaster when they were partners. They had been trying to do it as a straight picture for years. They were envisioning the old westerns from the 1930s. They wanted to do it again in the 1950s and were still trying in the 1960s.

Harold Hecht was such a—I shouldn't tell war stories—but he could be difficult to work with. One of the writers, Walter, said in a conference one day, "You know, the trouble with this goddamn thing is that every time I get to a typewriter, the gun seems funny to me. I begin to write it as a comedy. I just can't do it." Someone had the commonsense to tell him to write it as a comedy. Walter went away, and he wrote it as a comedy but just ripped it through his temple, came back, threw it on Hecht's desk, and said, "I can't take this shit anymore!" Hecht said, "This is a great picture. This is a very funny picture." They had commitments in hand at that point for Ann-Margret to play the part as played by Jane Fonda. Oh God, who played the Turk in *Lawrence of Arabia*? Ferrer? Yeah, José Ferrer was supposed to play the Lee Marvin part.

But they had commitments with them to start shooting in September, so they went back to get the screenplay, now written as a comedy. There were just two or three scenes that showed what the audience eventually liked. I was working across the street with a group of writers at Screen Gems. We were John Cassavetes; Jack Nicholson, who was still a writer back in those days; Bob Altman; Carl Reiner; and—who the hell else was there?—Bob Rafelson. It was great. Oh, we all got fired the same day. [*laughter*]

This is literally true. We got a new guy to run Screen Gems, so I didn't want him to get rid of all of us. However, we all have terrific contracts by television standards but very cheap by movie standards, so suddenly Columbia looks at all of us and says, "Well, we have all these crippled projects that we want to finish as cheaply as we can." So they asked me if I would do *Cat Ballou* because by their standards, it was very cheap, and they only needed me for a few weeks to kind of do the second draft, and by the time we finished the second draft, Ann-Margret had a contract to go to Las Vegas, so she went, and Joe Ferrer started a play on Broadway.

Jane Fonda, who was also inexpensive to hire because she had just finished *Barbarella*, which had fallen out of the gate. Lee had drunk himself out of Hollywood. No one was willing to work with him anymore because he was such a handful when he was drunk all the time, but he suddenly went on the wagon, and he was going out to parties with the script in hand. We never found out how he got that copy, and he'd play the big scene at cocktail parties. [*laughter*] Finally, somebody at Columbia saw him and said, "Listen, you better go and do that for Harold Hecht," and someone arranged it, and he was in the picture.

LEW: So, getting the aha in the two incidents you've described here: You've sort of backed into them.

FRANK: Well, with *Cat Ballou*, when I read Walter's script, and I came across the key scene where he introduces himself as a gunfighter, though, I wound up rewriting that. It was really just a matter of saying, "God, this is almost here. I can do this." So it was pride in my craft. It was feeling like, "Oh my God! I've caught the brass ring here." So it really had a lot less to do with the quality of the project itself and more to do with a feeling of God having touched me. You know, golden fingers.

LEW: Okay, you have the project at hand, and it's an original. Do you work first with character and then story, or do you do them simultaneously?

FRANK: The first thing I do is make an outline in terms of thinking of the principal character, the one I'm identifying most strongly with, as a voyager. What is the voyage this character takes? That makes me answer some questions. Again, I'm so stupid, I write them up on the computer screen and so on. What does this character want? What is preventing him from getting it? Where does he go to seek it? Why does he think he deserves it? Or any kind of aspect of it?

So these things would draw out my understanding of the character and who he is and where he might go because if he's driving the story or she's driving the story, that person is going to go to places, seeking whatever it is he or she wants. That suggests to me places where things can happen. We're going to suggest also characters that are going to either facilitate or provide the conflict, and that comes out of asking questions about the character. I'm that character. Where do I go? Why do I do it?

LEW: Do you have a process where you ask yourself and develop, "What's the movie about?" I use that because Arthur Miller said that he wrote his plays in a process that is not dissimilar to your putting questions on the computer screen. He types out words that remind him of his theme and tapes them to his computer.

FRANK: I guess I do something similar to that, but it really all has to do with the principal character, the one I'm identifying with primarily. Sometimes it's two characters, and it changes as you go along. As you're working on a story and rewriting and reworking it, you find more and more out about it. A lot depends upon whether you know where the character is going at the beginning. Sometimes I don't. Visual stories change more often than not. I know even with an original story. I'm always trying to develop where the story ends. I may not be able to articulate very clearly why he ends up in that spot and so on, but I know that he winds up dead, or I know he winds up married to the girl and lives happily ever after.

LEW: Were you influenced by Joseph Campbell because some of the stuff you were talking about?

FRANK: No. I know he talks about the hero dying for the greater good, which kind of relates back to the hero dying in the end of certain pieces, but to always have that, it instantly takes out the order of creative thinking and feeling that is the process of writing. He puts a philosophical distance instead of being right in there, sweating and bleeding with these characters.

LEW: Have you been influenced by Aristotle or Egri in your developing life?

FRANK: Yes, Egri. My mother was a screenwriter. When I had first revealed that I was interested in screenwriting, she gave me a copy of Lajos Egri. That was in 1945. It remains for me—perhaps because it came to my life at a very early point in my thinking about all this—it remains for me the best source book of that kind because it deals with these things in terms of character issues rather than talking about the mechanics of what happens on page 13 or the act breaks and all that nonsense. She wasn't so enthusiastic when I put the principle as I had understood them to work on writing one of her screenplays. [*laughter*]

STUDENT: What was your mother's name?

FRANK: It was Loretta Randall Pierce. There's no reason why anybody should know it. She did do the production rewrite on *Mildred Pierce*, for which she got credit.

LEW: Now getting into story: Do you outline? Do you use cards? How does that process work for you?

FRANK: I used to do cards. I do outlines now because you can rearrange an outline so easily on the computer. I don't try to stick to the outline so much, as I keep making outlines as the story evolves. I find doing a single-line outline is very hard to write. I only learned to write them when I began to get into production, but you know, it gives you a pretty clear sense of where the story is going in the most bare-bones kind of way.

LEW: You basically one-line or two-, three-, four- that sort of thing? You don't do prose, like short-story telling?

FRANK: No. I'm doing a treatment if I have something I want to sell to somebody. Like we're working on a project for HBO right now. An outline isn't going to mean anything to them. If you want to sell a pitch, you have to write the story in some detail. It can be a lot of wasted effort because you're doing the process of writing but not script writing, and no one may buy it. It's almost like talking about a script too much in a very early stage. It's very destructive in a way, although, I don't know, I do that. I find myself telling the story to my friends because it's evolving, you know. You listen to it, so you can hear how it sounds.

LEW: I've always found, I leave my fight in the dressing room if I'm too detailed in the outline.

Okay, now, you're in the script. What are your personal work habits? Do you have so many pages a day as a goal?

FRANK: No, every morning, I sit down at ten o'clock and do not answer the telephone. I'm very surly with my wife, and I kick my dog. I work from ten to twelve every day, and then I'll go off to lunch. In the afternoon I'll come back and take a look at what I did in the morning and reread other pages and fool around with it until I go to bed at midnight. The next day I sit down from ten to noon. It's a habit that's been so many years standing, it's become like an addiction. If I don't do it, I get very unhappy and very unpleasant. I do it seven days a week, on Christmas, New Year's, and every day.

LEW: So that ten to noon doesn't necessarily have to be for a script? You could be working on developing a character?

FRANK: The main rule I have for myself is that I never lighten up. Very often it's a matter of just sitting there and saying, "This scene is not working. What will it take for it to work?" I need to go back. That's when I begin to write questions on the screen. Why doesn't it work? Conflict, conflict, where's the conflict? Nine times out of ten, or I'll do exercises, like saying, "Okay, maybe I don't understand the character enough."

So I put the character in some fictional situation. The ones I like best is having him change a tire on a freeway or how to get change for a hundred-dollar bill in Detroit after midnight when you're white, and this is not a place you feel comfortable in. How would this character handle it? Would he handle it with grace and aplomb, or is he stupid or what have you. Any kind of situation that a character isn't used to is a place to develop and understand that character better. In the tire situation, would he be like Warren Beatty? He pulls over by the median, where the cars are traveling faster, and the first thing he does is take off his shirt while he's changing the tire. Or does he pull off on the right-hand side and drive very, very slowly so that he ruins the tire? Does he wait until he gets to an off-ramp?

Somehow or another, doing these little stupid exercises and so on, you learn something about the characters. It's amazing how often you pop them into a situation like that, and it winds up in the movie.

LEW: Do you break up a script into the three acts?

FRANK: I'm just beginning, middle, and end. Act breaks, to me, are a handover from theater.

LEW: Are they writer's shorthand, though?

FRANK: They are writer's shorthand, but in thinking of them, you tend to look for closure. The way movies have gotten now, it's like the beginning of the next scene is the response to the climax of the scene before.

LEW: Explain that a little further, please.

FRANK: Well, we used to start scenes and write them out. For example a taxicab drives up in front, and a guy gets out, walks into the house. The door opens as he meets the girl, and the whole entrance scene, the whole body of the scene, and then you have the end of the scene, where you discover they're husband and wife, and he's telling her that he's sorry, but he's going to leave, and he says, "Look, I've had as much of this as I can. I am really, truly sorry, but I don't think we should put each other through this anymore. I see the pain you've been in. I don't want to talk about my pain. I just think the best thing for both of us is to stop here." She says, "You know, I think that's a good idea. I'll have a drink on it." She goes to the kitchen, and we see her rattling glasses and so on, but she pulls out a drawer, and there is a butcher knife and so on so. She's making all the sounds of pouring a drink for him out there, but we see she has the knife, but there's a lot of different ways of handling this. I don't know where that came from, why I invented that. [*laughter*]

LEW: I like the concept of the one scene being in response to the scene before.

FRANK: Let me try and illustrate that further. The knife comes out. Of course, the way they make movies now, you see the knife go in, and the blood come out, but in older days, even if you carried the scene that far, you would for sure have some reaction shot of the person who's done the stabbing before we move to the next scene. I think now what we tend to do is see the hand pull the knife out, and the next shot is the police car coming through the camera. They don't tell you what happens in between the two scenes. You take a leap ahead.

LEW: Why do you think that's changed?

FRANK: I think everyone is thinking a lot faster. I think the audiences are up to speed. Actually, audiences by and large today are much faster than the filmmakers, especially the studio heads. They're way behind. I work on it until I can't think of anything more to do with it. Nothing is ever finished. Nothing is ever done, especially movies. There does come a day when the best thing to do is turn and walk away because you just can't do anymore. You can fiddle with it until you're dead.

LEW: Is it almost like the point where they get the joke? Will the studios or whoever clearly be able to understand what I'm trying to say? And it's time to turn it in.

FRANK: Yeah, and I just reach a point where I want to get a reaction. I try to work with people—and I'm in a favorable position to do this—who give the best advice. There are people I trust. They won't betray me. They won't get angry because it isn't done yet, and they fully understand the difficulty with turning it in to studio. Because studios, they tend to react to everything as though that's your final statement, the best you can do, and you're not going to be able to do anything better, and if they don't react to it in the positive way, executives get terribly upset. And they don't know what to do when they're upset because they have nothing to do. The executives have no techniques to deal with disappointment except to fire people.

LEW: Yeah, and Spielberg said most people are fired because they don't see how the second act can be fixed, so they bring somebody in. Do you agree with that concept of the second act?

FRANK: Yes, but more movies are lacking a third act than they are a second.

LEW: Ah. Respond to this view, please. I said exactly that to Billy Wilder when he was here. I said, "Billy, when I first came to town, I'd go to say hello to a writer, and he'd say, 'I can't get my third act. I can't get my third act.'" And Billy said, "If you haven't got the third act, perhaps you haven't got the first act."

FRANK: That's right.

LEW: It's just as simple as that? Do you have any tricks like that? Like, you say, "Wait a minute, this is not working. Let me go back to the first act"?

FRANK: No question about it. If you've reached a point where the thing just seems to be fooling around. In fact, there's a script right now that

I just turned in to Ron Howard, and that's exactly where we are with it. He's gone off to direct another picture, so I'm waiting for him to get done with that. Exactly what I'm suggesting is we have to find another way of beginning this movie because everything in it will work even as it is if we get the right beginning. But there's something wrong with the beginning, and the thing is that because what is not working is the resolution of the story, right now the attention of the executives and story-development people tend to be directed at that.

There always comes a point where if they're not happy with the material, they tend to say, "Well, in that scene, I'm not happy with that. I think she should slap him in the face to precipitate this." You feel as though this is not right, but if everyone in the room is attacking the same scene and everybody's got a different suggestion about what line she should say or whether she should slap him and so on, the important thing is not so much the suggestions they are making, but the important thing is something is wrong here.

You have to think about the subtext of what's going on here. Why are they unhappy? What is missing here? There is something missing in the scene, or it's not been set up right. This is what you have to identify for yourself so you can write it. Sometimes you find yourself saying, "Look guys, don't try to write this thing for me. That's what I was hired to do. If you want to write it, get a stenographer in here to take down all your great suggestions. What I want to figure out is, why are you unhappy with it here? Does it seem slow? Does it seem boring? Does it seem that the character has changed or is not acting in character?"

LEW: When I was first starting out, Les and Tina Pine told me, "When they don't like something, there's usually one thing in there that is not coming through. Rather than say, 'Oh, yeah,' you should go the hell away and figure out what that thing is." Tell us about rewriting.

FRANK: I don't think I've ever done less than eight or ten drafts. In *Dog Day Afternoon*, I did them all for myself. By the time the studio had seen it, we thought we were finished. We took it to Sidney Lumet in London, and he asked what it was about. That was the first moment where I fully articulated what the movie was about. I heard myself saying it: "He's a magician who imagines he can fulfill wishes." Sidney said, "Well, I'd better read it." Al Pacino said, "I guess I'd better read it, too." So he read it and the next morning quit. He was so tired from just finishing *The Godfather*. He was so tired and depressed. He just didn't have the strength to do another movie. I said, "Is it the homosexuality that bothers you here?" He said, "No, no, I don't think it's that. I just don't want to do another movie. Maybe I'll do something on the stage. Maybe I'll do *Richard III* again." I said, "That'll cheer you up." [*laughter*] He said, "I'm sorry, I just can't do it." After he left, the producers said, "What do you think we should do here?" I said, "Send it to Dustin Hoffman." So we did, and briefly it was going to be done with Dustin and Bob Rafelson directing. It would have been a completely different movie at that point. Al heard it had gone to Dustin, so he asked to have it back.

LEW: A ploy?

FRANK: No, it wasn't a ploy. I think he really was exhausted but fascinated by it, too. He couldn't put his finger on what was bothering him. This sounds like a war story, but it has more to do with rewriting, and it has to do with the contributions an actor makes to the writer. After he came back on the picture, and Sidney Lumet was done shooting *The Orient Express*, he was back in New York, and he started preparing the picture.

Al essentially cast the picture because of Sidney Lumet's schedule, so he made a sort of repertory theater, as it were. We had one script conference where there were a couple of funny jokes that Sidney felt he had heard before, so I wrote in new jokes and some little transitions. It was very little. It took a day to do that rewrite. That was the first rewrite that I had done at anyone else's request. All the other ones had been for me as a means of grappling with the story problems that came up and finding a way to resolve them.

We got into rehearsals, and our agreement on this picture was the great luck of having three weeks of rehearsal with the full cast. Because it was all in one place and all of the actors were present through the entire shooting schedule, it didn't cost any more to have them report three weeks earlier for rehearsal period. We didn't encounter the kind of carrying problems that SAG rules impose. Three weeks of rehearsal with the entire cast—that's such a blessing. The agreement was that Sidney would rehearse for ten or twelve days, by which time any problems in the screenplay would resolve themselves, and then I would come back and sit through a couple of rehearsals, and we'd work out how to solve any problems that had popped up.

About five days into rehearsal, I get this frantic call in Los Angeles to come to New York immediately. When I arrive, there is Sidney and two producers and Al in Al's apartment, very glum. I knew immediately. They said, "Al quit again." One of the producers said, "It's not a big thing. I think what Al really wants is just a polish," at which point Al got on all fours and ran out of the room barking. This is true. I said, "No. I don't think Al is talking about a polish." I think Al had been fighting with them for so long and was trying to communicate that they don't understand a goddamn thing here. I wish I'd had the presence of mind to say, "Al, what is it? You want a walk in the park?" [*laugher*] Unfortunately, I thought of that much later.

The gist of the story does have to do with writing. Al was just absolutely against it. He didn't say anything that really made any sense at that stage. He just said that he was afraid of doing it. He thought that it was going to be the end of his career. "I'll just have to drop out," he'd say. The producers turned to me again and said, "What do you think we should do?" I said, "I don't know what to do, except send it to Dustin Hoffman." Al said, "You know, he would be great for this. Dustin would be marvelous. But before you do that, let me ask you a question. I know enough about you to know that you've had a couple of marriages that had gone bust and one thing or another in your life. How often were the big scenes in a relationship between a man and a woman? In the big scenes—those moments of declaration of love, deciding to move in together, deciding to get married, deciding to break up, get a divorce—in those big scenes, how often does sex come into it?" I said, "Never. It's soon afterwards or not, but it's not what the scene is about." He said, "That's what I think you need to figure out here."

It's very funny because at that stage of the game, there were a lot of sexual jokes and scenes that were eventually written out of the picture that involve the sexuality of the relationship between him and his gay wife. It was great stuff, and that made most of it. It would have been a lot funnier picture if we'd shot that draft as it was. But Al said, "There's one thing here I want you to understand. If I'm going to do this movie"—by which time I knew he wanted his way back in—he said "no sex scenes and no mention of sex at all. No sex jokes." By the time he'd eliminated everything, I said, "In other words, you won't even appear in the same frame with the gay character, Christopher Sarandon?" He said, "I won't be in the same frame or the same room." Then I said, "That's tough. I don't know how do that." And he said, "I wish you'd try."

You have shown an audience that a man has married a man. You can't take away the audience's awareness of the gay aspects with this.

Their discomfort with it, their celebration, whatever their feelings are, are there. Al said, "Why do we have to make the story about that? Why can't you make the story about two people who love each other who can't find a way to live with each other?" I thought, "Oh my God. That is the real key to make this picture." I said, "You son of a bitch. Why didn't you think of that four months ago when I would have had time to really sit and think that through?" Al said, "Well, I wish you'd try."

So as a matter of fact, it turned out to be easily done. I listed all the scenes that were about the sexuality of the relationship and just took them out. Then it took about a day to write the transitions and to sew it all back together. Then there was the problem of how to show the relationship between the two of them, which was now limited to the arrival of the gay wife, their conversations with each other. The police are trying to talk the gay wife into going into the bank and talking the Pacino character out and what ensued between the two of them, which would have to be done now on the telephone.

In the original, there was a conversation between the two of them in the door of the bank, and what I loved about that particular scene was that you had two people who cared for each other deeply who were having to part forever, and their parting scene has to be played in the doorway of a bank: the guy inside with a gun in his hand and the other guy, outside with an FBI man behind him, holding him by the belt so that he can't be pulled into the bank and made another hostage. Two thousand police, all the residents of the town, and everybody from New York who could get there screaming epithets and yelling and throwing beer cans. These characters against that background have to play the one scene in the arc of their relationship that calls out most for privacy. I thought that was a wonderful concept.

Then, at the end, they kiss each other on the lips. Our studio head referred to that as the $10 million kiss when it came out of the movie. I said, "What do you mean by that?" He said, "The movie would have made $10 million more with the kiss in," but I think he was wrong. So it became a story about human values and not a story about jokes, about a homosexual marriage, or about anything explicitly homosexual. Let me finish by saying I'm eternally grateful for this because it was a huge step forward in the concept and depth of the story, and I thank God I was able to execute it in the short time I did.

LEW: *Dog Day* sounds a bit like *Lilies of the Field,* where they took three weeks to write it, three to shoot it, and three weeks in post. They just didn't have time to fuck it up. [*laughter*]

FRANK: There was a bit of it. There would have been struggles, but this is the major one. The other thing I'd like to talk about with *Dog Day* is the impact the acting had on the writing. I don't know how well many of you remember *Dog Day Afternoon,* but there is a character, Sal, who is his partner. He is a very dangerous guy. He's played by John Cazale, who was then thirty-five and who plays the part in a very threatening way, so you believe he is capable of killing all those people in the bank. He's the kind of threat that makes the melodramatic aspect in the film work, no question about it. However, in the screenplay he is described as a fourteen-year-old Botticelli angel. He was based upon a character John actually picked up when he was cruising Greenwich Village.

By the way, the people of Greenwich Village never felt that the real John was homosexual. They never knew why he was down there. Well, I finally knew why he was down there, in my mind. Remember, I never met him, so I'm making up this character. But I felt he was down there, looking for people he felt he could help. He picked up this real-life kid, who was a heartbreaker, probably a little slow and very sweet and very innocent. John picked him up, I think, to protect him from being repeatedly raped. The kid followed him around like a dog. The boy was a true innocent, one of God's innocents.

There was one particularly important scene. Part of John's voyage through the story is the progressive understanding of what he has done with his life. He has utterly ruined his life but also the lives of a lot of others around him by similar kinds of actions. This is capped by the climactic action of robbing the bank and holding hostages. How did that affect him? Did it change his feelings about himself as he understood things? Yes, it did. In fact, there are a number of places where we touch upon that in the course of the story.

The important one is in a moment in the middle, when they have a little space of time to themselves, and Sal, the Botticelli angel, says to him, "You know, back there, when you were talking about shooting the hostages and throwing the bodies out there on the street?" and Pacino's character says, "Naw, come on, Sal." And Sal says, "No, no, listen. That's what I wanted to say. You don't have to do that. I'll do it." It's at that moment that the Pacino character realizes the depths to which he has fallen because he has corrupted innocence, the ultimate crime. That's even worse than shooting a hostage, worse than robbing a bank. It's all been based upon the fact that he promised he could help people, and what has he done? He's done the one thing that the Bible says is the ultimate sin. He has corrupted a soul, who is now going to go to hell, who could have gone to heaven, if you want to extend the metaphor to the Botticelli angel.

Then I got to New York and found out Al had cast John Cazale, who is as far from a Botticelli angel as you can get. So I got Al aside and explained this to him, and Sidney—Sidney said nothing about it, by the way—and Sidney did nothing in the meeting we had in which Al was going to quit. Once, Sidney did say, "Don't worry. I'll get this son of a bitch. He'll see. I'm going to live longer than he does." But Sidney's forgotten he said that, but I never forget. That's the first rule of being a screenwriter: Never forget and never forgive. [*laughter*]

So I explained my theory of the Botticelli angel, and they didn't apologize for having read the stage direction where it described the angel. Al said, "You know something? That's really interesting. That's really, really interesting. Find us an angel, and we'll do it." So for three weeks, we went all over, up and down, all over the eastern United States, interviewing Botticelli angels. And Al—I've got to give him credit—he made an effort. He read the scenes with them, made his effort to make it work with him, but we never found a replacement, no Botticelli angel that would be quite as satisfying as John Cazale. Now, given that not a single word of dialogue was changed but what makes a difference in terms of an element in a story—then again, I don't know how important it is because the movie's a success. It works. It also works because of John Cazale, and his murderous authority to that character is scary. I don't know whether DiCaprio, who could have played the angel, in that part would have worked. I guess there's no way to tell now.

LEW: The Botticelli angel—that's what we want. A little poetry in the description as well as the dialogue.

Julius Epstein said, "After I see the rough cut, I go throw up."

FRANK: That's what they all say. Nobody's ever seen bad dailies, and nobody's ever seen a good first draft. I don't know if the first cut of *Dog Day Afternoon* was the very first cut. I know that it had been shown to an audience, and there'd been some editing on it, but you could see it was on its way to being a good movie. On *Cat Ballou*, I went into the director's office, Elliot Silverstein, and I destroyed everything that could be destroyed in the office, smashing on the top of his desk while he cowered underneath it. An array of responses all the way.

LEW: Are you angry at the writer when you're directing? With you yourself as the writer? Or do you deal with whatever compromise as needed?

FRANK: I was, early on in my career, but by the time you're shooting on a set you can't waste your energy. All you can do is sit down and resolve it. When you're on a set, what it comes down to is, okay, we have to change something. This is not working. You can't think about, "If I had another actor." You think, "Maybe if I can force them to do it. Maybe I can talk them into doing it." It's too much. Even George Bernard Shaw was an absolute tyrant on the issue of his authority as the playwright. Nonetheless, in one or another of his prefaces to his plays, he talks about this very situation. If you're that far along and the actor cannot say the line, then change the line because you can't change the actor. Also, you may be wrong.

LEW: Frank Pierson has been an icon for me as a writer and as an individual for many years. He doesn't know that I know him because so many mutual friends between the two of us that we sort of run parallel lives, but the thing I most admire about Frank, as much as I admire him as an Academy Award–winning writer and a variety of Writers Guild and various other awards, is for his work with the Writers Guild of America. He had been president twice. Twice.

I was asked to run for the board a couple of years ago and two things that I wanted. Obviously, I wasn't fit to run for the board on the two platforms, but one was copyright, and the other was I would want to try to elevate screenwriting to an art rather than whining about how we've been fucked over so many times. But the copyright, the copyright. Are we ever in our lifetime going to see screenwriters having some copyright control?

FRANK: It's funny because I just finished writing a note to a screenwriter's group that meets the last Thursday of every month and so.

LEW: Is that the one that Ron Bass said he was going to?

FRANK: Yes. It's an amazing bunch of people.

One of the things we were going to talk about at that meeting is the issue of copyright and what we're all trying to get into our contracts. The difficulty comes down to what I mentioned right at the very beginning, and that's work made for hire. The employer is deemed to be the author, and from that point on, it means that everything that we get is being ceded to us at great cost by the employers. We have, in fact, gotten many benefits, including residuals that resemble royalties that flow from copyright, and we get a piece of whatever they get when they're using our copyright to market their material. But it is their material, no question about it.

I hate signing those contracts where it says that Warner Brothers has the material under contract and are now deemed to be the author. It make me sick to my stomach every time. But the real issue is that it's something that cannot be won away from them now that the studios have it, except by organized action, and that means the guild. The difficulty there is that the guild exists as a union only because of the work-for-hire doctrine, in this sense that a guild is exempted from the Sherman Antitrust Act, which forbids people from getting together and conspiring to fix prices, wages, and so on. It includes the concept of work for hire, so they get us from both sides in that way.

However, because the guild pushes for copyright, we endanger the guild's status as a union and its ability to do anything at all. Part of the definition of what is work for hire is that the company defines what is made and defines the manner in which it's made, that it's made on the company property, that the company supplies the material, the company supplies the tools, and all of the conditions under which the work for hire is done. When you have a guild made up mostly of people working at home, buying their own computers and paper, who come and go at will during working hours, and one thing or another, it begins to be like the law is looking at us not as employees anymore but as independent contractors who are selling, not even a service, but supplying a product.

The Dramatists Guild, once a very powerful union, was disenfranchised under labor laws on this very score. The playwrights were deemed to be independent contractors who were supplying a product rather than being employees. That would enable them to join a guild, and the guild would operate as a union. So our guild is already in a very tenuous state, especially when you look at the show runners and producers in television who hire other writers. You can easily find a judge that's going to look at them and say, "Wait a second, these guys are not employees. They're employers—employers of the very people that make up the guild."

It's a very messy situation for the guild to go much further from where it is now because if they were challenged, it could be disastrous for us all. I believe if they did challenge the guild, they could disenfranchise us even as we are now, but I doubt that the studios would want to do that because they have an inherent advantage in being certain of all of the work that is done for them, they are deemed to be the author. So the benefit from the having the guild there: The guild does too many services for them, protecting them from lawsuits over the issues of arbitrated credits. So there is an inherent advantage for studios to keep the guild alive and what's keeping it alive now, in my opinion.

But what are we to do on this Thursday night group is to consider whether or not we can change it a bit. The law also says you can write an employment contract in such a way that you are definitely the author, but you are simply ceding or releasing to the employer your copyright in turn for employment. We think that that might be legal, and those of us that have the momentary clout—there's always about five or six people in Hollywood that everybody is so hot to hire—that maybe we can get that language into their contract. Once we do that, we can get it into more people's contracts and so on and just chip away. That's the way we got rid of the loyalty oaths that came out of the McCarthy era. There was a clause in everybody's contract called the loyalty oath, and what we did was we just simply crossed it out and initialed it and turned the contract in.

STUDENT: That was in the late 1960s?

FRANK: Yes. After a while, everybody was crossing it out of their contracts, and the contracts had been accepted so many times, the studios just got sick of putting it in, and they left it out.

LEW: So for my and your FSO companies, the language would be read a bit differently, but we could still be members of the guild under that concept?

FRANK: We hope, but I don't know. Maybe we can get some lawyers here to discuss it.

LEW: Yeah, well, Ron Bass himself. Questions, please. We all want you who become professional screenwriters to keep chipping.

STUDENT: I have a question about *Presumed Innocent* because compared to the movies you've discussed, it's a lot more mainstream. It's one of those movies where people actually don't say, "I liked the book more." It worked on the screen, and I was just wondering how you chose that movie.

FRANK: It's interesting you should pick that and interesting what you just said about it. I started writing the movie for Sydney Pollack. He was going to direct it. I liked the book a lot, but there are a dozen different movies there. It was a very rich book, but the theme of it attracted me enormously. Again, it's a guy who essentially is very much alone. He winds up bucking the system and, in this case, happens to believe passionately about the system of law and order as being our protection against chaos. He crosses the line once, has an affair, and that almost leads to his destruction. Again, the relationship between him and his wife is where I made that emotional connection Lew was asking about.

So I was passionate about it, but here are a dozen movies I was going to make. I had my first meeting with Sydney and said, "What do you want to do with this?" He said, "I don't want to talk about it too much. Why don't you just go write a draft, and then we'll have something to talk about. I don't want to talk in detail between us. We will work out some form of a treatment of what we're going to do with the book, and you go off and spend six months or a year or whatever it takes to do the first-draft screenplay, and inevitably it grows and changes while you're doing that, and it comes back to me, and I have in my mind an image of the movie we talked about. That's always in the way between my consciousness and the screenplay I'm reading. This character in the book isn't the way I envisioned him. I like to be surprised." I said, "That's lovely, great. I'd like to work that way, too, but just one thing: There are so many things this movie is about. Can you distill the essence of what the movie is about to you?" So he thought for a second and said, "Blood and sex." So I said, "Okay," and I went away and wrote a screenplay telling the story that's in the book but with the emphasis laid upon the blood and sex.

So it began with a scene in which two people are in a dark room and are making love, but we're only catching flashes, close-ups. White curtains are blowing. There is a night light outside, and we see that shadows that are constantly moving, with these bodies clashing about, and we don't quite know who they are, except, of course, we know they're beautiful, and they're making love. But gradually, it turns a little bit strange, and maybe the titles are rolling at this point, and then there comes a moment where there is this cry of orgasm that turns into a strangling sound. And then all of a sudden, things go very quiet, and we begin to have the feeling that light is coming into the window and more light, and now we realize that whoever the man was in the room, he's left. And the woman is still there, and we begin to see the light of dawn come upon her. We realize she's dead and tied up in some kind of thing.

Then we go closer to her face, the titles clear, and we begin to hear voices of people talking about her. The police are in her room. They're taking samples of tissue from her body, snipping her hair off, and things like that. It's all detectives and so on. Then Rusty, the Harrison Ford character, steps in, and we're not sure whether or not it was him at that stage of the game. That's how the movie began. We start with the act itself. The blood and the sex. As you see, I'm a very literal-minded man. [*laughter*]

I turned in the first draft that we worked on. We got through another draft and a half with Sydney. We were having a lot of fun. He's great to work with. He was producing *Rain Man*, and they got unhappy with the director that they had at that point, so Dustin convinced Sydney to take over, and he stepped down as director on my picture. The studio allowed him to do that on the condition that he find a director of equal stature, so he got Alan Pakula to come for him, and he read my screenplay and committed. I think Sydney lasted two weeks of the second go-around with Dustin before he quit the *Rain Man*. That was when they brought in Barry Levinson. Sydney was producer on everything.

STUDENT: The Rusty Savage character dies, too, because of what his wife reveals in the end. He didn't die, but all the faith that he had dies.

FRANK: Listen to what happens. Alan comes onboard the picture, and he had committed to the screenplay as it was: blood and sex. By the time I had a chance to meet with Alan a couple of weeks later, he'd read the book and he said, "I've read the book, and I like the book better. I want to do the book. I don't want to do the screenplay the way you've done it." So I said, "What is it about to you?" and he said, "It's about law and order," which is a major theme of the book. So I said, "That's a major, major change." He said, "That's the way I want to do it. Do you think you can?" I said, "You know something, I don't know. I really don't know because I've never gotten so committed, so deeply into one approach to doing a story, and then had to turn around," and he said, "I wish you'd try."

So we spent the better part of the next year reworking it. Of course, what I wrote for the law-and-order version begins with an empty courtroom and Rusty's voiceover talking about law and order and our hope for justice in this world and the only way that we're going to get it. I like both versions. I'd like to see both movies. They'd be very different.

LEW: Shelley?

SHELLEY: This is going to seem like a very obvious question, but I noticed in my work the climax comes around the end of act 2, and I always have a problem with my third acts. I don't know if this is anything you can articulate, but when you're conceiving the story, do you think about the climax? Or do you leave it as a choice at the end of the script when you get there?

FRANK: Gosh, I don't really know. Every picture is different in that respect. The way I think about the three-act structure is really in terms of movements. There's always, in every story, a point at which everybody in the story can go back to their previous lives, and nothing would be changed, but then something happens. It comes from the fundamental character of the hero of the story.

In *Dog Day Afternoon*, it's the moment where they've got the money in the bank, the police have not yet come, and to their knowledge they could get away. But then, one of the cashiers says, "I have to go to the toilet," and he stops everything and says, "Okay," and tries to arrange for the girls to go to the toilet. Things fall apart on him, and in the middle of all that, the telephone rings, and it's the cops outside. They've been trapped. So because he's Mr. Nice Guy, the guy who's always trying to make things good for people, it leads to him taking that one step too far, and he's trapped inside the bank, and they can never go back. They are now in an area of their lives, an evolution, where all the rules by which they have lived their lives up to that point no longer work, and they're going to have to find their way out of it.

So my second movement of the story is people trying to find and grope their way in unfamiliar territory. If you come to the metaphor of the traveler, he's now in the deep woods, without a map. He may even have lost his reason for being, and if that were the truth, he's lost his faith in where he's going, which is kind of what happens in *Presumed Innocent*. There's a period of time where he keeps trying to believe the law will save him, the long second. The film is in the courtroom where he suddenly realizes, "My God, my wife actually planned to kill me, and the plan is going to work." All concepts by which he's lived his life up to that point are now lost to him.

What does he do now? That's the second movement. Then you come to the climax of the piece in my mind, which is the moment when, if you take that metaphor for the story, he gains new insight into what he must do in order to escape from the situation or resolve it, or he regains his faith, and that gives him his way out. From that point on, the climax, it's a matter of how you get from there to the end in a way that's honest to the story. Those are all different in every story.

Dog Day Afternoon: What is the climax? It is the moment when he realizes the futility of it all, I guess. Actually, it's almost a matter of a musical rhythm in *Dog Day Afternoon* because one of the other aspects of the writing of that picture was that from the very beginning, the Pacino character is the guy who's driving everything. He's the guy who's saying, "Come on, let's get going. Da-da-da-da-da." The cops are always the ones saying, "Whoa. Slow down. It takes time for that. We've got to be sure people are safe. We've got to be sure we have the right airline. We have to get the airplane. We have to get it in place for your protection." He's saying, "Come on. Don't give me this shit. Just move it, move it, move it, move it." He's always pushing against them; they're always trying to slow things down.

That is, up to a critical point, and this is the moment when the bus comes to take them to the airport. By then he has realized—and we all know, everybody knows—he's never getting out of this situation. He'll be lucky to get out alive at all. So the last thing he now really wants is to go to the airport. When the FBI shows up, and they say, "Here's the bus," now the rhythm is reversed. From here on out, the FBI is saying, "Okay, come on. Everybody on the bus." He's the one saying, "Whoa. Let's take it slow and easy. Two at a time." He's still trying to control the situation, but at every step he's losing control. There's a musical rhythm, which supplies that shift in emphasis. I see that as the climax of *Dog Day Afternoon*.

LEW: Another question?

STUDENT: You were talking about copyrights, and I'm curious, with all of the screenplays that are being published now as books, what impact do you think that's going to have on all of us in terms of what we reserve back or whether we can reserve back certain rights? For novelists, there are certain delineated rights. I've been so screwed by one of my movies.

They've done a thousand things and made so much money, and I didn't receive a dime.

FRANK: In guild contracts, you do have separated rights on the novelization of your work. Did you know that?

STUDENT: No, I didn't.

FRANK: Most agents don't seem to know that, either. Studios don't. Actually, they often make a mistake and ask permission from the screenwriter to write the novel.

STUDENT: They did that on mine.

FRANK: You had the rights then. Check the guild contract. That's something worth the negotiating because for the most part, studios don't care. They usually don't see any real advantage in the novel.

STUDENT: With the Al Pacino character, he's basically a bad guy who's doing a bad thing.

FRANK: No, he's a good guy doing a bad thing.

STUDENT: Okay, but from society's point of view, from the police's point of view, and for us, standing in a crowd in New York, he's bad. But in your movie, everybody seemed to like him at some point. Initially they didn't really know what to think, so they didn't like him. Did you find it a challenge to make us care about this guy who is stealing money so he can give it to his lover?

FRANK: That was the argument the studio gave. They were not that all anxious to make this at Warner for that main reason. They saw it in that light. I felt a great affection for this character once I understood him, and I think I succeeded in writing him in a way that made him sympathetic.

Luke himself was not particularly an admirable character. He was a drunk, he was a troublemaker, and so on, but still there was something about him I felt very deeply for. I also think that when you write, you have to think in terms of a good person doing bad things. The temptation on the part of the executives is to say, "Maybe we need to see the scene which is the reason he does the terrible things." Sidney Lumet refers to this as the rubber-ducky scene because maybe he does it because when he was ten, his mother took a rubber ducky out of his bath. I suppose you can look at the mother scene in *Cool Hand Luke*, which I wrote for a very particular reason as I explained earlier, which in a sense is a rubber-ducky scene because it seemed to indicate the roots from whence he came.

STUDENT: That mother scene in *Dog Day Afternoon*: Same thing?

FRANK: I never thought of it that way because they're so angry at each other.

STUDENT: There's a long scene where Al is talking on the phone. You know, teachers and people who teach us writing stuff say, "Never do a scene where you're talking on a telephone," but that worked because of the dialogue.

FRANK: You're absolutely right, but I never would have done that if it had not been for Al quitting the film and saying he would not appear in any scenes or frames with his lover. The only time that they can ever communicate is on the telephone, so you first have the scene with Chris Sarandon and the cops, which sort of sets up Sarandon as a character. Then, the key eight-minute scene that you're talking about, where the two of them are talking, close-ups, and so on.

What I tried to do was to write that scene so contained so that it replicated the path of their actual life relationship. When they first started talking, they're sympathetic with each other, acting the role of Chris Sarandon as the victim, and Al is going to help him and support him. As the conversation gets more and more conflicted, finally it's revealed that Chris has been threatened by the cops, and he's going to be arrested. Pacino then realizes what's happened and says, "What? You've been talking to the cops? You're letting them try to use you against me?" So you see, their relationship disintegrated at the very end. They come to a very sad goodbye. So there is a tiny short story being told in the course of it, and that's what makes it work. But never on God's green earth would I have tried to write that from scratch.

LEW: We've unfortunately run out of time. I want to thank Shelley, who has been part of the process with almost all of the people interviewed. Tolstoy said, "We're all different. We're all alike. We're rivers, broad and narrow, warm and shallow, cold, deep." Every one of you are so very different and have so many different methods, and yet you all reach the same end, which is telling great stories. Thank you very much, Frank Pierson. It's been a wonderful honor to have you here.

16

David Ward

David Ward comes into our 434 screenwriting classroom, and he is home. The star of the class of '71 is happy to be here. After Francis, David is the most hallowed screenwriter from that time. David, like Francis, won his Oscar with one of his final scripts written at UCLA. David is a rarity, in that his range in genre is substantial, as one can see from his screenwriting résumé, which includes cinematic classics *The Sting*, *Sleepless in Seattle*, and *Major League*.

Now a professor of writing at Chapman University, David easily settles at the head of the 434 table. The class instantly becomes a tableau, silent, eyes widening. He's not only an esteemed writer; he's also movie-star handsome. One could light a match off the energy in the room. Everyone feels that something special is about to happen as David's mind becomes totally accessible. He shares the journey of becoming a solid screenwriting professional and tells the class how to get a studio head to say, "Let's make it!" David is a closer.

David opens our minds and allows us to acquire a clear insight into both Hollywood and humanity. No glamorizing, just facts and some lifting-up of the circus tent in order to better see the show. His words read like fifty angels dancing on the tip of a pen. Let's dance with David Ward.

LEW: We have a gentleman here now who is one of us. He was here where we are sitting. You were a 434 graduate student.

DAVID: Yes.

LEW: David was—like for subsequent generalizations of UCLA film students—there have always been a series of *whoas* at UCLA. I was here as a student, when it was the Sanders brothers. Then it went to Francis Ford Coppola, then to David Ward, along with Alexander Payne, Mike Werb and Michael Colleary, Scott Rosenberg, David Koepp, and I've watched all of these graduations. *The Sting* was the first movie you wrote that got made.

DAVID: No, it was *Steelyard Blues*.

LEW: Then, my favorite piece of yours, *Canary Row*.

DAVID: I'm glad to hear that. That was a movie very near and dear to my heart, but nobody ever saw it. Whenever I meet somebody who has actually seen it, I'm delighted.

LEW: Nick Nolte played Doc, and it's just a wonderful piece of material. I have such reverence for Steinbeck. When I was at Northwestern, getting a master's degree, I said, "Mr. Steinbeck, what can I do to become a wonderful writer?" He said, "Write," and walked away.

DAVID: That's good advice.

LEW: The only other reply that might be as good was from Jean Cocteau. Somebody asked him the same question, and he said, "Surprise me." So, anyway, we have *Canary Row, The Sting, Sting II*.

DAVID: *Sting II*, forget that. I tried to take my name off of it, but they wouldn't let me.

LEW: *Milagro Beanfield War, Major League, King Ralph*, and—here's a movie that if you asked nine out of ten people who have a pretty good knowledge of movies, they would say that somebody else wrote—*Sleepless in Seattle*. But there are actually three people credited, and David Ward came in and got the picture made with his draft. Is that fair to say?

DAVID: Yes.

LEW: To continue, we have *The Program, Major League II*, and you just finished writing *Zorro* for the Spielberg world. Steven didn't direct this, did he?

DAVID: No, Martin Campbell.

LEW: Is there anything else to add to this list right now?

DAVID: That pretty much covers it. They left out one or two, which I'm glad they did.

LEW: Oh, well, let's leave it at that. David mentioned something interesting about when we were coming here. We were really deep into the '60s, and everybody wanted to do movies like *Alice's Restaurant*, pictures having to do with the Revolution. David wanted to do "entertainment."

Now you're here for a couple of reasons. The most important reason for this small forum is we want to talk to you about the process. Most of these people have heard plenty of screenwriter war stories of how studios have fucked them over. And because students can't identify with these stories—to them, they are boring—and they don't help them get closer to becoming the writers they want to become. Of the twenty people we accept each year, about fourteen of them become professional writers, so I can say that of the eight people sitting around here, six will go on to be professional writers.

DAVID: And the other two?

LEW: Well, there's real estate.

DAVID: The mortuary business is also good.

LEW: Actually, the rest either become educators, and some are now going into CGI.

DAVID: Dirk Diggler was a graduate of my class. He's the guy in *Boogie Nights*.

LEW: Francis was coming into UCLA as I was leaving, and he told me, "Ah, I have this great gig to help pay my tuition." It was something like a porno.

DAVID: I was also asked to do a porno.

LEW: I was asked to write one, but I had two children at the time, and I didn't want to have to tell them what I was working on all day.

DAVID: I actually didn't shoot the sex parts. They had someone who was an expert. "Look," I said, "I don't know how to light that."

LEW: This is a sidebar thing for me and probably doesn't mean much to anyone else, but who was your favorite, most memorable professor?

DAVID: Probably two: One was Palmer Shoppe. Palmer's area of specialty was actually in design, but he was a great person just to talk to about the visual point of view in movies. The other was Paul Magistretti, who was my writing teacher when I was here. He was actually a part of the theater department. I never took a class from Bill Froug, not because I didn't want to, but because it just didn't work out that way. Paul was here only a couple of years, then he went off to become a story editor for *Baretta*, I think.

LEW: Paul was a student when I was here.

DAVID: Paul was an interesting guy, you know, a body builder, the last guy in the world that you'd think was a writer. He was buff and huge, with a thick neck. But he was incredibly well read, incredibly well educated, and a good writing teacher because he used examples from literature, from theater, and he was very good at relating what you were trying to do to what other writers had already struggled with or had an approach to. He was very memorable to me.

LEW: The Doors were here with you, too, right?

DAVID: I knew Morrison when he was here. There's also another guy I remember from those days. I can't remember his name. He was a photographer. I remember him because he was such a pompous ass. At every student's screening, he would say, "That was a wonderful celebration of life." His whole thing seemed to be to get the female students to his apartment to look at his photographs and to smoke pot and hope something would happen. He drove me nuts.

LEW: Ah, the bad old days. I've been interviewing, and it started quite by accident with Billy Wilder and Julius Epstein and Irving Ravetch and Harriet Frank Jr. I had them here, and after I looked through it, I thought, "I could do an entire interview book on the process of screenwriting from these award winners." So I've been asking the same fundamental questions on how everyone attacks their writing, and I've been getting such different points of view. Bruce Joel Rubin was quite special because he has such a spiritual viewpoint on writing and on living.

So onto storytelling: Other film students wanted to make statements. You wanted to tell stories?

DAVID: Yes, they wanted to do political movies. I wanted to do art; they wanted to do documentaries.

LEW: And you're doing just great. Tell us what you think about the relationship between storytelling and movies. Do you think it's like the oral tradition of sitting around the campfire, telling stories, as opposed to the theater?

DAVID: I think it's changed over the years. When movies first started, there were closer relationships to literature, not necessarily great literature, but popular literature. Literature, as well, and certain legends. Storytelling today is a little different. In the movies I admire, storytelling is still an essential part, but there is a whole genre of movies today that don't really tell stories. They sort of create atmospheres, they create worlds, and they try to create some kind of intense experience within that world. They don't necessarily proceed through any kind of narrative. You know, the "e-ticket ride" movies, the *Twisters*, and those types. They do have characterization and story points, but they are pretty perfunctory. You have to make some sense out of all of this. But it's really not the engine that drives the movie. It's not the reason people are there.

There are some movies that apparently don't need good writing to be successful. I really don't have anything against *Twister*. I sat in the theater, and there were times when I said, "Wow!" If they had spent more time with the story and the characterization, it might have crossed purposes with special effects. I don't say this is a pejorative way, but it seems the balance can tip toward spectacle over storytelling.

LEW: But then comes *The Full Monty*, and we're all like, "Whoa!"

DAVID: I think movies, like all popular culture, go in cycles. Something happens for a while, people love it, they can't get enough, then it's done. People get tired of it and want something else. I'm not sure if next summer you're going to see as many hardware action movies as you did this summer. I think audiences have become a little satiated.

How many times have we seen our hero running, and there's this ball of fire behind him? I've seen this now in six movies. There have been movies that have been combinations of good character and narrative with hard action. The first *Lethal Weapon*. The first half of the first *Lethal Weapon* I thought was great. Gibson's character, the cop who wants to commit suicide, and a partner who is two weeks from retirement—that's just great stuff. For the first half of the movie, they really bring some wonderful changes with it. The second half of the movie becomes pretty much a straight action movie. For me, the second half wasn't as interesting, and still, the movie works, there's no doubt about it. *Titanic* has, in addition to some amazing visualization, a very service-able and affecting story.

LEW: *The Fugitive* was like that for me.

DAVID: *The Fugitive* was one of those, also. They literally were rewriting the script every night before shooting. The studio thought the movie was going to be a total disaster. At first they weren't even going to do any promotion for it because they thought it would never work because they never had the script right. Well, that shows you never really know. But yeah, *The Fugitive* is a very good example: a good action and a good character movie.

LEW: Howard Suber, who heads our producing program, says we remember characters. Sometimes, in addition to the special effects pay-ing off and the characters being so memorable, they are what blows the story away. Before we actually talk about script development, what's the process you psychologically put on yourself. Do you do the same thing today that you did when you were starting out?

DAVID: Pretty much. I think that one of the things you discover as you write is how you write, and I tend to write best in the morning or late at night. I'm not very good between about eleven and four. I don't know why. I guess I'd rather be playing basketball. That's just the way I am. I also find that I can't write in complete silence. Silence is very distracting to me. I need ambient noise in the room, and I listen to a lot of classical music when I work. It's more difficult to work with music containing words because that's distracting. I start to follow and sing along.

For example, when I was writing *The Sting*, I wrote a lot of it in the Continental Airline terminal at LAX. I was married at the time and hav-ing problems at home, so I needed to get away. I needed to get away to where there was activity around me and where I could be anonymous and nobody could notice what I was doing. At the airport you can sit and write, and there are things going on, but no one really notices any-body. There were many nights where I was down there writing. I found a certain energy in that place that really helped keep me going.

The script took me a year. The first draft was about six months, and I scrapped it because I didn't think it worked. I thought I hadn't done the subject justice. Until I got the idea of having the movie con the audi-ence, as well as being about confidence men, that it really came together for me. Then I went back and wrote the whole movie again. But if you work on a script for a year, it can get a little stale. Also, when you're working on a story that is plotted with a lot of twists and turns, you can get confused. You can forget where you are.

But as far as the way I work, I usually start with either a situation, theme, or a character that intrigues me. I usually have a piece of music that reminds me of the feeling it. For example, when I was doing *Major League*, I always had this idea about "Wild Thing," about this character who is a complete rebel, punk kind of kid, who happens to throw the ball 99.9 miles per hour but didn't know where it was going. So I would listen to "Wild Thing," the X version of "Wild Thing," not while I was writing but whenever I got stalled. I would go to "Wild Thing," and it would get me back to where I started. It would remind me of the irreverence I wanted the movie to have. It kept me from getting too cute, and it kept me from getting sidetracked.

For some reason, doing *The Sting*, I was listening to a lot of blues from the period: Ida Cocks, Bessie Smith. And for some reason, just listening put me in the right atmosphere for the movie. One of the things you have to do when you're writing is to maintain concentration, to stay in the atmosphere of the screenplay. One of the things that makes writers so difficult to get along with is that you're always in that world. It's very tough, when you have a wife and children, for them to realize, you're physically there, but even when you're doing nothing, you're thinking about the script. I've learned over the years how to come out of the world and then reenter. The music-identification thing helps me get back into that world when I need to almost instantly.

I don't write on a computer. I write longhand, always have. I've tried to write on a computer, but somehow it just doesn't feel natural because I'm so used to doing it the other way. The intervention of the machine, it feels like the machine is waiting for me to do something. I feel judged. Having this thing here, waiting to have something on it, it intimidates me. I'm like, "Forgive me, computer."

LEW: Do you give yourself a page limit per day?

DAVID: I'd be dead now if did that. I would have committed suicide several times.

LEW: When do you know it's time to stop?

DAVID: Boy, I'll stop for almost anything. Mail is really great. Somedays I'll just write ten minutes. I mean, it's just not happening some days. I feel that I'm nowhere, just clueless. Other days I might write ten hours. It just depends on how I'm going. Also, it depends on the deadline. Sometimes pressure is good for me. If I'm not under pressure, I explore forty-five different ways to do a scene. If I'm under pressure, I'll just make a decision.

You hear these stories of how some writers have time blocks where they work and then take the rest of the day off. That's great. It's just not me. If I could explain it, if I could control it, I certainly would. There are just times when I feel a certain amount of anxiety associated with writing. A lot of people find writing relaxing; I find it terrifying. The anxiety for me is if I'm going to sit down and I'm finally going to have run out of ideas. It's all over. There's nothing left. That's it, Dave! You got your quota of ideas, and now they're going to find out that I've been just getting by. So when I write, I have to get into a sort of feeling of relaxation.

LEW: Do you still go down to Continental Airlines or some other place?

DAVID: Not as much anymore. I take long walks. Sometimes I'll just drive. If I'm not getting anywhere and I feel like I have desk fever, I just get up and try to do something physical, like go to the gym, shoot baskets, or something.

LEW: William Burroughs said being alone in a room for eight hours with nothing to do but writing is his idea of heaven. You don't share that?

DAVID: It's my idea of hell.

LEW: But you keep going.

DAVID: Well, I'm driven to do it, and also when things are going well, it's the greatest feeling when I sort of know where I'm going and I can see that it's going to work. The terrifying part is usually when I'm just starting. When I sort of know where I'm going and it's all going to come together, then it's fun. Up until that point, it's scary.

LEW: Ideas. Are there any set of mental configurations that signal you to go with an idea?

DAVID: I think the one, for me, is when you think about it, you get lots of thoughts. People come to see me with ideas that are great, one-line ideas, and nothing happens in my brain. For other ideas, I'll start to think, "Gosh, that's great if that happened," or "I could do something with this." Then I know something is happening with this idea, and it is engaging. It's true of all writers.

There is a lot of work out there that I admire, but I could never do it because for me, it's not my sensibility. It's not my experience. It's not my interest. I think you have to be intuitive about what is speaking to you and what isn't. Now, often, when you're professional and you've had a couple of divorces, something has to speak to you, even if it doesn't. Sometimes you just have to do a job. You have to be a professional. I've learned how to do that, but I don't think that's necessarily my best work, although some have turned out pretty well.

LEW: In retrospect, you say to yourself, "I thought I made this piece of shit into something that was actually rather good." Then you realize, you've been conning yourself.

DAVID: Well, I don't look back. I have never seen one of my movies since it was released. That includes *The Sting*. I tried to watch *The Sting* for about ten minutes, and then I couldn't do it. I just thought, "The dialogue sucks." I can't do it. I'm too critical.

LEW: Does that mean that you basically have different sensibilities today that may be better now?

DAVID: I'm sort of a perfectionist. When I look at something, I get right back into saying, "I could have done that better," "The scene is going on too long," or "I should have had this character come in here." It drives me crazy because there is nothing you can do. The picture is done and released. I just don't put myself through it.

LEW: Do you reflect back on things that you've done and say, "That was terrific," and it continues to be terrific, or are you always self-critical?

DAVID: When you direct a movie that you're so familiar with every frame of the movie, when it's released, you can run the film in your head. So you can harken back to certain things and think, "You know, I think I did that pretty well. I think that really worked." Then, other things you run through your head and say, "Gosh, now I realize what that scene should have been about as opposed to what I made it about." Sometimes you feel that way about an entire movie you've written, something you're more connected to than what the movie was.

I can remember every script I've written. I can't necessarily remember the movie, but I can remember the script. What happened in the script and what I did. When you're writing, you can learn from the movies made from your work because, God forbid, directors sometimes improve things. They really do. Or actors will come up with something you never thought of, and that's great.

Everyone has heard the horror stories of when it goes the other way, but you do have to be self-critical to evaluate your own work and try to be honest about what worked and what didn't. Some people naturally do that; other people think that everything they do is wonderful. I wish I were that person, but I'm not. I tend to think that everything I do is flawed, and people just haven't noticed it yet. Every time I hear *The Sting* is going to be on TV, I think, "Well, how many times has that film been on? This is like the twenty-fifth time. They're going to figure it out this time."

LEW: Maybe you should be more spiritual. In the Old Testament, those cats didn't take name credit. They thought it all came from above and beyond. Then you have someone to blame.

DAVID: I don't want to say that I don't enjoy writing, but it's a real battle for me.

LEW: I asked Billy Wilder if he thought of himself more as a writer or as a director. He said directing was just an extension of his writing. It seems in your case you feel you are completely two different people.

DAVID: You are at times. Sometimes actors force you to be that way because they have a different idea of the character. There are also times when you are writing the action of the movie, where you sort of have to fill out a paragraph that says, "Something wonderful happens here." As a director you have to figure out what to do. Those times, you separate yourself from the writers. As a director, you have to learn to be flexible.

When you write something, you hear the way everything is said. But when you have a living human being there, saying the words, and it doesn't sound like you heard it in your head, your first reaction is that it's wrong. However, it may not be. It may be a different way of looking at it, which may have some validity. That's a decision a director has to make. Sometimes an actor will come up with something you hadn't thought of, which is really great when it happens. Other times, you have to steer an actor toward your vision of what's going on because the direction you want to go, otherwise, even though it's heartfelt, may ultimately pull the movie apart. Sometimes actors have their own character, but they don't have a sense of how the overall movie fits together.

LEW: Tell us about your process on, say, an original script. Most of yours have been original. Do you do it by actors, and how long does it take before you type out "Fade in"?

DAVID: I usually start writing a few scenes from the first ideas I get about where this could go. I try to get a few anchors to put down. I know I want this, I know I want this, I know I want this. And usually I try, before I start writing in earnest, to know where I'm going to end up, what I'm trying to do, what I am trying to say, where I'm trying to get to. Sometimes that will change as I go along, but I need the security of having some idea of where I'm going before I start to write in earnest. Otherwise, it's very difficult to make decisions about which way to go or not.

LEW: You referred to what it's about, a phrase my students hear like a mantra. Also, I like how you say that sometimes it will change. Coppola said that at the theater is where he finally realized what *Finian's Rainbow* was about.

DAVID: Yeah, thematically, I want to feel like I know what I'm trying to do. I don't have a beat-by-beat outline before I start because I get a lot of ideas as I write. Certain characters start to become more important than I thought they would. Others really don't happen, so I realize I need another character to come in to do something for me. Then I use that character in a different way, and he or she becomes more interesting to me, and it may generate a subplot. I don't lay it out in acts. I've never written in acts. I think it's something I naturally do, but I don't think about it so much that by the second act, I have to have this happen.

LEW: But you really try to have the end, right?

DAVID: I really try because that helps me make decisions along the way. If you don't know where you're going, you can go anywhere for weeks, down some path that doesn't pan out. Now, that happens, but when you're writing professionally, you can't afford to do that. When I first started out and I was writing *The Sting*, I could take a year to write a script. I don't have this luxury anymore.

LEW: You came out of UCLA at a time when you weren't required to write a script in a ten-week period.

DAVID: Actually, *Steelyard Blues* started out as my thesis project, but it just kept getting longer and longer, and I couldn't shoot it with my own resources. So I turned in a feature-length movie and went from there. But for me, I really have to know what it's about. Is it about this character's journey to some understanding or redemption or whatever? I try to let the structure of the movie be dictated by the subject. *The Sting*, the structure of the movie was dictated by the way a con game unfolds. Maybe that's why I had the chapter headings, the setup, the hook, and finally the sting.

With *Major League*, the structure of the story unfolds like a baseball season unfolds. Same thing in *The Program*, the football season. Something like in *Sleepless in Seattle*, there was already a structure there because Jeff Archer was the original writer and basically laid out the structure. What I did was a lot of character work, particularly between Tom Hanks and the little boy.

LEW: How do you break the back of your stories?

DAVID: Sometimes you get it as you're going along. When I was doing *The Program*, it started out as a generalized movie about the gauntlet of playing big-time college football and some of the things the kids go through. As I was dealing with the main characters, I realized, basically, that the story was about a guy trying to kill himself before he became a failure. A guy from a family of drunks, a family of failure, and burning out. Here he was on top of the world, Heisman Trophy candidate, great quarterback, and the more successful he became, the more he felt that his fall was near, and the better he did, always thinking failure is just around the corner. So he did these incredibly self-destructive things, hoping to take himself out of the arena before this failure, which he didn't believe he could handle, actually happened. It's those kind of character notions that greatly help you write a character. In *The Program*, the movie is not solely on him, but you have these kinds of ideas about characters in order to write them.

In *Sleepless in Seattle*, the seminal event for me was when I first realized how the Tom Hanks character deeply missed his wife and how empty his life was. I read it and thought, "This is wimpy. A woman is not going to fall in love with a guy who calls a radio show psychiatrist and pours out his heart. No way." So I thought, "The son has to call because he's worried about him." You know, he's been trying to hide his pain from his son but unsuccessfully. He doesn't want his kid to feel this responsibility or this burden, but there's a certain amount of pain that he can't hide. Kids are always very tuned in to their parents, so this kid knows his dad is unhappy. As a kid, he doesn't know what to do, so he calls a psychiatrist on a radio show because he hears it at night. The radio is his nighttime companion.

The dad gets on, only for a short period of time, only to appease his son. He says just a few things in a short time. Once I made the switch of having the kid call, the movie sort of fell into place. Then it's the son who gets excited about the letters coming in, who likes this Annie because she mentions him in her letter. When I first read the script, I thought, "This is a wonderful idea Jeff has. I like this Meg Ryan character, but I didn't think she would fall in love with a guy who is still so emotional over his loss." Strangely, by taking some of his action away from the original script, I was able to get a grasp on this character, and I could see him, at least in my own mind.

LEW: What you just said triggered, for me, that Tom Schulman didn't like *Dead Poets Society* early drafts. Then he decided to make the kids really bright so that they could play off of the Robin Williams character, and that's basically what you did. You let the characters solve the story problems.

DAVID: You said earlier that what we most remember in movies are the characters. I remember them more if it's a good movie than if it's a bad movie. The main character has to lead you ultimately to a satisfactory story ending, as well. I mean, they are related, obviously. But character is where it all starts for writers. It's certainly the thing that keeps me writing a script. I can't write a script about a situation that doesn't have character. I mean, I just don't get ideas that way. It's the character that drives me, that interests me, that I get a kick out of.

When I was here at UCLA, the films we all watched were foreign films. It was the height of the New Wave, Godard, Truffaut, Antonioni, and their movies were all character driven. They very seldom had much in the way of plot. I was weaned on those movies. Yes, *The Sting* is one of the more heavily plotted movies you could write. Actually, I try to balance character and plot, but I tend to get more plot ideas off of the character than character ideas off of the plot. Rather than laying down the plot and then saying what characters do, when I need to make this plot work, I tend to say, "I like this character. What plot do I need to take this character on an interesting journey?" Some people work the other way. I'm not saying that my way is right. It just happens to be the only way I know, and you write the only way you know.

LEW: So the soul of screenwriting, if there is such a thing, would be the characters and how they relate to the story. I've always been interested in the soul of screenwriting, the interior aspects of a screenplay beyond plot.

DAVID: Well, the story is how you reveal character, so in that sense they are very closely related, and you don't just tell the people who the character is; you show people who the character is. You have to put them in conflicting situations where the character is revealed or tested or found wanting or whatever, and that's story. When you're deep into the character, it's going to suggest some story to you because you're going to want to put that character into situations where he or she is revealed in all of their glory or weakness or whatever it is that you're trying to do.

I find that when I have writer's block, I'm either trying to do something unreal, or I'm trying to force something. I may have a scene down the road here that I'm trying to get to, and the story doesn't go there. Or it's a wonderful scene, but it's not real. It's like, this would be a great scene if it were possible, but it's not possible, at least not in this story. So sometimes I have to give that up.

Or the other thing is, if I'm blocked, it's because I don't know enough about what I'm doing. I either don't know enough about the subject, or I haven't gone deep enough into the character, and I'm still noodling around on the surface. I've sort of used up everything that I know. I don't have anything more to say about the character because I don't know any more about the character. I have to think more about it. I have to give the character more complexity. I might have to research it more. I might just have to think more about the character and stop writing for a while to go deeper into what is really going on and not just have the character be a representation of an idea or be predictable or have one layer.

LEW: Was *The Sting* a spec script for you?

DAVID: No, but by today's standards it was. I was paid an option fee of like $1,200.

LEW: Tony Bill once told me that you gave him a script at a bar.

DAVID: That ties into *The Sting*. We were doing *Steelyard Blues*, and Tony was a production partner. He wanted to know if I had other ideas. I told him this idea I had about confidence men. "That's great. Could you put that on tape? A ten-minute tape we can take to Redford and see if he's interested?" I made a pitch and recorded it on tape and sent it to Redford. We set up a meeting, and he said he'd be interested, but he'd have to see the script. That's what most actors say. They optioned it for like $1,200, so I went and wrote it. *Steelyard Blues* was a complete spec.

LEW: You do have some parameters in your mind of the story since you don't actually step it out? You write 1, 2, 3, 4, 5 to some degree?

DAVID: Yeah, and I will do an outline as I'm going along so I know where I am and also to know if I'm proceeding strongly enough toward where I'd like to go.

LEW: So you really do have an outline, but it shifts and changes depending on things that come in? Kind of a road map, but it's not the kind of thing that one would turn into a studio?

DAVID: When people say, "Can you give me an outline?" I say, "No, you've got the wrong guy."

I don't know of a professional writer who says, "I'll whip something up tonight." But you have to have some idea of where you're going. Like I say, you have these anchor points when you think of the story. You have to have something specific in your mind when you're writing, or it's very difficult to make decisions about what goes and what doesn't, what's working toward the goal and what is really just practice.

LEW: Do you have a group of readers you give the script to before you send it out?

DAVID: I wish I did. Actually, there is one: my brother, who is also a writer. I give it to him to read, but that's about it.

The thing about giving it to other writers is that they don't always wish you well. One of the terrible things about this business is that some of your friends, not your best friend, but some of your business friends can carry a lot of envy, and there's so much competition because, you know, these are contract positions. They aren't stable. This is a business where you're always ten minutes away from being wealthy or poor, and that's what keeps people going, even when things are going miserably. If you have a film that has sold for a lot of money or a film that has done well, your superficial friends might be a little pissed at you because you're making them feel bad. Conversely, if you have a movie bomb, they love you. You've made them feel a lot better. I may be having a tough time, but I didn't have that turkey on my hands.

Sometimes you really have to know, when you're giving someone a script, what their point of view is because theirs might be totally different. For example, you mentioned Oliver Stone. Now, I haven't seen Oliver in many years. We used to spend time together, but then we drifted apart. He would be a strange guy for me to give my stuff to because his scripts are so different. He has his own point of view, so a lot of notes are not usable to me in terms of what I'm trying to do with the same subject. You have to know people's biases when you give them something to read. For example, there are people out there who just don't like anything romantic. To them, romantic is cornball. They don't care how restrained you are about it; they just don't like it.

LEW: So you cast your people to read, just as you might cast actors.

DAVID: Exactly. I think the main benefit of giving your pages to people to read is not the opinion of one person, but if you hear the same thing over and over from different people, then you probably know you have a problem. It's that old saying: "If three people say you're drunk, you'd better lie down." If you're going to give it to one or two people, you have to know they're on your side, but they'll be honest with you. There are some people who will just tell you that it's great. They don't want to hurt your feelings, but that doesn't really do you any good.

LEW: Did the Oscar change your life at all?

DAVID: Yeah, when I started out, I considered myself a filmmaker. I wanted to direct. When I won the Oscar, suddenly I was this huge writer guy. Nobody wanted to hear about directing from me. I could make a lot of money writing, and I was taken seriously as a writer in a way I wasn't as a director. So in some way it postponed my becoming a director.

I also had pressure to write big movies. The next script I wrote was a never-made script. I really like it, but it's this epic, historical western called *Amber Waves*. It's unfortunate one of the porno stars in *Boogie Nights* was called *Amber Waves*. We may have to revisit the title. One of the reasons it hasn't been made is that not too many people are interested in making a $100 million picture. There is a certain kind of pressure that came with it.

I also didn't want people to take me so seriously as a writer yet because I was still very young and still developing as a writer and person. I didn't want to start being treated as a veteran writer just yet. That was only my second script. I wanted to do other things, and I didn't want to be judged against the same standards that you would judge a Larry Gelbart. I didn't want critics looking at me because then they could tear me apart.

LEW: Two more questions, and then it flips over to the class. Is screenwriting an art?

DAVID: It can be, yes. Certainly.

LEW: So it's more than Jack Warner referring to us as the schmucks with the Underwoods?

DAVID: Certainly. I think what always happens is that people compare screenwriting with writing novels. In that sense, they always find screenwriting lacking because it doesn't have the same kind of psychological depth and can't go off into the flights of descriptive fancy. They are totally different disciplines, apples and oranges. There are really great novelists who can't write screenplays at all, and there are a lot of screenwriters who can't write novels. These totally distinct disciplines shouldn't be compared. When they are, screenplays are seriously wanting to serious students of literature. Yet screenwriting is very difficult. You have to write with a greater degree of economy. You have to be aware of a lot of factors that novelists don't have.

Novelists don't have to put up with interference from directors, producers, studios, actors. I think screenwriting in its purest form is an art. It depends on whether you make it an art or not. There are times when it is simply a craft. That's not so bad, either, because it's a difficult craft. There are times that you're working on a rewrite, you try to fit something in between something else, and it becomes a bit of carpentry.

LEW: Creative mechanics. Who is a screenwriting artist you admire?

DAVID: I hate to single out names because I feel bad about the people I left out.

LEW: Have them be dead.

DAVID: Mankiewicz is one.

LEW: Herman or Joe?

DAVID: I'll take either.

LEW: Are there any secrets to screenwriting? Tricks of the trade?

DAVID: Secrets in screenwriting? I don't think so. I think writing is so personal. Everybody has their own secrets that wouldn't be secrets to somebody else. Like you say, the thing you have to do is write. The more you write, the more you learn about yourself, the more you learn about what you do well or what you don't do so well, how you write and the conditions under which you write best. The more you write, the more you focus in on what it is you're about, and what it is you're about as a writer is what you have to say.

I think the impulse to write comes from a need to work something out, a need to understand something, to say something, a need to explore something. The more you write, the more you begin to understand what it is you're trying to get to. It doesn't mean you get to it because most things that are worth writing about are complex and there is no one truth about them.

LEW: Aristotle says superior drama is drama that allows us to discover ourselves. In essence, the idea of becoming a writer to discover ourselves gives us a commonality with the audience. We feel connected. Questions, please.

STUDENT: I am interested in your process of story development with producers and directors.

DAVID: Take a Valium. Having been on both sides of the equation, as a director and a writer, it's different now. Before I began directing, I was much more defensive and less likely to be flexible about the stuff I'd written. Having directed, unfortunately, I understand the director's problems.

The thing you have to keep in mind, when you're with executives or other creative people, they can get on this feeding frenzy. They'll get an idea and get all excited about it because you're triggering ideas. Sometimes these ideas have nothing to do with the script that you have written, and you have to be aware enough of how your script works so that you can be articulate about why their idea will, as good as it sounds, rip your script apart, which they usually don't want to do because it's major money. I think the way you prepare for these meetings is just to be articulate about what the script is trying to do, why certain things are where they are, and why moving them or eliminating them or going off in this direction is going to create tremendous problems. You have to do it without being hostile about it because if you're hostile, they think you're being a defensive writer and that you're not really listening. You have to listen to them but also defend what your work is about.

There are times when you have to walk away. I did that on *Steelyard Blues*. They started making a movie I just didn't understand. You also have to keep in mind who is in the room. If you have studio executives whose job it is to make comments, then they're going to make them. Then, once having made them, they're finished. So if you let sleeping dogs lie.

LEW: Sometimes your best response is, "I'll take that under consideration." Then you continue on your path. You can't do that with Sydney Pollack, though, right?

DAVID: No, if you're dealing with Sydney, then you're dealing with a peer, with somebody whom you respect and who knows what he's talking about. You listen to what he says. The problem is, by the time you turn in the script, you have already struggled with so many different options and combinations that to have to open it back up again and more surgery is sometimes a really hard thing to accept. But there are times when somebody will have an idea that's just really good, that really makes it better.

You have to be open, while at the same time, don't get steamrolled into something that is just going to tear it apart because even if you do what the studio wanted you to do, and it's bad, they're going to see that it's bad, and they're going to blame you. They're not going to remember that it was their idea. They're going to say, "Ah, we have to get another writer. This person is finished." That's the way they think.

STUDENT: What would you do if you were a student today?

DAVID: What would I do if I were just starting out in the business? I'd probably do what I did, which was just start to write the best idea I had, write it, finish it, try to get an agent interested in it, and go from there. I don't know any other way to start.

There are a lot of people who try to psyche out what's hot in Hollywood and try to write that, and by the time they have written it, it's not
hot anymore. It may not even be what they do well, and people say that
Shane Black jumped on the action-movie bandwagon, but that's what
Shane likes to do. He didn't jump on any bandwagon. He did what he
wanted to do. People say, "Steven Spielberg is really a clever commercial
filmmaker," but Steven didn't make *E.T.* because he thought it would
make half a billion dollars. It was the kind of movie he wanted to see.
You've got to go and write your movie.

LEW: Shane literally says, "I love this shit."

DAVID: And that's why he does it so well.

LEW: The difference today from when you and I were here as students is
that this is now a two- to three-year program and all older, beyond the
age of twenty-five. When they finish, they have at least done five feature
scripts, so they have a stockpile of work in hand. They have a learning
curve that they go through, as opposed to you and I, who had to learn
writing on a professional level during on-the-job training.

DAVID: Well, I was very lucky to sell my first script.

STUDENT: Were you in an interesting situation with *Zorro* when you
started with one director and then got switched to another?

DAVID: That happened more to me on *Sleepless in Seattle* than *Zorro*.
Robert Rodriguez was no longer on the movie when I came. Martin
Campbell was the only director I worked with on *Zorro*. On *Sleepless*,
Nick Castle was the director when I started writing, and then after my
draft, Meg Ryan decided she wanted to do the movie, and she didn't
want to do it with Nick. That's when Nora came in.

STUDENT: With *Sleepless*, did the switch of sensibilities from Nick to
Nora affect you at all?

DAVID: Not too much because ultimately Nora was going to do a draft
of her own. She wanted to punch up the humor because Nora's funny.
I also had to go off and do *The Program*, so I said, "Nora, you might as
well take it and run with it at this point because I don't have the time to
do much more writing."

One of the strange paradoxes of directing is that on two films that I
directed, I desperately pleaded with the studio to get me a writer because

I was so busy preparing for the movie that I didn't have time to write, and I felt that more writing needed to be done. Tom Schulman did a draft of *Down Periscope*, but the studio said, "You're a writer. Why do want us to spend extra money to hire a writer?" So I said, "Because I can't do it. I don't have time to do it, for the thing I need in the script. I think if a writer is very good, they can do better than me." It's strange. When you're a writer, you can't get things like that.

STUDENT: What was your affiliation with the *Milagro Beanfield War*?

DAVID: The book was written by Nichols, who had done a draft of the script. Redford called and said, "Dave, I want to do *Milagro*, but this draft is not yet ready. Would you come in and work on it for a few weeks?" I was starting *King Ralph* at the time, so I had to go to Sydney and ask if I could go to New Mexico for a couple of weeks. I forgot something.

I did a draft, but the problem with *Milagro* was this was a book with a wealth of wonderful anecdotes and incidents. It didn't have a narrative line to hold it all together. The story sort of meandered here and there, with all of these wonderful characters and things, but you can't possibly put them all into a movie. The job was to figure out which characters to keep and what story to tell. John, because he wrote the novel, wrote the script with everything sort of swirling around. It was an interesting script, but it didn't have enough focus for Redford. The word he kept using was *focus*. So I wrote a script with a narrative line, and then I went and wrote *King Ralph*.

Bob called me two weeks into shooting and said, "Dave, I need you to come down and do a little more work, just a couple weeks." Because one of the things that that happened was, he had hired Melanie Griffith to play one of the parts just because he loved her as an actress. He loved her quality. There was really no part for her. I thought what is she going to do? There were like two pages for this character. What Bob did, the first couple of weeks, was shoot a bunch of stuff with Melanie and try to work it in into the movie, and he realized, feeling guilty about hiring her, that he had lost his way. So he told me to come back to get him back to square 1 because he felt a little diffused.

I went to Sydney and said, "Bob wants me to come and write for a couple of weeks more." Sydney said, "You know it's not going to be just a couple of weeks. We'll see you in about three months." I said, "No, believe me. It's just a couple of weeks." Well, fourteen weeks later, I finished. What was weird about it was I didn't do anything much different than I had done on the original draft, except Bob would always want to have two or three versions of a scene to make sure the one we were shooting was the best. He'd say, "Why don't you try this scene from this point of view?" Then I'd go and write the scene, but this new stuff, he'd never use.

Bob is also a guy who doesn't sleep. He's an insomniac. He sleeps maybe two hours a night. He would call me at like, 3:00 a.m., as if everyone else is up: "Dave, I have a great idea. Joe and I want you to see, What if he is sort of attracted to Sônia, so there's a love triangle between her and John Hurt?" I said, "Bob, he's happily married. He's got a family. His whole thing is trying to protect the water rights. I think that's his only distraction." He said, "That quite possibly could be, but let's just see if any sparks fly. Something else might happen."

So, I write it, take it to him the next day, and he said he didn't even read it. "You know, Dave, I thought about it and you're right." The whole thing he just wanted to have in case something went wrong with the scene, if something came up, but he basically shot what I had written before I ever got there. I spent a lot of time in Santa Fe, which is a nice place to spend time. *Milagro* was great because it was a beautiful place, and there were wonderful actors in that film.

STUDENT: How do you reference within yourself to write a movie about a different culture?

DAVID: I was married to a Mexican woman at the time who came from a family of ten, so just interacting with her family, I learned a lot about the culture. It wasn't specific to New Mexico, as there are things in the culture of New Mexico that are quite different from California. I spent a lot of time talking to the novelist, John Nichols, who was from New Mexico and has a wonderful feeling for life there. The Native Americans as well as the Hispanics in the area he knew quite well. He's a real student of culture. He loves the synthesis that creates a whole social situation unique to New Mexico, which is what he basically writes about. Just talking and going places and seeing things with him, and some of the actors also helped.

One of the things I had a problem with were all of the different accents. For example, Sônia is Brazilian, and she doesn't speak Spanish as her native tongue but Portuguese. Every time I listened to Sônia, it was like, "Wait a minute, she doesn't sound like she's from here." But she has such a wonderful spirit, it overrides her. She's a force, a real-life force.

I love that culture. I love the openness and warmth to it. It's the Milagro Beanfield. I think that that's what attracted Redford. Bob feels that he grew up in a repressed sort of cultural and family environment. He just loved the sort of freedom of the culture, and even though there are some real restriction and codes of behavior, there is something about its openness in the natural world that Redford really responded to. That's why he really wanted to make this movie so much. It just fascinated him that things that might seem fantastical or paranormal was to them a part of everyday life.

STUDENT: Did your desire to be a director first help your writing?

DAVID: Like most writers, I didn't really realize what I didn't know about directing until I actually directed my first movie. I think that being a director has hurt my writing a bit now because I tend to be too cryptic because I know the director is going to figure these things out himself, and the art director is going to do this, and the production designer is going to do that. Before, I tried to write the script with some style about what the tone of the movie should be. Now I find myself not doing that much. I have to remind myself to do it because that's one of the things that makes a script compelling to readers. Now I find myself becoming a little perfunctory.

LEW: Goldman says that he puts a lot of things in the selling draft, then when he sits with the director, he takes "half that shit out."

DAVID: You want the script to read well. You don't want it to be a chore for people to read. That's not going to help you.

LEW: Well, David Ward, I can speak on behalf of everyone in this school and room that we are so proud to have you as one of us.

DAVID: Thank you very much.

17

Horton Foote

Horton Foote is a very special writer to me because he has a bucolic background. We're from the same pastures, so to speak: Horton hailing from Texas, me from Nebraska. We shit-kickers have always stuck together and understood one another. Ah, to have his talent! But that aside, to have written the screenplays for his Oscar-winning *Tender Mercies* and *To Kill a Mockingbird* would be just to die for. To a major degree, the Horton Foote dialogue is, perhaps, my favorite.

Before the 434 screenwriting course had begun, Horton told me he had been working on a screenplay, and the night before, at three o'clock in the morning, he woke up with the solution to a scene he had been working on. I asked, "Did you get up to write it down?" He fired back, "Yes, immediately!" Horton's fire burned on for all eighty-eight years of his life. What a role model!

What you are about to read is exhilarating to me, and I pray it will be for you as well, dear reader.

LEW: Mr. Foote.

HORTON: Mr. Hunter.

LEW: I'm so thrilled to be interviewing you especially for this book because you've not only won one but two of the little gold devils. The idea is I want to talk to you about the process—not how you became a writer or playwright or performance writer but how you do it. It's very much pegged off my own inspiration in life, which was: the Writers at Work Series, do you remember, from the *Paris Review* a number of years ago?

HORTON: Oh yeah.

LEW: I thought it was very useful to young people because it made the process appear accessible to them. That's really what we're doing here—rather than how one became famous or how one became a screenwriter—was being a screenwriter as opposed to becoming famous. In your case, you've had such a wonderful variety of media you've worked in. I would assume, to start off, you really consider yourself, no matter what media you're working in, that you're a storyteller? Would that be safe to say?

HORTON: I think, when I get down to it, I think that's how I would characterize myself, even though so many people think my plays and screenplays are what they call character driven. It's essentially a story I'm interested in telling.

LEW: Do you ascribe a good share of that to your Texas heritage?

HORTON: Yeah, I think so. I think it's certainly a Southern heritage. In the South—at least when I was growing up, I think in some ways it's still true—we have a great oral tradition, so vivid in my case that often, years I wasn't even on the earth became as real to me as those I lived through.

LEW: Did you have a storyteller in your family, like my aunt, who was also my mother-in-law because I married my cousin? She was born in Waxahachie, Texas, and she used to tell stories and stories and stories. Do you have that person?

HORTON: I had about fifteen of them because I had a large extended family growing up. The other thing I learned very early on is that stories vary and are very subjective. In this case, so many people told the same stories and told their variations of them, so I learned early on you had to listen very carefully, and it was interesting, the subjectivity of the stories.

LEW: I've been a professional screenwriter since '69. I've not written plays, but I've written a number of screenplays, both television and motion pictures, and I've also been involved with screenwriting professing since '09, and I'm always trotting out Ecclesiastes, the part where there's nothing new under the sun. But I would suggest that your uniqueness is what is new. That probably leads to this lovely concept of Rashomon, the same story told many different ways.

HORTON: Yes, and that's exactly true. But the thing that's difficult sometimes for a young writer to grasp but very important is not to learn to write about someone else but to find out what your particular talent is and what your particular gift is, and that's your strongest suit. I don't mean that you don't have models that you love and watch and learn from, but I hear of young writers so often saying they watch television shows to get the formula. That just chills my blood. I don't understand it. I'm sure each of those writers inside themselves have marvelous things to say. It's a question of trusting it.

LEW: I grew up ten miles from Red Cloud, Nebraska, and if my memory serves me correctly, you were at a Willa Cather conference about two years ago, and I was keynote speaker last year. They really came down when they got to me, but nevertheless I was proud to be there. But my grandmother roomed with Willa Cather. They had a boarding school there, and Willa Cather, of course, is an icon in my personal and professional life. She said, "I became an artist when I stopped admiring and began remembering." I should think that the basis of what you've written—and I've seen a great deal of your work—a lot of it seems to have a great deal of remembering.

HORTON: Yes, and I just reread a novel by Willa Cather the other day.

LEW: Which one?

HORTON: *Lucy Gayheart.* The thing that's extraordinary about her is she takes the memory, but it isn't reporting. It's why I think she's almost impossible to dramatize because she finds a way to use events in a very unique way in a way that's very personal to her style. You almost wonder how she does it. The things she withholds and then tells you at the end of the story, what she tells you at the beginning, the way she kind of leads you on emotionally, and then—wham!—she'll change the subject, pull the rug out. I, too, lectured at her conference. I was so deeply moved by being at her house, imagining that little girl growing up in that house.

LEW: You can imagine how I felt on that second floor, which is where my grandmother and she lived together for a year. My grandmother reported that Willa Cather said, "I'm not like other girls." Perhaps a lot of that ascribed to her gender situation, but I much more ascribed that to the intellectual depth she carried in that world.

HORTON: But that must have been a burden for her. When you see pictures of her dressed—she called herself Will Cather—she really dressed as a boy. But whatever. She used it wonderfully.

LEW: Yes, she did. I'm fascinated, since I'm sixty-three years old, that I grew up as a young man pushing a broom on the floor of a television station, preparing for the next show as one of my entry-level jobs, and watching *US Steel Hour*, *Studio One*, et cetera. That is really an area that was sort of your gestation area in growing up as a screenwriter.

HORTON: That, of course, was live television. When television started, I don't think consciously but unconsciously, two schools played there. I think one school wanted to turn it more cinematic. I was a playwright with two plays done on Broadway, and really when I went to television, I wrote a series of one-act plays. Of course, it was live then, and you couldn't stop it, and I felt it was very much like theater. I think Paddy Chayefsky, who I was very fond of, felt totally different, and of course, he won out because television has become totally cinema now. I used it really because no one wanted one-act plays in those days, and it was a chance to get them done and wonderfully acted and directed.

LEW: When people ask about the so-called golden age, I reply it was somewhat of an elitist age because most of the men and women, and most specifically men, that started in television were predominantly intelligent men, and they came from the theater. Also, most people couldn't afford a television at that time because it was so expensive. Consequently, it was people who were the upper economic class that could afford the television, and they, of course, would be much more appealed to what you all were doing as opposed to today, where we have the Stephen Cannell, Aaron Spelling type of school.

HORTON: In all truth, it wasn't all golden. There were a lot of mistakes made and a lot of heartbreak, a lot of things that didn't work.

LEW: In your career, how have you identified the idea that you want to spend a bit of time on—whether it's a week or a year or a month or whatever—how do you say, "That's the one I choose"? What's your process there?

HORTON: My original work, I don't choose it so much as it chooses me. I also do work where I adapt the film, and that is a much more difficult choice for me because I've found over the years that unless I really like something, and I mean in the deepest sense, I really can't serve it. I'm not a craftsman in that sense. I just can't find a way to emotionally attach myself to anything. For instance, I just finished working for Universal *Little House on the Prairie*, not the television series, but it's going back to the original work.

LEW: From the Laura Ingalls Wilder book, sure.

HORTON: I had no idea when they asked me to do it that I'd be attracted to it. But I did find it in a sense, maybe not as good as Willa Cather, but it has the same kind of mythic sense of life in the past.

LEW: I was an executive at NBC at the time, and I was involved in the initial development of *Little House*, and it very quickly became Michael Landon's *Little House on the Prairie*, as opposed to Laura Ingalls Wilder.

HORTON: I've never seen the television show.

LEW: It wasn't bad.

HORTON: It was certainly popular.

LEW: Yeah, it was, but it did not have that Willa Cather element to it.

HORTON: I hope I've captured that because I have a lot of respect for her. It's been a great journey for me because I've gone back and done research and learned things about our past that are very useful to me.

LEW: It seems like you're identifying an idea, whether it's an adaption or if it's an original piece, as a journey you would like to take.

HORTON: Absolutely. Otherwise, I just don't think I would be of any use to anybody because, as you know, in the given state of our profession, you'd better enjoy the journey because sometimes other obstacles present themselves.

LEW: I always tell my students that if you pay so much mind to consequence, you're going to possibly be terribly disappointed. Because I can't believe in the movies I've seen, with *Trip to Bountiful* and *Tender Mercies* and *To Kill a Mockingbird*—specifically the ones you are most known for—that you didn't have a wonderful journey working with the characters inside of those stories.

HORTON: I did, no question. As a matter of fact, I've had few bad experiences. I've been very fortunate that way. I've also done a series of independent films, which are also not well known, but they mean a great deal to me. And then, *Of Mice and Men*, which I did with Gary Sinise, was a wonderful experience. He's very gifted. I was spoiled because my second film was *To Kill a Mockingbird*, and Harper Lee and I are still very close friends.

LEW: How did you get that opportunity to write that?

HORTON: I had worked with Mulligan and had known Pakula well. As a matter of fact, he wanted to do *The Chase*, but we had gotten to be friends, and they had offered it to Harper, and she didn't want to do it, and I was the next in line. They said if Harper and I got along, it would be a done deal. And we did. We got along.

LEW: Oh, so you hadn't known her before?

HORTON: No, but I'm devoted to her now.

LEW: Tell us a bit about your work habits, if you will.

HORTON: They're very different, depending if it's my own work. I've just finished a very different, strange territory for me: the memoirs of the first seventeen years of my life. I've just finished that. Right now, I'm searching around for something, either a play or a screenplay to work on.

That search is very important to me. Sometimes the ideas come very quickly. I do lots of notes, do a lot of thinking. Whatever the process is, it tells me, "This is something that I want to spend a journey on." I begin the process of being more specific in working through the characters and the story and where I want to go. My first draft, I don't edit at all. I just sort of write it out full.

LEW: Do you outline?

HORTON: In my own way. I kind of make milestones. I make a lot of notes. I make a lot of test scenes for myself, trying out certain things. I've just gone back before you called, looking at some notebooks I've had in the past, projects I've done. I realize that this is in some ways the most difficult period, but for original work, it's probably the most valuable period. It's not censoring and just sitting and thinking and trying to find something you really want to be involved with.

LEW: When you find it, do you make sort of a rough notation, either in your mind or on paper, what you wish?

HORTON: Yes, and I've always found I don't trust my memory. Any impulse I get, I write down immediately. Even when I'm very involved, I get really obsessive, and I might even wake up at night and start to work.

LEW: Do you have a piece of paper by the side of your bed?

HORTON: Yeah, I do.

LEW: Do you ever—Robert Benton, last week, said he wakes up in the morning and sees what he wrote last night, and he thinks, "My God. How could I have ever thought that was worth putting down?"

HORTON: Absolutely. But I still don't dare not put it down.

LEW: Do you make some sort of a beginning, middle, and end sketch for yourself before being more sophisticated?

HORTON: I just had an experience that I had a season done at the Signature. They did four of my plays, and the last one, they wanted an original, one that had never even been done outside New York. I was struggling around and thinking, "My God," and then I remembered, when I lived in New Hampshire many years ago, I had worked on something, and I'd gotten to a certain point and found out it just didn't work. But I've learned to save everything. So, for some reason, I thought, "Let's look that up." I had about eighteen pages, and I read it and thought, "That's pretty good, but I still don't know what to do with it."

I took a ride in the car and went by a house that was all boarded up, and I realized that was the house I was writing about. Then I was invited to a lunch, and a lady came up to me and said, "Do you remember me?" Of course, I didn't remember her because I hadn't seen her in maybe thirty-five years. This was the woman whose story I was trying to tell, about her as a young girl. I don't know what that opened up inside me, but I went home, and I began to find answers to things I hadn't been able to find.

LEW: My, my. So this is more of a subconscious thing: the house as well as the woman?

HORTON: I think so.

LEW: So I must assume you've gotten to the point of where you seek or at least be open to that subconscious?

HORTON: I don't think you can call upon it. There is an exercise that actors often do, which is effective memory when they want to call up an emotion. What they've learned is, if you concentrate on the emotion, it's not going to appear. What you do is you begin to think about the circumstances, what the room looked like, the clothes, all the physical things, and that somehow triggers it. In that sense, that's what happened to me, although I wasn't consciously doing it.

LEW: Yes, that awareness just came to you. What we're talking about here is in the area of gestation/research, right? And then when you really start to focus on the parameters of the story, do you write down a beginning, middle, and an end in a page or two, or do you just have it in your mind?

HORTON: Sometimes I do, but I don't always stick to it because as I go along, new ideas may come.

LEW: But as you said, it's always necessary for you to write it down.

HORTON: Exactly. Just something I can go back to even if I say that's not what I want to do.

LEW: Then are you more sophisticated in like a step outline after that beginning, middle, and end?

HORTON: No, I'm never that specific. I have my own kind of outlines, and they're very difficult to describe because they only mean something to me. I know writers that do that, and I think it's wonderful. They're very organized. I wish I could do it, but so often I find, and this is why I object to treatments, I think you write it out.

LEW: Oh yeah. You leave your fight in the dressing room, is the way I like to put it when you're too detailed. But you just have a generic set of notes that show you the beginning, middle, and end?

HORTON: That's right.

LEW: Do you generally have a pretty good idea of what the third act is going to be before you start going into the script?

HORTON: You know, in the theater we don't have any third acts anymore.

LEW: I always tell people, "The third act is screenwriting shorthand for Aristotle's beginning, middle, and end." Somebody told me one time. Maybe you know. I talk about this. I always say, of course, that theater is only two acts. Why are there two acts? Because people have to go to the bathroom. But somebody said that perhaps it's because in the '20s, they had to catch the eleven o'clock train to get to the suburbs.

HORTON: Probably.

LEW: Maybe a little of both.

HORTON: When we think of films, we don't stop films.

LEW: Well said.

HORTON: I was talking to someone about doing a play of mine on television, and they informed me that they have seven acts.

LEW: Shakespeare's *Julius Caesar* had ten acts. Most of Shakespeare's plays had five. So it probably becomes an opportunity to sell popcorn or Jujubes at break, doesn't it? It gets back to commerce.

So then you sit down in the writing process. Do you have a particular set of hours that you give yourself for your script pages?

HORTON: I'm a fairly obsessive writer. I wish I weren't so. I mean, I admire writing so much that I start at ten o'clock in the morning and break for lunch, read in the afternoon. Once I get started, it's very hard for me to stop. Often I get on tangents, and I do work that's not useful. But I don't seem to be able to stop that.

LEW: Actually, in point of fact, what's past is prologue, but I would say, in your case that's excellent because it has served you very well in your career to have that obsessiveness. I find that that obsessiveness with all of the Oscar-winning people. I've had similar discussions with these people in this book. They all are going to the same ocean, but they all do it so wildly differently. But one thing: They all are very smart people, they all are very feeling people, and they all are obsessed, but their obsession manifests itself in different ways. How does yours manifest itself? Just sitting down and getting a first draft done without censoring in a few days?

HORTON: I simply cannot rest once I get started. Even when the process, which I'm going through now, of thinking—I can't say I didn't stop to listen to Ken Starr this morning because I did, but even in the back of my mind something was trying to figure out something. I get started into the actual process of writing. As I say, I wake up in the night, and I have to get up and get to work on it.

LEW: Do you assign yourself so many pages a day?

HORTON: No, I don't. I have a compulsion to get that first draft done. Once that's done, I begin to feel easy, and then I begin fixing what I call mechanical work, the architectural work.

LEW: Bless your heart. These people that say writing is rewriting. I always say that the first draft is so important because from then on, you're on the downhill. It's more of a mechanical process because that's when your intellect kicks in. Before, you were working on your visceral sense, right?

HORTON: That's right. That's what I feel.

LEW: What are the most pages you've done in a day?

HORTON: I don't think I've ever counted.

LEW: Would you say twenty?

HORTON: Yeah.

LEW: Tom Schulman, who wrote *Dead Poets Society*, said that he has a little garret that he has a few blocks away from home, and it's about six by twelve. He'll have a little mat, and when he gets tired, he'll sleep. Otherwise, he finishes his draft in about twenty-four to forty-eight hours.

HORTON: I understand that.

LEW: Then the obsession has that combination of success and self-confidence, and with age, the obsession has not subsided, I see.

HORTON: No.

LEW: That's to be admired. I have a number of my friends who are in their sixties and seventies who don't get at it quite as much anymore.

HORTON: If anything, it gets even stronger for me.

LEW: Oh my. What makes you rub? What causes that?

HORTON: I think part of it is my wife passed on about three or four years ago, so I have a lot of time.

LEW: So the writing is a companion for you, I suspect, too?

HORTON: Absolutely.

LEW: I just love the fact that Arthur Laurents one time said, "I'm not alone." People say, "Isn't it lonely?" He says, "I'm not alone. I'm with all those characters."

Oh, talk to me just a bit about rewriting. Is rewriting more in that mechanical process that you were describing?

HORTON: I'm a little shy of using the word *mechanical.*

LEW: You're right. Perhaps I should say more craft; the craft kicks in.

HORTON: Right. Usually, rewrites come from—I'm talking about my plays, though with my screenplays I've been very fortunate. I hear these horrendous things that some writers go through. I've never gone through them with studios.

With rewrites, I've had a few hair-raising experiences. I've found the dissatisfaction grows inside me. I don't know where the dissatisfaction necessarily comes from because often when I finish a draft, I feel very confident and very good about it. And then this little voice will begin to speak a little doubt, and I go back, and I think, "I don't like that very much." Then the process starts all over again. And if I'm working with a director, which I do, that I mostly admire, I'm very attentive to their notes. Usually, they're people of goodwill and are not demanding, and if I don't agree, they're very open to my disagreements.

But I find that helpful. But mostly I'm on my own, and I have to be tough on myself, as tough as I can be.

LEW: When you're working with a director or some other person, do you generally go to them or they to you, or do you do it via machinery and via e-mails and phones?

HORTON: It depends. Working on *Little House*, which is the last big studio project I've done, I worked with a woman at the studio, and she came here first, and we had some talks. Then I sent some drafts in, and we talked on the phone, and we got notes back and forth. It was all very pleasant.

Lew: When we talk about screenwriting, what would you say is the soul of screenwriting, the most important part of screenwriting?

Horton: I have very particular likes and dislikes. In one sense, I'm not really a great authority, as I don't see as many films as I perhaps should see. But the films that attract me, I find that what attracts me is something that's very personal about them, something that's very unique, and it comes because of the individuality of the personality of the writer. I'm not very interested when I feel things have been contrived to make a certain kind of effect or even to make money.

Lew: *Tender Mercies* was an original?

Horton: Yes.

Lew: Was that personal? Did somebody bring you that notion, or is it something you'd been living with it for a while?

Horton: Actually, I wanted to start writing and had some experience with young men who had tried to start a string band, a country western band. So the experience reminded me much of when I was beginning in the theater as an actor, getting started. I had never done what they call "pits," but I had been working on a series of plays, and I needed a project, and my agent said that this is a very easy thing to do, and she knew someone that liked my work, and she said to just go and tell them a few things, and they would underwrite it.

So I did that, and to my surprise I didn't have to say much, and they liked it and sent me to someone higher up, and they talked, and said, "I like it very much. I only have one idea: I think there should be an older man in there somewhere." I thought about that. He said, "I'd like to make a deal with your agent," and she came out and opened the trades, and that day he'd been fired. But his suggestion stuck in my head for some reason, and out of that came Mac Sledge. By that time, I'd become interested and didn't really want to get involved with the studio until I had done it.

Lew: You wrote what we call a spec script, then?

Horton: That's really what I do with all of my stuff.

Lew: Yeah, that's what you've done with your originals. Just simply writing it, and if somebody likes it, fine. Otherwise, you simply keep on going. That's so wonderful. I so admire that. Part of it is because I do the same thing. I do it with my books, et cetera. Just do it, and if somebody likes it, fine. Most young writers have to be paid up front, or their agents provoke that thought.

HORTON: When I was raising my children and having to put them through college, I'd have to go look for work, but those days are gone. I don't have to do that anymore.

LEW: When you first went to New York, did you go with the hopes of becoming an actor?

HORTON: Uh huh.

LEW: Aha! Because I am always pushing on young writers, particularly here in film school, to know more about acting, and I suspect you would share that concept, right?

HORTON: Exactly. To me, it's like the conductor knowing the orchestra.

LEW: Well said.

HORTON: I mean, you know the instruments. You really should know what's actable and what's not actable.

LEW: How'd you get veered into writing?

HORTON: Oh, goodness. I've told this story a million times, but I suppose I can tell it again to you.

LEW: Oh, okay. I said I wasn't going to talk about it, but it's a fascinating question.

HORTON: I started with an Off-Broadway company, which turned out a very distinguished group: Jerry Robbins and Mildred Dunnock and Valerie Bettis and Joseph Anthony, who became a very famous director. Agnes de Mille came down to do a project with us, and we were all kind of doing improvisations to help understand the different sections of the country we came from, and she casually suggested I write. I thought about it but then thought, "No, I never had." She said, "I think you should."

So I don't know why, I wrote a one-act play with the lead for myself. With those strange circumstances, a critic came down to see it, and he liked it, and he liked my acting, so I thought, "This is how it's going to be. I'll write plays that I can act." So I wrote a three-act play. At that time, New York was a very provincial town, and word got around that I had some talent. Brooks Atkinson, who was the dean of the critics, came down, and he loved the play but didn't like my acting so much. So I was determined to show him, but I went away that summer and did a lot of parts, and just suddenly, it left me, and I decided I wanted to write.

LEW: I'm going to let Rita Augustine ask a few questions representing both herself and our sixty-two-member student graduate body. Rita, what comes to your mind?

RITA: You said you write your first draft straight through. Is that what gives you the spine of your story?

HORTON: I do that, but sometimes I stop in the middle and say, "This isn't working at all."

RITA: Right. It just sounds like once you get the story, it's easier to change details and minute things. We get forced into the same thing here because we are forced to write a screenplay every quarter, and we have three quarters in a year, so we can relate to this.

HORTON: I should join that class to make me work harder. [*laughter*]

LEW: Actually, it's a two- to three-year program, so when they get out of here, they've done anywhere between five and eight over a two- to three-year program. Not only of their own—but that's a small tutorial—classes of eight people, so they've been involved with the development of almost a hundred screenplays over the two- to three-year period.

HORTON: That's wonderful.

RITA: When you finish your draft, how long do you let it sit before the dissatisfaction creeps in and you go back to it?

HORTON: Not too long. Maybe that night.

RITA: Do you purposely leave time between your projects?

HORTON: I like to, but sometimes I don't do it. But I really like to do it. I like to just cool it, as you might say, and walk around or listen to music or go and see a film or a play. Sometimes I like to read something entirely different. Something that kind of cleanses my mind so I can come back to it a little more objectively.

RITA: Do you have a person you show it to at that stage?

HORTON: I gave it to my wife for a long time, and I'm very close to my children. I usually share it with one or two of them.

RITA: I was intrigued by the thing you said at the very beginning. Even though people consider your stories character driven, you consider yourself a storyteller.

HORTON: Yeah.

RITA: I wondered if you could expand on that just a little, just to say what does character driven mean versus what does being a storyteller mean to you?

HORTON: I'm only telling how people characterize me. I think when I was asked the question, I'm interested in stories, the stories of people, of lives, and that usually gets me going.

RITA: When you say the idea that you have to write, that it chooses you, are you hearing characters or seeing situations?

HORTON: I've taken a very peculiar task for myself. I mostly write about a small town in Texas. Only a fool would do that. I was told from the very beginning to "give it up, buddy." [*laughter*] Nobody cares about it.

So I'm saying that this chose me. I didn't choose it. It isn't always easy, but that's what I had to do, and I don't know how else to describe it, except that I just know when I can't do it. I think it's a remarkable talent. Some writers can sit down and objectively plan something out. I just can't work that way. It's just more of a feeling. If I get the feeling, that's very difficult to describe, and I wish I could be more specific.

RITA: No, I think most writers understand exactly what you're talking about. I was wondering, a lot of our people in our program have come from playwriting, too. Are there specific things you've learned from going from plays to movies that you would recommend for people to watch?

HORTON: The first thing is you have to realize that they are very different mediums. But the things I like best in both mediums I share. I think you have to watch out in both mediums for the clichés.

For the playwrights, the first thing they have to be wary of is when they say to them, "Open it up," because it could become a travelogue if you're not careful. It could just be dazzle, dazzle, dazzle. I don't think a lot of locations make up a good story. I think it could be marvelous if you've got a good story. I mean, *Little House* is a long journey and is very important.

Also, *Trip to Bountiful* I did originally for Lyndon Gershowitz with Philco in live television, and we did it in the theater. When we finally came to film, the first thing I realized was that I could take the journey because in television, we were only allowed three sets, and on the stage we obviously couldn't. So I just think you have to search out the strengths of each medium. I think actually, theater has taken more from cinema than cinema from theater because so many of the new techniques they use in theater, like dissolves, are all cinematic techniques.

RITA: Would you agree with what I hear a lot about, that playwriting is that it's the words that are what's important? It's almost like you can create more intellectual ideas on a stage than you can in a film, where it's much more subconscious and emotional.

HORTON: I'm not an intellectual writer in that sense. I don't really think in terms of ideas. I think primarily in terms of characters and language. Language means a great deal to me, but certain kind of language is important to me. I don't particularly like obvious language. I don't teach playwriting or any kind of writing anymore, but when I did, the first thing I taught them to do was really train their ear, to really learn to listen, not just to be reporters, but to get down deep into what they hear, because no matter how cinematic we get, words help if they are used properly.

LEW: I don't know whether I came to this myself or whether I heard it, but that really doesn't make any difference. I think that good dialogue in terms of film or television or a play is dialogue that illuminates what characters are not saying. *Trip to Bountiful*, for instance, is my favorite piece you've done, I guess, because it so ties into women I knew growing up and still do know, quite frankly, in the Midwest in Nebraska. How did you come to that notion in the first place? Was it based on someone you knew?

HORTON: Yes, often composites, but there was someone I knew. As a matter of fact, it's interesting technically. When I first worked on *Bountiful*, I was always fascinated by this story, which is the story of my family about a woman who had not been allowed to marry because it was her first cousin, and she married someone else. Then she lost the husband, and she came back to this town, and the man she had wanted to marry was married to someone else. They had a very formal relationship, but they still cared for each other very much. So I started out writing it the day of the wedding, where she was being forced or urged to marry the second guy, and it just didn't work. So I put it aside, and again, there is this period of thinking, and I began to think about her at the end of her life. So it was just a memory, and that was something that she could tell about, and that was the genesis of it.

LEW: Now this was initially before you brought it to television, right?

HORTON: No, I did it first for television.

LEW: Oh, so you were thinking of doing it for TV, then set it aside and came back to it days, weeks later?

HORTON: No. As a matter of fact, I had a deadline because in those days, they commissioned you. I was paid all of $5,000 and glad to get it, let me tell you. So I couldn't get out of it. Thank God in about three days it came to me, and when it came to me, I wrote it very quickly.

LEW: You must have sparked, then, when I told you my wife and I are first cousins.

HORTON: I'd forgotten that.

LEW: I have just one more question, Horton. My publisher, and I'm one person that doesn't complain about my publishers, said people pick up these kinds of books to pick up the secret of screenwriting. Is there anything you could define as a secret of yours that we might focus on?

HORTON: I get asked this question all the time in my playwriting and screenwriting. My only advice is to find something you really want to write about it and write it. I don't think there are any secrets to the actual technique of it. Essentially, what you have to have is a story and some passion for getting it done, and listen, if you have that, the technical things you can learn very quickly. Don't you think?

LEW: I think so, I keep saying two things: Do things you care about, and do what you know about. Then, I also feel very strongly, beyond passion, that they should work quickly, so you've tied very well in the way I teach because I think the subconscious is where the true creativity is.

HORTON: I think so often that people get stuck on a screenplay or a play and just stop until something happens to it.

LEW: I just say, "Just put something down, and keep right on going, and you'll get back to it, and you'll fix it."

HORTON: Or sell it.

LEW: Or sell it, right. It's just been absolutely delightful to talk to one of my favorite dramatists. I feel honored to be including you in this book. I think you'll be very pleased to be in this company, and I wish you were in front of my class right now. I would say to have you in this book is to have you before them, to have you before Rita and myself, akin to having God come to divinity school.

HORTON: Oh my God.

LEW: That's pretty lofty stuff. You're obviously not going to accept that as Billy Wilder accepted it: with a smile. You, on the other hand, said, "Oh my God." It's lovely to visit with you. I hope someday you come to Southern California or back to Willa Cather land, and we can connect up in real life.

HORTON: I'd love to.

LEW: Thank you so much, Horton Foote.

18

Ron Bass

Here is the most gregarious screenwriter in our magic twenty-two. Ron Bass is equally mesmerizing as he illuminates the heart and soul of we writers— passion and passion and passion. Part of his process is paying students to have at him, as the jury would do, and to defend his choices. He notes he was an attorney, one who worked for writers. He's also a great legal resource for the Writers Guild. My 434 students were quiet in their chairs, and I have never been more on my toes, as he, as opposed to most writers, is not an introvert.

Get out the popcorn, and enjoy Ron Bass, as we did. You'll learn a lot about writing and also that he's a great man.

> LEW: 434, the date is what? January 29, 1998. We are delighted and pleased to have a man here who has written *Code Name Emerald, Black Widow, Gardens of Stone, Rain Man, Sleeping with the Enemy, Joy Luck Club, When a Man Loves a Woman, The Enemy Within, Dangerous Minds, Waiting to Exhale,* and the most recent to have come out to our theaters is *My Best Friend's Wedding.* There are other screenplays on this list, Ron: *Snow Falling on Cedars, Edge of Eden, Professional Athletes, What Dreams May Come.*
>
> RON: What a bizarre collection. That includes films that are in production now and some written twelve years ago.
>
> LEW: You currently have five movies in production.

SHELLEY: And there's something really remarkable I just learned about *My Best Friend's Wedding.*

RON: What was that?

SHELLEY: About the amount it made.

RON: Oh. This is funny as a story on studios. This is the first comedy I've ever written. I've written over eighty scripts. Two weeks ago, it surpassed *Sleepless in Seattle* as the highest-grossing romantic comedy of all time in film. Then, right after that, it passed *Jerry Maguire* as the highest-worldwide-grossing romantic comedy in film. So it's both the highest domestic grossing and the highest worldwide grossing.

I called the guy who's vice president up at Sony, where I now have worked exclusively for three years, and said, "Maybe you could have an ad that says that. It's kind of nice isn't it?" And he says, "Well, we don't eat our young over here, and you know, *Sleepless in Seattle* and *Jerry Maguire* are also Sony films. So, we'll make sure that your film gets the recognition." I said, "We don't need the recognition. We did okay. It was fine."

But I guess they have a lot more to worry about than just that. It was a good education for me after all these years. I've been to work for seventeen years, and I never really realized that you have to take out your congratulatory ads with an eye toward not wanting to insult the people that you also work with.

LEW: Oh yeah, I used to be an executive for seventeen years before I went crooked and became a writer, and I was in charge of programming things, series and stuff at Disney and at NBC and ABC, and then I was the head of the story department at Disney, and boy, I tell you, we just cringe every time something came out in the trades because that meant we had to do damage control in about thirty-five other places in the context of the studio network, so that's what he's talking about there.

But isn't it exciting that you did *My Best Friend's Wedding*? What I thought was, it's just a wonderful movie and a terrific idea, just a terrific idea, an idea that just transcends boundaries and that can do so well worldwide. Isn't that exciting? Congratulations. Well, like we were discussing earlier, Billy Wilder and Julius Epstein and so forth, and they were pretty much in the contiguous United States. It was the impact.

RON: Well, because it was a different world.

LEW: You bet it was. You bet it was, Ron Bass. I have literally used the name. I have visuals here. I have turned down some things I don't even know if I'm going to refer to them or not. Oh, I guess one thing that was—is it honestly true that what we read in this "Written by Ron Bass" that number 2 pencils are your instruments?

RON: Well, I have a better pencil than that. I use a Sundance number 2.

LEW: Now I'm going to change your life forever.

RON: You'll never get me to try one. Won't happen.

LEW: Have you tried one of these?

RON: No.

LEW: I got them. I used to get so angry, right in the middle of a roll, and the fucking thing is dull, and I would, er, grind it up, you know. You never have to sharpen these.

RON: This is a great lesson in screenwriting. What isn't broke, don't fix it.

LEW: I actually really do most of my screenwriting on a typewriter that I got at ABC which was Ernie Kovacs. Right after he died, I walked by his office, and there was a typewriter. There was a 1918 Remington, one of those big iron things.

RON: Sure.

LEW: There was nothing else in the office. And about four days of seeing that, I stole it. And I've made every nickel as a writer, and twenty-six years as a writer, off of that soul in Ernie Kovacs.

But back to storytelling. Now, this gathering will be about writing scripts. It won't be about what Julia Roberts is really like or a lot of Bill Clinton jokes and Lewinsky and so forth but really about the process. You have a process that I think I heard audible gasps when you said you had written how many scripts?

RON: Eighty-six.

LEW: Eighty-six scripts.

RON: It took a lot of years, though. Over about fourteen years, though.

LEW: Well, I've written—I've been writing for over twenty-six years—and I've written a mere forty or so. Ah, no, that doesn't include television episodes. I guess I could get up to eighty-six, too.

RON: Well, you know, Brahms wrote four symphonies, and it's really not how many you write.

LEW: We have a lot of people here that think they're overwhelmed by doing three scripts a year in the context of these 434 graduate screenwriting classes.

RON: How can they be overwhelmed?

LEW: Well, they think it's a lot of work.

RON: That's different from if they think they're being forced to write faster than if it's coming naturally. That's two different things.

LEW: Elaborate.

RON: People talk of how much I write. I get tired of hearing how much I write because, as I said, it doesn't matter if you write nine scripts a year if nobody knows the difference. But I always say that it is true that I can't write faster or slower than I do now. It's just there when it's there. All I can do is spend more time in front of it.

That's the only control I have, is how many hours I spend with my notebook, as I'm sure everybody's heard, if you bother worrying about how I work. I do not own a computer. I do not know how to work a computer. I advise that no one write with a computer. I think it's a bad way to write fiction of any kind. I don't even know how to work one. I have a loose-leaf notebook and pencils and a plastic pencil case. You can only write as fast as you can write, and what I think is dangerous is, well, I got to deliver this because the syllabus says if I don't deliver this by Friday, then I'm not getting a grade on this script. That skews your writing.

But this class is unlike competing university film classes, where you write new scripts again and again and again and never rewrite your old scripts. I think that is so essential. It's shocking to think that there are film classes that have people rewriting their script again and again. You should never look at it again. You should just finish it, and the day you finish—no, not even the day—the moment you finish, you should just set it aside and line up the next one with notes. It's great to take all of the loose material, the stuff that you couldn't use in this one, and you keep spending hours each day filling up a notebook with notes because these can go in your next one. Then you're able to start with a time and a setting: Corey's bedroom, night.

You have to be able to just do that. You have to show yourself that it's a process of being a writer and not obsessing over this one thing. I think, the single biggest reason many talented writers don't make it is because they don't let that first one go.

LEW: Hear, hear!

RON: You have a lot of wisdom in having people write and keep writing, keep writing. But I guess I don't agree with the technique that says you've got to deliver it Friday because if it ain't ready, it ain't ready, and it's only good when it's good, and it's not always good when the time's up.

LEW: I was involved with setting up Sundance a number of years ago in the writers lab up there, talking to a now deceased head of Columbia, and he said, "When we spend our first year, we have exercises." He went through a three-year program with about, say, one script, which theoretically was the perfect script.

RON: What were the films that came out of that script?

LEW: That school?

RON: What, was it Cassavetes that came out of there?

LEW: You mean, Columbia? [*laughs*]

RON: Well, I'm saying, what was the success rate?

LEW: Well, there you are at NYU. You rewrite in one semester what you wrote the preceding semester, so in one year, you have one script. Your preparation to become a writer was probably in some ways not like other people. We all came from disparate areas. You came from law, right?

RON: Yeah, but I wrote short stories. I was bedridden as a child. I taught myself to read when I was three, and I was writing stories when I was five or six years old. By the time I was eighteen years old, I wrote a novel. I had worshipped novelists. That's what I wanted to do with my life. I never thought about writing for the screen. I never even realized that it even existed for me. My heroes were Dostoyevsky and Faulkner and Fitzgerald, and that's what I wanted to do. But because they were my heroes, therefore, it was assumed by me that of course I couldn't do it because it was the thing that only the best people in the world could possibly do, so therefore I couldn't.

I was actually at UCLA for six months before I went to Stanford because I was in the ice age when I was in high school, and you could graduate mid–senior year, so I couldn't get into Stanford until September, so I came to UCLA for six months. I fell in love with my English teacher, just a huge crush on this brilliant woman from Columbia University, who was my English teacher in 1960. I showed her my novel that no one else in the world had ever seen, not my parents, my girlfriend; no one had ever seen it. She read it, and she said, "God, Ronnie, this is, I mean, you're so talented. You really should really write." I said, "Yeah, yeah, yeah, but can we get it published? Like published in New York?" And she said, "Oh no, this is like a personal fantasy, this subject matter. You can't publish this book."

I went home, and I burned it, I don't mean throw away. I mean burned, with a match, in an iron bowl. Flames. Soot. Junk all over my book. The only copy of it that ever existed was gone. I never wrote another word of fiction for seventeen years; from nineteen to thirty-five, I never wrote another word of fiction. Became a lawyer, went to law school. I was just going to do what I felt my talents and IQ would carry me. It was like the voice of God, this woman I had a crush on, I couldn't be published. Eventually, I did write my first novel. It was actually reworking that same first novel. It was published. So, what do you know? Nothing. No one really knows anything.

LEW: Did you write the novel in the context of your job as a lawyer?

RON: Well, not in the context of the job. I had to write it against the context of the job.

LEW: Did you write in the morning, early, before you went to work?

RON: Yeah, I get up at three o'clock in the morning, and I would write from 3:00 to 6:00 or 7:00 a.m., and I would put on a suit, and I would go down and be a suit. Also, I would write on weekends, I would write on vacations, and I didn't know anyone was going to read it. I just had to do it for me. It was the most fun I ever had.

Because I was an entertainment lawyer, I knew everybody, and there was a guy in New York who was negotiating for the publishing house, and my client, Dick Clark, was doing his autobiography for him. I told the guy that I had written something, and he insisted I show it to him. He said he was quitting and becoming an agent. That's how it all got started and got published. I wrote two more novels and sold the last one for the screen. I didn't really look back till now.

LEW: Did you tie yourself into the screen one as a writer?

RON: You betcha. Otherwise, I wouldn't be here.

LEW: That was the deal?

RON: It wasn't a deal like that. It was just like, "Oh, you want to buy it? I'm the screenwriter." I mean, it was a deal breaker for me. They wanted to buy the galleys. They had seen the galleys and the third novel. I said, "You could only buy the literary rights if I write the screenplay." It isn't like, "I have an idea. Let me write it." I could write a novel. They didn't think it that strange that I would write a screenplay with my own novel.

LEW: Have you ever seen the woman you fell in love with at UCLA?

RON: Never saw or heard from her since 1960.

LEW: Is that right?

RON: I hope she's alive and well and happy.

LEW: You haven't gone back to show her the novel?

RON: Oh God, no. I didn't even think of it.

LEW: Oh, I see. I thought you might've wanted to see the reaction, have a true writer's love-story ending.

RON: No, no, no.

LEW: Do you still get up at four o'clock in the morning to write?

RON: Yeah, there was a long time when I was getting up in the 2:00 a.m. time frame, but then I was going to bed at like around ten o'clock. Now I get up around 4:00 a.m. I start working in the 4:00, 4:30 range, but I don't go to bed until midnight sometimes.

LEW: Do you work all that time?

RON: For the last six months, because of all these pictures and all this stuff I'm doing, there's a lot more working in the fives. By now I work until about ten, eleven o'clock at night. Then I've got to sit and watch

ESPN or FOX Sports or something for an hour; otherwise, I can't go to sleep.

LEW: Do you know Floyd Mutrux?

RON: Don't know him. I should know who he is.

LEW: Floyd was working one year, and somebody asked him, "How many hours do you write a day?" Floyd said, "It's not the hours; it's the pages. The pages." He assigns himself five pages a day. Do you have that sort of goal?

RON: I work from early morning. Because I produce and have all of these projects, there's a huge amount of my time where I don't write for six or seven days. In term of writing dialogue on a page, I'm working for six different directors now, all at the same time. I just came from a meeting with Phil Robinson.

LEW: He's not writing his own material?

RON: No, he's going to do mine. *Mozart and the Whale* for Spielberg, and we're working with Wolfgang Petersen and Wayne Wang and Vincent Ward and Jerry Zucker. Then there's two that are rewriting these, so they only call me once in a while: Scott Hicks and Chris Columbus. Directors do that a lot.

LEW: So your training as a lawyer was really invaluable in terms of juggling balls?

RON: Yeah, you know, that's really, really smart and great that you say that because most people think that the relevance of it is only in the business. The real relevance of it is the kind of lawyer I was, as an entertainment lawyer, was a negotiator. That's all I did. I never went to court. I negotiated the deals, so I would come in in the morning, and there would be sixty files on my desk, very neatly exposing the top thing that you could read which one it was. There would be like four or five lights lit on the phone, and every day you would just be punching one button, and you would argue with somebody for forty-five minutes or for two hours. You had to argue your side selectively in the middle of that, and it's very great training for these meetings and collaborations. It's also a lot of juggling, so I could write on twelve different things in the same day, and it's not an issue. Just when you're there, you're there.

LEW: I shudder because being an executive at three networks, I had probably about a hundred contracts in development with various firms, and so, like you say, be as good as you can be in that context, in that isolated moment.

Are there any tricks that you have to focus on, or is it simply habit over the years?

RON: It isn't tricks or habit. It is what my nature is. Everyone's writing process is different. I'm working with Meg Tilly. She is an actress who wrote an incredibly great script, a beautiful script. I'm going to work with her and maybe produce it, and I said, "Well, why don't you come with my development team, and we'll sit down and brainstorm for six or seven hours and get all these different ideas. You don't even have to use any of them." She was scared. I said, "If you're scared, don't do it."

Everyone's process is their process. My process is sort of like auto-writing. I'm very, very compulsive, very controlling in everything else in my life except my writing. My writing is the only thing in life where I trust myself. Whatever feels good is what I do, and whatever doesn't, I just avoid it like the plague. I take no advice from anybody about the process. I sure take advice on scripts and on notes and on specifics, but in terms of how I do what I do, when I do it, it's just when it happens. It's sort of like watching it and being it at the same time. You are all the characters. The writing really feels like it's coming through you. There's really no sense of calculation or sense of control in writing a first draft. In rewrites, it's completely different. It's a completely different skill, completely different muscles.

LEW: I hate it.

RON: There's no one who likes rewriting.

LEW: You have to solve these problems because either something doesn't physically work or doesn't work emotionally for it.

RON: Oh no, it's worse and worse and worse. Not that it doesn't work; it doesn't work for some jerk who's the vice president of the studio. If it really doesn't work for you, you'd have changed it already. So it's not working for somebody else, and nine times out of ten, if it's the studio, you aren't really agreeing with them. When you get a better idea, when your director says, "Why don't you do it this way?" and "Hey, that's better than what I had," you are thrilled.

So it's really never about ego, and it's never about doing what some-body else wants. It's all about whether somebody else can make you do what they want. There's no more unpleasant feeling when you create for a living than the knowledge that somebody else can make you do what they want. You know it's wrong, and you know it doesn't work. It hap-pens to me all the time.

LEW: You must have thought you died and gone to heaven working with John Calley, right?

RON: Yeah, he is the greatest executive I've ever known in thirty years in the business. He is a unique, brilliant, amazing person.

LEW: In the '70s he wanted me to write a novel for him called *The Search for Anna Fisher*.

RON: I was their lawyer, his lawyer.

LEW: Were you really? I said, "I can't take your money. I don't think there's a movie here." And he said, "Oh no, I'll get you $75,000." It was pretty good money back then. I said, "No, I can't take your money." He stopped, and he said, "You're the most honest man I've ever known in Hollywood," And I was just thrilled. And Jeff Sagansky used to be my intern when I was at NBC.

Talk to us about storytelling. Obviously, you enjoyed reading and then of course writing stories when you were quite small. How do you feel about the statement that movies are the most exciting way to tell stories?

RON: Absolutely not.

LEW: Not at all?

RON: A story is a story. When I first started to write for the screen, I really felt like, "Why am I doing this? I'm doing this to make money. I need the money." But my whole life I wanted to be a novelist. When I realized that there was absolutely no difference—it was very different in what you were doing, but there was no difference in the feeling of telling a story.

That rush I had from writing was a huge problem for me because for a lot of years, from 1984 to 1993, I really considered myself a writer and not a screenwriter. I really considered myself as a novelist who was sort of trapped in this screenwriting thing, where I could make a lot of money and have a lot of fun. I resisted rewrites, I was incredibly impossible, and I never connected with the process. I resented when it was taken away from me. I hated the fact that the film was never as good as my script. There was a project in 1992 called *The Joy Luck Club* that changed me. I decided to be a producer. To realize what I was doing was part of an overall collaborative process rather than what I had always dreamed of doing, which was writing in solitary.

People in my company, they're incredibly helpful to me mentally. My work is now very collaborative, and I work on a lot of things I don't write. I write more and more things than I ever did before. I found the joys of collaboration. The answer to your question, as far as I'm concerned, it's all storytelling, whether it's a short story, whether it's a novel. Peter Weir told me that we were going to do his project together. He said, "If we do this, the first thing you're going to have to do is write a short story for me of what you're going to do as a screenplay. If it doesn't work as a short story, I know it's not going to work as a screenplay. It will have to analyze those problems." He made it very good.

LEW: Don't we screenwriters call that an outline?

RON: No. Oh no, a short story is very different from an outline. A short story has only a fraction of the information that you have in an outline, but it has to capture the emotion and the heart and the spirit of what you feel or what you're supposed to feel when you read the whole script. Writing an outline is not art. Writing a short story is art.

LEW: But you don't write an outline for the—

RON: For anybody but me.

LEW: Outline is such a bastard form of writing because it's not screenwriting. It's not a short story.

RON: Never write an outline for anybody but yourself. But you have to write it for yourself.

LEW: Let's talk about that process now. I think you have a good idea. If the idea isn't worth doing, nothing's going to help you: not the outline nor the script. Wouldn't you agree with that?

RON: This is the problem with screenwriting classes and with abstract conversation generally. We were sharing stories about our formative stuff, and I said, "When I was at Stanford in 1960—I guess it was in

September of '60—and Wallace Stegner, who was at that time best of American novelists, this legendary guy, he was six foot four, gray, and gorgeous, and every girl was like, "Oh my God." They were all dating him as fast as they could, every freshman, every sophomore. His talk was always peppered with "Tommy" for T. S. Eliot and when he was in Paris with Scott and Tommy. I mean seriously, this was all legit. He was really close to all those people.

I finally got the guts to come to him after class, and I say, "What writing courses at Stanford do I take?" And he said, "Never, ever take a writing course. Never take a writing course. Do you hear me kid? Never take a writing course because the moment that you take that fucking course, you are saying to yourself, 'There is somebody who can tell me how to do it.' And believe me, I can't tell you how to do it, and you'll never get a course from anybody as good as me for the rest of your life."

His course was literature; his course was not writing. He said, "You read everything you can read, and you steal, steal, steal, steal, steal." Believe me, you're not stealing because it has to come through your own horn anyway. It's got to come through you because there's no other place to come out of but you, so it's not stealing. Just take in the stuff that's great, that inspires you, and just do it.

I so firmly believe that. I think there's a great value in criticism and a great value in people evaluating your work and making good comments about your work. However, when it gets to rules, as Syd Field and I came together as extras on a movie I wrote and produced, we sat there and determined, there are no rules. He and I were sitting together as extras in this scene. You know, he makes a great living. God bless him. But there are no rules.

LEW: You think so? I would think the opposite.

RON: I would think there's more craft in novel writing because the way in which you use all the words is significant. I'm the only screenwriter I know who writes in as novelistic a style as I do, who has as much prose, who dwells on looks and glances and internal feelings in the prose of my screenplay because I was told in the beginning that that was really going to irritate the hell out of everybody. It only irritated the hell out of the studio. But director after director and actress after actress said, "I'm so glad that's in there because I get your intent. I get why. I get what I'm supposed to be feeling and thinking when I'm reading that. I mean, I disagree with you completely, but that's okay. I want to know what you thought."

LEW: But that you can teach.

RON: I don't think so.

LEW: I don't mean teach, but I mean, do you believe people can get better with guidance?

RON: I don't want to spend the argument over this, but what I mean is this: There's a lot that you can learn from other people, but you don't learn it by general rules. You learn it by exposing your finished work to someone, hearing their reaction to it, and assessing in your own mind without giving them any authority at all how I feel about that. That's something new. I didn't think of that. Or I thought before that I shouldn't do it that way, but you know, what he's saying, I kind of like the reason. Maybe I don't want to do what he said, but over here, two pages earlier, if I did this, that's going to make this work better. That's kind of the way other people help you.

But I don't think they help you by saying, "My process is a three-act process." I can tell you an awful lot about my process. I can talk to you for hours about my process if you want. But it can have value only in the sense that someone says, "Yeah, I like that. I think I'd like to try that. That sounds interesting to me." But not because this guy makes money doing it, so, therefore, he must know what he's doing.

LEW: Now, you say your act is a three-act process. Does that come from your studying Aristotle early on?

RON: Hell no. It just comes from the rhythm of it. It feels right. I have three sheets of paper. I have one line per scene. I have a headline for every scene. On three sheets of paper: act 1, 2, and 3. And I know my act-outs before I know anything else. And that's how I write. And the reason it's good is that it's good for me. It feels comfortable and right, and of the eighty-six scripts, I think there's one or two that are in four acts. There is maybe one that's in two acts. Doing the math, there are eighty-three that are three acts.

LEW: See, I've always felt that the three acts is a definition. It's just writer's shorthand for beginning, middle, and end. How do you mean two acts versus four acts because certainly in theater, Shakespeare, some of his plays are ten acts long?

RON: What I mean is that is basically, when I say it's three acts, I mean the movie changes significantly twice. It becomes something qualitatively different from the other turns that it's taken all the way through, what your act-out is, what turns it that hard, so that suddenly you're elevated to a completely different level that you're doing something else, and then it happens one more time.

Although, the three acts are not necessarily all of equal length. It is not forty, forty, and forty at all. But as I say, very, very rarely, I have found I couldn't really fit it in three acts. I really needed three sort of equal turns instead of two, or once it was only, there was only really one turn in the story.

LEW: So it's turns. Now, back to the idea: identifying. Identifying the "Aha. Yeah, I want to work on that." Is that a visceral thing, or do you have an idea beforehand?

RON: I don't know if it's visceral, spiritual, paranormal, or whatever the hell it is, but it's something that you can't analyze. That's what got me off the track to talk about teaching. When people say, "Gee, where do you get your ideas? How do you identify your ideas?" Once you ask that question, you're a dead duck because that implies that, oh, you can learn something about how to identify an idea, but you can't. You hear it, and it sounds to you like what it sounds to you. It sounds great. It sounds awful.

And I'm telling you, I'm exclusive to Sony; they're spending a fortune to have me there for three years. I sit down with a guy who's the vice president of the company, who's a really bright guy, who's produced movies for years and years and years. And I pitch him things from my heart that I love, that I think will make $500 million for Sony, and he hates them. It's like, is he right, or is he wrong? I don't know. In the good old days, I got to go down the street and pitch it to somebody else and write it and prove that it'll make $500 million. Now I don't get to do that anymore. Now I just save them up. I harbor my grudges for three years, then release all these scripts that they like, or they don't.

LEW: What's your process in developing the story? Do you do anything beyond those three pages that you have? Or do you think beginning? Do you noodle it out all in your head?

RON: You want to take time to give you my process? I can give you my process, but it takes a few minutes.

LEW: Please. That'll be fine. I want you to do it. That's what we're here for.

RON: The first thing in the process is deciding that you want to write this. Sometimes it's an idea you heard one second ago, and you know the second you heard that idea, you want to do it.

Sometimes it sits with you for years, for a long, long time until it's right. *My Best Friend's Wedding*, for example, is a combination of four different ideas, four separate things I always wanted to do that kind of gained a critical mass when I got to the third one, and I said, "You know, I could—you know, wait a minute, it could be one story where," and so sometimes it happens in that composite way. Once that happens, and this is sort of part of what I said a little bit before, that what's essential to being a writer is continuous writing. What makes you a continuous writer is that you are preparing your next thing while you're writing the thing you're writing. If you don't, you're dead. If you do, you never have a break, you never have a block, and you never have a blank, you're never facing a blank page.

So long before anybody was working for me, when I was only working alone, I would be writing on script X, and I would have realized a while back that I want to write script Y, so I would be working, let's say, a seventeen-hour day, a fourteen-hour day, whatever it was. It's long hours to do this. This is a long-hour job. If you want to do it seriously, like a business, and that you love to write a lot. If you hate writing and you're doing it to make a living, I don't know how you can only write a few scripts a year. Talk to Alvin or somebody else who writes one a year.

But when you want to write as much as you can write, you start with just a lot of walking around. I start with a lot of walking around. A lot of stuff I'm afraid to pick up the pencil because anything that I write down, I'm going to start myself too permanently on a path. So there's just a period of time where I ask myself, "Why do I like this? Well, who is she? Well, what's that about? What's this and what's that?" It just kind of transitions, so that soon I'm writing. Let's say I get up in the morning, and I'm writing on the project I'm going to do next—let's say, is *The System*, when I get out of all these rewrites. So I'm writing a rewrite on *The Children of Angels*, and I get up every morning, and I'm working at four o'clock on that, and then at two in the afternoon, I say, "Okay, I got four hours, and I'm going to spend those working on *The System*," which is the next thing I'm going to write for Will Smith. The first step is, it's just all walking around, feeling confused, feeling very anxious.

The best part of it is, you're feeling anxious. You're scared it's never going to work. You're never going to have enough. Let's forget this thing. It was too thin. There was never enough there. It never made any sense. You see all the contradictions. Ah, it's derivative. I've done this before, or there's nothing profound about this. It's just—ah, forget it. And you just keep doing that, and then you keep thinking of other things, and you just keep thinking, thinking, thinking, thinking.

Then there's the day when you pick up a pencil and you start to write down as fast as you can on these yellow sheets of paper because I don't have a computer. I'll tell you why I think that they're terrible later, but I still write everything I can think of. It's sort of one line a piece, with a hollow circle next to it, is my process. This blank circle, this thought, which could be plot, it could be theme, it could be character, it could be anything. Totally uncensored and totally unordered. Just write 'em down, write 'em down, write 'em down, write 'em down. It's kind of like I'm debriefing myself on everything that I've been walking around, worrying about for the last few days.

Now, after that, I start thinking, with the pencil, with me writing, writing, writing. I get to a stage where this is sort of the black hole. I call it the "critical mass stage" because at some point I just know that I'm tired and antsy and irritated of doing this, and I better start preparing my outline. So what I have to know to prepare my outline is, I have to know how I start. I have to know the last scene of the movie, how it ends. I have to know both of my act-outs, where it turns big. I have to know all my people very, very well. That's 90 percent of it. Also, who they are and why they do what they do and why I care about them. I really don't write about people I don't care about. Even psychotic murderers, I care about them.

I did a film called *Black Widow*, and if you saw that film—it's, well, you probably weren't even born when the film came out. I love the character, though, and we've talked about doing a sequel. Because they all come out of you. You're all of them. You're the perverts. You're the murderers. You're the people that are of opposite gender from your physical gender. You're all those people.

My outlining process is the most important time of the whole script. It usually takes place, like, in one day. It's like one big bang theory. If I have enough stuff, I excitedly have these three sheets of paper. This is all before I had my team. Now it's all changed, and it's all less romantic and much better. But right now, you can't afford to hire anybody. You're doing it on your own, so you're back where I was when I was.

Then I start on act 1, and I make all these blank circles that we talked about before, and there are all these pages of notes, every single note, every thought, has a blank circle next to it. I write the first scene of the act and the last scene of the act, and I work toward the middle. Once I know the first scene, I know what the next thing is going to be and the next thing and the next thing. And when I get kind of tired of that—I kind of, sort of feel like I'm running dry—I start working backwards and up from the end of the act. Well if this happens, what has to happen before that? That's usually the way that it goes, and it used to happen all in one day or two days at the most.

Now that I have a whole team, my God, it takes forever because they've got so many damn ideas, and some of their ideas are so stupid and so wrong. I go through the process of explaining to them, which is a useful time because as I explain to them, I explain to myself, and I understand things much better than I would have if I just accepted my word on faith. So being challenged is very valuable.

Once I have that outline done, then the next part of the process—and this is far and away the most time-consuming process till you actually write—which is what I call blocking. Blocking means—oh, by the way, on the outline, every scene is immediately page-budgeted to the half-page and includes guessing how many notes I can do for that scene. For example, I can do this scene in three and a half pages. I can do this scene in half a page. And man, if you are over four pages for any scene in your estimate, unless it's the last, really big mother of the movie, and it's going to take that seven pages because you're reconciling twelve people in the family in one scene—other than that, just once you're over four or four and half, start scratching your head and make sure that you really need it for that, and maybe you do that for a bunch of reasons.

It will, of course, change as the outline itself will change many, many times in the course of the process. But the reason for page-budgeting is, not only at the end of it do you see, well, if you come out to somewhere around 120 or 130, you're a happy guy. If you come out to eighty-five—it's never happened to me—you don't have enough story. If you come out to 160, which happens to me all the time, you got too much story, and you have to decide what you're going to cut or what you're just going to gut it out, try to write tighter, and try to trim, or whether you want to fundamentally reexamine your story. But what it's really there for is to help you in the blocking. The blocking means you prewrite every scene.

You start off with a sheet of paper that has a 1 on it for scene 1, and now you've had to remember all those notes that you took before with the blank circles. Well, now you have something to put in all the circles because you have a number for every scene in the movie. So, you go back over all your original scenes: "Well, this fits in scene 7. Let's put as a 7. This fits in 3. This fits in 4. This doesn't fit anywhere; forget that. This fits in several scenes." And you have 4, 7, and 12. You want to remember this thought because it plays to the last.

Now, you go and you collect all the ones, and then you start thinking a lot more about everything that could be in scene 1. And the fact that you originally thought that you could do this in two and a half pages tells you that you're not going to do some big, huge opening that's going to take twelve pages to do because you figure that if you're going to bust your budget on this thing by anything substantial, it's going to have to come out of somewhere else. So you have to sort of then reexamine how substantial this scene is, and what are the emotional highs? What are the emotional lows?

When I write with someone who's never done screenwriting before— and I partner about 20 percent of my writing—and Mrs. Amy Tan, who is, of course, one of the best novelists, and we shared *The Joy Luck Club* together, and we began this process. She thought this helped her in her novel writing enormously. The page-budgeting process, I mean, because, I would say to her, "What you write twenty pages for we write two and a half pages for. So, forget about all the fun texture. Forget about all that stuff. What is the guts of this? What's got to happen in this scene? Where does she come from? From here to where to what? What is surprising in this scene? What is what you didn't expect to happen in this scene?"

If there's one black-letter rule that I would risk giving for everybody, it is: Every time you do the thing that people wouldn't have expected you to do, you're going to feel good. Every time you do the thing that everybody exactly expected that you would have, you're going to feel like shit. There's a reason for that because it is satisfying to have your expectation fooled. Now, of course you're going to have to be smart about why a character is doing the opposite thing. Why is there more to this than meets the eye?

You wind up even in a really simple film like *My Best Friend's Wedding*, which sure ain't Shakespeare, and it ain't the most profound thing I ever tried to write, but just the idea that the girl was doing something incredibly selfish. Just the idea that Julia Roberts wouldn't get the guy at the end of the movie—my God! It's talked about like I revolutionized romantic comedy. It's remarkable how people don't realize the satisfaction level of surprise, of setting something up and then doing the opposite, because it just draws you in, as opposed to making you laugh through popcorn because you've seen this before.

So you block every scene, which means you write down everything you can think of that's going be in the scene. My team is much more full now, in that I have people doing it for me. But I get a fax from every one of the people who I have on blocking, and it's grown now to maybe there's maybe there's five or six that send me blocking, but there's a core three or four that are my real people, and there's two that are my really right hands, that I really love, and that I really look to. What they're writing down is everything I've ever said in all these staff meetings we've had, so now I don't lose it anymore. I don't have to remember to write down what I said because it's there.

They dress every set. They're walking into a teenage girl's room, determining, What are all the things you can see there? That stuff is fun to do yourself, but when you want to write nine scripts a year instead of two, you start some time management, and you start to say, "Well, I'm going to have other people doing some of the stuff for me, some of the research, where it might be nice to research William McKinley's first inaugural ball." So Brooke does that for me now, and she sends me a fax that says what's there.

Instead of sitting and staring at a blank page and trying to figure out what this teenage girl's room looks like, I've got several people that wrote versions of it, and I read all those versions, and sometimes I do something completely different from anything anybody said. But on something like dressing the set, I frequently will say, "This is great, this is great, this is great, this is great." Also, when you're blocking is temp-track dialogue. It's lines that come to you, that you think are cool. It's what everybody's feeling in the scene. It's what the changes are that are in the scene. She comes in wanting this, and she goes out because this happened to her instead. What it gives you is two things: One, you're never facing a blank page. You're always facing more material than you could ever fit in. Now, you may hate it all. You may never use any of it.

I frankly go through scenes—and I hope this doesn't find its way into your book or get read by them because they'll be dispirited—but I go through scenes where I never even read the blocking of all these people because I'm just rolling, and I know if I'm rolling, I want to write scene 19 right now, even if Jane's got a better idea than I have. I don't care. I got to get it out. It's coming now. But when you know that it's there, even if it all came from you, as it did from me in my first ten years, you have a huge confidence level that you are selecting and deciding from more interesting, different ways to go than you thought that you could.

The other thing that it teaches you is that every scene has to count for something. Structure is important, but I am heretical in my belief that structure is overemphasized. It's necessary, but it's overemphasized. What really makes a film work is in the scene by scene. You have never seen a film where every scene was just incredibly great that you hated, no matter what garbage it was, if it made no sense, if it wasn't about anything, if there was no theme, no structure, if it wandered. If you loved every moment of it, you loved the film. Conversely, you may have seen many films that made a lot of sense, were really brilliantly structured, put together, and you didn't have any fun. You didn't have any engagement in two-thirds of the scenes, and you hated that movie.

Every scene has to count for something. Every scene has to be terrific. Never accept a dry scene because you want to get from here to there, and I just, well, there's got to be the scene where she comes in and tells him this because I can't think of another road. You better find some way to make it funny or heart-warming or angry or mysterious or surprising or something that's going to have somebody watching it because you cannot afford to lose them once. This is the big difference between what film and fiction is. Fiction is what happens within people, and film is what happens between people. That's the difference in your writing.

When I wrote novels, when I worked with Terry McMillan or Amy Tan or novels, and I try to help them adapt to writing for screen medium, you are reading a book, and you can pick it up, and you can put it down; you can turn it back. What we're writing, guys, is going to go by them twenty-four frames a second. It's just going to blast by them twenty-four frames a second. You do not think of, "They're going to buy the video and stop it and turn it back." Forget it. You're not writing for video. You're not in the directing video days yet. Still writing good, old-fashioned films where you go with your sweetie, and it just runs by you twenty-four frames a second. And it's got to have impact. Once you lose 'em, you've lost 'em.

There's a lot more pressure on a screenwriter than on a novelist. You have to be far more concise. It is a little bit as short story is to novel. It's a little bit that. You have to think about visual, you have to think about what's being seen, and you have to think about the emotional content of what is happening in a whole different way. This is all, so at the end of it, when you start to write, the last thing to say is, the second you realize that you're going to change your outline, you stop writing, and you change your whole outline. If it's in the middle of scene 1, you stop and change it. You don't keep going, figuring you're going to fix it later because, believe me, it comes in so handy to know what's in scene 19 when you're writing scene 1 because you may need it. It may come in real handy, and you don't really know until you get there.

When you think your page budget is wrong and you're running five pages over, stop, and rebudget because it's telling you something. You're not going to be allowed to be young screenwriters if you turn in 145-page scripts, so don't make all your adjustments at the end.

LEW: You talk about your staff. You see, these people really do have a staff because that's one of the necessities of going into the business. Of our eight writers here, six of them will become professional writers.

RON: Which six?

LEW: Well, that's what we're going to find out.

RON: The three that raise their hands first are the ones that are going to make it.

LEW: But they help each other. We all help each other. So basically, as proctor, as facilitator.

RON: It's always going to be that way. When you have a community of friends who are also doing it, it's great.

LEW: Kurosawa. You know that Kurosawa did something similar to what you're doing. He would go out into the countryside, outside of Tokyo, live in a motel room with about six people. And okay, today we're going to do the script of what he tells her when he realizes he doesn't love her anymore. They go off for a full day, write it, and at the end of the day, they give it to him. He either takes it or doesn't.

RON: Sounds like Mike Leigh. Mike Leigh improvs, you know. They improv all the scripts. They improv not on the day but in rehearsal, and he's kind of writing the script to what he's watching them do. An interesting process, but you've got to be a director.

SHELLEY: And the investors have to invest without having a script.

RON: But the good news is, when you make all of your films for $3 million apiece, you can get away with it.

LEW: Let's talk about the script. Now we know you've gone through this process in terms of developing the idea, developing the story, but script. How's your process in script writing?

RON: We always did script before that, but let's say we just now finished *Children of Angels*, and I'm picking up *The System* today. I'm writing scene 1. Certainly on scene 1, I'm going to read all the faxes of my own notes, in your case. I always write when I'm alone. Even with a partner, I only write when I'm alone. I have all my own idiosyncrasies. I can't hear a human voice. A jackhammer doesn't disturb me, but a radio or a human voice will pull me out of it because my process is that I'm just there. I'm just lost in it. I'm just there. I'm nowhere else. And it's just happening. And sometimes it's very joyful, and sometimes it's very painful. But it's very taxing, it takes a lot out of me.

I write with pencil, which I think is very good for me because it's very physical. You're crossing things out, and you're circling things, and you're creating something with your hands. I have two boxes of pencils, one sharpened and one unsharpened. There's hundreds of them.

One of the things about computers—that I promised I would say why you shouldn't write on a computer is, and everyone I've said this to says, "Well, yeah, that's right." You don't say every word you write. Sure, at the end of the day or the end of the hour or whatever, you were ruined at the time of stop. You can say that. But what you don't say is, "She walked in the door with blood in her eye." Ah, fuck, "blood in her eye." "She walked in the door with something else," and five minutes later, "Why did I say that? What did I say? No, I like the first. What I did, what was that?" It's gone. When you take something off your computer, it is gone forever. You are making every decision you make literally is a permanent decision on your word processor. For me, it's a terrible way to write.

Writing by computer, it's slower. I watch Amy, Terry, other people doing it, and I see it happening. It slows them down. They go slower, and they're more thoughtful because they know when they take that sentence out, they don't really have it anymore. Suddenly, it's like a debate already. They're already rewriting themselves because of that limitation. What is the point of that? Everybody says, "I can take my laptop anywhere." Wrong. They really don't take it everywhere because they only have so many batteries, and the batteries run out, and outside, the screen, well, the sunlight, you know, hits the screen. And when you've got a pencil and a notebook, man, that is everything.

LEW: My wife talks about my sitting by my mother's dying bed or my daughter giving birth, with my sitting there working on a script.

RON: Yeah. Well, when my dad was dying of cancer, I would go to his house every day, and I would do all my work at his bedside so we could be together and talk when he was in shape to talk. If I had a laptop, I wouldn't have done that. He would ask what I was writing, and we would talk about what I was writing. It was the most fun, or the most out of himself that he was.

LEW: I went through that thought process with the electric typewriter. When everybody else was getting an electric, it would sit there and hum at me. It would be like, "Come on, Hunter, come on, come on." A computer doesn't even hum; it just sits there. Never mind. Nobody wants to hear that in this room.

RON: The other thing, that I'm really an incredibly insecure writer. I'm a great arguer and a passionate arguer for my thing, but I'm also really insecure that it's no good. I love that insecurity, and I always want that insecurity, and when I look at directors, actors, or writers who I know, and I think their work has gone south, it's almost always because they started to believe what people write about. But the corollary to keeping your self-doubt is you have to struggle to keep your confidence up. So when one of my people reads the pages and calls me the next day and says, "Boy, this was awful because yadadadada." I say, "Man, I don't want to hear from you for the next four weeks. Just forget it." Because you've got to have some level of confidence in what you're writing.

Now, in working with six directors, these guys are all used to getting pages from writers. You understand what pages mean? It means, as you're writing, they don't want to wait until the draft is done. They want pages. I've told everyone of them, and I had a real discussion with Wolfgang Petersen. I said, "You have to find somebody else. I won't take a phone call from you once the draft has started. We can design and design and design for twenty years and meet every day for five hours, and that's great. I don't care. Let's really get every damn thing in this rewrite down and design so you are really thrilled. After that, lose my phone number, man. I will not take a call. I will not hear somebody give me a bright idea today that rips out a scene that I spent my heart's blood on last Thursday because then I can't do anything. Then I'm just waiting. I'm looking at the phone and waiting for you to call and rip out what I know I can make work." So when my job starts—forgive me for ever calling movies art, but that's my little piece of art. That's my thing that I'm doing. That belongs to me. I've got my march in order, see you when it's done, and then we'll do another one. Then we'll hark on my mistakes next time.

Keeping your confidence up is very, very important, and it's only important when you have the balance in understanding that you really don't deserve to have any confidence because no matter how many pictures that were successful—and boy as I have, when you write nine things a year, I turn in stuff that they hate. I just turned in two things to Sony within four days of each other, and one they loved and put the director on it, and one they just hated. But the one they hated is ten times better than the one they loved. It's a $500 million movie. It's a huge, huge special effects, fabulous movie. Everyone on my team happens to love it. My agent happens to love it. We're going to try to get it back and maybe sell it someplace else. But five consecutive people in that studio hated it.

There is no accounting for the subjectivity and reaction of material. There's no way around the fact that it is essential that it destroys you when anybody doesn't like your stuff. If you can laugh off anybody not liking your stuff, you're not a writer. Forget it. Really. If it doesn't come out of a place that means that much to you, that anybody's disapproval hurts, for example, if you had a baby, and the biggest jerk on the street said, "Your baby is really ugly, man. That is the ugliest baby I've ever seen," and it didn't hurt you, I wouldn't believe it. So you have to be in that rocky, emotional place, where you don't know if what you're doing is any good, and your passion is just there, and it's this high, emotional state. One of the things that's hard about rewrites is not only that your rewriting is somebody else's design. But by the time you're down to rewriting, and you've worked with them enough so that it's really okay, and you shove them out and make it okay, you can't quite get the same flow and the same passion and the same thing going on a rewrite because when it first comes out of you—man, it is the most fun, it is the most beautiful thing, and my fantasy is not doing what I'm doing now. My fantasy is going to Maui and just having a condo on the beach, and writing ten, twelve originals a year and sending them off to CAA. I don't even want to know which ones sold. Here's the bank account. Put something in the bank. If ever get within a $100,000 of going dry, let me know. I'll get a job. That would be heaven. That would be absolute heaven.

LEW: Willa Cather said, "The journey is all. The end is nothing." Do you get off on the writing even more than the actual movie itself?

RON: Yes, it's so obvious that it's hardly even profound. But it's the most important thing that you can realize is that, like the rest of life, it's only about the journey. There is no destination. If you don't enjoy the process of writing, then there are only two people that are in these classes: people who want to write and people who want to be a writer. The first people have a chance of succeeding, and the second people have no chance of succeeding. So you want to be a writer. That's what it's about, that, like, it's cool to do what writers do. You can never withstand how horrible it is to be a writer. The only real compensation for it is it's so great to write. That's the only real compensation.

LEW: You were talking about people telling you, people trying to break away your self-confidence?

RON: Well, they're trying to help me, too.

LEW: Well, they're trying to help you, but then are they? I go home to Pamela, my beautiful wife, and I say, "But Pamela, I gave them everything they wanted!" Now how do you deal with that one?

RON: No, I really learned that you don't pitch outlines to people because even though they sign off on it, that's just the guy that's going to hate the draft when it comes in. He's got this thing in the back of his mind, like, oh, he's going to tell me now that I'm supposed to like it because I heard it all before. But I didn't see it on the page, and this guy can't write. There's no percentage, unless there's a very specific reason, in telling anybody too much about what you're going to write before you do it. But that's a tough one.

LEW: Well, actually, I'm pretty tough in rewrites, so I go back, and I rewrite it, and I've heard it said, "Don't give them what they want. Give them what they think they want."

RON: No, you have to give them what works. When you find out that what they wanted didn't work, even though you thought it was going to work when you agreed to do it, then do something else. Because nobody takes the heat for something that doesn't work except for you. You never get any brownie points for, "Well, I knew this was going to suck. You told me to do it, so here it is. Right? See how right I was and how wrong you were? Let's go back to the old ending, right?" Forget it.

LEW: Tying off: You're in the script. Do you have a goal for yourself if you're rolling?

RON: I do an actual, a little homemade, handwritten—because I don't have a computer—or writing schedule with all the weeks of a six-month period and every day. When I start, I put down the number of pages that I want to achieve per day.

LEW: What is the consistent page count? Does it depend upon each sheet? Must be close to ten pages at least.

RON: Oh no, because there's never a day when I can spend more than a fraction of it writing. I have sixty phone calls to return a day, and I'll have two or three or four meetings a day.

LEW: Don't you get most of your primary writing in in the morning, from three to ten or something like that?

RON: Well, from 4:30 to 6:15 a.m., till my kid is up, and I have to help her put her homework together. But yeah, if I can write at least five hours in a day, that's incredible. I usually say to myself, "If I could average four pages a day, and a day for me is seven days a week, well, that's twenty-eight pages a week." That's a full script in four weeks. That ain't bad. That's a guy who could write twelve in a year. So when I'm writing, I will usually try and do eight to ten pages a day. Like, especially weekends, when it's more free, I can get ten.

LEW: Are you angry at all the meetings and phone calls and so forth that get you away from that process?

RON: Absolutely.

LEW: Yet you want to be a producer because of the producing and collaboration aspect?

RON: It's a tradeoff. Everything is a tradeoff. Right now, what I'm going through is how many stories can I touch in a year. The reason I'm exclusive to Sony is that once we work through the backlog of everything for all these other different studios, then we will be able to have me rewriting lots of other films of theirs, supervising other writers, producing things that I don't write, partnering with people, and we kind of want to see if I can make a contribution on a really large number of films. That's something I'm going to try for three years, and John wants to try it. We'll see. I'm probably going to write like three of my own instead of eight of my own.

LEW: It really sounds like you're designing a life for yourself not unlike Spielberg. Steven wants to kind of juggle but on the directing thing, but you want to do the writing sense of it. Juggling lots of, you know, schedules.

RON: Steven and I talk a lot about how we structure our lives, and he pretends to admire mine, and I genuinely admire his. But the key difference is, Steven can structure his life where he can make all his own decisions. As a screenwriter, the only way this works is that John will make all these decisions.

LEW: One of our students, Brad Silberling, directed *Casper, the Ghost.* He said they showed it to—

RON: Brad was one of the three or four guys who almost directed *My Best Friend's Wedding.*

LEW: Oh, is that right?

RON: He's a lovely guy.

LEW: But he's one of those six out of eight people that have done well. He said that they showed *Casper* the week before it opened to Universal.

RON: How is that possible?

LEW: They must not have even seen the acer print to make that happen. That's what he said. but you know, writers lie, right?

RON: Wait, are you saying that Amblin distributed themselves?

LEW: No, Amblin worked through Universal on *Casper*, and he said nothing.

RON: Must be just a predistribution.

LEW: Must have been a distribution deal. Questions? Anybody got any questions?

STUDENT: Because you worked as a lawyer first, are you at the point where you're saying you can tell someone, "I'm not going to give you the outline. This is how I operate." I mean, is that the advice you mean to give to us but not on our first script to the studio? Or can we? Should we as writers have more say?

RON: That's a great question, but there's no real answer. It's all contextual. What I'm telling you is, do what's best for your own process. Have I compromised my own process because I really wanted that job? Absolutely. It just depends on what it is, and I've definitely pitched outlines, and I'm sure I will again. There are reasons and times and places where it makes sense to do it.

LEW: Another question, please?

STUDENT: Do you find it useful to have table readings with actors as you're writing the first draft to see if the dialogue is coming across in a roundtable kind of a thing, where you're critiquing as you go?

RON: No. I now just barely have the guts to let the people who work for me call me and say the dialogue sucked in this line. It so hurts me when I hear it that I'm very, very careful about how they call their shots. While I'm writing—that's two totally different times of life—while you're writing is when you have to get your confidence up. Once it's over, forget it. Then you put on the thick skin, and you let everybody kick the hell out of it because you want to hear what they have to say and evaluate it. But it's not destroying the next scene you're going to write because my God, I can't write anymore, and this is already horrible, so what am I going to do over here? So similarly, with table readings.

I'll tell you something else about table readings, just another little anecdote. *Black Widow* is, like, my second script ever. I'm just out of the law practice. I'm nobody. Debra Winger, who had been my client, so I knew her, but I was a little lawyer, so I just knew her, like, the little lawyer knows the big star. She was then a huge star, 1986, does anybody even know who Debra Winger is anymore? Nineteen eighty-six, she was, she was God. She was one of the top two or three actresses alive. She came in an hour and fifteen minutes late for the first rehearsal and sat down, and she's eating an apple while she's reading the lines. She looks up to her girlfriend, Theresa Russell, who she had cast, who she had insisted on, her costar. She wouldn't accept anybody else but her girlfriend to be the costar. Winks at her girlfriend and starts to do this ridicule reading of my lines. Just this ridicule reading of my lines. It goes on for a whole scene.

Everyone's kind of looking at me. This is a true story, and I could have gotten fired off this job real simple by doing this because she's a real pistol, and she's fired people. I've been fired by actresses, more than one. The director, Rafelson, said to me, "Well Ron, what do you think?" I said, "I think Deb and I should switch seats." I said, "Apparently she can write the script better than I can, and I know I can read the lines better than she can." Rafelson said, "Well go ahead and do it." And I did. I read her part. Read her part for about fifteen pages. When I was done reading, I looked up to Theresa Russell. I said, "Who read it better?" She said, "You killed it." I looked at Debra, and Debra said, "Okay, maybe it is better like that."

There's a phone call the next morning, and she just decided to move on. She decided she wants another voice. She just, you know, won't really be for much, just wants to dial-in a couple of scenes. And, man, next time you turn around, every word, every dialogue is run on. Film's on the screen with your name on it, and you hate every word of it. So it's a very risky game to be a big shot and shoot your mouth off. I've done it right, and I've done it wrong.

LEW: Another question?

STUDENT: I'm interested if you've ever written a script where you haven't done enough research. The corollary of that is, Can you do too much research before you start writing a script?

RON: Yeah, of course, a script when you haven't done enough research, I mean, you can always stop and do the research you realized you haven't done. So have I ever decided, "Yeah, I don't care. I don't care that I find I haven't done enough"? No, I've never done that before. Now that I have people working for me, that's one of the fundamental things that they do. It's not about doing too much research. It's about falling into the trap off feeling that research replaces thinking and decision making and judgment and choices. You can't think that this lovely, fascinating thing that you've learned is going to be fascinating to anybody else. All it's there for is to adorn your drama, but it's the drama that you're doing that's what it's about. Some people get lost in the research because it's easier to do than writing.

LEW: For me, one time, it was procrastinating. I suddenly realized, "What a minute. I got to do the script." I'm telling people who've lived through this Japanese-American division before, during, and after, who've lived through this terrible experience. I'm telling them what happened to their entire world. I got to write the script. Stop. Stop with the research.

STUDENT: Can you talk a little bit about your character development because they always seem to be idiosyncratic and vulnerable, just full of surprise?

RON: That's the people I like. I really don't write people to the best of my ability who I don't like and who aren't interesting. That's why I basically write for a female lead every chance I get because I find women much more likable and interesting, as a generalization, than men. It goes back to this thing Lew was saying about the journey versus the end.

Men as a generalization, and this great line in the Brooks movie about, "How do you write women?" "I write a man, take away reason and accountability." It's a Jim Brooks line from *As Good as It Gets*. A huge number of the men that I know, of all ages and across the board and all levels of success, a gigantic number are result-oriented people, which means they don't really want to have a communication with their inner life if it's going to fuck 'em up. They don't really want to feel scared or insecure or anything that can get in the way of getting the job, getting the girl, getting the account, getting the A, getting the whatever it is that they want to get. They want to get where they want to go.

Women, as an overwhelming generalization, in my experience, are the opposite. They are process-oriented people and not result-oriented people. They want to know what they feel even when it hurts them, even when it screws them up, even when it keeps them from getting where they want to go. It's that knowledge that makes a character interesting to anybody who is in their inner life.

What has made me able to write successful movies that executives thought were chick flicks when I started and were, like, amazed that men go to the movies and really, actually enjoyed them once the woman in their life brings them to that movie because they enjoy having their inner life reached; they're just kind of afraid to do it. So, all the characters, remember, come out of you. You're always looking for, "Why do I care about this person? Why is this person interesting? Why is this scene interesting? Why is this line of dialogue interesting? My God, of course, she can't say that. That's what she said in every movie that anybody ever wrote. She's got to be the opposite. Why is it the opposite? What's really going on here? What am I actually feeling?" This dialogue all happens within you, and you sort of are all those people, and you're having this argument with yourself. You see, in *When a Man Loves a Woman*, there's that scene, the big argument, the big break-up argument, that's this nine-page scene. I turned this in to a studio that says, "Who's going to want to come see a movie about alcoholics? And Meg Ryan will never do that." And I said, "You can't take a word out of this argument. This is a nine-page argument. Unfortunately, it's all of a piece. It all came out of me at once, and everything leads to everything else, and nothing would make any sense if you pulled any part of it out." We tried in rehearsal to pull parts of it out. Both of the actors insisted that it all stay in, and it actually got to the screen. Nobody objected to it in previews. We should talk about the previewing process.

LEW: Okay.

RON: The previewing process is really a wonderful, important process. The previewing process is when you hear writers say, "God, it's terrible letting some bunch of jerks tell you what your film ought to be." Yeah, because they really know. They really, really, really know. What's astounding is, you preview the film in the mall out here in Fallbrook, and then you fly to Kansas City, and you go to Scottsdale, and you fly to Portland. Boy, the cards are the same. Cards are always the same. Quadrants are always the same, too. Above and below twenty-five, eighteen quadrants. The focus groups sound alike.

There is actually—and you've actually created a thing, not a thing that is different to different people—there is a thing that you've created, and the people will tell you what you've created. Listen to them because they're telling you what's not working. We got up at the end of *My Best Friend's Wedding*. We didn't have to see the cards were seventy-two. We got up. The director wanted to kill himself. He was just, like, devastated. We were watching it play before there was a focus, and we knew that it didn't work. We walked out of the hall, and Calley was there. I said, "It's no sweat. We bring George in at the end. It's all the stuff that I wanted to do in the beginning. It's this thing that Jerry said to do over there. We're going to need five, six, seven scenes." Calley said, "Meeting tomorrow. Two o'clock. Tell 'em what you want to do." Jerry and P. J. and I have lunch. I say, "Here are the six scenes I cooked up this morning. Six scenes." They hear them all. They love them all. We go in, and we pitch them. What a great—this is why I work at the studio—what a great studio. It's a fortune to spend. I pitched all six scenes.

Lucy Fisher says, "We're doing it. They're great. We're doing every one of them. Call Julia. Get her onboard. Call Rupert. Get him onboard. We're going to do this." They did it. They never cheaped out. They never said, "Can we get away with four of them?" In the next preview, the cards are, like, eighty-eight, and the film made a lot of money. It was the audience that told us what worked and what didn't. It's such a useful tool.

Shelley: Can you say what the original ending was?

Ron: The ending that you saw in the film was the ending I always wanted. The heads that prevailed felt they did not want Julia in the arms of her homosexual best friend because that will make people feel that Julia is down and depressed and has not recovered from her devastating blow. We need to see her in the arms of a handsome, young man. "Not that we're going imply, Ron, that that's going to be her boyfriend. Of course not. But just because she can smile and laugh in the arms of a handsome, young man, we know she will find true love one day."

We had this huge fight about it because I said, "You know she's going to find her true love one day because she's Julia Roberts! I mean, look at her! For Christ's sake! No one's going to walk out of there thinking that she's going to go join a nunnery! Plus, she learned the lesson that she learned. Believe me, she's going to be taking applications." But she's not going to be happy dancing with some stranger. This is about my best friend's wedding. She has a new best friend. It's the guy she cares about. She's going to be happy being in his arms at the end of the movie because it doesn't matter if you're going to have sex tonight. There's an intimacy, and there's a relationship, and there is something there that really will warm her because that's someone she feels great to be with. There's more to life than the chase for the perfect mate. Isn't that an important thing to say? Isn't that what this movie is about? Guys? Folks? Everybody? I lost. In the end, when you win, sometimes you lose, and later on, you win. In the end, everybody said to them they were wrong.

By the way, just to balance it off, there was something that I was incredibly wrong about. The most popular scene in the movie I resisted like crazy. The crab-house sing-along? I said to P. J., "You know, *Muriel's Wedding*? It was an ABBA fest. Great, everybody likes to sing. But you know, we're stopping the dramatic movie in the middle of the movie to do eight minutes of singing, also my favorite song." I said, "At the end of that scene—which they will all have loved—they will all mark on their cards it's their favorite scene in the movie. I understand. It's a crowd pleaser. At the end of it, they will be derailed, and they will not get back into the third act, and you will lose them."

Well he was right, and I was wrong. But, well, maybe not for you, but I'm saying I sat in the theater in the first preview, and I'm waiting, and I'm waiting and waiting. That's the only thing I'm really waiting for. I knew they were wrong about the end of the movie, so I'm waiting, and I'm watching the audience loving it. The second they were right into the next scene, and they were right there with us. They were right there. They were laughing, they were interested. I said, "Son of a gun, the guy is dead right." He gave the film its big, signature scene, and for the focus, I mean, there's always going to be exceptions, but a huge number of people didn't get derailed by it.

LEW: Two more questions.

STUDENT: When you were thirty-five and you got back to writing that novel, what made you decide to turn to writing again? Do you still write fiction at all?

RON: Well, for me, writing screenplay is writing fiction. It's got its own form, but it's like saying, "Now that you're writing haiku, are you still writing poetry?" It's fiction. I don't write prose fiction anymore because I haven't got the time because I'm committed for three years down the road, and I'm writing nine things. Everybody says, "Well, when you retire, are you going to go back and write a novel again?" Yeah, I will. I do miss it because it's different, but I also love what I do.

I envy the life of a novelist. When Terry can, you know, get an $11 million check in advance for one book, and she can knock it out in a little bit, and then she can take the rest of the year, you know, traveling. Hey, that's a nice life. But the reason that I went back to writing was that I was getting divorced from my first client. Twenty years ago, I was getting divorced, and I was so lonely, and so I didn't want that divorce, and I was so unhappy, and I was so miserable. There wasn't anything I had in my life that could make me feel good. The only thing I had ever really wanted to do was write, and I said, "You know something. Write this damn thing. You'll never tell anybody. You'll never show anybody. Just write it because you will feel good writing it." It made a huge difference. Before I was done, I was with the woman who I am now married to for twenty years, and she was really supportive about it. That's why I turned back, to make myself happy.

LEW: Boy, you are a lucky man. To have a woman right there, something like getting up at three o'clock in the morning.

RON: She gets up at four.

LEW: [*laughing*] Pamela does not get up at four o'clock.

STUDENT: I'm just curious, if you have a project go into turnaround?

RON: About five a year.

STUDENT: I'm assuming so. What do you do at that point if your passion for the piece and your possible insecurity because it's gone into turnaround has made you want to make changes at that point?

RON: I have never voluntarily made changes in something that was in turnaround before I turned it out because if I didn't think it was done, I wouldn't have turned it in. So you can see the movie and what I write. You don't know which changes to make because you're making them for some brand-new person who you don't know who he is yet. So they'll tell you what they want you to change. They don't expect it to be a shooting script when they get it. I've sold lots of things in turnaround. *What Dreams May Come* is a movie that's just now finishing—Robin Williams's movie—which is, I think, my favorite thing I ever did. I think the best movie I was ever involved in. It was a turnaround project.

Turnaround happens a lot because when they develop it, you never met their expectation. They had a platonic script in their mind that they thought they were going to see, and it was always the best script they'd ever read, and yours isn't. You're up against that, and you turn it around. They're just ruining what you give them. You say, "Hey, I can steal this. Hey, I'd buy this. Let's make this movie."

LEW: My publisher says that when people get these books, when people go to these classes, go to the seminars, go to the workshops—oh, Richard Walter, by the way, my fellow chair, says hello.

RON: He's my buddy.

LEW: He said that they pick these up because they're expecting to find the secrets. Do you feel there are any secrets in screenwriting?

RON: There are all kinds of secrets, but they are the secrets that we each have for ourselves. I have all kinds of things that are really, like, embarrassing and weird and psycho that I use to motivate myself or chill myself out. It's all about babying yourself. It's all about being good to yourself and getting the most out of yourself and knowing when to kick your own butt and knowing when to try to love yourself and knowing when to shut everything out. It's all about getting the most out of you. There is no such thing called screenwriting. There is you screenwriting. It's only in the context of you and who you are. You can't write like somebody else. You can't be somebody else. You can't adopt somebody else's process.

LEW: Each writer's uniqueness is probably the most valuable thing that they have as a writer.

RON: It is not only the most valuable thing. It is the only context in which they can work and see themselves. The big danger of reading books and taking courses and even hearing advice is to honor someone else who may have greater talent, may have greater experience, may have, you know, a greater command of principles of fiction or drama or writing or filmmaking, but they still aren't you. It's still got to somehow come through in a way that you can use it and you can feel comfortable with.

LEW: Finally, you used the words *screenwriting* and *art* earlier in the same sentence. Expand on that just a little bit as a go-out.

RON: Screenwriting is an art. Any writing is an art. You are creating something that didn't exist before you created it. Even in the most literal, lame, hack screenwriting, unless you're assuming, and I'm not talking about writing for documentary; I'm talking about writing fiction. Once you're writing fiction, you are writing a metaphor. You are trying to illuminate something that is real by writing something that is unreal, and its unreality illuminates reality. That is art. We can make lousy art. We can be bad at it. I don't mean that because we are artists, that this means we are something lofty and great and talented and wonderful. But every day that we're writing is creating art. Who would ever think that it wasn't? Who would ever think that it doesn't rise to the level of novels or poems or paintings or sculptures or symphonic music?

LEW: I was asked to run for the board of directors a couple of years ago, and I used some variation of what you just said. I said, "When screenwriters stop whining about how they've been fucked over by people in the studios, we'll get closer to being regarded as artists." But I was drawing a blank look from their faces.

RON: People are going to regard you the way they're going to regard you. You can't do too much about that.

LEW: Last question.

STUDENT: I just want to ask, do you feel the artistry of it when you first began to sit down and write a screenplay, or did it take you a while to sort of find that?

RON: No, the rush of creating something that wasn't there and making something that didn't exist before. I remember when I was six years old, writing the little stories, but it was certainly there when I was nineteen.

STUDENT: I know, but when you came from novel into screenwriting, did you feel that?

RON: It was exactly the same rush. I didn't think I was very snobbish, and I really thought, you know, "Now I'm selling out, and I'm doing this commercial thing because I need the money," because I really did need the money. It was exactly the same process, if you do it with the same level of care and observation. It's easy to do screenwriting badly because you don't have to have all that descriptive prose. But if you do it with the same love and the same attention to detail and the same level of observation and level of thinking, there's no reason that it's anything other than it's just, like, you know, a great sea bass versus a great rack of lamb or something. I mean, it's something that's different, but how can anybody say that it's lesser? If they really have done both, I don't think anybody does.

LEW: Thank you very much, Ron Bass. You are the most introspective screenwriter I have ever met, and so right. Thank you for your voice, all of your voices, tonight and on the screen.

19

Alan Ball

I've always noticed that television writers are trying to get into feature, and feature screenwriters are trying to find a way into television. Alan Ball is wonderful in that he is very good at doing both; however, he acknowledges that television can be wonderful or it can be too constricting. Thankfully, he had an experience where he felt too constricted in television, and from that came what will remain a classic picture of the twentieth century: *American Beauty*. *American* Beauty is special because it garnered mainstream attention without being a mainstream movie. Mr. Ball didn't expect to be able to sell it, and he was more surprised when Spielberg showed such an interest that he recommended the script not be optioned but instead be sold outright.

During the interview that you're about to read, Ball was just beginning on *Six Feet Under*, which we now know was a critical and commercial success. *American Beauty* perhaps enabled him to do exactly what he had always been itching to do as a writer, and in so doing, he's become one of the most successful screenwriters in the industry. Yes, he is nice, and he is smart, but he is also very thoughtful and funny. He has a lot of experience to share with us in the coming conversation, and it's just so delightful to have him as part of this work.

LEW: The thing that everyone has responded to is how we don't want to talk about how you became rich and famous. We want to talk about how you do it, the process. As Bill Goldman says, "The horror of it all is we all do it so differently." To take your fabulous success with *American*

Beauty, a midlife crisis is not the newest story in captivity, but the clothes you put on them were fresh and wonderful, and everybody here is excited to have you here.

ALAN: Thank you. I'm excited to be here.

LEW: I have about four questions that have been kind of the general tone of everybody we've talked to. But you are also working on *Six Feet Under*.

ALAN: Mm-hmm.

LEW: Good, good. Great title. I was an executive on *Till Death Do Us Part*. It became *All in the Family*. We hated the title. I spent about seventeen years as one of them, as a program executive for ABC and CBS and NBC. I was cool. [*laughter*] Imagine being sent into a room to give notes to Neil Simon or Paddy Chayefsky: [*voice cracking*] "Mr. Chayefsky." The good thing that came out of those notes is he said, "Lew. It is Lew?" I replied, "Yes. Lew. It's Lew." I said, [*voice cracking*] "Geez, I just think you're terrific, and I just feel like such a piece of shit." He said, "Listen, just tell me what you got to tell me, and let me take it from there." He took it from there, and it became *Network*. He got so enraged at the people upstairs.

ALAN: Oh, that's great.

LEW: So I have a little bit of pride in being at least the beginning of it.
    Let's talk about storytelling. How do you see storytelling? Is it closer to the oral tradition of storytelling?

ALAN: I started out as a playwright, which is a very word-focused medium. I certainly was a big fan of movies ever since I was a kid. I can very clearly remember the first movie I went to see and what kind of magical experience it was. It was a movie called *My Six Loves*, and it starred Debbie Reynolds as this famous actress who discovered six adorable homeless orphans living on her estate in New York. She very quickly realized that she didn't really want a career. She really just wanted to be a mother. I've seen it, and it's just dreadful. [*laughter*] Yet, it was my first experience at looking at something on the big screen.

LEW: How old were you?

ALAN: I think I was five. Screenwriting is very different from playwriting in that you want to tell the story as visually as possible. Although

I do think, as human beings, we communicate with each other mostly through spoken word, so, I mean, I'm not one of those people who just picks up a script and goes, "Oh, that's too much dialogue." I think, that's completely arbitrary. You don't know that. I've been very leery of blanket rules, like, when they say, "Never use voice-over."

LEW: Some of those Chayefsky speeches in *Network* are like six or ten inches of script.

ALAN: Right. That being said, I think film is such a visual medium, and if you can tell the story visually, that's what I like about it. That's something you can't do when you're writing a play.

LEW: I'm thinking that there was a saying that became cliché: "Radio is theater of the mind, and television is theater of the mindless." [*laughter*] You, of course, have not experienced that in your forays into television.

ALAN: Yes, I certainly have. I spent many years in the trenches of network sitcoms, and on the one hand, I really am thankful for that because I learned a lot about structure. I studied acting when I was in college. I'd never taken a writing class in my life, so it taught me a lot about the nuts and bolts of screenwriting and making sure that each scene has a purpose that takes you to the next level, or else you can cut it. Doing 125 episodes of TV back to back, I had bootcamps in terms of teaching me how to tell a story.

You know, I had eighteen months left on my TV deal after *American Beauty*, and I thought, "If I have to do another network sitcom, I'm going to kill myself." So I'm doing this thing for HBO now, which is really fun because you don't get the same notes you get at the network. And you don't have broadcast television standards to deal with, you don't have arbitrarily imposed commercial breaks to try to hit a false cliffhanger four times in an episode, that kind of stuff, so it's really fun.

LEW: Most of the screenwriters in this book have not had the experience in television that you've had. Only three in terms of professional playwriting: Horton Foote, Ted Tally, and Alfred Uhry. They kind of go back and forth between the two areas. Obviously, you have tremendous value both in terms of playwriting and screenwriting. But television—some of these folks here scorn television, and others can hardly wait to get into it. I'm telling them that it's almost like when you were a teenager—er, teenage boy: "Just let me put the crown in, you know."

Do you sort of feel that way that enough of it but not too much? How was your response to that?

ALAN: I feel like it was really valuable for me. It taught me a lot in terms of just tools. It taught me a lot about what I hate. Because I was a playwright in New York, I'd written a play, and I'd gotten this offer to come to Los Angeles and write for television. I didn't even watch TV at the time because I worked with this theater company. I'd go from my day job to rehearsal. I'd come home. I never watched television. I did watch *The Sopranos* and *South Park*. Those are really the shows that I go out of my way to watch, and I don't really care about anything else. I just got satellite, and there's every movie that I haven't seen in the last four years, so it's like, "Yeah. I'll watch that." Plus, I guess I'm becoming an old fart because I'm really fascinated by Animal Planet and the Discovery Channel. [*laughter*]

LEW: But if I see another incredibly pretty, anorexic woman trading insults with a buff guy on a set that's too bright with a canned laugh track, I'll just kill myself. [*laughter*]

ALAN: I did a show last fall that tried to do that.

STUDENT: Can I just ask, as you're talking with us, what shows you've worked on, so we can have a point of reference?

ALAN: My first job was on *Grace under Fire*, the second season.

LEW: Was Kathy Stumpe there?

ALAN: Yes.

LEW: Kathy's one of ours, from this program.

ALAN: Oh, fabulous. I love Kathy. She's on *Everybody Loves Raymond* now. That was kind of like the best first job I could ever have in TV because nothing could ever be that bad. [*laughter*] It was really an eye-opening experience because I came out of the theater, where the writer has a certain amount of power and a certain level of cash, but you can't make a living. They can't change the script without your permission. It was a madhouse. It was the most amazing experience, and just watching the kind of self-indulgent, self-destructive, creatively destructive behavior not only be tolerated but also sort of be enabled. I was really angry. But I was making money for the first time in my life.

Then I spent three years on *Cybill,* which was equally upsetting. But at the same time, it gave me a financial stability that I never even thought I would ever have. It taught me a lot about basic storytelling. Then I took a year off when we were shooting *American Beauty,* and then I wrote a pilot episode for NBC called *Oh, Grow Up.* And I did thirteen episodes of that. It died a slow and painful death.

LEW: Those are the magic moments in television, those of you that get into it. [*knocks on table*] "Susan?" You remember knocking on dressing room and trailer doors? [*knocks again*] "Susan? Can we talk to you for a moment?" Mmmm. Talk about being an old fart. I was thinking as I was driving over tonight that most of these people that are in our graduate program are in the average age of thirty or thirty-five. They're going to have to join the ageism committee lawsuit immediately for the Writers Guild, aren't they?

ALAN: Yeah, but I think network TV is dying, and I kind of think it deserves to. I think certainly within the next five or ten years, we're going to see a big change in programming. My main beef with network television is, I think when television first became a popular entertainment medium, sponsorship and advertising supported the programming, and I think that has totally changed now. I think programming is serving the marketing. First and foremost, it's a marketing medium. I think that really permeates the whole market. Even if you just look at network television, the most interesting, the most well-shot, the highest production values, the most kinetic, the most visceral imagery is always in the commercials.

The programming itself because the networks are scrambling and they're losing viewers at such an alarming rate and the infrastructures of the networks are so bloated and are at cross purposes and there's so many conflicts of interest going on with the networks all owning programs and that type of stuff—I just think that they don't have the courage of their convictions, and that's why everything you see is so incredibly formulaic and to the formulas that have been successful in the past. This is why I'm very excited to be working with HBO, where I actually am realizing that while I learned a lot writing for television, just in that it made me much more disciplined as a writer. You've just got to do it until it's done.

I also became very adept at anticipating network notes. In my opinion, all of the network notes that I've gotten with television can be

condensed into two sentences: Articulate the subtext, and make everybody nicer. Those are enemies of good writing. If you make everybody
nicer, you drain the conflict out of it, and drama is conflict. If you
articulate the subtext, then it's all there on the surface.

LEW: Exposition, too.

ALAN: Yeah. If you can't have the subtext, then you can't give the actors
something besides the actual lines that they're saying. It's just superficial.

LEW: I've never figured it out. When I was doing a movie for NBC and
I ran into Steven Bochco on the lot, and he said, "Fuck 'em. Tell 'em to
go fuck themselves." I said, "Great. That's great." He had Grant Tinker
behind him at the time. But it never got to the point where, you know
how in old times editors used to, well, with the old time Moviolas, when
they had a bad cut, the editor used to jiggle or readjust the frame a little
bit so you wouldn't notice it.

ALAN: Right.

LEW: There used to be tricks back in the old radio days when Bob Hope
would put in jokes that he knew he wasn't going to get away with so he
could keep the ones he wanted. Ergo, two lines on the air because of that
technique: One was Bob saying to Lana, "Meet me at the pawn shop,
and you can kiss me under the balls." The other one was, "If women's
dresses get any shorter, they'll have two more lips to paint and another
head of hair to comb."

ALAN: Wow. [*laughter*]

LEW: I wasn't able to do that when I was doing series television. They
picked up on it. They have so many bureaucrats involved. At any rate,
how many feature-length screenplays had you written before *American
Beauty*?

ALAN: Three. I had written one just to teach myself how to write within
the medium that I never let anyone read. I had done an adaptation of
the play that I wrote that got me the television job. At the same time,
it was optioned by Columbia Pictures, and they flew me out first class,
and I sat next to Richard Gere, and I stayed in the Westwood Marquis,
and I thought I was so fancy. I went to a story and development meeting
at Columbia and sat in a room with four people who all talked at once
and basically just threw random ideas at me, and I took them all down

and put them all in the script because at that point, I just assumed that's what you did. That was your job: to take down all their notes and just put them in.

It's a terrible screenplay. The play itself is about these bridesmaids at this wedding in Memphis, and they all hate the bride. They hang out in a room and smoke pot and talk to each other. You can get away with that in a play because the actors are actually in the same room with the audience. There's like a whole energy connection that's going on.

STUDENT: The audience can smell the pot.

ALAN: Yes. Exactly. But that's a dull movie. Everybody in the same location and talking for a long time. Although it takes place in the South, it's got a whole New York sensibility. It's very ironic and postmodern. They wanted there to be flashbacks, too, when they were little girls and the moment when they all banded together against a common foe, and we're cheering for them at the end. You know, exactly the kind of movie I hate. [*laughter*] Yet exactly the kind of the movie that many times, if all the elements come together right, are huge hits. So I tried to write that, and I'm just not that kind of writer.

I also did a rewrite of a high-concept romantic comedy for WB about two divorced lawyers who used to be married. And now they are representing a high-profile couple getting divorced, a rock star and a model, and in the process fall back in love. They represent the opposite sides. I did, like, three drafts of it, and they were really happy with it. Then someone decided that lawyer movies weren't making money. You know what? I read that script now, and it's not very good either. What I did in both of those scripts: I was trying to give someone what I thought they wanted because that's what I did all those years of TV.

That's the big mistake I made with my television series. The last years was I was trying to do my version of mainstream network situation comedy. My biggest success has always been when I write what I would like to go see. Granted, my tastes are not particularly mainstream, which nobody was more surprised than I was that *American Beauty* did seem to appeal to as many people as it did. First of all, I never thought it would get made, and second of all, once it got made, I thought this will be a weird, little, arthouse movie. If I've learned anything, it's been that I'm best writing about things I really care about. Anger fuels my best work a lot. Anger with mediocrity.

This whole thing for HBO I wrote when I was furious because I'd just spent six months of my life working around the clock, trying to give them what they wanted, and once they got what they wanted, they decided they didn't want it, and they canceled my show, and I was really pissed off and upset because by that time I had gotten attached to it, which a lot of people say you shouldn't do, but I can't not do that. So I'm not saying that that's the only thing that you should do because there are a lot of people who are purely crafts people and who can look at what people want and give it to them, and that's very successful, and it's really good work. For me, I have decided and I'm lucky enough to be at a point in my career, and I don't know how long it will last, but I have decided to focus on the stuff that I really feel passionate about and that I'm only going to write the kind of stuff that I myself would watch.

LEW: They heard me give a speech last week, and I said, "If you're going to fail, fail on your terms, not on their terms." The pillow's easier at night. There's also some sense, specifically, at your level—this isn't particularly true at the beginning level, but at your level—that at some sense that, as Harriet says in her interview in this book, that the sexiest word in Hollywood is *no.*

ALAN: Oh. Yeah.

LEW: A half a dozen times, I have made a lot of money saying, "Oh, I don't want to do that. I'm not the one. Not me."

ALAN: They can tell if you're not really into it, and it just makes them love it more. When I had to pitch this TV series for ABC, I was like, "Okay, well, I'd gotten this TV deal." I knew I was expected to come up with a pilot, so I went, "I lived in a house with three other guys in Brooklyn, and there was a dog, and it's about these three guys who live in Brooklyn, and they have a dog." I was just sort of like wishy-washy, and they sort of liked it, and they said, "Go write a pilot."

So I wrote a pilot, and they made me do like five or six drafts of it. Then they called and said, "We want to do a reading of it." And I thought, "I don't want to do some reading with badly cast actors who are available that night, and then I get huge series-changing notes because they were badly cast." I just said, "You know what? Just don't do it. Just cancel it." I really meant that, but the next day, they were like, "You know what? We're going to produce it." [*laughter*] It wasn't like I was angry. I was just like, "You know what? Let's just don't do it." Because

I will have fulfilled my contractual obligation, and then, you know, I'll write a new pilot next year.

LEW: Listen to the sensibility that's inside of what he just said in terms of the badly cast. I think specifically in television but probably in motion pictures, too, because I have learned and I teach, too, that we don't remember what in God's name was the plot of *The Fugitive* or the plot of *Lethal Weapon*. But boy, do we remember the characters. The characters are beautifully cast. A lot of directors say 90 percent of it is in the casting. If you get shitty people, good words unfortunately are probably not going to come off terribly well if they're not well read.

ALAN: Absolutely.

LEW: So what he's saying there is very, very important, and that's all of you, too. Because I really encourage these writers to definitely be involved with the producing process because if they really want your material bad enough, sure, you can be a producer, coproducer, or line producer, whatever. We've gotten a lot more directors out of the writing program than out of the actual directing program at UCLA, with Brad Silberling, Coppola, and Colin Higgins and so forth. So many of our directors are busy working with the machinery as opposed to the casting. So don't forget and listen to that: casting.

ALAN: It's so important and so key. Because there was another director besides Sam Mendes who was going to direct *American Beauty* for a period of about a week. He was kind of a well-known guy, and his ideas for casting the leads were Kurt Russell and Helen Hunt. I heard that, and I was like, "What? Are you crazy?" I called the producers, and I said, "That's awful. That's really a bad idea." They went, "Well, yeah, but he's got a deal with Dreamworks, and if he decides to do it, he'll do it." So, then I was thinking, "No!" But then luckily it fell through.

LEW: How do you recognize the idea, the "Aha," the, "I want to spend X number of weeks, months, years on this idea"? What's your method of saying, "Yeah. That's the one I want to work on"?

ALAN: For me it always starts with character. In my best work, character fuels plot and not vice versa. I think, I'm probably mildly crazy, and so I have this sort of really palpable connection with my subconscious. As a kid, I was pretty much totally neglected. I became very used to entertaining myself.

Lew: Were you an only child?

Alan: No, but I came very late in my parents' marriage. My older siblings had pretty much moved on. I have a brother who's nineteen years older than me.

Lew: So almost like an only child.

Alan: In a lot of ways. And it's a very instinctive thing for me. I started out as an actor, so I'm very used to imagining other personalities in other people. I think one of my strengths as a writer is when I write, I'm sort of able to inhabit the characters as opposed to thinking of them as pieces you move around a chessboard. The flip side of that is I always have to go back after my first draft and remove my performance choices from the description because a lot of them just don't make any sense by then.

Lew: And you endanger the selling process with those, too.

Alan: Yeah.

Lew: Because you might find someone that hates Helen Hunt, for instance, and someone else loves Helen Hunt. So someone might want to pay attention to the script, and someone else might not.

Alan: But also, for me, you want to put as much information down as you understand what's going on with the character, but you also want to give the actors freedom. Although I will say this: I think when you write a draft, you write a draft that is to be read by people in the studios, by readers, by producers. That's a very different thing than writing an actual shooting draft. I think your first draft is basically a presentation in which you try to make the movie itself as clear as possible.

When I wrote *American Beauty*, I was very specific with shots and very specific with imagery because I was just writing a movie that I saw. A lot of people said to me, "Don't do that. Don't do that. That's the director's job and everything." But I think one of the reasons that the screenplay attracted as much attention as it did was that you sort of saw the movie as you read it. All the rose imagery was in the first draft. I very specifically had his point of view (POV), reverse angle, all that kind of thing. To me, when you're writing in a visual medium and you're writing in film language, you have to write it that way. If you just write a blank scene, you might luck out and get a great director with a great visual style who really understands your script and knows how to inform it, but you also might get somebody who—

LEW: Goldman says he writes the selling draft, then the director's draft. He says, when the director comes onboard, he takes all that shit out, you know.

ALAN: Absolutely.

LEW: Because it's already sold. But not all of it. But enough of it.

ALAN: Yeah, but when you're writing that shooting draft, hopefully the people that are reading that script will sit down and be able to visualize the movie. If you don't put that stuff in, then it's just words on a page.

LEW: Well, let's just use *American Beauty* as an example. How did you get to that idea where you said, "I want to spend a lot of time or a little time on that"?

ALAN: I had done two seasons on *Cybill*, and I hated it. In the middle of every season, she'd have a big breakdown, and she fired half the staff, and those of us who stayed, they would lure us back with promotions and money, and I'd done that for two seasons, and I was really feeling like a big whore. The third season, they said, "We want you to come back. We'll give you all of this." I thought, "Okay, well, I can do this, and I can just do it for a year, knowing that I'm just doing this to stick all this money in my bank account so that I can have the freedom to do something I really care about." You know, you can rationalize it like that, but you're still a big whore. I just felt so awful, and by that point she was dictating what the shows would be about. She's crazy. She would come in and say, "I have a bad haircut. Let's do a show about that." "Okay, Cybill has a bad haircut."

It's no mistake that *American Beauty* is a story about a man who hates his job and sort of hates his life and rediscovers the forgotten passion he had about living because that was sort of what was taking place with me when I wrote it. I tried to write a play with these characters like eight years ago. I had had a kind of epiphany moment with a plastic bag myself that had always stayed with me. I just knew that I had to write something about something and not just filler between commercials, or I was in danger of—forgive me for being dramatic—but I was in danger of losing something important.

Lew: What was the epiphany with the plastic bag?

Alan: It's everything. When Ricky describes that moment with the plastic bag, it was that. I was walking home from brunch with some friends in New York, and I was in front of the World Trade Center, and this plastic bag just flew out of nowhere and just circled me about eight or nine times. And it was so graceful. It was such a moment of such stillness and such grace. It was a really Zen moment. It was one of those weird moments when everything just sort of comes together and everything feels incredibly simple and yet complex at the same time. It always stuck with me. I never thought, "I'm going to write a movie about this moment," but I was writing the script for *American Beauty*, and Ricky says, "Do you want to see the most beautiful thing I've ever filmed?" And the next thing I know, they're up in his room, looking at the television screen, and I'm like, "Whoa. Well, what is this going to be?" I just thought, "Well, that's the most beautiful moment I've experienced."

Lew: Again, in the book, you'll read that Eric Roth talks about he had the feather from *Forrest Gump* from the beginning. The feather meant the whole thing to him, and he was working on a script at that time that never got made. It was about the CIA, and he just had this vision. In New York, there's a hat on a busy street, and people are walking over it, walking around it, and just that one image pulls him forward through the process of that particular script. Dennis Potter. I'm sure you admire Dennis Potter.

Alan: Oh, yeah.

Lew: He's exactly out of the Dennis Potter book. And he did a whole thing about the plastic bag. This was before *American Beauty*, and it turned into a suicide club story and into Dennis Potter. The idea of having that image is something that very few people talk about.

Alan: For me, when you do that and you map it all out in detail, then when it comes time to do it, to me it's like writing a term paper, whereas if you have an idea where you're going. I always know where I'm going, except for the pilot of *Six Feet Under*. However, in *American Beauty*, I knew Lester was dead. I knew that's where I was going to end. It's sort of the process of discovery that is so much fun, that I try not to map everything out so that when I actually do the writing, it is a journey. It is a process. Things are revealed.

Like when I got to the scene in *American Beauty* when she can't sell the house and she starts slapping herself. That just happened. Again, that sounds really flaky, and it probably is, but I didn't really know who that woman was until that moment. It was then that I realized, "Oh my God. Not only is she incredibly unhappy under this veneer of perfectionism, but these things that she's saying to herself are things that she's heard at some point." "Weak. Stupid. Baby. Incompetent." Those are things that her parents said to her when she was a little girl, and they are firmly ingrained in her, so she doesn't even question that. I don't know. I'm just saying that it's a very instinctive process.

LEW: But you knew that scene was going to be there with her?

ALAN: I knew that she was trying to sell the house, and she didn't do it, and she was upset, but I didn't know she started slapping herself.

LEW: But that's where the rough outlining in your head, in your case, is needful, I suspect, right?

ALAN: Right.

LEW: Because normally, you know, practically every other person says, "Why don't just sit down and write it." That reminds me about Truman Capote. Somebody asked him what he felt about Jack Kerouac as a writer, and he said, "He's not a writer. He's a typer." Because obviously Capote wrote outlines, even very sketchy outlines.

ALAN: But also what I'll do is I'll get a burst of inspiration, and I'll just sit down, and I'll just start something not knowing where it's going to go, run out of steam, get lost, put it aside, years later pick it up, and go, "Oh. What you have to do is this." It might be then that you realize this goes there. You occasionally need a little distance from it.

LEW: Now when you're in a script, what are your habits? Do you assign yourself so many pages a day, so many hours? What kind of regime do you have?

ALAN: Well, it depends. I mean, if I'm writing something for myself on spec, I tend to rely on inspiration more than just being disciplined about it. If I'm contractually obligated to do something, and I have to turn it in by Friday, you know, that's a big motivator. I'm not saying that's some of my best work. I think I really look at these stories and these characters as things that exist in and of themselves, and they have their own rhythms and their own schedules of making themselves obvious.

Believe it or not, I do have a lot of technical know-how, but there's a certain element of mystery to the writing process that I don't ever want to lose because I feel like if I totally understand it, then it becomes only craft and that whatever that intangible thing that happens, you lose that, and I don't want to lose that.

LEW: You become like a stenographer almost?

ALAN: Well, no, you just become a technician. And you certainly need to have technical skill, and you certainly need to have a process and be disciplined, but at the same time, if you're going to try to do anything that is, um, and I hesitate to use the word *art* because I know you're supposed to apologize for that in this business. Everybody looks at that, and they're like, "Elitist, snob, fuck you." [*laughter*] But I am somebody who aspires to do that. I like it when the work has some real meaning to it.

LEW: Mm hmm. How long did it take you to write *American Beauty*?

ALAN: Eight months. I was working full time as co-executive producer on a sitcom. But I hated it so much that I would come home at three in the morning, and I would be so excited to sit down at the computer and write because I didn't have to listen to anybody's notes. My first draft of *American Beauty*, he totally sleeps with the girl.

STUDENT: I read that and then saw the movie. I thought for some reason that Hollywood had said, "No. He can't do that."

ALAN: I was given the note that it wasn't so much he can't do that, but it was that perhaps it might inform his sort of mythic journey if he had a moment of epiphany before the tragedy occurred. Because I was so sick of the, "Oh, that's so unlikeable. Everyone has to be nice." In the first draft, she still revealed to him that she was a virgin, and he said, "I can't do this," and then he said, "No, no. I want to." And it became a moment about making love as opposed to sex, but that's such a fine line and such a very subtle delineation that I don't think anybody could ever see beyond the actual sex.

No, but what I was saying was that I was so angry at my day job, where I would come in, and they would go, "She's really sarcastic. We're going to hate her if she's so sarcastic." I was like, "It's Christine Baranski. You love her if she's sarcastic. What are you talking about?" and they would reply, "No. They shouldn't be mean to each other." So I say, "Okay, we'll make them not mean and not funny." Then I'd go home from these constraints and be like, "Yeah, and he sleeps with the girl, and the kids get accused of the crime, and they go to jail." [*laughter*]

LEW: Did you close the door and work on your own stuff during that time frame?

ALAN: No. I was actually running the show at that time, so I couldn't do it.

LEW: I produced five shows and wrote on the shows. Cybill was on the *Yellow Rose*, and she was on her good behavior. She was terrific.

ALAN: She's always on her good behavior in the beginning.

LEW: Well, the show ran one season. That's probably part of it. But I could never figure out what good is going to come out of minds at two o'clock in the morning. Have you figured that out yet? Do you do that here on this show?

ALAN: No. No way. We're very much ahead of the game. We're shooting episode 3, and we have scripts through 7, and we've broken stories through. Actually, in broad beats, we've broken down the entire season. Also, it's only thirteen episodes, which is so much more civilized than twenty-two.

STUDENT: And it's called?

ALAN: It's called *Six Feet Under*. It will be on HBO. It's an hour-long single-camera series about a family of morticians in Los Angeles. It's very twisted. It starts in June.

LEW: When I was head of development over at NBC, I always wanted to do a mortician show, and you're doing it. Yay!

ALAN: Really? Well, it's a very interesting world, and I've learned way more about the funeral industry and embalming and stuff than I ever wanted to know about, but it's a great premise for a series because everybody comes through there.

LEW: Oh, you know what you'll want to do, too? When you go to different towns, inform the local morticians, and they'll let you use the hearse. Ben Alexander, he was Jack Webb's sidekick on *Dragnet*, owned a mortuary. So I came into town and asked if he could send me a limo. He said, "Sure. Oh, I'd love to do it."

ALAN: It sounds like an interesting premise for a series because I feel like, as a culture, we are very much in denial about death and the presence of death in our lives. I thought, "People who live with the presence of death on a daily basis, how does that affect them?" It affects some of them in good ways and some of them in bad ways.

LEW: Now you finished the script. Again, we'll use *American Beauty* as the model here. You've finished the script. What can I do about rewriting at the spec stage?

ALAN: It was 150 pages. I knew I couldn't give that to anybody, so I went down to Laguna and locked myself in a motel room for a weekend and cut twenty-five pages out of it. Then I gave it to my agent. He read it, and he said, "Wow." Because he had asked me to write a spec script because I had switched agents because I felt like the place I was at just really thought of me as the television writer. I'd go, "I really want to work in features, too," and they'd go, "Mm hmm. Yeah. Fine. We'll set up some meetings for you, but keep sending the television commission our way."

So I actually switched agencies. I went to UTA because UTA had pursued me, and also, they packaged *Cybill*, so they didn't accept commission on anybody who worked on *Cybill*. I thought, "Well, they're putting their money where their mouth is. They're really going to try to make a features career happen for me." My new agent, Andrew Cannava, met with me and said, "You have to write a spec script." I pitched three ideas, two of which were pretty high-concept romantic comedies. You know, I was still sort of in the mind-set of, "Well, I'll write what everybody wants. I'll write the thing that you can put Julia Roberts and Hugh Grant in." But then I pitched *American Beauty*, which is difficult. You can't really pitch it because at the time and in the first draft, it takes place within the context of this big media trial where the two kids are on trial for murder.

So there's a big media trial, and you think you know what's going on, but the real story is way more twisted and these two families and this guy who's sort of given up on life, but he's rediscovering it, and then next door, she's like shut down, and then underneath it all is this meditation on the nature of reality, you know, and I'm just expecting him to just not get it at all. I was surprised that he said, "That's the one you should write." I said, "Really? Why?" And he said, "Because it's obviously the one you're the most passionate about." That's the best piece of advice I've gotten in my life. Later, he told me, "I never thought I could sell it. I just thought I'd have a very interesting writing sample." [*laughter*]

LEW: I have often felt, because I've done that myself and I try to tell people that that's a great way to use an agent, I don't need to know from an agent on page 44, "Why don't you do so-and-so," but tell me one of these three ideas, one you can sell and one that you like and sometimes they're different ones, as you well know.

ALAN: It worked out because 80 percent of the agents in town would have said, "Write the Julia Roberts one."

LEW: Oh. Sure. Absolutely.

ALAN: And I would have written another movie where I was trying to write something to give people what I thought they wanted, and it wouldn't have been authentic.

LEW: So you cut out twenty-five pages, and then you what?

ALAN: Gave it to him. He read it. He called me back and said, "Well, this is something. I really like this. I think it's really interesting. I think it's really unique, and with your permission, I'd like to start talking it up." What he did, he was pretty brilliant the way he sort of marketed it. He started talking about the script to people that he was dealing with, people in the industry, and then he put together a very specific list of people who would get it when it went out. People would say, "I heard about that script. Can I read it?" He'd say, "No. You're not on the list." Again, *no*, the most powerful word in Hollywood. It became this sort of prestigious thing even before it went out.

LEW: So it had to go out as an auction spec, but he had a very specific group.

ALAN: Yeah, he targeted very specific people who had deals at all the studios, and a lot of people passed on it immediately because they were like, "Oh, it's so dark, and he sleeps with the girl. No, we could never make that." I had a lot of meetings at October and Lakeshore, those smaller independents, which is where I expected it would end up if it ended up anywhere. You know, I was actually prepared to sell it to one of those places. My agent called me and said, "Hold on from making a decision because Steven Spielberg is reading it tonight." I'm like, "That's a waste of time. He'll hate it."

STUDENT: Mister commercial, you thought?

ALAN: Yeah. I was thinking, "*E. T.*? He'll hate this." But he didn't.

LEW: But you actually didn't do a tremendous amount of rewriting at that level, did you, before you sold it?

ALAN: No, I didn't do any rewriting on it until we had a director, and then I went through it with Sam and did a pass on it before it went out to actors.

LEW: In the rewriting or after you've finished, after you climbed the mountain, do you read aloud to yourself is one of them? Do you have any tricks or things that you do just to see if you've checked off everything to see how it feels to you? Do you have friends you show it to?

ALAN: Yeah, I have friends I give stuff to. I have a handful of friends whose opinions I respect who have tastes that are very similar to mine.

LEW: Do you read it aloud?

ALAN: No, but it's interesting that Sam had me read the script aloud to him. So I finally got to play all the roles.

LEW: I was at the Beverly Hills Tennis Club one year waiting for a lunch date, and I looked over at the pool and saw a man reading a script. I said, "Oh, that's Neil Simon. Hey, he's reading his words aloud." I thought, "Way to go, Neil." I like to read my stuff aloud, too. I also have an acting background.

ALAN: It was totally fun when he asked me that because I was like, "Hey, great. I get to play all the roles." And I got to be Lester, but I also got to be those teenage girls, so it was really fun.

LEW: Did you do a lot of rewriting with Sam?

ALAN: We continued to tinker with it. The two main changes were that he did not sleep with her and there was a flashback. The colonel had a flashback to his experience in Vietnam, where this other soldier was his lover, and they were ambushed, and he saw the guy get gunned down in front of him, and he sort of went crazy and killed the guy who killed his guy.

STUDENT: Why did they take that flashback out?

ALAN: Because it totally tipped where you were going. It completely gave away the ending of the movie. But it was something that I needed to write so I knew his backstory and knew where his whole thing of pain and anger and self-loathing came from. Because I think he looked at that incident as proof that God punished him. But also, the thing that no one knows is he named his son after that guy. We took that out because it totally tipped where we were going. But everything else was fairly tonal detail. There's a lot of the first draft in the movie.

LEW: That was *Men of Honor* today. I was talking to Chris, the director, about *Men of Honor*. I just knew what was going to happen in every next scene. I can actually see the story meeting up there, which is sometimes really horrendous.

ALAN: Oh God. Ninety percent of the movies I go see, I see the studio notes: "Oh, we gave her a child so she's more grown up."

LEW: Did you see *Billy Elliot*?

ALAN: No, I haven't.

LEW: You don't quite know where it's going, but once it gets there, you're glad it's there. My publisher publishes my stuff. Great company. But they said that people buy these screenwriting books to find the secret. What beyond character is a secret that you'd want to throw out to these folks here?

ALAN: That's hard. I don't believe there is a formula. I think there are certainly things you learn, that you pick up along the way. There are things that work, but I'm very leery of trying to assemble a bunch of stuff that has worked together previously because it ends up seeming very familiar and very, kind of, derivative. At the same time, I feel like one of my strengths as a writer is I have written and/or produced a hell of a lot of stuff, a lot of it I'm not proud of. But I know about production. I write things that are easily shot. I write things—one of the things I'm doing now with each episode is little rules like, "If that's going to be a location, we need to have at least two scenes there to make it worth our while to go to the location." Things like that. The same thing when

I was a playwright. I would say, "Let's have one set and five actors," because that means it will be much more likely to be produced because it's cheap.

LEW: *Same Time, Next Year.* Bernie Slade was so pissed off at NBC at the time—you're helping me drudge up old memories of people who were upset—he decided he was going to make a fortune. He was going to have one set and two actors, and that was it. So he did *Same Time, Next Year.* But these folks are really, really fortunate. I think they are aware of that.

We have a producing program. Joe Roth is in it, Tom Sherrick to talk about distribution, so when they come out of the two- or three-year master's program, they really have a lot of information that you had to pick up, by gosh and by golly, and through just being in the trenches because that is the one thing about television: It gets you into the trenches, and you learn how to read and write day after day.

ALAN: I have nine days to do each one of these episodes, and *Six Feet Under* really rests on the characters and the performances. I'm saying, "Let's really simplify the production schedule so we can focus on those moments and we can focus on getting the exact nuances of those performances, and let's keep the camera still." I don't want to spend a lot of useless, busy camera work like a lot of TV shows do to disguise the fact that it's basically the same old stuff and the same old formulas that we've seen over and over again repackaged. We have great actors. Let's give them the space to do their stuff.

LEW: Questions?

STUDENT: Lew was talking about characters as what we remember in a film. My question is, When you write, do you put faces to your characters, and how much input did you have in *American Beauty*'s casting?

ALAN: I don't think of specific actors when I'm writing. The characters themselves seemed real enough. However, when Sam came on as director, he said, "Who did you have in mind for these roles?" I replied, "You know what? I really didn't have anyone in mind. I mean, since then I've thought of certain people, but who do you have in mind?" He said, "Kevin Spacey and Annette Bening." I said, "Okay. That's good." Because they were so perfect. I mean, right off the bat. I was like, "Yeah. Let's try to get them." Then we did. There were instances in casting where I—for example, everybody was interested in seeing Christina Ricci play the daughter, and I felt like we'd seen her playing that role so many times that the minute she came on-screen, you would know exactly what you were getting. Not because she's a bad actor because she isn't. She's really terrific. But she had played so many characters, so many disaffected teenage American girls.

STUDENT: *The Ice Storm.*

ALAN: Exactly. I really fought for the kids to be three faces that you didn't know so that when they came on, you would sort of get to know them as characters as opposed to actors' personas. And actually, they listened to me. I don't know why. Maybe she was unavailable.

LEW: I want to thank you, kind sir, for enlightening us today on your forays into both television and screenwriting. I sincerely believe your unique voice resonates in American mainstream and will for a very long time. Hear, hear, Alan Ball.

ALAN: Thank you, Lew.

20

Callie Khouri

Callie Khouri is an American original from Paducah, Kentucky. She is the most passionate writer I have ever met—a hell of a statement. Her dialogue here will certainly prove this. Only one with this much passion could have conceived *Thelma and Louise*. I wholeheartedly support her and all that she stands for. I am so proud of our verbal exchange. We do not have enough female screenwriters in the Oscar tome. Callie details how writers can craft, make their art come alive, and maintain some form of ownership of what we all hope to birth, which is a wonderful story. She is also very adamant, and very right, in saying that there are not female writers who tell female stories or male writers who write male stories, as Hollywood likes to label. There are only writers telling human stories. Callie can tell a human story like no other, and she tells her own journey as a writer here. And it's as incredible, as you will see.

LEW: We are doing a book right now called *Naked Screenwriting*. I want Academy Award–winning screenwriters to bare their art, soul, craft, and secrets. We're going to talk about the process and about how you became a screenwriter. Would you say screenwriting is storytelling? Is it theater? Do you have some kind of definition for screenwriting?

CALLIE: Let me think, let me think for a second. What it is, is just a giant pain in the ass.

LEW: That's empowering to all of us.

CALLIE: It's a hassle, but you know, it's also such a unique form of story-telling. I'm on the board of the Writers Guild, and about screenwriting, I'm with screenwriters a lot. They are the most interesting, fascinating people in the business, no matter what the outside perception is about actors making up their own dialogue. I always say, if I can get an idea in my head and not actually have to sit down at the computer and write it out, if there's some way I could show it without using words, then I could actually find happiness.

However, I actually have to put it through the process of finding the right words and subject it to the limitation of verbal explanation. I find that so incredibly frustrating. I should be able to draw it in pictures or find some way to animate it. I've had some really frustrating conversations with directors over what we call a "vanity credit." You know, the words "a film by," who that actually belongs to. We're so vehemently opposed to giving that up because it's basically other people claiming credit or authorship over your original idea.

I was having a conversation with a director who I completely love and respect, but he said, "You know, until I come along and do it, it's just words on paper." And I'm like, "That doesn't mean it's what it's meant to be." The visionary is the person who sits down and comes up with the idea, manages to force through the very difficult process of language. You try and use words to describe your idea as Monet used paint to show his—it's kind of the feeling I have when I'm writing, which is that it's difficult, but at the same time I love the language. I love the people talking to each other. I love all that goes with it. When you find the right combination of letters and words and phrases, it's just sublime. It's so rare, though.

LEW: When Billy Wilder was with us, I asked him if he considered himself a writer or a director. He said, "Oh, I am a screenwriter. Directing is merely an extension of this."

CALLIE: That's exactly the way I feel. I wrote *Thelma and Louise* to direct. I begged and pleaded to direct *Something to Talk About*. Every single time I write anything, I drop to my knees and plead. I've got to say, I've been having a lot of conversations with people about what's going on here. I don't know why I can be accepted as a writer but not given authority to direct my own work. I should be. I don't know what the problem is.

LEW: It's called deal directors.

CALLIE: I mean, I do have deals to direct.

LEW: David Koepp, you know, Ed Soloman, were ex-UCLA people who were around this table. I kind of tease them and say, "We didn't teach you to write this shit." They say, "Oh no, but the next one is going to be for me, and I'm going to direct it." They use this to wedge in.

CALLIE: Let's face it, if you're going to work in this business, you're going to be forced at gunpoint to write some shit. You are. I mean, it's terrible because of the development process. Fifteen people grab a hold of it, and you've written from your heart. They will then also ask you tell a story about another character, and they want that character to be their mother. They want you to write as if it's their story, which is an impossible task, to tell another's story inside yours. You end up trying to serve a lot of masters who have incomprehensible agendas.

LEW: Dan Pyne was one of our professors. He wrote *Pacific Heights*, *White Sands*, the last few seasons of *Miami Vice*. He told his class, "This is the last chance you have to be as good as you can be. Right here. Right now."

CALLIE: Man, you're not kidding.

LEW: There are no compromises because we as professors don't say, "No. You've got to do this."

CALLIE: It's like we want you to do exactly what it is that you do, only we want to be able to take credit for it.

LEW: Nora Ephron did a very clever thing in—you may have heard this—after she wrote *Sleepless in Seattle*, she said, "I want to direct that." They said, "No, no, no." So they said, "Well, if you get a cinematographer, then maybe." So she went out and got a very famous cinematographer, Sven Nykvist, and then she goes, "Any further requirements?" This is also the way Colin Higgins was able to direct *Harold and Maude*, which he wrote in one of these 434 classes.

CALLIE: Can I get in this class?

LEW: He finally got to the point where every time he asked, they'd just whistle and walk away, but he kept asking, and finally they said, "Hey wait, we'll surround him with Peter Heralds, the best line producer, and make sure he gets the best cinematographer, too. It can't go wrong if he's got the best." He finally got to direct it.

CALLIE: That's starting to happen for me.

LEW: Quinn Martin once told me, "Never work with anyone dumber than you are."

CALLIE: Right.

LEW: Let's talk about your writing habits. Do you write in the morning? Afternoon? Middle of the night?

CALLIE: It's different every time, unfortunately. When I wrote *Thelma and Louise*, I was working. I wasn't a working screenwriter. I was producing music videos, and as anybody who's had the incredible misfortune to do that for a living, you know, you shoot eighteen-hour days, twenty-hour days, sometimes two or three days in a row, if you get enough money to shoot that long. You're in production for two weeks furiously, and then nothing for a while. So I just wrote whenever I got a chance or whenever I could.

It was actually such a fantastic experience. This is the thing that's so great, too, and you guys are experiencing right now because I didn't have to please anybody but myself. I just wrote something that I liked. I didn't know if anybody was going to ever see it. I just said, "Can I get to the end? Can I start something and actually finish it?" I've never done that before in my life, for anything of my own. But I could make these crappy music videos that are basically nonsense on the one hand. On the other hand, I'm very grateful for that experience because I learned how to make a film backwards. I was going to say something to her, then I have to put the camera over there, and so on. I learned a lot technically about how to get an image on film, and that was incredibly meaningful to me as a writer. But it was just hellish as a daily grind. I started thinking, "If I can do that every day, why can't I finish this?" That was the only goal I had in mind when I started writing *Thelma and Louise*.

LEW: Had you had any particular training?

CALLIE: No.

LEW: But what was the thing that drove you to do that script?

CALLIE: The idea. I was just, "Oh my God, I have to write this idea out."

LEW: Longhand?

CALLIE: Yeah, and I would go to the office where I was working, and they had a computer there, but it didn't have a screenwriting program on it anywhere, so I was just typing. You know, I could back it up in case the house burned down or something. You know, with all of my luck at that time, it was a possibility. So I would, you know, toodle up to this office. It was on Hollywood and Vine, you know, this office where I was working, actually a little further south than that. Because I was working freelance and I would just kind of toodle around with my little floppy disk and, you know, go in and type on whatever word processing program was there.

I don't know, it was just like, I would sit in there, and I'm having the greatest time in the world. So I would write longhand to get a scene done and then put it in the computer and kind of refine it as I went along. It was just one of those things where I loved being with those characters so much. I would get ideas for a joke line. I would be lying in bed late at night and think, "Oh, that's funny." I'd jot it down. I was having the best time. It's still the most fun I ever had in my life. I always say that because it is when you're doing it just for yourself, you make it as good as you can make it. There is just no greater joy than that.

LEW: Have you been writing for hire most of the time since then?

CALLIE: Unfortunately, yes, I have.

LEW: Because some of our ex-students who say, "Ah, fuck it, I'm just going to write a spec." Well, Shane Black went off into the woods and did *Lethal Weapon* and just did it on spec. Have you been tempted?

CALLIE: Yeah, I mean, the only thing that's stopping me is, you know, I haven't had an idea that really has excited me the way *Thelma and Louise* did, you know what I mean? That, like, you know on the first puff on a cigarette being a stick of dynamite. It's just like nothing else really. I have moments of that in everything that I do now. I touch it, brush against it, and I went, "Oh God, I've got to do this!" I couldn't wait to write when I was having that idea. I have moments of that in everything thing now. I have learned that the more you do it, the more likely you are to have those moments, but there's also that fear I have, that I will run off the road, and I am just writing dreck. That's a tremendous fear. Once fear comes into it, then you're just in this death struggle. That's like the most debilitating thing and, I think, useless but probably very common.

LEW: Do you have people who read your material and vice versa?

CALLIE: Yeah.

LEW: Do they help you say, "Oh, maybe that's not too bad after all," or maybe, "Oh God, that's really great"?

CALLIE: I do on the one hand. On the other hand, it's like I always want my stuff to be mine so much that if somebody goes, "I don't know, what about this?" I'm like, "Give me that. You don't know anything."

LEW: How and when do you write?

CALLIE: If I get blocked, because time is really important, I turn on the computer, and I'm like, "I can't do it anymore," you know, then I'll pick up a pen and go off somewhere different, just kind of change my location a little bit. There's this woman, Cathy Coleman, who teaches a creative writing class that's more prose. My husband took a class with her, and I had a very short window of time to do it, and I was just not in the frame of mind to do it at all, so I hired her basically to babysit me while I wrote. It's pathetic. It cost me a fortune. I had to pay this woman like a shrink. But that's what it took, you know.

STUDENT: What did she do?

CALLIE: Well, her writing classes are sublime. She does writing exercises that just free your mind. She's not a screenwriting teacher, although she has, from working with so many screenwriters, really started to get inside that process, too. I actually found her incredibly helpful in that process. She just starts asking you questions until you're more in touch with what you're doing. I can't tell whether I just get irritated with having to answer questions and it's just easier to go write. I don't know what it is exactly. But her whole thing is about just kind of silencing your inner critic, which, you know, as I said before, mine is strong. Mine works out at Gold's Gym.

LEW: I always liked that Aleksandr Solzhenitsyn's wife—perhaps this is a good concept for your husband—his wife locked him in the basement with two pails. One had water and a loaf of bread. One pail was for drinking, and the other, for elimination. He couldn't get out till one was empty and the other was full.

CALLIE: I write for short bursts, unless I'm doing a production rewrite, where I will literally sit there till I can't sit there anymore. But you know, for the purposes of creative inspiration, I won't ask myself to do more than four or five hours a day.

LEW: Do you assign yourself hours or pages a day?

CALLIE: Hours. Because I would rather have a good half-page in five hours than, you know, five shitty pages. Because five shitty pages just undoes me. That's when I start going, "Okay, it's over."

LEW: You know, one of the exciting aspects of this book about all of these writers is everyone does it so differently, yet they all have the same goal.

CALLIE: I was talking to Tom Schulman this morning.

LEW: Oh, she's got a story. Go ahead.

CALLIE: I said, "Every time I finished with a screenplay, there's a part of me that's just like, 'Who did that?' I didn't even do it. I feel like it was elves. I don't know. I don't remember it." You know, I think, I've never had a kid, but I always liken it to childbirth. It's like I'm going through it. I'm like this tragic mess. As soon as it's over, I'm like, "That was easy."

LEW: Tom Schulman talks about an office. He doesn't have a bed, but he has a rug that he will roll out, and he'll sleep and then keep going for hours.

CALLIE: Jesus.

LEW: Floyd Mutrux one time said, "Well, it's not the hours. It's the pages." Ernie Lehman says he always has ten to noon. If he gets nothing done, he wrote for those two hours.

CALLIE: When I'm good, though, I can get five or six pages.

LEW: How do you know it's a good day? Just a visceral feeling?

CALLIE: It just feels good. It just comes. At times, if I write with a specific goal—and that was the other thing that really helped working with Cathy because she helped me mentally organize the scenes I had to write. Just going, "Okay, so let's just write that scene." Then, I'd limit how long the scene can be in a very loose way. Can't be more than, depending on how many people are in it, then, let's just say four pages. It forces me to be really hard. If I have a little short scene, I'll write that afterwards. My favorite things are two-and-a-half-page scenes. You can really zing in there.

LEW: Do you get a feeling, as you're developing the outline, how long the scenes should be?

CALLIE: Well, yeah, in a very general way. I don't go in for this thing of exact rules. That's just not my nature. I like for everybody else to follow rules but not me. That's the way the world works. If a studio executive were ever to say to me, "You can't have a five-page dialogue scene," I would probably go off on a mission to collect every brilliant ten-page dialogue scene that's ever been written. I'm afraid this stodgy rule thing is something that's happening now in the way films are made, and it's getting too formulaic.

LEW: I was thinking when you're building the outline and you say, "Oh, that feels like four and a half pages."

CALLIE: I don't care about how long a scene is going to be when I'm doing an outline.

LEW: So you don't feel them?

CALLIE: I don't care. It's not that I won't know. It's just that it's not important to me at that point how long it's going to be. Because the outline and all that stuff is great, but then you have to make room for the creative process, too.

LEW: The idea. I remember you were speaking at the Writers Guild maybe two or three years ago, and you said—you got out of your car— and you said, "Two women go on a crime spree," and then you went inside the house, and six weeks later you have—

CALLIE: No, six months.

LEW: Six months? See, my anal-retentiveness heard six weeks. Six months later, *Thelma and Louise*. Now, obviously, that was synergy. The spark that creates the fire: Is that how you recognize a good idea?

CALLIE: Pretty much, I mean, but in a more contained way in a scene. There's a certain kind of rhythm. I'm not sure what to call it. You're writing and observing the scene at the same time. You are in it, and you're not in it. You start to see ahead. You know that the character needs to say this. It's like if you're skiing and, you know, find the exact stance and have the confidence that you'll make it down without falling, but you're no longer thinking about it. You're just there, doing it. It's effortless. It's like everything else. If it's working, you don't feel it. There's no pain. It's good. You know, it's like for me, cooking is the only time when I'm not critical. I don't give a shit. I'm just doing it. My cooking, it's good, but I'm not all over myself, judging and worrying. I'm just into it. When writing can be that, it's good. Usually the writing that you do in that frame of mind, it's that thing of not serving any other master. You're writing to tell a story. That's it.

LEW: So you have this idea, and then how do you develop your idea? You did scene cards at one time?

CALLIE: I do some form of that.

My husband can just do an outline like [*snaps*] that, you know. He gets the idea, and he does an outline, and he's made me start to do that. If I won't do it, he sits down, and he makes me. Otherwise, I pace like a caged animal, and sometimes he writes it as I pace and talk it out, and he prints it out. From that, I can start doing cards. When I did *Thelma and Louise*, I didn't do any of that because I didn't know what the hell I was doing. It was such a totally organic experience. I picked up one of those Syd Field books, started thumbing through it, and I was just like, "This is going to fuck me up." No slight to Syd. It's just that I didn't want to know. I was just afraid that if I imposed anybody else's idea of what something was going to be, I was screwed. Because I knew it was impossible, what I was about to undertake anyway. I knew it was impossible.

I didn't tell people I was doing it because I didn't want to have to, like, explain that I, too, was writing a screenplay. Yeah, I just couldn't bear it. So I mean, like, two or three of my closest friends knew that I was even writing anything. But now, of course, I have to do it, and that I'm not writing with, you know, divine inspiration. I need it. I really need it. I really need the structure. I really need to go, "Okay, I'm going to just jump ahead and write that scene." Because, at least, you know, you have an idea what that scene's going to be. Sometimes going ahead can be really beneficial. It helps you to get an idea for something that when you go back, you have even more than you did.

LEW: Are your outlines particularly detailed?

CALLIE: No.

LEW: Because other people can be detailed. Like Paul Schraeder is wildly detailed. For me, I always worry about leaving my fight in the dressing room.

CALLIE: Right.

LEW: It gets back to, I was an only child. Were you an only child?

CALLIE: One of four.

LEW: Bringing one of these four children up into people. I just kind of hate rules, too. And for the Jane class—Campion was here—she said she read Syd Field but that she got the most out of Flannery O'Connor. Has any reading helped you out in any way?

CALLIE: I started reading really young. I don't actually remember a time where I wasn't reading. My parents taught me to read and then to eat. I grew up in Paducah, Kentucky, and there ain't much going on in Paducah, Kentucky. I read voraciously. In fact, one of my oldest friends says her permanent image that's seared into her retina is of me at her house, spending the night, under the covers with a flashlight. I think I was reading Dickens. It could just or possibly does ingrain a sense of story into your being, and this might be the single most important thing you can possibly have.

I think one of the things that's kind of left out of a lot of discussions about screenwriting is that screenwriting, in its own way, is a kind of performance. I think there is a little bit of the theatrical in screenwriters, and in me, you can tell if you've spent a few moments in my wildly gesticulating presence. I love just talking to people, and I love trying to take them somewhere or just try and get them completely wrapped up in the moment. I like to make them laugh without knowing that it's coming. I like to be able to do it visually. It's so much fun.

LEW: T. E. Kalem, who was a critic for *Time* magazine, said, "In theater, the drama is thrust at the audience, and in motion pictures the audience is thrust at the drama." I've always liked that because you're part of the process.

CALLIE: The first time I saw *Thelma and Louise* with an audience, you kind of have an idea about what's going to work and where people are going to laugh. But the first time I actually heard an entire movie theater full of people, you know, spontaneously burst out laughing, I just thought I was going to die. I mean, I couldn't believe it. I was laughing and crying and shaking at the same time, all without actually moving. I couldn't believe it. I just couldn't believe it. It was the most exciting experience I ever had. It just makes you a total junkie for that because you got to do it more and more.

LEW: So then the pleasure is worth the pain. The selling process is the thing that drives me crazy, which is really a lot of what you're talking about: trying to persuade somebody into your line of reasoning or trying to get something you believe in sold. Do you have any particular techniques—let's say, a less pejorative word than *tricks*—for trying to persuade somebody into your line of thinking when you're in a story meeting?

CALLIE: You know, it's weird. I mean, I'm fortunately extremely persuasive in those kinds of meetings. I can generally demonstrate what it is I'm talking about. I just recently was doing a rewrite on something that was just a production rewrite. But I was talking with the director, and I just knew that she wasn't quite where I was, and I was like, you know, "This part where she does this and he says this," and I said the dialogue for him, and she's like, "Ah, God. I feel like such an idiot. It's just that I didn't read it like that. That makes so much sense."

So when I start to feel doubt, I just make sure that they know what it means. Now if somebody just disagrees, then I'm like, "Well, you're wrong. This happens to be what I do. I'm not going to tell you in which order to return your phone calls, and I don't think you should be telling me how a story works." I get real righteous and indignant. Sometimes that works, and sometimes I lose.

LEW: You really utilize your acting background not only in your writing. We know that very clearly.

CALLIE: I think so. It helps, which is why I always get frustrated with the limiting, to people reading words on a page, when it's so much more than that. It's really open to broad interpretation based on the life experience of the very different people that are reading it. That's why writing for me is just not enough. I want to direct it, as well, because it's not vague to me. I'm writing something very specific, and I want to convey this. I was never an actress, but I did study it for a long time with Peggy Fury.

LEW: At Lee Strasburg. You've got a nice background.

CALLIE: I dedicated ten years of my life. I was a drama major in college.

LEW: Purdue.

CALLIE: I understand that you can always bring more to something than you would think, the words on the page. But you know, there are very few people who are going to be able to bring more to it than the writer intended. Scott Frank always goes, "Sometimes it's even better than what I what wrote." I haven't had that experience. I don't know what that says, but he's a very good friend of mine, and we kind of let each other have it on a regular basis.

LEW: React to Bruce Joel Rubin's line here, if you would: "I think you only have strength in something based on your ability to leave it behind. The only real strength comes out of detachment. If your happiness is based on material achievement, then you're going to be in trouble because you become addicted to the things they gave you."

CALLIE: Totally right.

LEW: We complain on the one sense about the journey, but on the other sense, the journey is quite thrilling.

CALLIE: When it's good, it's good. When it's bad, it's like a gravel road lined with only Motel 6.

LEW: That's a good line. Questions?

STUDENT: There's a great moment in *Thelma and Louise*, where she sees this old woman putting on lipstick, and at that point you know she's not going to grow old. Was that in the original script?

CALLIE: Actually, the moment that was in the script was that she started to put on lipstick. And she looks at herself in the mirror, and at the point in the screenplay, it was like, she went from no longer being able to look at herself, which I think is a real common thing. We all—not we all—but people imagine the world looking at them. She was no longer the object of the world looking at her; she was now looking out. So whatever she did here, she couldn't see this. There was a lot of mirror imagery to her looking into a mirror and trying to figure out who this person was, and at that moment, trying to change who she was, was pointless.

STUDENT: It was slightly different. It was the interaction with the lady behind the glass, which I loved because that was great pathos and that she was never going to do that. She was never going to become that woman. She knew, then, part of her destiny.

LEW: Another question?

STUDENT: How soon did you know what the ending was going to be?

CALLIE: I knew it instantly. I saw the whole thing.

LEW: That goes back to Harriet and Irving Ravetch. When asked how many rewrites it takes to get something right, she replied, "We try and get it right the first time."

CALLIE: I'm with them.

LEW: You clearly got *Thelma* right the first time. Now, subsequently in your other scripts, how do you feel about rewriting?

CALLIE: I feel like it's great for other people. I like to get it as close as I can the first time. I want to believe in it. You do want to get it right the first time is believing in it wholeheartedly. I hate turning things in, which I've had to do, and kind of going like, "I don't know." Once you don't know, believe me, you are knee-capped, man. You are not getting out of there alive.

LEW: But really didn't have much changing to *Thelma and Louise*, right?

CALLIE: No.

LEW: So again, this plays off the visceral aspect. Another question, please.

STUDENT: Lew was describing and you confirmed that you had the idea and saw the characters in the situation. It was a film that inspired so much general debate on politics and issues. How much of that was something that you wanted to do? Or was it purely about those two characters?

CALLIE: I've always been one of those people who speaks in overly broad generalization, kind of a bad habit. In hindsight, it's not surprising, but at the time, I was shocked into silence. For the first time in my life and not again since, I couldn't believe it. I couldn't believe it was causing so much debate. I was just like, "You people have just gone completely off the deep end. This is insane that you would think." I swear to God, some of the shit I heard people saying about this movie.

SHELLEY: *Time* magazine.

CALLIE: I mean, not even that. I was in a situation very similar to this classroom setting at Vanderbilt University, and this one woman, she raised her hand, and she said, "Well, I just want to say, that I don't think this was a very feminist piece of work because all I could see was that Louise was just depressing Thelma." She started critiquing how it could be this, and if it were really feminist, they wouldn't have used guns, and they would have done something else. And I'm just like, "Would you get a fucking clue. Jesus Christ. It's an outlaw movie! It wasn't a tract, you know. It's an outlaw movie." I wasn't trying to do anything. I was trying to get in touch with that spirit, that we as women have been completely denied. An outlaw movie that isn't about men, with women waiting for them. The only women outlaws that you see in most movies are prostitutes because it's like, that's the only way that women can be demonstrably sexual, is if they're being paid for it. Otherwise, they're the villain? So here were these two women who were completely independent from a sexual standpoint now. The rape in the script was an attempted rape. Every act was an act of independence in a way. I couldn't think of one outlaw film, honestly, that didn't have to do with a woman who was ultimately a bad person.

I think it satisfies something in a really deep place in a human being, to be able to have that vicarious experience. But we're part intellectual, and we're part animal. There are times of just understanding that the rules will fall apart and work against you. I think it's something every person can relate to. It wasn't thought out, as a critical studies thesis, but it was a feeling of wanting to bust out of a mold. I wanted to realize all of the things that had been significant in my life. You know, riding in a car with my best friend in the seat next to me, in this encapsulated, metal thing where you are free and nobody can get you and nothing bad is going to happen because they're there and you're here and there's just the road. Maybe it wasn't overintellectualized, but it was well felt.

LEW: Another question?

STUDENT: Do you have a technique or a process which you use to write male characters or characters of the opposite gender? Something that helps you identify with them?

CALLIE: No. I mean, as odd as it is because I am, like, the "woman writer," I think I write men at least as well, if not better. I am half man. I admit it. I just feel like I get it. The good, the bad, the ugly. All of it. It's not that much of a mystery to me, even though in certain ways when I am, like, in totally inhabiting my complete feminine self on the rare occasions, I can be like, "What the fuck?" Like a lot of women, but on the other hand, it's like, I do know what the fuck. I empathize with everyone.

I mean, to make generalizations about men and women: There are women who I find absolutely incomprehensible, and if anybody mistook me for one of those, I would go insane. I'm sure men have the same experience. To make those generalizations about gender is a waste of time. The real question lies in, Can you relate to a character? I just did a rewrite on this movie that I hope will someday get made. I was like the fifth writer on. It's a baseball movie. I swear to God, people are just going, "These guys. Man, people are going to find out that you can write a film. You are going to be in business." I had so much fun because I could just be that. You can't limit, ever, being inside of a character. We have all written each other for centuries. Gender is not that important to me, only in terms of how well the story is told, for its archetypal significance.

LEW: Another?

STUDENT: I'm very intrigued by your career change. You were working full time, sort of scribbling notes at night? Is that how you wrote?

LEW: This one is a lawyer but trying to not to be.

STUDENT: Yes. Desperately trying to break out. Were you anxious to break out of that particular profession or to become a screenwriter?

CALLIE: I was working all the time. Years and years ago, I went to see this psychic, and she said, "I see you as a screenwriter, as a director. Definitely a director and writer." I was working as a waitress at the time. I'm thinking, "I just paid this fucking bitch to tell me what every other idiot comes in here wanting to hear. I am never going to be that." I didn't even know what it was. I didn't know what a screenwriter was. I came from small-town Kentucky. I was like everybody else. I thought the actors were doing it. I didn't know the most important thing, which is the screenwriter or the person who comes up with the story and actually gets it through that birthing process might also be the only creative person in the process. That every single other part of that process is interpretive. I could have saved myself years of doing acting exercises.

LEW: Irving Thalberg said, "The most important person in Hollywood is the screenwriter, but we must never tell the sons of bitches." One more question.

STUDENT: Was the way it was interpreted very different from what you thought you were setting out to do?

CALLIE: I think the general feeling came through. All of the political yammering that went on about it afterwards and before. The most important lesson I learned is you cannot control people's perceptions when you send something out into the world. This is the detachment Bruce Joel is talking about. You have to let go of what people think because people will think what they will. There's nothing you can do about that. There are far more people who got the movie and really had affection for it. Sitting in that dark room, they experienced what I was trying to give. This may sound corny, but you have to feel a real love for the people who are going to get your piece. You're writing for not just you but also for them. I want to make them feel better. I want to make them feel something. I want them to be happier about being a human being. I want them to feel happy and sad or both, as long as when you feel something fully, emotionally, you are enriched. You have to really give of yourself. I liken it to performance. When you're performing, you're totally giving everything you've got, but you have to do that in writing, too.

LEW: Question?

STUDENT: When I walked out of *Thelma and Louise*, I remember crying afterwards. I was thinking of every girlfriend who could have been in that car. I think that was a gift of the movie. I saw it here, and I saw it in Germany. That point where she shoots the would-be rapist, there was one in the audience, and he was screaming and yelling and clapping, which scared me a little.

CALLIE: It scared me, too.

STUDENT: But in Germany, silence.

CALLIE: I wish I'd gotten to see it in Germany because that's what I thought. I thought people were going to realize, "Oh shit."

STUDENT: That's what I thought, too, and so it really scared me when everybody was hooping and hollering. And yet, in Germany, they were just silent.

CALLIE: I love knowing that this happened somewhere because it's very disheartening to me, like someone throwing a punch and it knocks over a baby, and then you hear people cheering? I went to *Total Recall*, and there's Sharon Stone at the end, getting shot at point blank. I was there with my husband and another couple, and we all just looked at each other, and it was so unsettling because the audience cheered.

I was just like horrified, but at the same time I understood. I know I had to make Thelma emotionally justifiable, and I think that you had to understand why she was doing it. You had to understand that in that moment of time, even though it was totally the wrong thing to do, it was also completely emotionally understandable. You know because the film was about those women. I mean, for me, I wanted to be in that world of you don't know who you're talking to. Nothing is black and white, you don't know who you are. You don't know what's inside of you. You don't know that a certain set of circumstances can occur, that they will stack up, and that will bring out something you could never in a million years have imagined was there. I love those ideas about just how completely unknowable we are to ourselves.

LEW: What? Oh, Shelley, go ahead. I can't deny you.

SHELLEY: Talking about the ending, I have the same reaction as many. In one of our classes here, we talk about transcendence in movies a lot. That's like one of the few modern movies I can see where, even though those characters were dying, the way it was detailed, and they live on in our memory. It was so exuberant for me, to feel all of these things at the same time.

CALLIE: It's the half-full, half-empty glass of water test, you know. I mean, some people come and go, "How could you have killed them?" I'm like, "Well, did you see them hit the bottom?"

LEW: I have another question, maybe the next to last: Tell us, do you see screenwriters as artists? What can we do to push ourselves closer to the artist's mantle?

CALLIE: I've spent literally thousands of hours in this exact conversation, and our biggest problem is we don't own our copyright.

LEW: Hear, hear!

CALLIE: I'm going through something right now where American Greetings Cards used *Thelma and Louise* in an ad that I found really offensive, and MGM kind of signed off on it. They didn't check with me. They're fighting with each other. It's a huge mess. But basically, it wouldn't have happened if I owned the copyright to *Thelma and Louise*. They would have had to check with me, and the thing is, because I'm a screenwriter, once I decide if I will let it go to the next step, to its intended purpose, which is to become a movie, I have to give up all rights. They say, "But you sold your screenplay." It's a really fucked-up thing. We are trying to figure out a way to not have that happen.

But right now, I would suggest going the independent route and getting your own financing for films and making sure that you, as the writer, make the film yourself. Honestly, as crazy as that sounds, if it's something that you care about, keep it yours. *Thelma and Louise* is as a child would be to me. It will always be a part of me and a really important part of me. It was a life-changing experience. It was the culmination of everything I had ever dreamed of in a very mixed-up way, but nonetheless, on paper, I don't own it. You know, even though it is mine. It is crushing.

STUDENT: If it were a novel, you would own it?

CALLIE: I would own the novel.

STUDENT: Or as a playwright?

CALLIE: If I hadn't made it into a movie, the studio would still own the right to use those characters in whatever way they see fit. Once a studio buys it, it's theirs to do as they choose. They're never going to give you copyright.

LEW: That's right.

CALLIE: The only way is to make your own films. Produce, bring on your director, find outside financing. I mean, look at the way the screenwriter is now. I cannot name a screenwriter, and there are probably one or two, that are given the same—and I'm talking about the biggest writers in the business—that will be given the same profit participation that the movie star, the producer, that the director will have, even if it's an original screenplay. I'm telling you, I would be a hard-ass from the very beginning. I would get the meanest, most aggressive lawyer I could possibly get. There is a group of us fighting for this tooth and nail every single day, trying to figure out a way around this problem.

Part of it is, you know, now, as much as screenwriters get paid in the upper echelons, it's still nothing compared to what the directors are getting paid. It's not even close to what the stars are getting paid. When they can hire five writers for every one director, it even further diminishes the power of the screenwriter. So the only power you have is you. It's a sad thing to say that the screenwriter alone is not enough to gain the respect. Because every single person, every producer, every director, every studio head, everybody in this universe will say, "Without a script you have nothing. By the way, don't let the door hit you in the ass on the way out."

SHELLEY: Are there may writers who choose to rewrite other writers?

CALLIE: Absolutely. Yes.

LEW: Absolutely?

CALLIE: Oh yeah. Because if you're doing a rewrite, I mean, listen, I recently got sent a script that was written by Audrey Wells. I like her writing so much. She is just funny as she can be. The director said he wanted to speak to me personally and all this kind of stuff, and I got on the phone, and I was like, "I am sorry, but you guys are insane. There is nothing wrong with this. If you guys start messing around with it, you're going to ruin it because this is magic, what you have here." I went through the whole thing and strongly made the case to cast the movie, do the read-through, whatever changes should be made for specific actors. But the structure was as sound as a dollar and that they should just get on with it and make the movie.

So, then they decide, okay, that's good, and they give it to the head of the studio to read, and then I hear from the agent. Well, you know, the unnamed studio exec, he's read about twenty-five pages of it, and he needs, he thinks he's going to want a rewrite. I'm like, "Well, you know, it ain't going to be from me. And it ain't going to be on the strength of reading twenty-five pages. Because when I read twenty-five pages, I would have thought it needed, it too. But I got all the way to the end and know it works. The goddamn thing works, so don't come back to me with this." If anybody is doing any rewriting, it should be her. I called Audrey—and that's the other thing, if it's a peer, if it's someone that I know, if it's not a script that's been laying around for five years that knows there's four other writers in front of me, and I know the original writers are just so long gone, then maybe—otherwise, I always call the writer.

LEW: Actually, we're supposed to. Do you know that?

CALLIE: Oh, yeah, but you're also discouraged. This is a new thing that's happened, too. I think it's happened in the last couple of years. We have started really talking to each other and really kind of baring our souls to each other. We get together every so often, and we just go, "You know what, I have a script that's out there right now, and if somebody calls you to rewrite it, please say no because this is mine, and they're going to fuck it up, and just don't do it."

LEW: That sounds like a big step toward the screenwriter becoming an artist.

CALLIE: Exactly.

LEW: Being considered an artist is something that we get there, through ourselves. But it's important to get there through the public, too. We're going to go the roots on this. I was very touched by this last statement in this book: "My father buried me very early with the idea that if you're going to do something, it should be original. Otherwise, you're just making noise."

I think that's one of the things that has prevented me from doing anything for so many years; I feared that it wasn't going to be original. It's a burden because it permeated my consciousness so completely that it's like, finally, after all of these years, I can say, "Well, there. There you go. What do you think?" My mother is thrilled beyond description, and of course, she always thought it was a matter of time. She's always been my biggest fan. So she's happy because she thinks, "See, I was right." But going through this period, I have just wished that my father could have been around for it, that he could see all this happening. You have a hell of a father-daughter story, don't you?

CALLIE Eh.

LEW: You'll get there. We love you so much and are so proud, Callie.

21

Robert Benton

Bonnie and Clyde, Places in the Heart, Kramer vs. Kramer, Bad Company, which Robert Benton is not, as this comprises just a few of his contributions to our screenwriting classics. You will find in this dialogue that Robert talks about learning. Every other page, Robert is "learning" in his ongoing history as a screenwriter.

From the time Robert was a kid and his dad took him to the movies on school nights to all of the movies he's written and the many that he also directed, Robert was learning. Walt Disney was a special friend of mine, and he, too, emphasized how much he was always learning. This acknowledgment is what may divide the wannabe writers and directors from the will-be writers and directors: an openness to and realization that we are constantly learning.

You will be thrilled to hear the journey Robert takes in his learning, and we will be learning, too. We will learn to be in the mind of this great man, so read on, my dear reader.

ROBERT: Mr. Hunter.

LEW: Mr. Benton, may I call you Robert, and please call me Lew.

ROBERT: Okay.

LEW: I met you when you brought *Places in the Heart* to UCLA. You had been a very conscientious student of Hitchcock then. I recall you said, "Well, I think I'll try and do a Hitchcock," later saying it was the hardest type of film to do.

ROBERT: It is. It taught me to never do that again.

LEW: Fortunately, I learned from your experience. I worked with Hitchcock on *Alfred Hitchcock Presents*. I was an executive on that show. I was in a constant awe of him at the time and thought maybe I could do it. I decided not to.

ROBERT: Yes, stay away from Hitchcock.

LEW: Nobody but Hitchcock can do a Hitchcock, I'm afraid. Now, what I'm doing here is developing a book of award-winning screenwriters. Most have come to class at UCLA, but since you're geographically not available to us, we're doing phone, same as we did with Ted Tally.

ROBERT: He's a friend of mine.

LEW: Not surprised at all. You East Coasters have to hang together against the philistines in the West, right? Kind of an interesting trade-off, here, using phone. What we lose in eye contact, we can make up for in concentration.

ROBERT: Sounds good.

LEW: How do you relate screenwriting to storytelling, and how did storytelling affect your life before you became a professional storyteller?

ROBERT: I was always into reading. Unfortunately, I was seriously dyslexic, so reading was very difficult. The one thing I could do that would allow me to concentrate, as I also had a short attention span, was to draw. I had ambition, when I was in high school, to be a cartoonist for Walt Disney and also to be an artist. I also loved movies.

From the time I was very young, we would go to the movies two or three times a week. My record is seven movies in one day. That was almost without eating. My father, who was first addicted to movies, would come home from work and instead of saying to me, like any normal father, "Have you done your homework?" He'd say, "Let's go to the movies." A fool would have said, "I don't care if I get an A. I'll settle for a C." I was so interested in movies, but I never thought I'd get involved in the making of them.

I remember in high school, the first film I ever sat through twice was *The Red Badge of Courage*. The first five minutes are shot like a neorealist or documentary film. Then it goes back into that regular Houstonian, expressionistic way he shot most of his early films. I was so mesmerized that when the movie ended, my father said, "Okay, let's go." I said, "No, I'm going to stay and watch it again." It was a small little town where we lived, so I could just sit through it again, no problem.

LEW: Waxahachie, Texas?

ROBERT: Yes. Anyway, it was an involvement with a form of storytelling that I could deal with because of dyslexia. I loved stories, and slowly the dyslexia got better. I was able to read, first comic books, then mysteries, because what would hold my attention as a reader was narrative. I could read for long periods of time with pulp fiction, detective, or science fiction. This drove my father crazy, but I loved the concept of storytelling.

I went to college to study art, but my dyslexia got better, so I was able to take a lot of English. When I came to New York, I still wanted to be a painter and supported myself by doing commercial art and ultimately went to work for *Esquire* magazine as the assistant to the art director. The thing I loved about this job was the combination of reading and artwork, and throughout all this, I was going to movies.

Also, the influence of the New Wave, which was radically different form of storytelling, exerted a great deal of influence over me. This whole new generation of filmmakers, like Bogdanovich and Arthur Penn and Coppola and Scorsese, this generation was deeply influenced by European film, and the generation following that was a very American group of filmmakers. People like Lucas and Spielberg—I mean this as praise—they are great American artists. The New Wave essentially taught me to examine American film, to go back and look at Hitchcock or Hawks as more than entertainers, to see them as kind of artists, and to understand that you can be a very popular artist and also be a great artist.

LEW: That's an interesting juxtaposition, but I was at UCLA at the time of Francis and bunch of others as a screenwriting student. Why do you use European films as a frame of reference?

ROBERT: Because that's when I grew up. At certain times in my life, films have been a life raft for me. I had been flirting with this girl in college, and she had fallen for someone else. I was crushed. I came to New York to get as far away as I could and to try to go to graduate school to avoid getting drafted during the Korean War. At that point, *A Place in the Sun* was playing. I know I saw that film at least ten times. It was the beauty and the structure—it was so intelligently done. It taught me a huge deal about storytelling, that themes echo themselves through the picture like musical themes. When Shelley Winters and Montgomery Clift go to get the wedding license, they're standing in front of the room where he's going to be tried for murder. All of these themes repeat throughout the picture. It's an extraordinarily well-made movie.

Later, when I had been involved with another girl and we broke up, I saw another movie at least eight times without being deeply influenced. At this time, New Wave was profound, and in New York, it centered around a critic, Andrew Sarris. Andrew and Peter Bogdanovich wrote for *Esquire* in those days with David Newman and myself. Oh, also, there was Ben Talbot, who ran the New Yorker Theater, which was revival. I don't think there are any revival theaters left. You can get anything you want digitally now. But it was extraordinary in those days. You could go to the Modern Museum of Art and see the most astonishing films. All of the conversations we would have would be about movies, not books, not paintings. It was an incredibly exciting time, and then the process of trying to write, trying to figure out the form. David Newman and I, when we did *Bonnie and Clyde*, we didn't know how to write a screenplay.

LEW: What screenplay did you use to get the form?

ROBERT: We didn't even have a screenplay. Somebody told us that you indent, and you do this, but I don' think we ever saw an actual screenplay. We wrote this treatment. We've got it somewhere in the files. It was about eighty pages, and it was in some ways just what the picture turned out to be. All of the shots were listed but not the dialogue. It got to Truffaut, and he was interested. He came over with a woman who later became a good friend, Helen Scott. Truffaut sat with us at the Regency Hotel for two days. Those were the only formal lessons I had on screenwriting.

LEW: Nice teacher.

ROBERT: Great teacher.

LEW: And a wonderful human being, as you know and as I know, too.

ROBERT: There were secrets Truffaut dictated to us line by line that are still in *Bonnie and Clyde*, and at that point, with the explosion of the European cinema, which was about breaking rules. As Godard said,

"Every good movie has a beginning, middle, and an end but not necessarily in that order." It left us free to examine everything from the ground up, and it was a wonderful time in Hollywood because at that point, there was an enormous explosion of new talent coming into Hollywood and new ways of doing things. That was when PBS got started. That was when there was such a rush that let a lot of fish into the net. It was an extremely exciting time. We really learned the form by watching movies. No one ever told us what the form was, and we learned by trial and error. It may be one of the reasons why I rewrite forty-fifty times because I know I don't get it right the first time. I depend a lot on rewriting my own material.

LEW: In my class I talk about going to quality writers to write so-called commercial movies. I use you and David Newman as an example of coming off of *Bonnie and Clyde*. Did they get an action and adventure writer to do *Superman*? No, they went to you to do it. The idea of trying to get quality writing superimposed on so-called commercial ventures is very common.

ROBERT: *Bonnie and Clyde* took four years to sell. David and I used to have this off-the-cuff humor that we would be ninety years old and still peddling this script. Finally, it sold, and the movie was successful. We got a writing contract at Warner Brothers. Kenny Hyman was running the studio, and he decided he wanted us to do a prison western, and he wanted it to be very violent. Then he gave it to Joe Mankiewicz to direct.

We were so lucky to work with the directors we did. We worked briefly with Truffaut and then Arthur Penn, who is a great teacher and filmmaker; then Joe Mankiewicz, who is also a great teacher; then Bogdanovich on *What's Up, Doc?* rather than *Superman* because with *Superman* I really only cowrote one draft with David. After the first draft, David and his wife did several others, and then they did *Superman II*.

LEW: My point is, the two of you had established yourselves as quality writers, and so rather than going the traditional, this writer does the action and adventure route. They were interested in reinventing *Superman*. Remember, it was coproduced by Salkind, who was European and had great success with *The Three Musketeers*.

ROBERT: What they did with *The Three Musketeers* was try and reinvent and do a movie that was both *The Three Musketeers* and a commentary on *The Three Musketeers*.

LEW: Probably humanizing it, as well. You were probably asked and expected to humanize Superman and Lois Lane. To get away from tradition.

ROBERT: To create another kind of Superman. I think everybody was saying, "We now live in a more sophisticated time, and what's called for are more sophisticated characters." If we're going to do these figures, they've got to be richer than the cartoon characters. They can't be like the television shows of comic series. They've got to have fun and character. Mario Puzo had written a story for *Superman*, and by its very nature, *Superman* had to be narrative driven rather than character driven. Our job was to simply beef up the characters, to take aspects of Puzo's script and string it together, to make the characters more memorable.

LEW: Do you find that motion pictures are more closely aligned to storytelling than theater or any other art form?

ROBERT: It's very different from the theater. I think that, first of all, there is often a relation to where you sit in a theater and where you sit in a play. Wherever you sit in a movie theater, you see the same movie. It is much more akin to having someone tell you a story. You lose yourself in movies in a very different way than you might approach theater. When you walk into a movie theater, you disappear into the movie, assuming the movie is halfway good.

LEW: I've always been fond of Kalem's line: "In theater, the drama is thrust at the audience. In motion pictures, the audience is thrust at the drama." Have you heard that?

ROBERT: I've never heard that, but that's absolutely correct.

LEW: Have you developed your relationship with Godard?

ROBERT: We were friends at one time. After Truffaut said, "I will do *Bonnie and Clyde* if I don't do *Fahrenheit*." *Fahrenheit* came through, so he gave the screenplay for *Bonnie and Clyde* to Godard. It was in the days when they were very good friends. Godard came over for the New York Film Festival. He said he wanted to do it. Again, learned classic differences between American and European organization. In France, specifically, a producer is someone who has the money or can get the money and then gets the director, and they make the picture. In the States, the producer is someone who gets a screenplay, then gets the director, then gets a star, then goes to a studio with what's called a package.

Bonnie and Clyde was optioned for two or three years by two wonderful people, and they gave us money to do it and were good friends of ours. They were trying to put the picture together in American film sense. Godard showed up in October and said, "I have to go back to Paris. There's a picture in December called *Alphaville*. I want to get out of it. I want to come here and do *Bonnie and Clyde*, and by December, we can be shooting." These people, they didn't say what they probably should have, but they were young, as we all were at the time, that they needed some time to raise money. Also, the picture was written for summer. Don't you think it would be better if we shot the film in the summer? Godard stood and said, "I'm talking cinema, and you're talking meteorology," and walked out of the room.

LEW: Is that the last time you saw him?

ROBERT: No, we saw him time and time again after that. Because when *Bonnie and Clyde* opened in Paris, we had dinner with Godard, and he said, "Okay, now let's make the movie the way it should be made." *Pierrot le Fou* is really his commentary on *Bonnie and Clyde*.

LEW: Really?

ROBERT: [*laughter*] Remember, I am dyslexic. I loved reading, but I cannot spell. I am grateful to spell-check. Whoever invented that should get the Nobel Peace Prize. I cannot punctuate. I took one creative writing course in college and flunked that. But I always loved movies. I would not dare write a piece of prose. The great thing about writing a screenplay is they are like a blueprint. Those things are torturous to read. They are useful tools. The difference between a book and a screenplay is like the difference between a blueprint for a house and a painting. I'd been working for an art director and was about to get fired.

LEW: You were given a warning?

ROBERT: They never paid me too much, so their guilt ate into them, I think. They said I would be a consultant for three years, so I had three years to rethink my life. No one would hire me as an art director on any magazine I wanted, and no advertising agency would hire me.

I had a friend who had been paid $25,000 to write a treatment for Doris Day. That was more money than anyone had ever showed me in my entire life, so I thought I'd write a screenplay. But I couldn't write. I had this wonderful friend named David Newman who was and is a wonderful writer. I spun him my dreams of being a screenwriter, my first great lie. We decided to write a screenplay, but we didn't know how. What happened in the next few years is Dave Newman really taught me to write. I write still in a style that's largely lifted from David Newman. I learned to write on the job.

What I really always wanted to be was a co-screenwriter, and then after *Bonnie and Clyde*, we did *There Was a Crooked Man*. David really wanted to direct, and we had this enormous fight. He said, "I want to direct." I said, "Okay, David, if you're going to direct, I want to direct." A friend of ours said, "You really have great value as partners, so write two screenplays as partners. Each pick a subject matter to direct, then do the two screenplays and send them out to the studios. That's how you get started." We agreed to it. The picture I wanted to do was a very low-budget western, as I felt it would get made. It wouldn't cost any money. That's still what should govern what you do. Of course, with the kind of irony that governs Hollywood, the studio picked my picture. If David had not been in the office the day they called for me, I never would have mentioned directing. I would have lied to David and said, "Look, let's forget this nonsense and go back to being screenwriters."

LEW: That was *Bad Company*, right?

ROBERT: That was *Bad Company*. We had a meeting with a young man from Paramount, and I said, "I'm attached to it as director." I kept waiting for him to say, "What makes you think you can direct?" He did ask, "Have you ever directed anything?" I said, "No." I kept waiting, but if you don't want something in Hollywood, they give it to you. If you do want something, they withhold it. He thought about it, they had a conference, then asked if I would do a screen test. It would be a test for actors, but it was also a test to see if I could actually direct. So I called Bud Yorkin because David Newman and I had done a screenplay with Bud Yorkin and Norman Lear that had never gotten made, but we'd become good friends, and he said, "Just say yes. I'll guide you through it."

So we were finished with the first draft of *What's Up, Doc?* David went off, and I stayed and spent two weeks preparing this test. I didn't know what I was doing. You've never seen anyone come that close to drowning on dry land in your life. It was horrible. On the way to that set that morning to do the test, I remember thinking, "This will teach me not to lie." One little lie and out of it comes enormous personal humiliation. I got there, and I started to work. After about half an hour, I thought, "If I don't do this for the rest of my life, it's going to kill me." Suddenly, I go from not wanting it to really caring about it. I desperately wanted to direct it. They let me.

LEW: Did you have a memorable cinematographer when you were working on that?

ROBERT: Yes, it was a wonderful cinematographer. They also provided me with Anthea Sylbert, who did the costumes. We shot on that back lot at Paramount when they had the old western street. We did it in the simplest way we could do it.

LEW: You had a good group?

ROBERT: Very good. They gave me the most extraordinary crew. When they said, "Okay," and let me do the picture, I had wanted a few people who worked for Peckinpah. Stanley said, "There's a guy I really want you to see. His name is Gordon Willis. I'm going to let you see *The Godfather*." What I saw in that was just so mind-boggling. Stanley was and is a great producer and has become over the years a great friend of mine. Gordon said very wisely, "You're going to have your hands full dealing with the actors. What you shouldn't have to worry about is the camera." So we sat down for two months, going through the script scene by scene, laying out a kind of crude storyboard, so by the time we got to set, we knew exactly what the camera was going to do.

I've always believed the Truffaut notion that from the first shot you make in a film, 80 percent of your options are gone because what you're going to do must be consistent with that first shot. I also believe Robert Altman's thesis, that screenplays are only fully written in a camera, finally. As much as I love and respect screenwriting, there's a certain part of a movie that's written in a camera, and what I love about movies is whether we like it or not, they're so vastly collaborative. They are the most collaborative form of art I can imagine.

LEW: When I asked Billy Wilder if he was a director or a screenwriter, he said, "I'm a screenwriter. Directing is merely an extension of my screenwriting."

ROBERT: I agree. Someone asked me if I would direct a movie I didn't write, and I said no. I'm still writing when I'm directing. Wilder is absolutely right.

Lew: While editing is the final rewrite.

Robert: Exactly right.

Lew: Someone told me, "There are a handful of cinematographers who will not let a director shoot a bad movie. Gordon Willis is on that list. I grew up in Nebraska, so I'm a western maniac. I thought *Bad Company* is simply a classic that needs to be brought back out.

Robert: I know.

Lew: Tell us about your work habits. Ron Bass is up at three o'clock in the morning. Others cannot function until midnight. Such wide diversification in all areas of all projects. First, how do you identify something that you want to spend a good portion of your life on?

Robert: I keep about four or five movie ideas that come to life or they don't. They're always sitting there. Somebody will come along, and I'll say, "That voice is a great voice, and I'll add that piece to that little rag-bag collection of stuff." Either it forms and becomes cohesive, or it doesn't. Sometimes, in the case of *Nobody's Fool* or *Kramer vs. Kramer*, somebody will give me a book, and I'll say, "This book is terrific. That's what I want to do." Sometimes it's just simply reading a piece of material. Sometimes, like *Places in the Heart* began as a radically different kind of movie. What was a minor character in the first draft became major the next draft over.

Lew: Your grandmother, right?

Robert: Right. She just sort of pushed everybody out of the movie. I truly love writing. I get up in the morning and do whatever it takes to get on my feet and moving. Then I go to work at long stretches. Then I go for a walk for about half an hour, then go back to work. I return phone calls at a certain specific time during the day. Usually because most calls have to do with Los Angeles and are made between four and seven in the evening. Oh, sometimes, if my wife is reading or doing something, I'll do some work in the evening. I have no format in terms of time. I work seven days a week. I may physically write only a few hours during some of those days, but I do work seven days a week.

Lew: How do you structure after you've identified the idea, whether it's a book or an original. How do you start developing the form, the structure?

ROBERT: Usually I start by trying to work through the characters because everything I've done, the story has been character driven. I'm trying to experiment now, to see what happens if I can do a movie that's narrative driven, just to see what it's like. It's the difference between doing a Hawksian movie and a Preminger movie.

If you look at a movie like *In Harm's Way*, which is a lovely movie, all of those characters change because of narrative. The narrative isn't affected by the characters so much as the character is by the narrative. It's an interesting way to think. I've decided to try and do that as a kind of discipline to see what it's like. Generally, I'll take the character and set him or her in motion. Then, I will do an outline. I will then start working my way through it and inevitably to a place where something that has happened in the screenplay that makes the outline not work, so I've got to go back and decide whether the outline will change, or do I mandate a different outline?

LEW: When you say an outline, are you talking about a step outline?

ROBERT: I do a thumbnail description of, not necessarily scenes, but blocks of scenes. This one now has sixty-two numbers.

LEW: Some people recently refer to it as a beat sheet. You don't do anything like prose for yourself, just professional notes?

ROBERT: Yes, and now what's happened is the last few days, I've hit something in the screenplay. I'm on page 84, and now I've got to change certain things in the last act. Generally, I don't start a screenplay until I have the ending set. When I have the ending set, then I know I have an arc for the characters to go through, and I hate that word, *arc*.

LEW: Me, too. Having been in story meetings as an executive for seventeen years with all three networks and Disney and Paramount, I never once was in a professional story meeting and heard the word *arc* until screenwriting teachers started utilizing it. Then it got into the screenwriting consciousness. It's kind of a nice word, but I hate it simultaneously because *arc* does not infer character progression.

When you're writing, do you focus on what the movie will be about?

ROBERT: At some point I do, but I've found that if I have an abstract idea of what the movie's about, it's never the fact that I have a scene that says to me, "This is what the movie is about." If the script shows it, I don't have to make the picture explain the polemic about what it's about.

I've generally got a scene that will essentially explain, even if it's just for me, what the movie was about. In *Places in the Heart*, it's the last scene. The whole movie was about nothing for me, except the last scene.

LEW: But then, when you walked out of the movie, you knew what you had just seen. For instance, last night in *Living Out Loud*, I just think Richard LaGravenese is a sensational mind. He's also a wonderful person, but I don't know what the movie is about. It can be so small, as in *Raging Bull*. Now I'm doing my teaching thing here, so forgive me, but *Raging Bull* is one line: "That poor son of a bitch would be a loser even if he did win the championship." The whole movie is right there.

ROBERT: Exactly. That's what it is. When we did *Bonnie and Clyde*, we remembered a line in a John Toland book that said, "They were not only outlaws. They were outcasts."

LEW: How much time do you spend before you really get into script pages?

ROBERT: I spend a lot of time before writing, trying to find not only what the movie's about but also trying to find the tone of it, trying to find the voice. Before I did *Late Show*, I had a terrible time trying to figure out this character for my script. There was a woman writer for *Rolling Stone* who had this extraordinary sense of language, and I went to her and said, "Would you sit and just talk into a tape recorder for two days?" She created that character, and once that character was there, everyone else fell into place. If you do the homework ahead of time, even though writing is always filled with revisions, you know the mind-set you're on. You know roughly what it is. You know when it's right and when it's not right. I've written scene after scene after scene, and suddenly, it said at the end, and it's, "This isn't right. They're nice scenes, but they're not what this movie's about." Half a movie is what you rip out of it, what you choose to erase.

LEW: When you're in a script, do you assign yourself so many pages a day?

ROBERT: No. I hit a real wall yesterday. It was very frustrating because I'm on the downhill float, and there's a part of you that just wants to get it finished. I hit a wall on this script, and I couldn't feel what it's about, and I had to go back like four scenes and say, "Something's going wrong here." What it's going to dictate is a change in the next four or five scenes beyond the scene I'm writing. Eight or ten scenes in the picture have become very fluid, and I have to work it through. I just began to get some notions this afternoon. The hardest thing is when you get this great idea late at night, and you write it, thinking, "I've solved it!" You wake up in the morning and think, "What gibberish is this? What insanity drove me to write this down?"

LEW: The pad by the bed.

ROBERT: Which can be the road to hell.

LEW: I was sitting in the UCLA audience, astonished when you showed *Places in the Heart,* and you confessed that your first draft was almost 250 pages. Was that before your grandmother was the heart of the movie?

ROBERT: There were enormous sequences with my father's side of the family. I kept on writing and writing. That was one of the cases when I thought I knew what it was about. I started writing, knowing where I was going, and suddenly, right in the middle, I stopped and realized the movie was about something totally different. This character had just taken over. I had to stop and go back and just work through it with her.

LEW: This doesn't happen to you often because you pretty much know everything about it before you start writing.

ROBERT: On any screenplay I've done since *Kramer vs. Kramer,* I've always gone through forty drafts, a minimum of forty drafts. Between forty and sixty drafts.

LEW: How extensive are each draft?

ROBERT: Sometimes they're really redrafts. Sometimes it's changing only three or four scenes, but most drafts are changing at least eight scenes.

LEW: I want Rita Augustine to represent herself and our sixty-two students in the program.

RITA: I'm still reeling at the forty to sixty rewrites.

ROBERT: It's very hard to be a writer now because there are very few really good producers. You're writing for an audience and for yourself and for the director and for these actors. You'd better utilize these actors as well as you can. You'd better give them all of the help that you can and make them as secure in their role as you can make them. Don't leave them with an egg on their face just because you had a good idea sitting in front of a keyboard. Altman used to say the heroes of the movie are the actors because it's very easy for us to write, "Do this, or do that." They're the ones who have to get out there and convince an audience.

LEW: The quote I use from Altman is, "The true heroes in movies are the actors we send before the cameras to tell our lies." You are one of the few actor-friendly directors without an acting background. How did that happen?

ROBERT: I was very lucky because I had a lot of directors to teach me when I was writing. When I started directing, I was very lucky because I had a lot of actors to teach me. Dustin Hoffman was a great teacher and taught me so much about acting and what acting is. Meryl did this, too, as did Sally Field and Paul Newman. There's not a time when I start making a movie when I don't say, "I'm going to learn something from actors." My job is to listen.

There was a moment when we were doing *Places in the Heart* in the very early days of monitors. The cinematographer relied on the monitor to check the framing. It was warm and very crowded to get by the camera. I was standing by the video monitor, and I heard Sally Field's voice twenty feet away: "Will the goddamn director get out from in front of the goddamn monitor and stand behind the goddamn camera so the goddamn actor can see?" From that day until this one, I never left the side of the camera.

Sometimes you learn something about giving an actor freedom to try to do something different. If it doesn't work out, then fine, do it your way. But trusting the actor. Sometimes it's learning to just stand beside the camera. I've always believed the less directing you do, the better director you are. You direct when you pick an actor.

LEW: That's what Marty Ritt says. He says 90 percent of the struggle is picking the actor. He said the other 90 percent is picking the actor who is closest to the part in real life as you can possibly get. He certainly paid that off because Paul Newman was Hud in real life, and Sally Field was Norma Rae.

RITA: You have such a full body of work. Is there one particular screenplay that you have a deep affection for?

ROBERT: It's probably *Places* because it's semiautobiographical. I have never gone back and looked at any of my movies once they're finished. Some time ago, I was at my apartment, and the television was on. I went through the apartment looking for something and thought, "That's a good voice. Who is that?" When I got there, I saw it was Dustin Hoffman. Then I realize it's a scene from *Kramer vs. Kramer* and walked out of the room. It's not having anything to do with not liking the movie. It's just that once I finish a movie, they no longer interest me. I've worked through it, and I don't want to see it again. It's out of my system.

RITA: Are you only writing for yourself to direct now?

ROBERT: At times with Truffaut, we've talked about projects I would write for him to direct. *Kramer* started out for him, but he couldn't get his schedule to work, and they let me direct it. I occasionally do rewrites, which I love. They're an enormous amount of fun.

LEW: Because you don't have ego involved? Is that part of it?

ROBERT: Part of it. I did one that will go nameless last year. I had so much fun and learned so much. It's like further learning your craft. There's some part of it that's just technical, in the best sense of being technical. It's very easy when you get involved in your own work to forget how important the technical aspect of doing a good screenplay can be, how important it is to have a certain rhythm, how important it is to move the story along in a certain way, how important it is to alter the humor to something else. It is a huge amount of fun, and you can learn a great deal.

RITA: Since you started around the New Wave influence and learning the freedom of breaking the form down at first, do you feel less free now when you're writing your stories, or have you found other ways to get at the excitement you had with your first script?

ROBERT: Some of those anarchic notions, which were so lovely in the late '60s, have come to seem slightly dated now. What I hope I have learned is that to make a screenplay that's as close to handwritten as I can, screenplays that are clear and as personal as handwriting and to make things simpler and simpler. It doesn't mean making a movie in one shot. It means be eloquent but also a minimalist.

Lew: Something you might like to have that I use a lot is that Einstein one time said: "Make it simple but not simpler."

Robert: Right.

Lew: I think that's so true in screenplay writing. Good for you. Two more things: One, you almost continuously use a word I don't think we've heard from any writer yet. You continually use the word *learn*. Learn about writing. Learn about acting. Learn about directing. Learn cinematography. That's so far away from, shall we say, the chutzpah of contemporary screenwriters. How did the word *learn* become such a part of your drive?

Robert: Necessity.

Lew: Do you think it started due to being dyslexic and being forced to learn things differently than perhaps others were learning? Maybe it put you into a state of constantly wanting to learn and relearn, which really makes you special as a writer and a director. It might have given you a gift that others don't have.

Robert: I was just constantly, in making a movie, forced to deal with things that I didn't have experience with. There's always something different on every picture. You can't fall into, "Oh, this worked last time, so I'll use it again." That's always a mistake, to think something will keep on working. Things change constantly, and the need to learn comes with the change.

The periods of art that I most admire are early Renaissance and Greek art. I once wanted to teach art history, but I wasn't good at that either. I love the times where the form hasn't resolved itself, where the people who make the form are still exploring possibilities. Once the Renaissance occurred, the style was locked in. I love the changing periods. One of the wonderful things about movies is that they haven't been around long enough to be locked in. It's like the first one hundred years of the novel. We have no notion of the enormous possibilities of movies. It's absurd to think we have any idea of what they are. It's what makes it a thrilling occupation. It's brand new.

Lew: Well said, all of this. I also think it's exciting to be a writer because you're always learning something new on your subject and also about yourself. I regret that I won't live long enough to write everything that I want to explore.

ROBERT: Me, too. Totally. One of the great advantages of being in your sixties is you now think, "There's so much to learn and still so much further to go."

LEW: I started teaching in 1979, and just the idea of sitting with these gifted 434 people and later on seeing so many of the classic movies that were written in these 434 courses, like *Harold and Maude*, to name just one of many, involved the development of the writers' lives, too. I hope they're using you at NYU back on the East Coast.

ROBERT: I've been talking about teaching.

LEW: Oh, talk to venerable Herndon at NYU. He's a beautiful human being. He also wrote *Alice's Restaurant*. He met me and my wife at a Village coffee house at three o'clock, and we stopped talking at about the same time in the morning. NYU, to me, is really the East Coast version of UCLA in terms of screenwriting. I have trouble teaching at an undergraduate level because the undergraduate can only write about the funniest thing that happened in the dorms or at a party. They haven't acquired enough experience just yet for the majority. I often advise undergraduates to study something else and do their graduate work in screenwriting so they can bring in experience and learning from other areas, too.

I have one last question, dear Robert. People often buy these books for the secrets, at least this is what my publisher says. Do you have any secrets? What has helped you be as good as you are?

ROBERT: I think the real secrets aren't secrets of technique. The real secrets are the secrets of character that make you say, "I'm going to see this through with this. I'm going to hang in there." The real secrets are the ability to take all of the imperfections of this business and somehow use them to find something helpful and useful.

LEW: I know I speak for myself and the readers of this book when I say, "Your collage of secrets have really come out in this talk and found a place in our heart."

ROBERT: Thank you.

22

Billy Wilder

He was frail. He was wizened. He was dabbing his nose with a handkerchief. He was suffering the residuals of a cold. He was ninety-two years old. He was a giant. He was Billy Wilder. Only four people have received three screenwriting Academy Awards each: Charles Brackett (one of Billy's partners) and Paddy Chayefsky, neither one of which are with us any longer; our first subject, a healthy Francis Ford Coppola (the only one still alive); and our last, the late Billy. *The Lost Weekend, Sunset Boulevard, The Apartment.*

My friend Sam Thomas, who wrote the Best American Screenplay series, set me up with Mr. Wilder and gave me his phone number. After six months of repeated attempts to get him to my 434, he finally said, in his Viennese accent, "Vell, all right, my boy."

You are often told to "save the best till last." The *New York Times* had called me a few weeks before and asked me a question I had never had in my forty-one years of the business of show: "Who is the greatest screenwriter ever?" All of the possible choices riffled through my mind in the speed it takes to make a decision while driving a car when an animal appears in your headlight. Finally, then, I responded with nonwavering conviction and spoke a moniker I denied myself in our dialogue: "Billy Wilder." Before the 434 warriors, I said, "I cannot call you Billy. May I call you Mr. Wilder? Billy cannot come from my respectful lips." Mr. Wilder replied, "Yes, anything you say." And thus, our mutual turf was established.

Mr. Wilder's screenwriting range, from the consistently voted best comedy movie in film history for *Some Like It Hot* to *Lost Weekend* to *Witness for the*

489

Prosecution to *Love in the Afternoon* to, of course, *Sunset Boulevard* is unparalleled in that same film history. Mr. Wilder told me privately, "I did not vant to be a one-trick pony." He was also one of the last century's greatest quipsters who also had a recognizable range, from "slipping out of this wet bathing suit and into a dry martini" to "those who don't believe in miracles aren't realists." A good number of biographies and other words well reveal Mr. Wilder's wit, but his own words captured by Cameron Crowe in *Conversations with Wilder*, for me, towers above all.

Here we also have Mr. Wilder's own speech, his simple, profound insights into writing screenplays. Albert Einstein said, "Make it simple but not simpler." I chose not to add or subtract words or to "straighten out" his language for a perfect English rhythm in his transcription, as it would not be the pure Billy Wilder. In his exact words is the wisdom, wit, and charm that is not only his but also of a well-lost generation. As said, these words were simple and profound, which was not what was expected by any when Mr. Wilder and I settled before my 434 people. I cleared my throat with the steadiness of a hummingbird and began.

LEW: This is May 18, 1995. We are sitting here in the 434 class of Lew Hunter. We have some distinguished guests with us today, in addition to the people around the table. Mr. Wilder, this is Howard Luger, who was a film star. He was a professor and co-runner of the producer program here. Richard Walter and I are both chairmen of the screenwriting program, and we have infected the world with our screenwriting books. Mr. Dana Gousten is one of our screenwriting professors here. You know, of course, Richard. He took good care of you. And here is Dean Crusoe, who is also one of our screenwriting professors. All of these screenwriting professors are or have been professional writers. Hal Ackerman is another one we couldn't keep away. They're not in our class, but they have been. They're Pat Gillan and Shelley Anderson.

BILLY: If I had known this was going to be filmed, I would have brought my makeup.

LEW: You need no makeup! I have a tiny introduction, and it's only this—I'm going to name titles, by the way—this is Mr. Billy—I cannot call you Billy. May I call you Mr. Wilder?

BILLY: Yes, anything you say.

Lew: Anything I say. This is Mr. Wilder. I think that the titles *Sunset Boulevard, Sabrina, Seven Year Itch, Spirit of St. Louis, The Lost Weekend, Some Like It Hot, The Apartment, Love in the Afternoon, Witness for the Prosecution*, and many more will explain your background to all reading. The thing I find, having spent twenty-five years myself in the Writers Guild, as a writer, the idea of having even one of the films to my name would be a huge thrill for me.

Billy: I'll give one to you.

Lew: Just one is fine. You have had a lot of partners over this period.

Billy: I have had a lot of partners and a lot of different kinds of pictures. You see, Hitchcock, he made it very simple for himself. He always did the "Hitchcock" picture. He never did anything else. So when people said, "Do a Hitchcock movie," they know immediately what it's going to be. It will be a suspense thing but beautifully done. However, it would be very boring for me to just do one type of picture, but I made one to show him off, which was *Witness for the Prosecution*. I quickly ran into, I don't know, some ridiculous comedy, like *Some Like It Hot*. I had to change all the time.

To begin with, I'm surprised that you are all writers here because the world has changed to such a degree. When I was a kid, I wanted to be an Indian, I wanted to be an FBI man, I wanted to be a detective, I wanted to be all kinds of things. Now, everybody wants to be a director or a writer. Are you going through the process by preparing yourselves for directing by writing screenplays now?

Lew: No, this is our screenwriting program, an average of 180 people who come through our doors. This is a graduate program. These are all grown-up people; they are not undergraduates. Of 180 people, 114 of them have become successful screenwriters, so our average, we think, is pretty good. Now, some of them become directors, like Colin Higgins in *Harold and Maude*, or Neal Jimenez directed *The Waterdance*. Some become directors, too, but most are here for screenwriting. We also have a directing department, and there is some overlap: Directors want to get into these 434 writing classes, and some screenwriters want in the directing courses.

Alex Cox and Francis Ford Coppola also came out of our program and did both, but this, here today, is screenwriting, and we want you here today for your knowledge on this, as well as your existence as a producer and director.

BILLY: I think that if you have a really first-class script and a mediocre director, you'd still come out with a good picture. If you have it the other way around—if you have a bad script and a first-class director—he still won't be able to do much with it.

LEW: Did any of the movies we've talked about here and other movies Mr. Wilder has written—I was looking at the Writers Guild listing. You have at least twenty movies before I think the first picture that really broke you through, was *Sunset Boulevard.* Is this right?

BILLY: No, no. Before that I had already won an Academy Award for *The Lost Weekend,* years and years ago. The first picture that I got a chance to direct was *The Major and the Minor.* That was about in the late 1930s.

LEW: The thing that fascinates me is that you worked very hard in Germany, and then you came here. So it just didn't happen instantly, or do you feel that it did happen quite quickly for you?

BILLY: Well, it did not happen that quickly. I'm remembering the first years when I arrived in America. We were forming the Screen Writers Guild. There was no guild. It was 1933 or 1934. That was the day when they started a fight between the so-called contributors to a picture. Are we going to name names? That was five or six years after sound pictures came out. That was when a big group of New York playwrights came out here because they knew dialogue. Actors that are all kicked out because they hit the wrong voice, and the directors could not direct dialogue, so they had dialogue directors come from New York. But it slowly kind of arranged itself. I feel it's been seventy very hectic years that I spent in the picture industry.

LEW: I'm going to pay attention to my beautiful wife, who just walked in with the camera. This is my wife, Pamela.

PAMELA: I've been looking so forward to meeting you. My husband has been so excited about your coming.

LEW: The whole room is excited. Do you want some water or some mineral water?

What we want to focus on is writing, and I'm so impressed with your range. As you said, not just the same thing but the range of your writing.

I'm so impressed with the fact that you were the cowriter of movies and with many different collaborators. But one of the consistent things is that they were all good movies. There was not that roller coaster that you see with so many writers.

BILLY: I did not become a director because you're the most powerful on the set. You're on the set, and people are following you with a chair for when you want to sit down. I became a director, unlike most other directors of this era, because I wanted to be as involved as I could with the picture. I was lucky to start like this without trying to be an assistant. Many assistant directors are always going to stay assistant directors because they need you. Never become an assistant. I also became a writer because I wanted to protect the script.

I was asked one day whether it was helpful if the director is a writer, too. "Absolutely not," I said. It's not necessary that he or she knows how to write. He has to learn how to read. Then they ask, "How do you mean? Because I don't quite see that." When I was at Paramount writing for twenty years, they would take me off the set when I was watching them shoot our script.

There was this one anecdote. We were writing for a guy called Mitchell Leisen. He was a practical director, not in the lower class, but in the higher class. But he was afraid for the writer to be on the set. We would be already writing for the next picture—as a matter of fact, in this particular case, was a picture called *Hold Back the Dawn*. There was a scene in the picture, it was the story of a French gigolo who would like to come in the United States, and he's caught because he has no visa. He's left there, sleeping all day, and he's planning as to how the hell he's going to get into the United States. Charles Boyer was playing him, and there was a cockroach that was climbing up the wall, the dirty wall, up to a mirror, and he would take a stick and talk to the cockroach. "What are you doing? Where's your visa?"

So we are still working on the last act of this, and we are having lunch at a restaurant called Lucy's, which is across the street from Paramount. We finished the lunch, and he passed the table where Charles was having lunch. He was having red wine, as a Frenchman, and then he says, "Hi Charles. How are you?" He says, "I'm fine." He says, "What are you shooting today?" "Today we are shooting where I'm in bed with a cockroach," and I say, "That's a very good scene, the way you talk to the camera." He said, "Except we did not do it this way because it was very silly for somebody to talk to something that does not answer." I said, "That's very important in the picture." He said, "No, no, we did not do it this way." They didn't even ask us. So I was still writing the third act, and on the way out, I told the director, that son of a bitch, you know, that we will no longer write a single word of the last act. Everything is going to Olivia.

LEW: So Olivia got in on the third act?

BILLY: Yes, she got the last act.

LEW: Have you always worked with collaborators as a writer?

BILLY: I have, though in Vienna, where I went to school, when you're ten years old, you had to choose a dead language, either Greek or Latin. So when you were thirteen years old, you had to choose between the French and English language. Everybody went to French because that was then. It was diplomatic, higher level. It kind of died down. They spent bucks to see an American picture in Paris.

LEW: So you used a collaborator at that time to help you with the language?

BILLY: Yeah, because I had to learn English. I sold a couple of stories, and I did the best I could; however, I made myself very unpopular with a group of chairmen and Austrian refugees because I surrounded myself only with the Americans. I wanted to learn the language. After we came back from the studios, everything started in German, German, German, and I just said, "No, that's not for me." I started writing then. I'm very grateful to Charlie Brackett.

LEW: Was he your first partner?

BILLY: He was one of my first partners, and it was Charlie Brackett who was associated with the Ivy League colleges. Williams, I think it was, and I learned English. I had only English girlfriends, and so it develops. I found it very helpful and very practical to work with a good collaborator, and every time you see me with another writer—

LEW: Well, names like D. M. Marshman Jr., Raymond Chandler, Edward Bloom—

BILLY: This is a whole chapter by itself.

LEW: I heard.

BILLY: That's a whole week.

LEW: Now all these people, you actually didn't work with them in a room?

BILLY: No, I didn't. I left Charlie Brackett immediately after *Sunset Boulevard* because we kind of felt like a box of matches. You have the match here, and you strike it against a surface, and it makes a fire, right? One of the scenes was missing or something, and there was no fire anymore. We just really suffered through *Sunset Boulevard*. We kind of broke up. But then I worked on two or three pictures with some very good collaborative writers.

LEW: Is that the time you worked with Chandler? During that time?

BILLY: During that time, yeah. I worked with Chandler.

LEW: That was then.

BILLY: Yeah, and then I stumbled upon I. A. L. Diamond, and I was with him through the years until he died.

LEW: Wow.

BILLY: If you have a good collaborator, if you understand, I will tell you the method I use with Diamond and with Brackett, as well. With Diamond, for instance, he would be sitting at a typewriter, and I would be walking around, either dictating or writing something on the yellow tablet, and he would be writing something, and he would look at me, and I would say, "I don't like it either."

LEW: Oh, you liked the matching?

BILLY: Yes, there was no facts, no nothing. He suggested something I did not like. It was over. He did not persist. I would say a day later or a week later, "That was really good. Let's do that." But writing, I think, as I got used to it, and I expanded it by becoming a director. I did that with the help of Brackett. I did it with the help of a producer, and then they gave me the first picture.

LEW: Which one was that?

BILLY: That was *The Major and the Minor*. It was a picture with Ginger Rogers. I always had a very good agent because she had just won the Academy Award for *Kitty Foyle*. My agent wanted me to have Ginger Rogers for the part. I said, "But she's not going to do it. My God, she's an Academy Award winner." So my agent then was—and then he became a producer—was Hayward, and he talked her into that. So that was already a big step forward.

LEW: He was the producer of *Spirit of St. Louis*.

BILLY: Right.

LEW: So you did things off and on with Hayward?

BILLY: Yeah.

LEW: Because he wound up producing all of your pieces together, in addition to directing them, right?

BILLY: Yeah, well, I hate the things they are producing now. As you look at any full-page ad, there are so and so "pictures" that are "produced by," but I don't see names. There's "light producer" and "associate producers," but nobody remembers the names. You can no longer mention a name of any really good individual producers, like Goldwyn, because of the studio. Now the producers are pairing with the writers because the writer thinks, and rightly so, they should appear before the director but not even before the producer.

LEW: You, of course, know the writers now have moved their credit up next to the director, which is a problem for the producers, of course.

Back to I. A. L. Diamond. Tell us how you got to the line, "Nobody's perfect."

BILLY: All right, I will tell you.

LEW: You all know what I'm talking about? In *Some Like It Hot*.

BILLY: We always would know exactly what the third act was going to be. We would sketch it out, and then we knew exactly.

LEW: Now, say that again. When I came to Hollywood, I would say, "Hello," to a writer, and the writer would shake his or her head, and rather than saying, "Hello," in return, they would say, "I can't get my damn third act." We don't hear that anymore.

BILLY: If it's in the third act, then something is wrong with the first act. That's always the same story, so then go back to the first act. But in any case, that's the way we did it.

We had the scene half down, but we didn't have the final dialogue. But the scene was coming up. It is the last scene in *Some Like It Hot*, and it was coming up, like, next Monday, and this was like it was on the Thursday before, and we stayed on it, writing the dialogue with the guys. Miss Marilyn Monroe and Mr. Joe E. Brown were at the scene where they are running away from the gangsters now. She comes on a bicycle, you remember? Then he tells her—Tony Curtis was the actor—he tells her that he's not really Mr. Shell Jr., but he's actually the saxophone player. They confess, and Lemmon also confesses to Julie Brown that she cannot marry him and explains why and "I can't have any children." He tries to do it gently and slowly, and finally he says, "I am a boy." Then Diamond said, "Well, nobody's perfect." So, we said, "Pretty good, but you can do better." However, the script would be distributed by the end of next week. Let's leave with that line, "nobody's perfect," and then let's fix it up until Monday next week, and then we can shoot it. But he had never thought of anything better.

LEW: Now, I talked one time to I. A. L. Diamond, and I asked him the same question, and he said that he was behind the typewriter, and you were laying on the couch, and he said, "We came to the line 'I am a boy,' and you, laying on the couch, said, 'Nobody's perfect.'" So, we'll never know. Now, he gave that line to you when he told me the story.

BILLY: How do you know I worked with him on this?

LEW: Is that the truth? Oh, okay.

BILLY: We are always standing around after the preview. He said, "Well, you talked me into this." He was a gentleman.

LEW: Yes indeed. Talk to us about the identification of an idea that's worth doing. Were things given to you? Did you run out and find things? Did they fall out of agents' briefcases? You must have gone through a great number of ideas to say, "This is the one I will work on."

BILLY: Well, I'll tell you. The most fun we had was with original ideas, the ideas I had or the idea he had, and then we started developing it. But it depends, you know. He would come to the studio with the question, "How do I tackle this screenplay?" Well, is it from a play? Is it from an original script or a novel? What is good? But that kind of suggested the idea that we should make a script and a picture out of it. It had different categories, but the most fun, as I said, was to do an original story because there's very little to go on.

I remember the idea of *The Apartment*. We were working with Lemmon. That was my first experience with him, and I also know it quite well. I very much admired him, and as we were coming to the end of shooting *Some Like It Hot*, I said I would like to make another picture with Lemmon again because he's just outstanding. So I was going to a drawer in my desk, which had kind of little notes, little bits of dialogue, of the first act. I was going through that same thing, and I came about a piece of paper, which was dated ten years back. The idea I got from Noël Coward's *Brief Encounter*, which was an illicit love affair between a married woman and a man. There was all this meat. He would always take her to the apartment of the friend of his chum. When it was written, I said, Noël Coward, and in front of him, I said, "How about that guy has to crawl back into the bed that strangers have been using at his place?" That was the basic idea that we had. Then we started talking about it, and suddenly there were three acts.

LEW: Do you feel like the idea is the most important part of the process?

BILLY: Just the idea, you mean?

LEW: I mean Noël Coward. That little scrap of paper there. By the way, obviously you have a drawer or something where you get ideas from, the same as everyone here.

BILLY: I take stuff out of there the whole time.

LEW: But in that drawer, like the match, do you believe that to be the most important part of the process?

BILLY: The most important part of the process is to find something that is an appeal to the good theatergoer. It must be at a certain level. You cannot bend too far back. But the idea is to find something popular, which you can inject at the highest possible level, popular as it is.

LEW: Bill Walsh, do you know that name? He wrote *Mary Poppins*.

BILLY: Yeah.

LEW: He was one of my mentors when I worked for Disney. He said he felt it was most important that people got to know, got to care about, the first reel of the picture, your people, and then you could go anyplace with them.

BILLY: But if you go any which way, then you might lose them. The more you like them, the more you dislike them, then you can do something wrong. But that doesn't make me fall in love with the guy or the girl the first five minutes. But that's, I don't know, everything I do or plan is always in three acts. The first act is the most important one because it plays off of the end.

Now, the first act, the difficulty with the first act, is that you go to preview night, and no one knows anything about it. It's not like when you go to the theater, and you get the program, and it tells you, "The action takes place in Chicago in 1911." It's all explained on that program. However, you have no information like this when you preview a movie. You have to start asking questions to answer the puzzle of what the whole thing is going to be. You have to curiously watch and be in the mood to play that game.

LEW: The word *puzzle* is interesting because we don't hear it in screenwriting often, but *puzzle* is a good word. So in comedies or dramas, the word *puzzle* for you is important?

BILLY: That is important. What is important is that you give them information, and you tell them. You step in front of them, and you say, "We're going to play a new game that I invented." Hopefully they say, "Yeah, that's great. Let's stick around a few minutes and see where this game goes." If it's good, they stick around forever. I want to tell you, I can't take them out of the scene. The puzzle is puzzling enough, and if they've fallen in love or have learned how to hate, it all gets bigger. They would like to see how the picture develops. Where does it go?

LEW: But you also say, running along with our puzzle, is a simplicity to what the story is about.

BILLY: Of course, there are two ways of writing and directing a picture. We take a very complex, gothic, curled idea, and you try to uncurl it to show them what it is, or you take a very simple story, and you curl it yourself. That should tell you what your ornaments are like.

Lew: The thing that actually got me was in *Double Indemnity*. I hadn't read the screenplay before, and I read it in Sam Thomas's *Best American Screenplays*. So again, Pamela and I were looking at *Sunset Boulevard* last year, before we went to see the play, and I'm sure you must be very conscious of this: There isn't a single word, neither in the description nor the dialogue, that has something to do with what the movie is about.

Billy: We do one thing. There is a dictatorial air about it. When a guy starts screenwriting, and he starts putting the screenplay on paper, he tries to impress the director with his technical descriptions: "Fade in slowly" or "A rosy sun was on the horizon" or "The camera moves from the long shot past the couple, then through a keyhole. Through the keyhole they discover that the wife of the one who is in bed with the other." Even though the camera is moving all of the time, I don't want that in the script. No director likes that. Just write, "Living room."

Lew: We say just write, "This is the master scene."

Billy: Except if you have a very important camera playoff that needs the camera to pan a little bit, so you see that, and you underline it. The first time I saw this, I remember, I said, "Jesus Christ! Those directors, those asses, they screw it all up." That was a silent film in 1929. Nobody was born yet in 1929. That was kind of a little shindig dance or something. There was on a blackboard, it was written, "Must wear shoes. Must wear tie." So our director at the time expected the shoes on the guy, and then the guy comes with a beard, and it was very long, and he pulls it up to see if he's got a tie on. How do you think the director reacted to a tiny bow tie?

Lew: Take it off.

Billy: It was a joke, but this is very typical, you know.

Lew: What is your reaction to Lubitsch Touch?

Billy: That is an absolute genius.

Lew: One time, when Robert Riskin, the legend goes, put a ream of paper in front of Frank Capra and said, "Here. Give it the Capra touch." Have you read that?

Billy: No. It's a tough time because he became a director for one picture. For Paramount, they wanted me to fall on my face, and they wanted me to go back and be a writer with Bracket and practice again. But, with Lubitsch, that was, you see, that was a whole different story. They only shared the Lubitsch Touch in Germany. He made this big picture. We made *Catherine the Great* and very big, serious pictures with big sets, but we saw Swedish pictures by a director, I don't remember, and it was called *Marriage Go Round*, and that was the origin of the Lubitsch. That is the technique, whereas the American director, in this case, or the European director, when he would come in and hammer it to death. He would just say, "Two and two is four, and one and one and one and one is also four." Lubitsch would say, "Here is two, and there is two, and the audience would just add it up." That is the trick.

LEW: My favorite was the one where he put the pants on, and they don't quite fit, do you remember? He suddenly realizes that his wife is cheating on him.

BILLY: Do I remember? I concentrate on Lubitsch's scripts, and I do that more often than I go to church.

LEW: One more thing, and then I know people are bursting with questions.

BILLY: Yes, one more thing.

LEW: About structures, Bill Goldman said one time that screenwriting is three things: structure, structure, structure. Do you feel that way also?

BILLY: Yes. Structure, structure, structure. That is very good. Did you know how to hide it? How to ornament it in such a way that it is the blocks that you're going to need later? They should look like wonderful chairs that you sit down on. They don't even know that this is a preparation for something big to come. You have to hide that, you see?

You know, it depends, if you buy a novel, you must have an idea for one or two or preferably four characters. Scenes must be photographed to be really first class. It is absolutely necessary that a shot of two or three guys talking, talk, talk, talk, talk, no matter how bright, how wise, how funny, it's not going to do it. Because why did you promise me there's going to be something good about that? I must get out of that setup there. I must do something, and you leave the theater.

LEW: I get the feeling that you are really, at all times, writing for an audience and not yourself. You always have the audience on your mind.

BILLY: Once or twice, I'll do a little scene for me.

LEW: Questions?

STUDENT: Mr. Wilder, if you had anyone but William Holden and the cast you had in *Sunset Boulevard* and *Double Indemnity*, do you think the picture would be as successful?

BILLY: William Holden wasn't in *Double Indemnity*.

STUDENT: No, I mean in *Sunset Boulevard*, and in *Double Indemnity*, Frederick MacMurray and Edward G. Ross, Barbara Stanwyck. Would it have been successful with any other actors, you think?

BILLY: That's very difficult to say because Holden was not our first choice. Our first choice for *Sunset Boulevard* was Montgomery Clift, who was a brand-new actor that just came from New York, and we were very enthusiastic about him. But he could have been just as good. Maybe a little better, maybe less good, but a week before we started to shoot, his agent, a woman, came and said, "Mr. Clift decided he does not want to start his career by being in love with a woman who is twice his age." That was the end of that.

For *Double Indemnity*, I went to every actor in Hollywood. I went through the list of actors who have a contract with Paramount, and then see Fred MacMurray, and I said, "Why not? I know what he's going to tell me, but maybe I could talk him into it." I was not very enthusiastic, but I thought he'd be the man. Because at MGM, with a script prepared for Clark Gable, and Gable was two weeks unavailable, so they get Spencer Tracy. They really had all the stars in the world. Paramount had fewer but also very good ones. But the only one that could play that, I think or I thought, so I talked to him, and he says, "Gee, Wilder, this is why I was acting." I talked him into it, and it became his most successful picture.

Another time, again, it was Fred MacMurray, he had called for *The Apartment*. We wanted him for the boss of the insurance company. Lemmon had called for Paul Douglas. You remember Paul Douglas?

LEW: Very well.

BILLY: Wonderful, wonderful actor.

LEW: Just great.

BILLY: That was on a Friday, and the telephone call from New York: He had a heart attack, and he died. There was nobody there on Monday to shoot. So I went to Fred MacMurray, and I tell the story: "No, not interested any longer, very happy the way I am." He wouldn't play this guy, the president of the insurance company had an affair with the elevator girl. He says, "I can't do it. You just put my children into poverty." I said, "What are you talking about?" He says, "I'm under contract to Disney. I play that crazy director with the Volkswagen flying around. I'm not playing a guy who had an affair." He says, "I can't do that." But on Monday, he was there.

LEW: Another question?

STUDENT: You said toward the end, when you buy a novel, look for one, two, preferably four characters?

BILLY: Four good characters, yes.

STUDENT: You look for four?

BILLY: I don't know. Four is better than three. If you just have a blank piece of paper, and on it, "A guy rents out his apartment," and doesn't really rent it out because we cleaned it up considerably. People hated me. Some critics hated me for that picture. They said, "It's a dirty character." But it won awards. I just said, "Why?"

This is not a guy who has made a career by letting people use his apartment. He explains it very clearly. Mr. So-and-So, who is head of the department but still below Fred MacMurray, he comes and says, "Look, could you do me a favor? I understand you have an apartment on Fifty-Ninth Street, and because I have my tuxedo and tie, and I have to change into it because my wife is coming from Atlanta, and I have to be dressed for the theater because we're going to the theater tonight." So the guy got his tuxedo. Then suddenly the guy, Lemmon, realizes that he was made a sucker of because it's too late now. Obviously, they make a victory. Jessie finds out, and the boss asks him, "Is it true?" and then he says, "Can I have the key?" How could he make a girl work every floor? Then the boss, the character, says, "It was a suicide attempt. It was all kind of very lucky to have a key to the window as well."

LEW: But you say the "four characters" problem. I'm suggesting one of the reasons why you have four characters is that people have to play the scene with each other. It's more interesting dialogue.

BILLY: Yeah, it's juxtaposition. Two people agreeing, they don't make a scene.

LEW: Richard Walter?

RICHARD: I'm just wondering, do you have a favorite among your films?

BILLY: *Battleship Potemkin.*

LEW: *Five Grains to Cairo.* That's a movie that I saw years ago. Did you wind up liking that?

BILLY: I really don't much think about what I did. When I was younger, I would like to remake them and make them right. Every picture has something wrong with it. If the stuff that is good is overwhelming, it's a very big success. If not, then it's just too bad.

LEW: Now, the criticism, put me in my place.

BILLY: Yes, sir.

LEW: The criticism I had with *Sunset Boulevard*, the musical, is that you notice that in the movie, I did not perceive her to be mad. By the end of the play, which I'm sure you have seen.

BILLY: Yes.

LEW: Glenn Close plays her as being insane.

BILLY: She has to be quite mad.

LEW: But in your movie, I got the feeling that she simply slipped into one of her fantasies.

BILLY: Maybe she makes a little too much of it.

LEW: Ah.

BILLY: I went to London to see the opening there. Then, when she did the opening, I went to New York. The critics are always waiting for me. Then, when they're going to grab me. Finally, I found the line that got me out of it. I get up and simply say, "This is going to make a very fine picture someday."

LEW: Julius Epstein was in our class. You know Julius Epstein?

BILLY: Yes. I love him.

LEW: Julius Epstein was in the class, and he said that when he's asked questions like that, he puts on this somber face and says, "No man is an island." That gets him out of anything.

BILLY: You know, for producers, they like to make themselves very studious and very deep, always searching: "Yeah, I read your script, and it's quite good, but what is the scene? I would like to know." When people ask me, "The scene is very simple. No man is an island," And, "Oh, of course." Any kind of cracks like this.

STUDENT: You just said you would like to do some of them over. Now that *Sabrina* is being remade do you have any thoughts on how—

BILLY: *Sabrina*? I know, but they're remaking four of my pictures, and I never get to see any of them. Because it was before 1960, before somebody knew that that little machine there, that little television or whatever may be behind it, is one day going to be bigger than all of us. I ran into Jack Warner, and he said it was a very happy day. He says, "Come on and have a drink with me." He says, "I sold a whole bunch of crap. Everything for $25 million." If he were alive now, he would find out that he could get $50 million for *Casablanca* alone.

LEW: He was relating to Paramount back before they sold everything to Lew Wasserman.

BILLY: He sold it to, I forget, I think, MCA.

LEW: Well, to MCA, Wasserman. Everything before 1946, I think it was. Enormous library. Shelley?

SHELLEY: What do you think about the screenwriting you see in theaters today compared to your pictures?

BILLY: Look, dear, they are making to me very few pictures. The industry is very busy with television, but once in a while, they lay out their money for $3 million or $5 million, or they make a picture with the best goddamn special effects that you've ever seen. They look over your shoulder. Good God! This age where we have to throw out all the secretaries and all the policemen because they're afraid that they may lay a tremendous egg, and if you wake up at Paramount, and you say the word *waterworks*. Oh. Somebody just made a picture, and if the picture did not work, they're shooting the middle of the next one. It was just not all that important. But when you bring up a picture in the middle of a little cheap picture for, I don't know, for $12 to $15 million dollars, you spend the very first day on advertising in New York and in Los Angeles, even more than the entire *Gone with the Wind* costs, which was $5 million. Two pages, triple pages, they go crazy!

LEW: Mr. Wilder says something that I think relates, that line I want to key in on, where you talked about disguising the structure. Today, sometimes, I think you can see the story conference up on the screen.

BILLY: They would like to get the stupid ones in there, too.

STUDENT: I was just curious. You talked about theme earlier. When you were coming up with these story ideas, when you were writing, did you think about them, or did you think mostly about story?

BILLY: There is a theme of *War and Peace*. I'm just telling a story actually, trying to do it as elegantly, as skillfully as you possibly can. Do it for intelligent people, and give them a little more credit than you do.

LEW: The word *puzzle*. I remember working with Jim Poe on some of the things, do you remember?

BILLY: Oh, sure.

LEW: I liked him a great deal, and they used the word *puzzle*. They talked about constructing a form of a puzzle. I hadn't heard that for quite a number of years, actually, because we don't use that in writing classes.

BILLY: Sure.

LEW: Okay, one or two more, and then we'll wrap up. We don't want to take advantage of you, okay?

STUDENT: Just to follow up on one thing. When you first get your idea, do you go directly to try to figure what the big moments are going to be in your three-act structure and fill in, or did you find yourself going at it some other way?

BILLY: No. It's not all that easy, and suddenly you have all three acts. But I think if I think it's healthy and the scene is good, it can be next to the second act. It can open the first act. I don't know. But all the good stuff that you accumulate will then automatically divide into three acts. In *The Apartment*, it's very simple. The first act is where he thinks he's making a career out of it. Meanwhile, the chief thinks about Nixon, the vice president. End of first act. End of the second act is where the girl lets the brother pick her up. He thinks the girl attempted suicide, but she was knocked up or something. [*laughter*]

LEW: We'll stop right there then.

BILLY: In the third act is where everything straightens out now. She's getting a divorce. Mr. Fred MacMurray, he cannot marry the girl, but it's New Year's Eve, and when the light goes on, she's gone. She's running back to the guy. It's a short third act, but every one of the pictures automatically falls into the same.

LEW: The second act I have always found to be the biggest problem in terms of the first one. The second act is a complications area, and what that really says is that I'm not really working hard enough on my puzzle, I suspect. Right?

BILLY: Yeah, there has to be a release. Just like the release in a chorus of a song, you know.

LEW: Right.

STUDENT: How did you first come up with the idea of *Sunset Boulevard*?

BILLY: I had an idea to make a comedy out of it with Mae West. She was just the proper age, but then I said, "But it's not the proper link between silent pictures and sound pictures," because Mae West made quite a few sound pictures, and we needed a silent star who has lost her career but who has money. So then we started working on this thing. The writer we had, the characters we knew inside and out. You know, of course, because I myself didn't stay at the hotel. I was staying at a wonderful, one-room apartment.

LEW: How much was it?

BILLY: It came with a little kitchenette and for $70 a night. It is now higher than $150 a night.

LEW: True.

BILLY: That is a different story.

LEW: Yes.

STUDENT: You don't have to say if you don't want to, but who was the nicest actor, male and female, that you worked with?

BILLY: I don't know who's the nicest. But very few of the actors, few less actresses, have become my personal friends. Two of them were actually Holden and Lemmon. I'm a great admirer of Lemmon since he's just in bloody shape that he's getting older. He can play absolutely anything. And the girls?

STUDENT: The sweetest?

BILLY: Sweetest? Sweet is not good, but the nicest, the most serious when it came to play the scene, the woman who never forgot a word, knew everybody's lines, she would be Sandy.

LEW: Richard Muller.

RICHARD: It's so exciting to see you under any circumstances, especially to see you so well with your cold. You just seem so strong, so sharp, so good. Do you want to work more? Are you thinking about making a movie?

BILLY: Of course I would like to make a movie, but under certain circumstances, I wouldn't make a movie. I would not make the movie where there are three head producers, three line producers. That's absolutely impossible to work, under the circumstances. I just fool around with some stuff. I have a half of a script here, three scenes there.

LEW: The drawer. He still has the drawer with the scraps. Finally, to wrap us up, was that where you got your line, "slipping out of a wet bathing suit and into a dry martini"?

BILLY: No, no. That was not the line. That was the line that began in the first picture, *The Major and the Minor*. We gave it to the men who I thought originated the matter that especially played the part. I said, "That scene. I'm going to give you a line of your own." I said that it's not mine, but as long as everyone accused me, I suffered.

LEW: Have you seen a movie in the last couple of years that you really liked?

BILLY: Yes.

LEW: Which ones?

BILLY: I really liked *Forrest Gump*.

LEW: We had Eric Roth right here last fall. Do you know him at all?

BILLY: No, but the idea of spending that much money doesn't not achieve a victory. To play someone who is half a step from being silly— it's so touching. It was a movie that people knew, and people like that in school. Some people recognized themselves in it, you know. It was just absolutely a wonderful, wonderful movie. Wonderful structure, wonderfully played, it was a great pleasure.

LEW: You know his father, Leon Roth?

BILLY: Yeah.

LEW: Another movie, any other movies?

BILLY: I would make a movie under happy circumstances. I never make a movie that was more than $2 or $2.5 million. But maybe I'm a little too old for them. I don't know. I just study it. I've had my share of good luck, and I don't go and beat my chest and say, "I'm not done yet!"

STUDENT: Did you see *The Piano*?

BILLY: Oh, yes.

LEW: Did you like that?

BILLY: Not very much. It was a little bit too much reach. It was done with a stamp of "I'll be dignified here" and "I'll keep making something absolutely unique." It's not common enough for me.

LEW: By the way, I can spend the entire hour with you talking about your late art collection.

BILLY: Oh, I have new things now.

LEW: God, I wish I could have seen it. Mr. Wilder was collecting Picassos and so forth and the pieces before they became well known.

BILLY: There are still a few very good collectors here. There was Robinson, who collected a lot. Can I leave now?

LEW: No, I just want to ask you one more thing. The one thing I want to ask you is, tell us how you came into the country, that circumstance with the man.

BILLY: I told that. That was very simple. It was not very simple. It was very complex. I wanted to pitch to America. I was a refugee from Germany, but I was in France, but that was not far enough for me. I wanted to go farther away. I wanted to go to America. Even with Adolf Hitler being in Germany, I always wanted to go to Hollywood because every picture maker wants to go to Hollywood. So I was here for six months before I wrote the script in German for Columbia, which was never made. My visitor's visa was expiring, where in order to apply for immigration, you have to be out of the United States and at the embassy or whatever. It took forever to show the papers, so I went to Mexico to a town called Mexicali, Mexico. Mexicali was on the other side of the world. That was the first counsel year. I showed the few papers that I had with me.

Everything was missing. I needed a paper that said I had no police record. I needed a paper that I don't have or have never had tuberculosis or another disease, and this was required. I said, "I'm sorry, but this is all I have. I need to go back so I can write movies." So he circled me and circled me. He finally took my papers and stamped it two or three times, and said, "Make good movies." I said, "I'll try. I'll try."

LEW: You kept your promise and then some. Thank you so, Mr. Wilder.

I have just finished reading the interview with Billy Wilder, and I am awash with tears. Several of the screenwriters of this book have since gone to their substantial rewards. May they rest in peace, as we still behold the magic they have left for those of us who remain.

I started this adoration of screenwriters almost seven decades ago. I look forward to seeing them by looking through the gates of pearls and laughter. I tell you, dear reader, I have already been in screenwriting heaven throughout all of this journey in collecting these secrets, troves, war stories, and writing journeys of love and passion. I can barely wait to join them at the sacred writer's table and to hear more stories that will surely be as good as their Oscar stories.

All twenty-two are just wonderful as people, screenwriters, and in doing this book, their conversations far exceeded my expectations; the intellect, the spirituality, the generosity of all are breathtaking. I know my brothers and sisters in the Writers Guild of America will surely be mesmerized with the insight and brilliance of the immortal twenty-two, living on this earth or no longer, while their creations continue to live on forever. I love screenwriting, and I pray that all writers, aspiring and professional, come to this book and leave with a stronger sense of confidence and clarity as to what it is that they must do.

I firmly tell my past and present UCLA students an old screenwriting mantra: Less is more. I will adhere to that for you here as well, my dear reader, and close out with a Ray Bradbury prayer that is also in my previous Screenwriting 434 book. Students, past and present, along with those I have not yet had the pleasure of meeting but who I have spent time with in this book.

Ray Bradbury's been onto this forever. Ray delivered the invocation to a Humanitas Prize gathering, and every UCLA 434 man and woman since has been blessed with Ray's words. Now, dear reader, it's your turn. Rest in peace, beloved Ray, a man who also carries the name of my beloved father. May they both rest in peace.

Dear Lord,

Help us to remember the gift of excellence that lies with us if we but call and bring it forth. Help us to recall that in excellence is surprising profit, for the soul, for the mind, and for the life we live, beside that soul and with that mind.

Help us to know that only in our loves can we create and out of that creation change some stray, small part of the world we touch. Help us to love ideas and their creation, even as we love our neighbors and, because we are proper creators, ourselves.

Tell us to lie down with that one inescapable person, our lonely selves, knowing that if the work of the previous day was a surprise of joy that we stumbled upon through curiosity, true need, and rare zest and the energy that comes from wild discovery, we are good company for the night.

Teach us not to hesitate atop cliffs but to leap off into our writing without wings. And teach us, with passion and love, how to build wings on the way down, hoping for a soft landing. We ask these things because, poor creatures that we are, we do forget and must remind ourselves, as you remind us, that love is the final answer; and excellence, its hallmark; and profit, which is peace of mind, its everlasting residue.

Write on, with love from Lewis Ray Hunter!

About the Author

Lewis Ray Hunter is a Nebraska-born screenwriter, author, educator, chairman emeritus, and professor of screenwriting at the UCLA Department of Film and Television. Lewis Ray spent many years working as a film and television executive creating and producing television episodes for Disney. His personal projects include many examining the oft-ignored Japanese internment camps. Lew was also a pioneer in penning teleplays examining issues many shied away from, such as child pornography in the early 1980s.

Lewis Ray's first book, bestseller *Naked Screenwriting 434*, has been called the "final word on screenwriting" by Richard Donner, director of *Lethal Weapon IV*, and has been read by most, if not all, aspiring screenwriters. Lewis Ray is also credited with creating the American Screenwriting Association as well as UCLA's extension writer's program. Both addressed Lew's desires of an all-inclusive writer's network and more access for screenwriters and screenwriting students to the best the industry has to offer in education and support.

Many of the Oscar-winning scripts over the past twenty years have been written by students of Hunter. His former students and advocates include Allison Anders, Michael Colleary, James Dalessandro, Lon Diamond, William Missouri Downs, Sacha Gervasi, Pamela Gray, Laurie Hutlzer, David Koepp, Chuck Loch, Paige Macdonald, Don Mancini, Adrienne Parks, Alexander Payne, Robert Roy Poole, Dan Pyne, Robin Russin, Diane Saltzberg, Joel Schumacher, Tom Shadyac, Brad Silberling, Darren Star, Megan Steinbeck, Kathy Stumpe, David Titcher, Mike Werb, Greg Widen, Robert

Wolfe, and many others. Steven Spielberg has called Mr. Hunter the "best screenwriting teacher going."

Lew resides with his beautiful wife, Pamela, wherever the wind takes them but most often in Arizona. He is working on a second book of interviews with Oscar-winning screenwriters.